MW00719793

REAL ESTATE APPRAISAL

WILLIAM M. SHENKEL

PROFESSOR OF REAL ESTATE
UNIVERSITY OF GEORGIA

COLLEGE DIVISION South-Western Publishing Co.

Cincinnati Ohio

Sponsoring Editor: Jeanne R. Busemeyer
Production Editor: Sharon L. Smith
Production House: BBE Associates, Ltd.
Interior Designer: Craig LaGesse Ramsdell
Cover Designer: Lamson Design
Marketing Manager: Scott D. Person

FL60AA
Copyright © 1992
By South-Western Publishing Co.
Cincinnati, Ohio

ISBN: 0-538-81375-X

1 2 3 4 5 6 7 MT 6 5 4 3 2 1

Library of Congress Cataloging-in-Publication Data

Shenkel, William Monroe.
    Real estate appraisal / William M. Shenkel.
       p. 509   cm.
    Includes index.
    ISBN 0-538-81375-X
    1. Real property—Valuation   I. Title.
HD1387.S484 1991
333.33'2—dc20

91-13218
CIP

Printed in the United States of America

CONTENTS

Contents   v

PREFACE

The text comprehensively explains *real estate appraisal principles* in the seven chapters of Part I. Starting with a description of the *professional appraisal industry* (Chapter 1), the next four chapters include introductory material essential to the practicing appraiser: *the market value standard* (Chapter 2), *real estate property rights* (Chapter 3), *land-use controls* (Chapter 4), and *real estate market analysis* (Chapter 5). Chapter 6 is a special feature that explains appraisal mathematics in detail. Part I closes with an intensive review of the *highest and best use* (Chapter 7), the principle that largely controls the valuation estimate.

Part II reviews the leading approaches to real estate value. Part II starts with the *appraisal process* (Chapter 8), and proceeds to *site valuation* (Chapter 9), *building analysis* (Chapter 10), and the *cost approach* (Chapter 11). Two chapters deal with the *sales comparison approach,* including a review and demonstration of advanced *statistical models* in Chapter 13. The two chapters on the *income approach* include a separate chapter on *real estate mortgages* that is important to understanding later chapters.

The five chapters on valuation practices in Part III demonstrate *cash flow estimates, lease valuation,* and the *appraisal of partial interests.*

The last two chapters, Chapter 19, *Appraisal Review,* and Chapter 20, *Appraisal Ethics,* are of special importance. The appraisal review chapter covers federal and state appraisal review requirements. The required review standards are preceded by a discussion of common *appraisal logic errors* with illustrations. A unique feature of this book, the logic errors are derived from appraisal practice covering some 25 states and a wide variety of appraisal assignments.

The chapter on *appraisal ethics,* Chapter 20, includes a general discussion of social responsibilities common to professional activities. Uniform ethical appraisal standards are discussed in a series of cases that demonstrate appraisal ethics, which are now a part of federal and state law.

Particular care has been taken to adapt the text to state laws enacted in compliance with Title XI, *Real Estate Appraisal Reform Amendment to the Financial Institutions's Reform, Recovery, and Enforcement Act* (**FIRREA**) of 1989. In pursuit of this goal, Chapter 1 summarizes current laws enacted in compliance with federal appraisal regulations. Also, the text appendix demonstrates an appraisal made with the *Uniform Residential Appraisal Report* required by federal agencies. To assist in preparing for license and certification examinations, each chapter has a glossary and the book ends with an alphabetical glossary.

I sincerely appreciate the invaluable contribution of several reviewers who materially improved the quality of this textbook. I am especially grateful for the contributions of:

Thomas E. Battle III
Center for Real Estate Education and Research
Indiana University
School of Business
Bloomington, Indiana

Billie Ann Brotman
Kennesaw State College
Marietta, Georgia

Linda L. Johnson
Appalachian State University
Boone, North Carolina

Further appreciation is extended to my assistants: Amy Reeves, an undergraduate, and Jim Sessoms, an MBA candidate. Their conscientious dedication substantially contributed to the final draft.

William M. Shenkel
University of Georgia

PART 1

Valuation Principles

C H A P T E R 1

The Appraisal Industry

After studying this chapter, you will know:
- The minimum requirements of a real estate appraisal.
- The purpose of real estate appraisals.
- Appraisal requirements for federally related transactions.
- State appraisal requirements that conform to federal law.
- Appraisal associations and their professional qualification programs.

Real estate appraisals are required in virtually every real estate transaction. To describe current appraisal practices, the chapter defines a real estate appraisal and explains standards required by federal agencies and the various states. The concluding section deals with professional appraisal qualifications of appraisal organizations.

REAL ESTATE APPRAISALS

Strictly speaking, an appraisal is a personal opinion of value. Real estate brokers, real estate salesmen, and contractors frequently express opinions on real estate values. Usually, such opinions are offered with little supporting evidence, and while they may be valid, they do not conform to the accepted definition of a real estate appraisal. Practicing real estate appraisers prepare *written appraisal reports* that document the value estimate.

Appraisals Defined

Though appraisals take different forms, an appraisal may be defined technically as an *unbiased written estimate of value*. In agreement with this definition, the written appraisal report includes:

Part I: Introduction
           Letter of transmittal
           Certificate of value
           Summary
Part II: Premises of the Appraisal
           Statement of limiting conditions
           Purpose of the appraisal
           Definition of value
           Data valuation
           Property rights appraised
Part III: General Data
           Property identification

Regional data/community data
Neighborhood data
Current zoning
Property tax data
Site description
Building and land improvements description
Part IV: Data Analysis
Highest and best use estimate
Land value
Valuation approaches
Sales comparison approach
Cost approach
Income approach
Part V: Reconciliation: Final value estimate
Exhibits
Qualifications of the appraiser
Photographs
Maps
Graphs and charts[1]

The estimate of value is a direct statement of value in dollars. Generally, the appraised value is not reported as a range of values—for example, $10,000,000 to $12,000,000—and it is *not* qualified by unreasonable conditions. Similarly, the appraisal date generally applies to the *date of inspection* and not the date on which the appraisal is signed or delivered. In some instances, the appraisal covers a specific date to satisfy legal requirements. The market value estimate, therefore, is valid for the stated date of valuation. The signature of the appraiser binds the appraiser to the documented opinion. Without the signature, the appraisal would be invalid.

The appraisal purpose and the value, as identified by the appraiser, guide the appraisal method and data analysis. For example, an appraisal of the leasehold interest (the tenant's interest) varies significantly from an appraisal for a highway right-of-way. The statement on qualifying conditions limits the appraisal findings to given conditions. For example, the appraiser makes no judgments over legal matters, errors in surveys, or other conditions not under control of the appraiser. The legal or land description identifies the precise location of the property, describes the property rights subject to the appraisal, and explains the ownership interest under appraisal.

---

1   Adapted from *The Appraisal of Real Estate*, Ninth Edition (Chicago, Illinois: American Institute of Real Estate Appraisers, 1987), 578-79.

The factual data is presented so that reviewing parties may verify appraisal data and its analysis. The required factual data covers information essential to the valuation estimate; namely, real estate sales, construction costs, land data, and annual income and expenses. With a written analysis, third parties may follow the appraisal logic. Additional supporting material such as maps, graphs, tables, and photographs further document the value opinion. Figure 1-1 illustrates a map that identifies the location of real estate sales used to support the market value estimate.

Figure 1-1   Sales Map That Identifies the Location of 16 Real Estate Sales Used for Appraisal Purpose

The Importance of Real Estate Appraisals

The importance of real estate appraisals is suggested by a review of common real estate activities that require real estate appraisals. In addition, the many sources of employment show the continuing demand for real estate appraisals. A review of typical appraisal assignments demonstrates the critical role assumed by real estate appraisers.

APPRAISAL CLIENTS

Appraisers serve a broad range of private clients, institutions, and government agencies.

PRIVATE CLIENTS. There are seven types of private clients who are served by appraisers.

Home Buyers and Sellers
> Buyers and sellers may employ appraisers to help them make rational buying and selling decisions.

Investors
> Investors in income property employ appraisers to estimate for many purposes: remodeling, rehabilitation, purchase and sale, and long-range investment planning. Frequently, investors require an appraisal of real estate income earned after income taxes.

Tenants
> Commercial tenants often rely on appraisals before negotiating leases, lease renewals, and related matters.

Accountants
> For asset accounting, for corporate mergers, for income taxes, and for related purposes, accountants depend on accurate values estimated by competent appraisers. Frequently, the financial sums involved more than justify the appraisal cost.

Developers
> Developers hire appraisers to guide decisions on project feasibility and the purchase and sale of development sites and projects.

Private Corporations
> Private corporations use appraisers for two main purposes: (1) To guide the acquisition, sale, and leasing of property held incidental to company operations. (2) To help in making optimum investment decisions.

Insurance Agencies
> Insurance companies and their clients determine recommended insur-

ance coverage by using appraisals. To settle insurance claims, insured parties frequently rely on professional appraisals.

LENDERS. Savings banks, commercial banks, pension funds, real estate investment trusts, insurance companies, and other lenders legally require qualified appraisals to determine the maximum allowable loan. Other financial organizations use appraisals for real estate investment, lending, and portfolio analysis.

GOVERNMENT AGENCIES. Agencies that require appraisals include federal, state, and local governments and their many administrative agencies.

Federal Agencies

Certain federal agencies active in real estate financing require appraisals by law. The Veterans Administration, Federal Housing Administration, Federal Home Loan Administration, Farm Home Administration, and related agencies must have appraisals to determine the maximum allowable mortgage. Other federal agencies depend on appraisals for operations, including the Corps of Engineers, General Services Administration, National Park Service, Fish and Wildlife Service, Internal Revenue Service, and the Post Office among others.

State Agencies

State revenue departments, housing agencies, public utility departments, and regulatory agencies depend on real estate appraisals for their operations.

Local Governments

Virtually every county and city relies on local appraisals in buying and selling real estate. The property tax assessor and local agencies that lease and manage real estate use qualified appraisers.

The list covers a broad range of appraisals commonly required for a market economy. Commerce that involves real estate and its acquisition, sale, lease, or financing depends on some orderly procedure to appraise real estate assets.

PURPOSE OF THE APPRAISAL

Appraisals vary according to their purpose. Appraisal data, and its interpretation, varies according to appraisal objectives. While the appraiser typically estimates market value, appraisals for various other purposes require value estimates adapted to other objectives, including:

1. A change of ownership.
2. Financing
⋇3. Eminent domain proceedings.
4. Taxation.
     Local property taxes.
     State and federal income taxes.
     Federal estate taxes.
     State inheritance taxes.
5. Estimating market rents.
6. Valuing property subject to a lease.
7. Valuing the leasehold (tenant) interest.
8. Insurance coverage or claims.
9. Corporate mergers or liquidations.
10. Bankruptcy proceedings or other liquidation purposes.

The first objective, the transfer of ownership, satisfies prospective buyers and sellers who conduct negotiations with market value estimates. Companies that relocate employees hire location specialists who arrange the sale and purchase of employee dwellings. Usually, the location specialist requires two real estate appraisals to establish a minimum selling price. If the two appraisals deviate by more than five percent, a third appraisal is often required. Relocation appraisals help ensure that the property is sold at the market value.

RELOCATION SELL AT minimum PRICE AT MARKET VALUE

Similarly, most federally regulated credit agencies must base decisions on valid real estate appraisals that meet required appraisal standards.

⋇ Eminent domain refers to the right of government and regulated utilities to take private property in the public interest. These appraisals provide estimates of the value of real estate taken for highways, power lines, pipelines, and other public improvements.

Real estate subject to property taxes is appraised by the local tax assessor. State or federal agencies require real estate appraisals for many state and federal tax purposes. In addition, appraisers estimate the market rent for office buildings, shopping centers, and other commercial leases. Other appraisals deal with corporate mergers, property liquidations, and bankruptcies. Finally, there are appraisals required by the courts to satisfy legal claims in proceedings such as divorces and estate settlements.

APPRAISAL REQUIREMENTS

Generally, lenders grant loans based on a percent of the appraised value.

Before July 1, 1991, appraised values were variously interpreted by state and federal agencies, lenders, and their clients. There were no nationally enforced laws governing real estate appraisals undertaken by federally regulated lenders. The result led to large-scale lending losses.

After lengthy deliberation, Congress enacted *Title XI, Real Estate Appraiser Reform Amendment to the Federal Financial Institution's Reform, Recovery and Enforcement Act of 1989 (FIRREA).*[1] This Amendment established minimum appraisal standards to be implemented and enforced by each state. A review of the main federal requirements precedes a discussion of state laws enacted in compliance with the Title XI amendment to FIRREA.

Federal Requirements

Real estate appraisals for federally related transactions must be completed

> *in accordance with uniform standards, by individuals whose competency has been demonstrated, and whose professional conduct will be subject to effective supervision.*[2]

Provisions of FIRREA are administered by a series of special committees and organizations starting with the Appraisal Subcommittee.

FEDERAL ADMINISTRATION

The Appraisal Subcommittee includes the five heads of federal financial regulatory agencies: the Board of Governors of the Federal Reserve System, the Federal Deposit Insurance Corporation, the National Credit Union Administration, the Office of the Comptroller of Currency, and the Office of Thrift Supervision. The Resolution Trust Corporation is also a member.

The Subcommittee monitors state certification and licensing of appraisers. It also monitors (1) state appraisal standards and (2) the appraisal standards of federal financial institutions. The Subcommittee maintains a national registry of state-certified and state-licensed appraisers qualified to appraise for federally related transactions. In exercising these duties, the Subcommittee delegates certain functions to the Appraisal Foundation.

The Appraisal Foundation is a nonprofit corporation originally chartered by eight national appraisal organizations (and the Appraisal Institute of Canada) to promote "uniform standards of professional appraisal procedure." The original corporation members included the:

---

1   *Public Law* 101-73, Sec. 1102.
2   *Ibid.*

American Institute of Real Estate Appraisers
American Society of Appraisers
American Society of Farm Managers and Rural Appraisers
International Association of Assessing Officers
International Right of Way Association
National Association of Independent Fee Appraisers
National Society of Real Estate Appraisers
Society of Real Estate Appraisers

Since incorporation, the American Institute of Real Estate Appraisers and the Society of Real Estate Appraisers have merged to form the Appraisal Institute. Other members include the American Bankers Association, the American Real Estate and Urban Economics Association, the Mortgage Bankers Association, the Real Estate Educators Association, the Urban Land Institute, the U.S. League of Savings Institutions, and others.

Title XI grants the Foundation authority to establish federal standards for appraisal qualification and appraisal standards. For this purpose, the Foundation appoints two advisory boards funded by grants from the Appraisal Subcommittee: the Appraiser Qualifications Board and the Appraisal Standards Board.

The Appraiser Qualifications Board studies and recommends education, experience, examinations, licensing, and certification of qualified appraisers. The Appraisal Standards Board recommends uniform standards of professional appraisal procedure and ethics. These organizational relationships are shown in Figure 1-2.

Figure 1-2   Administration of the Federal Financial Institution Reform Recovery and Enforcement Act of 1989 (FIRREA).

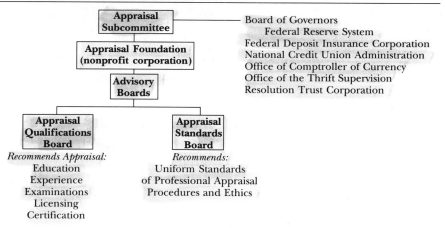

FEDERAL APPRAISAL STANDARDS

Under the amendment to FIRREA, a federally related transaction refers to any real estate related financial transaction in which a federal institution or agency or the Resolution Trust Corporation engages in contracts for the sale, lease, purchase, financing, investment, or exchange of real property. The Act covers real estate pledged as security for loans or investments, including mortgage-backed securities. Only state-certified or state-licensed appraisers are authorized to appraise real property for a federally related transaction.

Federal standards establishing minimum qualification criteria for state licensing and certification have been adopted by the Appraiser Qualifications Board. The Appraisal Subcommittee, based on recommendations of the Appraiser Qualifications Board, has issued an *advisory* to the states covering minimum qualifications for state licensing and certification of real estate appraisers.

States are required to meet (or exceed) minimum federal qualifications for state-certified or state-licensed appraisers. These minimum appraisal qualifications cover four main topics: experience, education, required examinations, and continuing education. Requirements for certified appraisers are higher than requirements for licensed appraisers. Generally, a *state-certified appraiser* is required for all transactions of $1,000,000 or more, while the appraisal of residential, one-to-four-unit properties (of less than $1,000,000) may be performed by a *state-licensed appraiser*. More complex residential property must be appraised by a state-certified appraiser.

LICENSED APPRAISER REQUIREMENTS. Qualifications cover minimum standards for experience, education, examination, and continuing education.

Appraisal Experience
> The Appraisal Subcommittee advises states to require, as a minimum, the equivalent of two years of appraisal experience, including at least 2,000 hours of appraising.

Education Requirements
> To sit for examinations for a licensed appraiser, applicants must complete 75 classroom hours of real estate appraisal and related subjects. Since the education requirement includes uniform standards of professional appraisal practice, most states require that 15 of the 75 hours cover professional appraisal practice and ethics.

Examination

> States must require applicants to a pass a uniform state licensing examination or its equivalent in order for the applicants to qualify as state-licensed appraisers.

Continuing Education

> The Subcommittee has advised states that they must require, as a minimum, the equivalent of ten classroom hours of instruction for each year of the license period preceding the renewal application. If the initial license for a state-licensed appraiser requires renewal at three-year intervals, 30 classroom hours of instruction would be required for license renewal.

CERTIFIED APPRAISER REQUIREMENTS. A state-certified appraiser is authorized to appraise all types of real estate. Because minimum qualifications are higher for certified appraisers than for licensed appraisers, states may require qualifications that exceed the federal standard.

Appraisal Experience

> Appraisal Subcommittee recommendations require a minimum of *two years* of appraisal experience, using a standard of 1,000 hours per year for one year of appraisal experience. In this instance, however, 50 percent of the experience must be in nonresidential appraisals. A residential appraisal is defined as an appraisal of a one-to-four-unit residential property.

Education Requirements

> For certification, states must require *165 classroom hours* of instruction in real estate appraisal and related subjects. A college degree, under certain conditions, may substitute for the 165 hours. Classroom hours must include uniform standards of professional appraisal practice. Educational credit is granted only where the applicant successfully passes an examination on each educational course.

Examination

> The Subcommittee has adopted recommendations of the Appraiser Qualifications Board that endorse a uniform state certification examination or its equivalent. A minimum examination standard assists in state reciprocity agreements for nonresident appraisal certification.

Continuing Education

> Like the state license requirement, applicants for certificate renewal require ten hours per year of continuing education. For example, over a two-year renewal period, the applicant must have completed at least 20 hours of classroom instruction at some time over the two years.

Federal Agency Appraisal Standards

While the preceding standards cover state licensing and certification, the regulations also cover federal agencies. Accordingly, the five federal financial regulatory agencies and the Resolution Trust Corporation have issued appraisal regulations as required by the FIRREA. As a guide, the types of appraisal required for transactions for federally regulated agencies and the Resolution Trust Corporation are shown in Table 1-1.

Table 1-1 indicates that transactions of less than $50,000 do not require appraisal under federal standards. Note that residential properties of over $1,000,000 and nonresidential properties over $250,000 require certified appraisers. Federal agencies may rely on state-licensed appraisers for the appraisal of residential properties of less than $1,000,000 and nonresidential properties of less than $250,000. The table shows that federal agencies may rely on certified appraisers for all types of property.[1]

Federal requirements specify *written appraisals* that include an opinion of a defined value, covering an adequately described property, assigned to a specific date, and supported by analysis. Written appraisals are defined as written statements which are independently and impartially prepared by a state-certified or state-licensed appraiser.

Table 1-1   Minimum Appraisal Standards for Federal Agencies and the Resolution Trust Corporation

Transaction Amount*	Residential	Nonresidential
Transactions less than $50,000	No appraisal needed	No appraisal needed
Transactions between $50,000 and $250,000	Licensed or certified appraiser	Licensed or certified appraiser
Transactions between $250,000 and $1,000,000	Licensed or certified appraiser	Certified appraiser
Transactions above $1,000,000	Certified appraiser	Certified appraiser

*   Refer to the specific agency which will be reviewing the appraisal to determine the current dollar threshold.

Source: The Appraisal Foundation

---

1   Consult specific agencies for current requirements.

State Appraisal Requirements

Under Title XI of FIRREA, each state must provide for state-certified or state-licensed appraisers and a certifying or licensing agency. In numerous cases, states have imposed higher standards than the federal law requires. In certain other states, it is uncertain whether state laws, at this writing, conform to FIRREA.

Selected examples of state laws show how various state requirements exceed federal minimum requirements. The chapter Appendix summarizes the general requirements of state laws. Consult state authorities for more current information.

State appraisal licensing and certification requirements vary greatly. While the states generally comply with federal appraisal standards and requirements, variations may be found in provisions for:

1. State appraisal boards.
2. Certified appraisers.
3. Licensed appraisers.
4. Experience requirements.
5. Minimum educational requirements.
6. Continued education requirements.
7. Exemptions.

In some instances, states have created additional appraisal classifications to meet individual state needs.

STATE APPRAISAL BOARDS. The state regulation of real estate appraisers is supervised by appointed appraisal boards. These boards operate independently of state licensing agencies for real estate salespersons or brokers. Board memberships range from the 15 appraisal board members in *Minnesota* to the minimum of five members provided by several states.

Board membership is usually dominated by certified or licensed appraisers. In a few states, all board members must be licensed or certified real estate appraisers, i.e., *Louisiana* (nine members), *Washington* (seven members), and *Texas* (nine members). However, *Alaska* requires that only two of its five members be certified or licensed appraisers. The other three members represent the general public, lenders, and an unspecified board member. Likewise, *Kentucky* requires only two appraisal members of a five-member board. In most states, the majority of the board members are certified or licensed appraisers.

CERTIFIED APPRAISERS

Florida distinguishes between a *certified residential* appraiser and a *certified general* appraiser. A residential appraiser is required to have only two years of appraisal experience in the last five years. The certified real estate appraiser must have three years of experience in the last five years.

Alabama complies with the federal statute by providing for a *licensed* real estate appraiser, a *certified residential* appraiser, and a *certified general* appraiser. Certified appraisers must pass a written examination on an advanced:

1. knowledge of technical terms.
2. understanding of land economics and real estate appraisal.
3. understanding of real estate appraisals.
4. knowledge of real estate costs and real estate mathematics.
5. knowledge of other appropriate principles and procedures.
6. understanding of real estate law.
7. understanding of appraisal misconduct.

Alabama does not require a license or certificate for the appraisal of real estate which does not involve a federally related transaction.

In short, the states generally provide for *certified residential* appraisers and *certified general* appraisers. The certificate for residential appraising is largely confined to the appraisal of one-to-four residential units and up to 12 units if the value is less than $1,000,000. The general certified category covers all types of properties.

LICENSED APPRAISERS

A few states, like *Georgia*, qualify appraisers as *certified real estate* appraisers who are authorized to appraise any type of real estate. Alternatively, appraisers may qualify as *licensed real estate* appraisers who may value one-to-four-unit residential property and up to 12 residential units if the value is less than $1,000,000 and if the property is appraised without reference to its income.

In *Colorado*, applicants qualify as licensed appraisers with 55 hours of appraisal education as approved by the board. Applicants must pass an appraisal examination. Colorado also certifies residential and general appraisers. *Nebraska* qualifies appraisers as either certified or licensed real estate appraisers. For the licensed classification, the applicant must have a college degree or 60 classroom hours of appraisal courses and 15 hours of instruction on standards of professional appraisal practice.

APPRAISAL EXPERIENCE

While most states conform closely to the federal law, they vary in the interpretation of experience requirements. In agreement with federal law, states generally require *two years* of appraisal experience acquired within the last *five years*. In *Georgia* and *Tennessee*, one year of appraisal experience equals 1,000 hours of appraisal work in one year. In *Idaho*, one year of appraisal experience must include 1,500 hours of appraisal work. *Michigan* defines one year of appraisal experience for certification as 2,000 hours of work per year, of which 1,000 hours must include appraisals on nonresidential property. *Missouri* defines one year of appraisal experience as at least 20 hours of appraisal experience per week for one year.

In *Florida*, however, one year of experience equals 120 appraisal reports completed in a format conforming to appraisal industry practices. To receive one year of appraisal experience, review appraisers must sign a minimum of 240 appraisal report reviews. Less than the required number of appraisals is permitted for appraisals that require more time or a higher degree of skills.

The states vary widely in activities that are considered as appraisal experience. The more liberal states include property tax appraisals, real estate counseling, review appraisals, feasibility analysis, real estate analysis, and the teaching of appraisal courses. Various states require documentation to support appraisal experience credits.

EDUCATION

The most common educational requirement includes 75 hours of classroom instruction or a college degree for *residential appraisal certification* and 165 classroom hours or a college degree for *general appraisal certification*. In both cases, 15 of the classroom hours must usually include professional appraisal practice and ethical standards.

For the general appraiser certificate, *Wisconsin* requires 200 hours of instruction in approved courses including 15 hours in professional standards, code of ethics, and state appraisal laws. An applicant for a *residential* appraiser certificate must have 120 hours of comparable education courses.

After July 1, 1993, *Idaho* will require an applicant for the certified general real estate appraiser designation to have a *college degree* which includes 165 classroom hours in appraisal-related courses.

In general, states that provide for licensed appraisers require 75 hours of classroom instruction, 15 of which must cover professional appraisal standards and ethics. Usually a college degree may be substituted for the 75 hours. *Utah* and *North Carolina* require a minimum of 90 classroom hours of instruction. State legislation or regulations usually detail course content and require course approval for classroom hour credit.

CONTINUING EDUCATION

While the prevailing standard requires ten hours of classroom instruction per year for license or certificate renewal, *Wyoming* requires 60 hours of continuing education preceding the three-year renewal period. For every two-year renewal, *Texas* requires 30 hours of continuing education courses, including seven hours on standards of professional appraisal practice and ethics. *Idaho* is among the states requiring *15 classroom hours* of instruction each year during the three years preceding certificate renewal. State laws and board regulations vary in the details that govern continuing education course approval and subjects covered.

EXEMPTIONS

State laws exempt certain appraisal-related activities from licensing and certification requirements. While some states, like *Alabama*, do not require an appraisal license for appraisals not involving a federally related transaction, other states such as *Illinois*, permit "noncertified" appraisals, provided the appraiser does not create the impression that the appraiser is "certified." "Limited certification" is permitted in *Alaska* to appraise property in sparsely settled areas if the cost of a certified appraiser would be unreasonably high, relative to the value of the property appraised. Such appraisals must be consistent with federal law, however.

Arizona issues temporary license certificates for one year if the appraisal board determines that there is a scarcity of state-certified or state-licensed appraisers. State-licensed real estate salespersons and brokers who give informed opinions of value incidental to a real estate listing and sale are generally exempt. Appraisers exempt from licensing and certification frequently include the exemptions as allowed in *Nebraska*, such as any employees of

the federal government,
state agencies,
insurance companies, and
financial institutions.

Licenses or certificates are required only if the sources listed above act as independent appraisers. Generally, as these comments suggest, exemptions under state law are quite limited and relatively unimportant.

State Regulations Summarized

States vary in their compliance with Title XI. However, a review of selected states shows a recurring pattern. States may delegate enforcement to a director, like *Texas* and *California*, which provide for a director and advisory committee to establish regulations that conform to federal requirements.

Probably the majority of states have laws comparable to *Georgia*, which provides for certified and licensed appraisers. This approach agrees with the Appraiser Qualifications Board position that *licensed appraisers* are qualified to appraise one-to-four-family dwellings of $1,000,000 or less, while *certified appraisers* are qualified to appraise all building types. These laws generally require a minimum of *two years of experience* for licensed appraisers and *three or more years* of appraisal experience for certified appraisers. Both designations require continuing education for licensing or certification renewal.

Other states, such as *Oregon*, enact stiffer requirements. *Oregon* and *Florida*, like many other states, require a detailed *log of appraisals* to verify appraisal experience. Some states prohibit appraisal designations unless the appraiser has been certified or licensed. In addition to appraisal standards, *Florida* and a few other states require applicants for the certified and licensed designation to be licensed real estate salespersons or real estate brokers.

In short, states administer appraisal certification and licensing laws similar to real estate licensing activities. Typically, states provide for a real estate appraisal board appointed by the governor, with the consent of the legislature. An appraisal advisory board, typically consisting of practicing appraisers and others, is appointed to work with board officials. Generally, state laws require *two to three years* of experience during the last five years and a *minimum number of class-approved hours* of instruction prior to taking qualifying examinations.

Examination content follows appraisal courses sponsored by colleges, approved proprietary schools, and trade associations. Appraisal examinations cover real estate instruments, real estate financing, and real estate law other than appraisal topics. States universally require a knowledge of appraisal codes of ethics.

APPRAISAL ASSOCIATIONS

Appraisal organizations serve the professional objectives of their member-ship. To this end, they support *educational programs*, sponsor *appraisal research*, publish *appraisal reference studies and textbooks*, and provide *member designations* earned by meeting qualifications of the organization. Designa-tions are earned by documenting experience qualifications, passing one or more examinations, and submitting demonstration appraisal reports for review and acceptance by examining committees.

National appraisal organizations tend to be dominated by the Appraisal Institute. The Institute was formed by the unification of the more than 22,000-member American Institute of Real Estate Appraisers and the over 20,000-member Society of Real Estate Appraisers. The two groups merged in 1990. Qualified members hold the designation "Member Appraisal Institute" (MAI) or the designation "Senior Residential Appraiser."

The current requirements of the Appraisal Institute are indicative of standards adopted by leading appraisal organizations in order to increase professional competence. Although subject to minor changes under the unification plan initiated in 1990, candidates for the Member, Appraisal Institute (MAI) designation require a passing grade in courses on:

1. Real estate appraisal principles.
2. Basic valuation procedures.
3. Capitalization theory and techniques.
4. Case studies in real estate valuation.

After taking these courses, candidates must pass a comprehensive ex-amination and receive passing grades on courses in *report writing, valuation analysis,* and *standards of professional practice.*

In addition, candidates must document *five years* of accreditable ap-praisal experience, of which three years must be in specialized appraisal ex-perience. Appraisal experience is reviewed to ensure that the experience level meets minimum requirements. The candidate must receive a passing grade on a *demonstration appraisal report* on an income-producing property.

To earn the *Senior Residential Appraiser* designation (SRA), passing grades must be received on *two courses*, including a course on Professional Practice. *Two years* of experience are required, based upon a minimum number of appraisal reports completed during a 12-month period. Candi-dates must submit a *residential demonstration appraisal* that indicates famili-arity with the narrative appraisal report format. Candidates for both designations must have an undergraduate degree from a four-year accredited college or have additional compensating experience.

Other appraisal associations have been formed by appraisers who are more specialized. The American Society of Farm Managers and Rural Appraisers issues qualified members the designations of AFM (Accredited Farm Manager) and the ARA (Accredited Rural Appraiser) for members who value and manage farms and rural real estate.

The International Association of Assessing Officers issues four member designations attesting to member qualifications: the CPE (Certified Personal Evaluator), the AAE (Accredited Assessment Evaluator), the CAE (Certified Assessment Evaluator), and the RES (Residential Evaluation Specialist). These specialized designations are earned by members who qualify to appraise property for property taxes.

The International Right-of-Way Association issues the designation of "Senior Member, Right-of-Way Association." Members qualify by meeting minimum qualifications for eminent domain appraisal purposes. Many other designations are issued by dozens of other appraisal associations. Their membership qualifications and education and experience requirements vary widely.

These member education and experience requirements show a rising standard for real estate appraisal qualification. State and federal legislation requires a minimum educational experience to meet legal requirements. Several state appraisal laws exceed minimum federal requirements. Given these minimum standards, appraisers then work toward a higher level of attainment by earning designations awarded by examination, demonstration reports, and experience in a specialized appraisal activity.

SUMMARY

Real estate appraisals are *unbiased written estimates of value*. The written estimate requires ten items common to a professional appraisal report:

Estimate of value	Qualifying conditions..
Date.	Property description.
Appraiser's signature.	Factual appraisal data.
Appraisal purpose.	Data analysis.
Value definition.	Supporting exhibits.

Appraisal clients include a wide variety of *private* clients, *business* clients, and *government* agencies.

Appraisals are completed for changes in ownership, financing, eminent domain, taxation, leases, and other special purpose appraisals that cover insurance, corporate activities, and bankruptcy proceedings. Appraisers may specialize in eminent domain valuations based on the estimate of *just compensation* for the taking of private property in the public interest.

✕   Title XI of the *Real Estate Appraisers Reform Amendment to the Federal Financial Institution Reform Recovery Act of 1989* establishes national appraisal standards that require real estate appraisals for federally related transactions. Such appraisals must conform to uniform standards prepared by appraisers who have demonstrated competence. The Act is administered under standards established by the Appraisal Foundation, a nonprofit corporation originally sponsored by eight national appraisal organizations. The Appraisal Foundation appoints two advisory boards: the Appraiser Qualifications Board and the Appraisal Standards Board. The Foundation establishes standards for the Appraisal Subcommittee which consists of five heads of federal financial regulatory agencies and the Resolution Trust Corporation. The subcommittee monitors state certification and licensing of appraisers. The Act requires each state to provide for *state-certified or state-licensed appraisers* for federally related transactions.

Title XI amendments to FIRREA require a state-certified or state-licensed appraiser to appraise real estate for a federally related transaction. Minimum qualifications for certified appraisers include:

1. Two years of appraisal experience.
2. 165 hours of classroom instruction, including 15 hours on professional standards and appraisal ethics.
3. Required examinations.
4. Continuing education for certification renewal of ten hours of instruction per year.

Licensed appraisers, qualified to appraise one-to-four-unit residential properties of less than $1,000,000, generally are required to have two years of appraisal experience, 65 hours of classroom instruction (including 15 hours on professional standards and appraisal ethics), a required examination, and continuing education of 10 hours per year for license renewal.

The various states, as required, appoint state appraisal boards to administer federal appraisal standards. The appraisal boards are usually appointed by the governor, with the majority of members drawn from licensed or certified appraisers. Selected states have exceeded the education requirements for appraisal certification or licenses. Some states require experience that exceeds the two-year minimum requirement under FIRREA. Several states have increased the continuing educational requirement from 10 hours per year to 15 hours per year over the renewal period.

Exemptions under the law are quite limited—real estate salespersons and brokers, and employees of state, federal, or financial institutions are usually exempt under the act. Other states have provided for temporary licenses or limited appraisal licenses to cover local appraisal conditions.

Appraisal associations are dominated by the Appraisal Institute. Qualified members hold the designation, Member, Appraisal Institute (MAI) or the SRA designation, "Senior Residential Appraiser." Other appraisal organizations qualify members by designations awarded after applicants have completed minimum experience and required examinations. The list includes the American Society of Farm Managers and Rural Appraisers, the International Association of Assessing Officers and the International Right-of-Way Association.

POINTS TO REMEMBER

appraisal report an unbiased written estimate of value.

eminent domain the right of government agencies and regulated public utilities to take private property in the public interest.

Appraisal Foundation a nonprofit corporation chartered by eight national appraisal organizations in order to promote "uniform standards of professional appraisal procedure."

Appraiser Qualifications Board a board appointed by the Appraisal Foundation to study and recommend education, experience, examinations, licensing, and certification of appraisers.

Appraisal Standards Board a board appointed by the Appraisal Foundation to establish and improve standards of professional appraisal practice.

Appraisal Subcommittee the Committee includes the Board of Governors of the Federal Reserve System, the Federal Deposit Insurance Corporation, the National Credit Union Administration, the Office of the Comptroller of Currency, the Office of Thrift Supervision, and the Resolution Trust Corportion.

federally related transaction a real estate transaction in which a federal institution or agency or the Resolution Trust Corporation engages in contracts for the sale, lease, purchase, financing, investment, or exchange of real property.

written appraisal a written statement that is independently and impartially prepared by a licensed or certified appraiser giving an opinion of defined value of an adequately described property, as of a specific date, and supported by analysis.

member designations appraisal membership designations awarded to qualified members who have obtained the minimum required appraisal experience, passed the required examinations, and submitted other evidence of their qualifications for a member designation.

QUESTIONS FOR REVIEW

1. Define an appraisal; what are the minimum requirements of a written appraisal report?

2. Summarize the common real estate activities that require real estate appraisals.

3. What are the main purposes of real estate appraisals? Explain fully.

4. What are the minimum federal requirements for a certified real estate appraiser?

5. What are the minimum federal requirements for a licensed real estate appraiser?

6. What is the function of the Appraisal Foundation? Explain fully.

7. What are the functions of the two advisory boards that serve under the Appraisal Foundation?

8. What roles do appraisal trade associations play in developing professional appraisal qualifications? Explain thoroughly.

PRACTICE PROBLEMS

1. You are requested to complete a market value appraisal on a 40-acre mobile-home park with 200 trailer pads. Your client requires an appraisal for a first mortgage from a federally regulated lender. The client requests your opinion on a one-page letter. How would you respond to this appraisal request? In advising the client, what data would you indicate must be included in a written appraisal report? Explain fully.

2. You are preparing for a career in real estate appraising. Discuss the course of study and experience necessary to be state certified. What steps are necessary to qualify for your selected industry appraisal designations? Explain courses of study that you believe would give you added appraisal competence not required for certification or designations. Explain thoroughly.

Table 1A-1   State Real Estate Appraisal Boards

State	Board Members	Board Composition			
		Appraisers	Public	Lenders	Other
Alabama	9	7	2		
Alaska	5	2	1	1	
Arizona	9	4	3		2(a)
Arkansas	Not available				
California	9	4	3	2	
Colorado	7	4	1	1	1(b)
Connecticut	8	5	3		
Delaware	9	5	3	1	
Dist. of Columbia	5	4	1		
Florida	7	5			2
Georgia	5	4	1		
Hawaii	7(j)	3	2	2	
Idaho	5	Not specific			
Illinois	7	5			1(c), 1(d)
Indiana*	7	5	1	1	
Iowa	7	5	2		
Kansas	7	3	1	2	
Kentucky	5	2	1	2	
Louisiana*	9	9			
Maine	5	3	1	1	
Maryland	9	3	3	3	
Massachusetts	No legislation to date				
Michigan	9	6	3		
Minnesota	15	8	3		4(f)
Mississippi	6	3			
Missouri	7	6	1		
Montana	5	3			2
Nebraska	5	3	2		
Nevada	5	4			1
New Hampshire	Not available				

Table 1A-1   State Real Estate Appraisal Boards

State	Board Members	Board Composition			
		Appraisers	Public	Lenders	Other
New Jersey	9	6	2		1
New Mexico	7	5	1	1	
New York	9	6	3		
North Carolina	5	3			2
North Dakota	5	3	1	1	
Ohio	5	4	1		
Oklahoma	7	4		2	1(g)
Oregon*	7	5	2		
Pennsylvania	7	4	2		1(h)
Rhode Island	10	7	1	1	1(i)
South Carolina	7	4	1	1	1
South Dakota	Nonspecific legislation				
Tennessee	9	6	2		1(a)
Texas	9	9			
Utah	7	4	2		1(e)
Vermont	5	3	2		
Virginia	9	4	2	2	1(a)
Washington	7	7			
West Virginia*	7	2	3	2	
Wisconsin	7	4	2		1(b)
Wyoming	5	3	1	1	

Source: Survey by author

* - Proposed legislation to date.
a - Member must be in business education.
b - Member must be a county assessor.
c - Member must be the Commissioner of Real Estate.
d - Member must be from the disciplinary board.
e - Member must be the Commissioner of the Department of Financial Institutions.
f - Member must be a consumer of appraisal services.
g - Member must be in real estate sales industry.
h - Member must be the Commissioner of Professional and Occupational Affairs.
i - Member must be the Director of the Department of Business Regulation.
j - Board consists of the board members of the Department of Commerce and Consumer Affairs.

Table 1A -2   State Requirements for Licensed Appraisers

State	Classroom Hours	Minimum Experience/ Years**	Continuing Education (Hrs./Yrs.)	Exam Required
Alabama	0		15/2 (a)	Y
Alaska	No licensing	---	---	---
Arizona	60	2/5	30/3	Y
Arkansas	Not available			
California	Nonspecific legislation			
Colorado	55	2/2		Y
Connecticut	60	2	20/2	Y
Delaware	85	3		
Dist. of Columbia	75	2		Y
Florida	No licensing	---	---	---
Georgia (c)	75	2/5	10/1	Y
Hawaii	75	2	10/1	Y
Idaho	No licensing	---	---	---
Illinois	No licensing	---	---	---
Indiana	No licensing	---	---	---
Iowa	No licensing	---	---	---
Kansas	No licensing	---	---	---
Kentucky	No licensing	---	---	---
Louisiana	No licensing	---	---	---
Maine	50	2/5	20/2	Y
Maryland	45	0	42/3	Y
Massachusetts	No legislation to date			
Michigan	75	2,000 Hrs	10/1	Y
Minnesota	No licensing	---	---	---
Mississippi	60		20/2	Y
Missouri	45	2/5		Y
Montana	75	Nonspecific	45/3	Y
Nebraska	75			Y
Nevada	No licensing	---	---	---
New Hampshire	Not available			

Table 1A -2   State Requirements for Licensed Appraisers

State	Classroom Hours	Minimum Experience/ Years**	Continuing Education (Hrs./Yrs.)	Exam Required
New Jersey	Nonspecific legislation			
New Mexico	60		30/3	N
New York	No licensing	- - -	- - -	- - -
North Carolina	90		24/2	Y
North Dakota	Nonspecific legislation			
Ohio	No licensing	- - -	- - -	- - -
Oklahoma	No licensing	- - -	- - -	- - -
Oregon	Not available			
Pennsylvania	No licensing	- - -	- - -	- - -
Rhode Island	No licensing	- - -	- - -	- - -
South Carolina	75	2	10/1	Y
South Dakota	Nonspecific legislation			
Tennessee (b)	45	2/5	15/2	Y
Texas	No licensing	- - -	- - -	- - -
Utah (c)	90 (d)	0		Y
Vermont	75	2	10/1	Y
Virginia	75	2/5	6/2	Y
Washington	No licensing	- - -	- - -	- - -
West Virginia	Not available			
Wisconsin	No licensing	- - -	- - -	- - -
Wyoming	No licensing	- - -	- - -	- - -

Source: Survey by author

* - Proposed legislation to date.

**- 2/5 refers to two years minimum experience in the last five years.

a - A standards of professional practice course is required.

b - Appraisers who apply within 180 days of the act are exempt from the 45 required classroom hours if the applicant has five years appraisal experience within the last seven years. Also, the examination is waived if the applicant completes 45 classroom hours.

c - The state registers appraisers in lieu of licensing appraisers.

d - A bachelor's degree in economics, finance, or related fields substitutes for the required classroom hours. The education and examination requirements are waived if applicant has two years appraisal experience or holds an approved appraisal designation.

Table 1A-3   State requirements for certified appraisers

State	Classroom Hours Res	Gen	Minimum Experience/Yrs Res	Gen	Continuing Education (Hrs/Yrs)	Required Exam
Alabama	75	165	2	2	20/2	Y
Alaska (a)	75	165	3/5	4/7	40/2	Y
Arizona	Not specific		2	2/5	30/3	Y
Arkansas	Not available					
California*	Nonspecific legislation					
Colorado	95	165	2	3		Y
Connecticut	75	165			20/2	Y
Delaware	75	165	2/5	2/5	10/1	Y
Dist. of Columbia		165		2		Y
Florida	60(b)	120(b)	2(g)	3(g)	45/2	Y
Georgia		165		2/5	10/1	Y
Hawaii		165		2	10/1	Y
Idaho	75	165(j)	2/5	3/5	15/1	Y
Illinois	75	165	2/5	3/5	14/1(k)	Y
Indiana	Legislation to be amended					
Iowa	Nonspecific legislation					
Kansas	75	165	2	2	10/1	Y
Kentucky	75	165	2/5	2/5	10/1	Y
Louisiana*	75(c)	165(c)	2/5(b)	3/5(b)	30/2	Y
Maine	85	165	2/5(c)	2/5(c)	20/2	Y
Maryland	75	165	2/5	2/5	21/1	Y
Massachusetts	No legislation to date					
Michigan		165		2000 hrs	10/1	Y
Minnesota	75	165		2/5	30/2	Y
Mississippi	75	165	2/5	2/5	20/2	Y
Missouri	75	165	2/5	2/5	30/3	Y
Montana (d)	Nonspecific legislation					
Nebraska (h)		165		2/5	12/2	Y
Nevada	60	120	2/5	3/5	20/2	Y
New Hampshire	Not available					

Table 1A-3   State requirements for certified appraisers

State	Classroom Hours Res	Gen	Minimum Experience/Yrs Res	Gen	Continuing Education (Hrs/Yrs)	Required Exam
New Jersey	Nonspecific legislation					
New Mexico	75	165	2/5	2/5	30/3	Y
New York	75	165	2/5	2/5	20/2	Y
North Carolina		180		2/5	24/2	Y
North Dakota	Nonspecific legislation					
Ohio	75	165	2/5	2/5	20/2	Y
Oklahoma	75	165	2/5	2/5	30/3	Y
Oregon	No certification currently					
Pennsylvania	75	165	2/5	3/5		Y
Rhode Island (e)	75	165	2/5	2/5	20/2	Y
South Carolina		165		2	10/1	Y
South Dakota	Nonspecific legislation					
Tennessee (f)	75	165	2/5	2/5	20/2	Y
Texas	95	165	2(g)	3(g)	30/2	Y
Utah	120(i)	165	2	2		Y
Vermont		165		2/5	10/1	Y
Virginia	165	180	2/5	3/5	20/2	Y
Washington	75	165	2/5	2/5	20/2	Y
West Virginia	Not available					
Wisconsin	120	200	2/5	2/5	30/2	Y
Wyoming	75	135	2/5	2/5	60/3	Y

Source: Survey by author

* - Proposed legislation to date.

**- 2/5 Refers to two years minimum experience in the last five years.

a - Limited certification is provided for sparsely populated areas.

b - Experience and class hours are on a point-equivalent system.

c - Applicants must hold a valid real estate appraisal license.

d - The state offers agricultural appraiser certification.

e - Applicants holding real estate licenses with five years appraisal experience qualify for real estate appraisal certificates.

f - An appraiser trainee license may be issued for one year subject to renewal.

g - A sales/broker license is also required.

h - Licensing and certification shall not apply to appraisers employed by government agencies, financial institutions, trainees, and appraisers testifying in court condemnation proceedings.

i - Applicants for certification must be state registered appraisers. Also, applicants may substitute a bachelor's degree in economics, finance, or a related field.

j - After July 1, 1993, the applicant must have a college degree (The 165 hours may be included in hours required for a degree).

k - 14 Classroom hours per year are required for residential appraisal renewal and 21 classroom hours per year are required for general certificate renewal.

C H A P T E R 2

The Market Value Standard

After studying this chapter, you will know:
- The meaning of market value and its implied assumptions.
- Leading concepts of value.
- Market value principles important to market value estimates.

Lenders, investors, and developers make rational decisions based on the market value estimate. Buyers and sellers both benefit by exchanging real estate at the market value. At the market value, the seller gains the highest possible price; the buyer in turn acquires property at the least cost.

Because of the critical importance of market value, the chapter starts with the concept of *value*. Given the idea of value, it is essential to review the meaning of *market value*—the next chapter topic. An understanding of market value is gained by a review of the many assumptions underlying the market value standard. The chapter closes with an explanation of market value principles.

THE CONCEPT OF VALUE

Value means *the power of one good to command other goods in exchange*. In this sense, *value is a ratio in which real estate is exchanged for other assets*. The definition does not imply that real estate has inherent qualities that determine value. Rather, value refers to a ratio determined by buyers and sellers in the market.

To have value, real estate must be relatively *scarce;* hence, a downtown commercial site may sell for $1,000 per square foot because downtown land is relatively scarce. Similarly, semiarid grazing land in the western states may sell for $50 an acre. Such land lacks the degree of scarcity to assume a higher value. Scarcity is measured in terms of the available supply and its consequent demand. Therefore, the value of real estate, in part, is measured by its *relative scarcity*.

To have value, real estate must also possess *utility*. Utility is the *power to increase satisfaction or decrease dissatisfaction*. To cite an extreme example, an abandoned, dilapidated dwelling in a declining neighborhood may have little value because of poor utility; its location and present condition lack the necessary utility to attract prospective buyers. Real estate assumes value according to its *relative degree of utility*.

The same idea also applies to real estate features. Consider the value of a two-bedroom house in a rural, lower middle-income community, with an 800-square-foot swimming pool. Though the swimming pool may cost

$25,000, the utility of the swimming pool does not justify a value equal to its cost. In other words, how much would the buyer of a particular two-bedroom dwelling pay for the added utility created by a swimming pool?

The central appraisal problem is to estimate the degree of utility that affects value. Accordingly, appraisers constantly review the utility of real estate and its components in order to estimate value. In short, to have value, real estate must be *relatively scarce* and it must have *utility*.

Market Value

Accurate appraisals depend on the correct interpretation of market value. Errors in interpreting market data are avoided by a clear understanding of market value. By modifying the term *value*, the word *market* adds a special meaning. A widely quoted definition of market value states:

> *Market value is the most probable sales price for which the property will sell in a competitive market, with the buyer and seller acting knowledgeably, and with neither party acting under duress.*

While definitions of market value vary in detail according to state law, definitions of market value rest on a fairly common set of assumptions:

1. The buyer and seller are reasonably well informed. Perfect knowledge is not required. In practice, the buyer is usually better informed on housing prices after reviewing perhaps dozens of houses listed for sale. The seller of a single-family dwelling generally has less exposure to the market. The typical house seller enters the market over an average of seven or more years. As a consequence, the buyer usually has superior knowledge of the current market.

The seller-occupant, in contrast, generally has better knowledge of the property utility. The seller knows about limitations, such as whether the central air conditioning system is adequate, or favorable and unfavorable features of the neighborhood. On the whole, however, the market value definition presumes that both parties are reasonably informed of the current market and property characteristics–and that they make rational buying and selling decisions.

2. Market value is based on a price realized after the property has been exposed on the open market for a reasonable time. The reasonable time requirement depends on the local market. The reasonable selling time for a warehouse may be six months or more. In an active market, the reasonable time for a dwelling may be 60 days. In other words, market value is that value which will be realized if the property is exposed for the customary marketing time common to the real estate appraised.

3. Market value presumes a cash price or financing terms typical of the current market. A typical single-family dwelling may be purchased with a loan equal to 80 or 90 percent of the appraised value, repayable over 30 years, with a fixed interest rate of 10 percent. Atypical financing would be illustrated by the same sale in which the owner agrees to take back a second mortgage with a below-market interest rate of seven percent. The market value does not cover prices resulting from unusually high loan-to-value loans or below-market interest rates.

4. Market value is the price realized, assuming many buyers and sellers. The number of buyers and sellers, ideally, should be such that the decision to buy or sell does not affect the price. To cite a common example, your decision to buy one dozen eggs today will not affect the price of eggs. Similarly, the market value estimate presumes that there is a sufficient number of buyers and sellers to avoid price distortion from the unequal bargaining power of a single seller or a single buyer. The market value estimate does not cover prices that result from monopoly advantages held by either the buyer or seller. Appraisers are aware of price distortions that may result from unusual market relationships. The market value estimate presumes fairly competitive market conditions.

Furthermore, it is acceptable to define market value as *the most probable selling price.* Because ideal, competitive markets seldom prevail, the appraiser reports that value which a buyer would be willing to pay and a seller would be willing to sell under *typical,* local market terms. This definition allows reasonable variations from the purely competitive ideal; market value would be that price which is typical under prevailing market arrangements. To avoid possible misinterpretations, appraisers cite their definition of market value in written appraisal reports or in court testimony.

Cost

The cost of real estate usually consists of the land, land improvements (land leveling, paving, and the like) and building costs. The real estate cost includes certain other "soft" costs such as legal services and financing fees. It is important to stress, however, that real estate *cost does not determine market value.* In fact, the cost of a poorly located building or a building of low quality construction or design may have a market value less than the original cost. An oversupply of housing or commercial space may lead to market values less than the current cost of real estate.

Conversely, market value may temporarily exceed the cost of land and the building construction cost. Generally, however, competitive forces lead to an increase in supply, with the consequence that cost and value tend to correspond. The equivalence of cost and value depend on the utility of the property and the supply of the real estate relative to the current demand. At this point, however, remember that *cost does not determine value.*

Market Price

Price is value expressed in money. Because of market imperfections, a given market price may be a distorted market value. An uninformed buyer or seller, below market financing, and other elements may result in distorted market prices.

Difficulties arise in interpreting market value because real estate prices vary among unique properties. Furthermore, it is probable that most real estate prices are generally changing either upward or downward. As a result, appraisers carefully analyze prices in the light of the market value standard.

Consider the residential lot sales shown in Figure 2-1. The vertical axis indicates the price per lot, while the horizontal scale plots sales over five

Figure 2-1 Residential Lot Sales Over Five Years

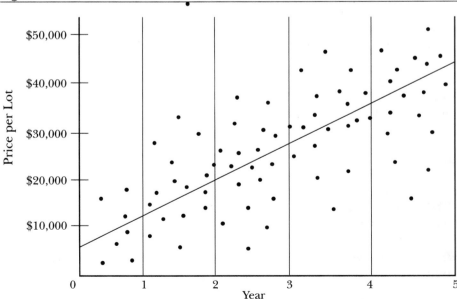

years. For lot sales in the same neighborhood, lot prices vary according to the size of the lot, the front footage, the topography, lot shape, locational advantages, and other features. At the same time, the lot prices of Figure 2-1 suggest an increase in value over time. If you were appraising property in year five, you would probably select a lot sale sold within the last year. Because lot prices vary, the appraiser must decide whether price variation results from lot characteristics, varying motives of the buyer and seller, financing terms, or a rising trend in land values.

Therefore, in this example, the appraiser must weigh the price variation caused by physical differences in the lots sold and the lot appraised, in addition to the variation caused by the rising lot values. The final value estimate, therefore, would be based on a comparison of the lot appraised with lots sold, as adjusted for the time of sale and differences in physical lot characteristics.

It may be readily appreciated that the interpretation of market value is fairly critical. That is, the appraiser would not reject sales sold in year five as a price distortion relative to the historical values that prevailed before year four. To help resolve these issues, appraisers are guided largely by certain value concepts that affect market prices and buyer and seller behavior.

VALUE CONCEPTS

While the concept of market value controls most appraisal assignments, other types of value are in common use. Some terms are special valuation concepts required by state statutes. Other value terms are commonly used by lenders, accountants, and others dealing in real estate. Familiarity with these terms helps appraisers differentiate between specialized values for specific purposes and market value for appraisal purposes. First consider, common valuation terms that are statutorily defined among the various states.

Statutorily Defined Values

State statutes define value for eminent domain purposes—the right of public agencies and regulated public utilities to take private property for public purposes. Similarly, state laws variously define value for property tax purposes. A description of these terms shows differences between concepts of value.

JUST COMPENSATION

The taking of private property by government agencies under state law requires payment of just compensation to the property owner. The courts have generally conceded that *just compensation means market value.* Just compensation may cover *severance damage*—the loss in value to the property remaining after a partial public taking of private property. Severance damages result from the diminution of value for that portion of an owner's property not taken for a public improvement. Other states may allow for *consequential damages,* which are payments for the decrease in value of an owner's property, no part of which was taken for public purposes. Consequential damages may be paid for the decrease in value arising from airport noise, even though no part of the property was taken for airport purposes.

With these technical qualifications, just compensation generally refers to market value—private property owners are entitled to just compensation or the market value of property taken for public purposes. Public utilities, as state-regulated monopolies, are subject to the same laws.

ASSESSED VALUE

Assessed value is the value determined for property taxes. Because the various states define the assessed value for property tax purposes differently, the term should not be confused with market value. For example, some states base the assessed value of agricultural property on its value for agricultural use and not the market value. Other states require assessors to base the assessed value on a given percentage of market value. Because of variations in state requirements and because of administrative deficiencies in estimating assessed values, the term should not substitute for market value. As a rule, the assessed value is a poor measure of market value.

OTHER STATUTORY VALUES

States vary in definitions of value for specific purposes. The appraiser may encounter local terms that refer to "just value," "fair value," "true and fair value," "normal value," "sound value," or "economic value." While these terms may have a legal basis, their interpretation is highly subjective. Usually, appraisers do not make ethical judgments over value implied in the terms "normal," "fair," "sound," or "economic." Appraised values follow the market value standard without the ethical connotation implied in these value terms.

Industry Value Concepts

Besides real estate appraisers, other specialists refer to specialized values common to their subject areas. Real estate appraisers rely on market value, while other specialists recognize differences in value concepts encountered in their subject areas. Value estimates are not confined to real estate appraisers. Engineers, accountants, and bankers regularly employ value terms for their specialty. Appraisers recognize the differences between value terms regularly used in business.

VALUE FOR ACCOUNTING PURPOSES

Accountants refer to *book* value, which is entered as the original cost of a real estate asset. In this sense, book value may be carried forward in succeeding years so that book value is actually a historical value—a value unrelated to the current market value.

Book value may also be based on the original cost, less depreciation. For accounting purposes, depreciation is a cost allocation. For example, the book value may be reduced annually by a depreciation factor that meets accounting standards. Consequently, *the depreciated book value* is the book value less the accrued depreciation allowable for accounting purposes. Again, this value has limited application for appraisers. Book value or depreciated book value may be quite unrelated to market value.

ENGINEERING VALUE

Engineers, dealing with property values for contractors and industrial clients, refer to *reproduction cost new,* which is the current cost of reproducing an exact building replica.

In calculating the depreciated value, engineers measure depreciation by the loss of efficiency. Asset depreciation may be determined by the degree to which serviceability is impaired, known as a *percent condition.* That is, an asset with a 98 percent condition is one that has a two percent impairment in serviceability. *Depreciation* is defined as *a loss in value from any cause.* Therefore, the depreciated value, in engineering terms, would be unacceptable as a market value estimate.

The concepts of value for specialized purposes is virtually unlimited. Lenders refer to the *loan value,* generally equal to a percent of the market value. Similarly, insurance companies refer to the *insurable value.* Insurable value is usually the reproduction cost new, less the cost of the foundation and of building plans. The important point here is that such specialized value terms have limited applicability to market value estimates.

MARKET VALUE PRINCIPLES

The interpretation of market prices and the selection of real estate sales for appraisal purposes depends on a thorough understanding of principles that relate to valuation. The appraisal principles explained here have gained wide acceptance among appraisers. In some instances, the principles are restatements of economic principles, while others have been derived from analysis of real estate investment experiences and from market observation.

The Bundle of Rights

The bundle of rights refers to *real estate ownership that consists of numerous property rights*—much like a bundle of sticks. The full bundle of sticks is known as the fee simple absolute. See Figure 2-2. Frequently, however, the appraisal problem does not cover the fee simple absolute title but only part of the bundle. For example, in appraising leased property, appraisers must consider the fee simple absolute subject to the lease—only part of the bundle is valued. In other cases the appraisal may require valuation of the interest held by the tenant.

Figure 2-2 An Illustration of the Bundle of Rights Concept of Fee Simple Absolute Ownership

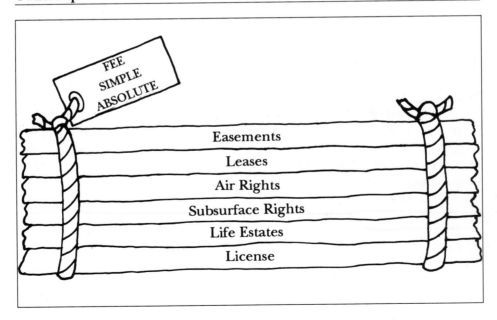

Furthermore, the fee simple absolute, the largest possible ownership, may be subject to the rights of others that have been granted easements. An *easement is a nonpossessory interest to use property for a specific purpose.* A single-family dwelling may be subject to rights of way for sewer lines, power lines, or natural gas lines. Such rights are easements that give others the right to install and service utility lines on private property. The appraisal of lots affected by such easements must consider the rights of others to use the property for a special purpose.

The bundle of rights held by the owner includes the right to convey air rights—the right to use the air space over the land surface. Substantial office buildings in Chicago and Atlanta are constructed on air rights over railroad property. Similarly, owners may convey subsurface rights for mineral and oil extraction. In some states, residential real estate is subject to solar easements giving adjoining property owners the right to the direct rays of the sun. Such an easement prevents a property owner from obstructing the direct rays of the sun to adjoining property. In short, because ownership consists of a bundle of rights, the appraiser must value property rights held by real estate owners.

Profit Maximization

Under our economic system, land is largely allocated among competing uses according to the market. Qualified by certain public restrictions imposed on property owners, the profit maximization principle refers to the *tendency of the market to allocate land for uses that earn the highest income.* If the market operates under reasonably competitive conditions, investors tend to develop land according to that use which is most urgently needed. The relative urgency is expressed in the form of market values and rents. Therefore, appraisal procedures imply operation of the profit maximization principle; it is presumed that investors and consumers act rationally in bidding for land uses that produce the highest income and values. Chapter 7, The Highest and Best Use, explains this concept in greater detail.

Anticipation

Anticipation means that *prices are an expression of the present value of future benefits of ownership.* Land purchased for $50,000 represents the buyer's estimate of the present value of future benefits—that is, the right to use land in perpetuity. This concept is particularly important in valuing income property that requires a projection of future income. The principle of anticipation means that market value follows from the present value of *future* benefits of ownership.   PV of Future income

Real estate may not be purchased for its present use or its present net income but for its *anticipated* use and the related future benefits of ownership. Hence, real estate appraisers must be well informed about real estate trends—local, regional, or national—that affect market value.

The Principle of Proportionality

For each property, this principle states that there is *an optimum combination of land and capital that maximizes income.* There is danger that too much capital may be added to land, leading to economic loss. It would be inappropriate to develop a 60-acre mobile home park at a cost of $600,000 (not including land) if the demand for mobile home sites is such that only five acres of lots would be absorbed by the market over the next five years. It would be inappropriate to build a one-story, five-unit apartment if the site could be developed and rented as a 200-unit apartment building.

Real estate can be over- and under-improved. The appraiser, in analyzing a given property, must make judgments on the ideal use of the property. The appraiser must decide if the present use represents the best combination of land and capital.

The principle of proportionality prevails in other ways. It would be unlikely that a modest 1,200-square-foot single family dwelling with two bedrooms would justify three bathrooms or a $30,000 automatic heating and air conditioning system.

In other words, there is some "ideal" proportion that conforms to consumer preferences in building design, in land use, and in combinations of land and capital. Appraisers recognize this principle by stating that elements of a property should be in "balance." Expressed in this way, the concept is known as the principle of balance.

The Principle of Contribution

Component parts of real estate assume value according to how much they contribute to market value; this is the principle of contribution. Appraisers are aware that cost does not necessarily equal value. The addition of a swimming pool that costs $50,000 does not necessarily increase the market value of a single-family dwelling by its cost. The value of a swimming pool depends on the additional price that buyers are willing to pay for a three-bedroom house with a swimming pool. It does not necessarily follow that buyers would pay $50,000 additional for a house with a swimming pool.

Hence, it is the *contribution* that the swimming pool makes to value that overrides its cost. In some cases, structures may contribute nothing to market value regardless of their cost. Appraisers are trained to estimate how much buildings or other improvements contribute to market value as shown by the market. In making these evaluations, they observe the principle of contribution.

The Principle of Competition

In real estate, this principle means that over time, *competitive forces tend to reduce unusually high profits.* Real estate buyers and sellers operate in a reasonably competitive market. Existing neighborhoods compete with newly developed subdivisions. A profitable, 5-year-old motel faces prospective competition from nearby new motels. The same principle holds true for investment property such as shopping centers, apartment dwellings, mobile home parks, and industrial property.

In projecting future benefits of ownership, competitive forces tend to correct for extraordinary profits and temporary shortages. By recognizing competitive market forces, appraisers adjust for unusual temporary profits and values, supporting their adjustments with concrete evidence of market trends.

The Principle of Substitution

Among most real estate markets, *real estate may be substituted for other real estate providing for similar utility or income.* This principle recognizes that buyers and sellers have options. For example, a dwelling with a market value of $40,000 is not worth $45,000 since the buyer has the option of purchasing another house with slightly less desirable features for $39,500, or a slightly more desirable property for $42,000.

The principle of substitution tends to set the maximum limits to value. A buyer would be unwilling to pay more than $150,000 for a dwelling if an equally desirable property could be constructed for $150,000. In fact, the substitutability of land and real estate is another way of defining real estate markets. If buyers are unwilling to substitute house A for house B, providing that prices are in proper adjustment and reflect differences in utility, then the properties are in different submarkets; for example, a dwelling in Seattle, Washington, is not a substitute for a dwelling in Tacoma, Washington. But in the same community a dwelling in neighborhood A may be regarded as a suitable substitute for a dwelling in neighborhood B. The substitutability of property is an important element in weighing market data and in estimating market value.

The Principle of Diminishing Returns

Students of economics recognize this principle as the principle of marginal utility. Marginal utility is defined as *the increase in total utility resulting from additional units.* It is implied that marginal utility decreases as additional units are added. Because of the assumptions that additional units have diminishing marginal utility, there is some point at which marginal utility equals zero. Appraisers confront the principle of diminishing returns or utility in virtually all real estate appraisals. For instance, in a single-family dwelling, attractive landscaping contributes to value, but there is some point at which additional capital invested in exotic and formal planting may add nothing more to value.

In income properties, developers attempt to combine land and building improvements to maximize annual net income. For example, in an apartment dwelling, an Olympic-size swimming pool may not add to annual net income compared to the contribution of a smaller swimming pool. In this respect, it is the main task of the appraiser to estimate the utility of the real estate and its component parts; the appraiser does not assume utility.

The Principle of Change

Real estate markets are subject to continually changing economic, legal, social, and environmental forces. It follows that these changing forces affect real estate market values. The immediate task of the appraiser is to estimate the impact of these changes on market value. It must not be assumed that real estate and real estate markets function under static conditions. Accordingly, appraisers give special attention to the direction and degree of change in real estate markets. Market values are affected by dynamic, not static, conditions.

Opportunity Costs

Opportunity costs are not actually costs but *the sacrifice of opportunities, or the cost of options foregone in maximizing choices.* Thus, by making a particular choice that incurs a certain cost, an individual sacrifices some other alternative that would yield an investment return. For example, consider the purchase of a 50-unit apartment building or a neighborhood shopping center, assuming identical profits from both investments. The opportunity cost of owning the apartment building would be the cost of the shopping center; that is, to own the apartment building, the investor foregoes the opportunity of owning the shopping center. In one sense, it is the sacrifice of opportunity that constitutes the principal explanation of costs and values.

THE MOST PROFITABLE CHOICE

Consumers and investors make decisions according to *the most profitable choice*. Consequently, prices are explained by the principle that buyers will select the most advantageous opportunity and, in making a choice, will deliberately forego other opportunities. However, each foregone opportunity constitutes a sacrifice. In compensation for this sacrifice, the option selected must earn a profit equal to or more than the profit that would be earned on the foregone opportunity.

It should be noted that opportunity costs are not actual costs; they are merely estimates or personal evaluations. Nevertheless, some authorities believe that opportunity costs are the chief force that determines market price. Viewed as an option relinquished, each good is a cost of every other good that might be chosen in its place. The estimate of the return that would be obtained from an alternative use is viewed as an opportunity cost, which is actually an alternative valuation.

FOREGONE OPPORTUNITIES

In short, *opportunity costs are foregone alternative opportunities.* The sacrifice of a second choice in the process of getting a first choice constitutes the true measure of cost; thus, with limited resources, it is assumed that individuals attempt to maximize their gains or to minimize their losses. In the selection of opportunities, each choice will be made with respect to the next-best alternative.

Following this, it may be held that a dwelling is not purchased on the basis of its construction cost but at a price buyers consider as the best alternative. For example, assume a single-family dwelling has a market value of $200,000. If the price were increased to $250,000, presumably buyers would select cheaper alternatives more nearly equal to the market value.

Similarly, the value of a ten-acre industrial site on a limited-access highway might be a suitable substitute, and therefore the best alternative, compared to a 20,000-square-foot site located in the downtown fringe area. This analysis assumes that the smaller parcel represents a foregone opportunity faced by a buyer who has the next best option of purchasing an outlying parcel with virtually the same utility.

Consider further the capitalization rates appropriate to income-producing real estate. Such real estate must earn a yield, given the degree of risk, that competes with other opportunities facing investors. Thus, if yields on a triple A bond are 10 percent, given equal risks, the real estate asset must earn a yield comparable to other available investment opportunities. In these instances the appraiser undertakes an evaluation of opportunity costs relevant to the property appraised.

Principle of Conformity

Real estate that conforms to surrounding property assumes maximum value. Generally, dwellings in a neighborhood of conforming dwellings have greater prospects for stable and rising values relative to neighborhoods with properties that vary by architecture, age, construction, condition, or size. A buyer of a $200,000 dwelling would favor a location in a neighborhood with properties of comparable value. Conversely, a dwelling that costs $200,000 sited in a neighborhood of $50,000 houses would be penalized by most buyers because it does not conform to surrounding properties. Buyers and sellers negotiate higher prices for properties that conform to neighborhood standards.

Use Value

Use value refers to the value for a particular user. Because of the particular circumstances of the owner who devotes property to a particular use, the property assumes a value to the particular user above the value in the market for persons generally. A textile firm with several branch plants located within a 500-mile radius of their central office and warehouse could profitably use multiple-story brick buildings for textile manufacturing. With a central warehouse, the firm could dispatch raw materials overnight from the central warehouse as needed by branch plants. Similarly, the plant output could be trucked to the central warehouse for final distribution. With central administration and central warehousing, the value of a particular plant would assume greater utility for this particular user than the value to other companies.

The concept applies also to agricultural property where the value assignment may be directed to appraising land according to agricultural use and not according to the market value in alternative uses. Value and use require that appraisers consider the utility of real estate to a particular user. The value in use contrasts to market value to persons generally.

Supply and Demand

Supply represents *a schedule or quantity that sellers offer at a given time under* a *series of increasing prices.* Demand refers to *a schedule of increasing quantities that buyers would take at the same time, at a series of decreasing prices.* It is the relation between supply and demand that sets the real estate sales price.

Figure 2-3 indicates that the equilibrium price is at point P, the intersection of supply and demand. At this point the quantity offered by sellers and the quantity buyers are willing to purchase at point P are equal. At point P1, sellers would supply a larger quantity, Q1, but at the higher price, buyers would take less because some buyers would drop out of the market. The reverse holds true for the lower price, at point P2.

Figure 2-3   Real Estate Supply and Demand Schedules

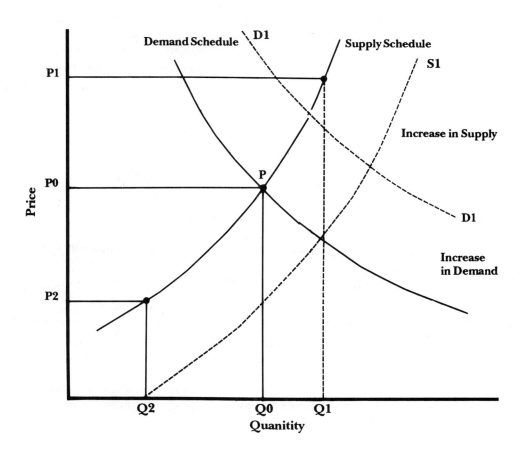

Note that point P represents the intersection of supply and demand, given the supply and demand schedule showing quantities offered and quantities willingly taken by buyers at given prices. This relationship should be distinguished from shifts in supply and demand. If the demand increases, buyers are willing to pay a different schedule of prices, given the quantity offered. The increase in demand is shown by the demand curve D^1. In other words, an increase in demand means that buyers as a group have shifted the quantity they are willing to take at a given schedule of prices.

Similarly, a shift in the supply schedule means that sellers are willing to offer a different schedule of goods at various prices. Suppose the supply increases as shown by the supply curve S^1. The increase in supply means that sellers are willing to supply a greater number of products at lower prices as shown by curve S^1.

Appraisers are careful to describe conditions of changing supply and demand. Movements along a demand schedule show how many units will be taken at various prices. Apartment property managers make this calculation in anticipating the number of tenants lost when given an increase in apartment rents. With an unchanging demand schedule, higher rents lead to a loss of certain tenants who move out as the result of rent increases. Some tenants are unwilling to rent apartments at the higher rent because of their unchanging demand.

SUMMARY

Value is the power to command other goods in exchange. To have value, real estate must be relatively scarce and possess utility. *Utility* is the power to increase satisfaction or to decrease dissatisfaction. *Market value* represents the most probable sales price, assuming a reasonably competitive market with the buyer and seller acting knowledgeably and with neither party acting under duress. Real estate cost does not determine value.

Price is value expressed in money. Real estate prices must be analyzed in the light of the market value standard in order to avoid unusual sales that do not conform to the market value definition.

Appraisers cope with certain statutorily defined values such as just compensation. *Just compensation* refers to market value. Government agencies and regulated public utilities pay just compensation to property owners if property is taken for public purposes. *Severance damages* refer to the loss in value of the property remaining after a partial taking of private property. *Consequential damages* are payments for the decrease in property value if no part of the property was taken for public purposes.

Assessed value is the value determined for property taxes. Assessed value typically is a poor measure of a market value. Other types of values such as fair value, true and fair value, normal value, sound value, and similar terms imply an ethical connotation not included in the market value definition. Accountants refer to *book value,* which is generally original cost unrelated to current market value. Book value may be reduced annually by *depreciation* or an annual reduction in value by a depreciation factor that meets accounting standards. Engineers refer to *reproduction cost new,* which is the cost of reproducing an exact building replica. For engineering purposes, depreciation may be determined by impaired serviceability. However for market value purposes, depreciation is defined as *a loss in value from any cause.* Appraisers face other value terms such as *loan value* based on a percent of market value and *insurable value* based on reproduction cost less the cost of the foundation and less the cost of building plans.

Appraisers observe the *bundle of rights* concept, which treats real estate as a bundle of property rights much like a bundle of sticks. As a result, appraisers value the property rights where the owner has only a limited property right. Appraisers follow other common valuation principles, including the *profit maximization principle* or the tendency of the market to allocate land to the highest use. Appraisers follow the rule that prices are an expression of the present worth of future benefits of ownership—the *principle of anticipation.*

Consider further the principle that component parts of real estate assume value according to how much they contribute to market value—*the principle of contribution.* Appraisers observe the *principle of competition,* which means that competition reduces unusually high profits. It is equally true that the *principle of substitution* operates so that real estate may be substituted for other real estate that provides similar utility or income. This principle tends to set the maximum limit to value.

The principle of *diminishing returns* refers to the tendency for total utility to increase with an increase in quantity. It is implied that as additional units are added, the utility of the last added unit decreases. It is also true that real estate is subject to the *principle of change*—real estate markets continually change because of varying economic, legal, social, and environmental forces.

Add to these principles the theory of *opportunity costs*—the sacrifice of opportunities or the cost of opportunities foregone in maximizing choices. Real estate values are affected by the *principle of conformity.* Property that conforms to surrounding property tends to assume the maximum value. Nonconforming properties are depreciated in the market. Appraisers confront the term *use value,* which is the value for a particular user.

Supply represents a schedule or quantity that sellers offer at a given time under

[handwritten margin note:] diminishing Return - a rate of yield that beyond a certain point fails to increase in proportion to additional investments of labor or capital.

a series of increasing prices. *Demand* refers to a schedule of increasing quantities that buyers would take at the same time at a series of decreasing prices. The *highest and best use* is that use from among reasonable, probable, and legally alternative uses that results in the highest land value.

POINTS TO REMEMBER

value the power of a good to command other goods in exchange.

utility the power to increase satisfaction or decrease dissatisfaction.

market value the most probable sales price for which the property will sell in a competitive market, with the buyer and seller acting knowledgeably and with neither party acting under duress.

real estate cost the cost of land, land improvements, and building costs including certain "soft costs."

price value expressed in money.

just compensation payment for the taking of private property by government agencies or regulated public utilities for public purposes.

severance damages damages from the loss in value because of the decrease in value to the property remaining after a partial public taking of private property.

consequential damage payments for the decrease in value of real estate, no part of which was taken for public purposes.

assessed value the value determined by the tax assessor for property tax purposes.

depreciated book value the book value less the accrued depreciation allowable for accounting purposes.

reproduction cost new the value based on the cost of reproducing or constructing an exact building replica.

loan value a value based on a percent of the market value.

insurable value the reproduction cost new, less the cost of the foundation and less the cost of building plans.

bundle of rights a concept that treats real estate ownership as a collection of numerous property rights, much like a bundle of sticks.

easement a nonpossessory interest to use property for a specific purpose.

profit maximization the tendency of the market to allocate land to uses that earn the highest income.

anticipation a principle that refers to prices as an expression of the present worth of the future benefits of ownership.

principle of proportionality a principle that states there is an optimum combination of land and capital that maximizes income.

principle of contribution component parts of real estate assume value according to how much they contribute to market value.

principle of competition competitive forces tend to reduce unusually high profits.

principle of substitution real estate may be substituted for other real estate providing for similar utility or income.

principle of diminishing returns the increase in total utility resulting from an additional unit. It is implied that utility decreases as additional units are added.

principle of change real estate markets are subject to continually changing economic, legal, social, and environmental forces.

opportunity costs the sacrifice of opportunities or the cost of options foregone in maximizing choices.

foregone opportunities opportunity costs in which costs are equal to foregone alternative opportunities.

principle of conformity real estate that conforms to surrounding property assumes maximum value.

use value the value to a particular user.

supply a schedule or quantity that sellers offer at a given time under a series of increasing prices.

demand a schedule of increasing quantities that buyers would take at the same time at a series of decreasing prices.

QUESTIONS FOR REVIEW

1. Suppose you were to dig a hole measuring four cubic feet. If your time was worth $10 an hour and you worked for five hours, what would be your estimate of market value of the hole? Give reasons for your answer.

2. Explain the difference between market value and market price. Explain fully.

3. Define the following statutorily defined values: just compensation, assessed value, loan value, and insurable value. Would you use these references as an indication of market value? Why or why not?

4. Give an example of how the following principles would affect a valuation problem.

    The bundle of rights   Anticipation
    Profit maximization   Principle of opportunity costs

5. Give an example of how you would apply the principle of competition in appraising an income property. Explain fully.

6. What is the significance of opportunity costs in the valuation estimation? Give an example to illustrate your answer.

7. Give an example of how supply and demand operate in a market showing a rising demand for residential property; a decrease in the supply of multiple family dwellings because of zoning restrictions.

PRACTICE PROBLEMS

1. You are assigned to value 100 single-family dwelling lots with a proposed tentative price of $20,000 each. To estimate the market value you propose a demand schedule showing the estimated number of lots that may be sold in the first 12 months. You estimate that in the first year 30 lots may be sold $20,000. (a) Prepare a supply and demand schedule showing this relationship. (b) On your graph indicate how many lots you estimate will be sold if the price of lots is increased to $30,000. (c) On the same graph show the estimated lot sale if the price were decreased to $15,000. (d) Now assume that demand increases so that 30 lots may be sold for $30,000. According to this demand schedule, indicate total lot sales at $20,000 per lot.

2. You are valuing 30 acres of redeveloped land in the central city area for industrial use. You find no similar land in the central area zoned for industrial use of more than one acre. You decide to base your appraisal on industrial acreage located ten miles away on the freeway selling for $.50 per square foot. What appraisal principles are you exercising in this case? Explain fully.

C H A P T E R 3

Real Estate Property Rights

After studying this chapter, you will know:
- Legal rights in real estate.
- Rights held under less than freehold estates.
- Easements rights: their creation and termination.
- Different ways to own real estate: ownership in severalty and concurrent ownership
- Four types of legal real estate descriptions.

The legal rights and interests held by property owners largely control the market value estimate. To the layman, ownership conveys a property right in land and buildings. The appraiser, however, must govern the appraisal according to *interests* held by property owners and the *legal restrictions* common to a particular property. While appraisers look to legal counsel to resolve legal issues, the appraiser requires a working knowledge of property rights associated with various ownership interests; appraisers must recognize situations where legal advice is necessary before making the final value estimate.

The chapter reviews minimum knowledge necessary to understand the main valuation issues: real property defined, legal rights held in real estate, and common forms of ownership. The chapter closes with an explanation of legal descriptions for appraisal reports.

LEGAL RIGHTS

In practice, the terms *land, real estate,* and *realty* are interchangeable. Simply stated, real estate is land and its attachments. Real property, in contrast, refers to the legal rights associated with land ownership. Legally, the term is defined as "the interest, benefits and rights inherent in the ownership of the physical real estate."[1]

Personal property is non-real estate property: movable items that are not permanently attached to land or buildings.

These definitions may assume considerable significance in valuation practice. For example, lumber and building materials temporarily stored on a building site are personal property; they are not part of the real estate.

---

1   *The Dictionary of Real Estate Appraisal,* Second Edition, (Chicago, Illinois: America Institute of Real Estate Appraisers, 1989), p. 248.

When building materials are attached to a permanent foundation, the resulting structure becomes real estate because it is attached to the land.

Consider a further example of a mobile home. A mobile home on wheels, not affixed to land, may be judged personal property and ineligible for a mortgage loan. However, if the mobile home is permanently connected to sewer, water, gas, and electricity and is supported by a foundation, the mobile home may be considered part of the land, depending on state law.

Appraisers deal also with *fixtures;* an article (formerly personal property) permanently installed or attached to land or buildings is part of the real estate, or a "fixture." Frequently, appraisers require legal advice in determining if an item is personal property or a fixture and subject to the appraisal. Dining room chandeliers especially adapted to a dining room would be considered a fixture. A stereo high fidelity music system or television unit specially fitted into wall cabinets or attached to the building so as to be inseparable and permanently affixed would probably be real estate. The determination of a fixture rests on four tests:

1. The way in which the item is attached to the building.
2. Character of the item.
3. Intent of the parties.
4. Relation of the parties.

These issues generally would require a legal interpretation. In the valuation of single-family dwellings, appraisers take care in itemizing personal property which may be included in the appraisal, i.e., appliances, draperies, curtains, carpets, and the like. Those items that are fixtures that would be included in the real estate appraised. State law generally controls the definition of trade fixtures, machinery, and equipment.

Estates Held in Real Estate

Generally speaking, real estate interests fall in two categories: *freehold estates* and *less than freehold estates.* The freehold designation, traced from the English feudal system, means an interest in land. Less than freehold estates cover leases, which grant use and possession for a limited time. Freehold estates are owned in two forms: *estates of inheritance* and *estates not of inheritance.* While states vary over the rights defined as freehold estates, such an interest may be held as an estate of inheritance or an estate not of inheritance. Freehold estates are shown in Figure 3-1.

Figure 3-1   Freehold Estates

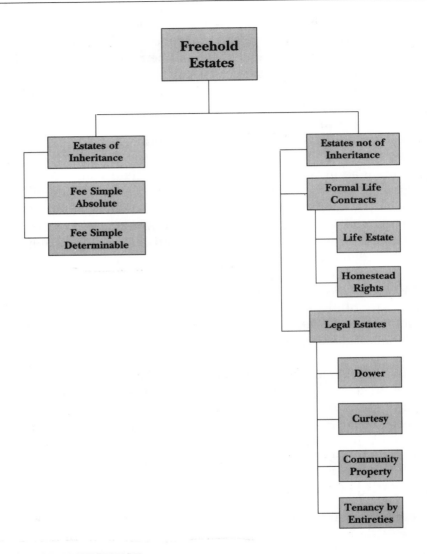

ESTATES OF INHERITANCE

Estates of inheritance, as shown in Figure 3-1, include the *fee simple absolute*, which is often referred to by language that reads the "life, his heirs and assigns forever." Consequently, the fee simple absolute (or fee simple estate) conveys title over the life of the owner which may be inherited without restriction. It is called simple to indicate that title is held without restrictions. *This is the maximum title that may be acquired in real estate.*

The *fee simple determinable* is an estate that terminates on the occurrence of a known event. The language that creates the interest reads typically "as long as, until, or during an event." For instance, a property owner may convey a fee simple determinable as long as the land is used for a church. The abandonment of church use automatically terminates the estate, and the title reverts to the fee simple ownership or his or her heirs.

ESTATES NOT OF INHERITANCE

Appraisers may confront estates not of inheritance in valuing single-family dwellings. These estates may be expressed by contracts or by operation of state law.

CONTRACTS. Figure 3-1 shows a *life estate interest,* which is an ownership that terminates upon the death of the person whose life measures the ownership period. The estate automatically terminates upon the death of such a person. To create this estate, an owner expresses his or her intention by deed or by will.

For instance, A transfers a life estate to B during B's life with the provision that the estate reverts to A upon B's death. A holds the *remainder,* which is an estate in fee simple. A is known as the *remainderman.* The life estate gives the life tenant the exclusive right to possess, enjoy, and use the property providing he or she observes limitations common to life estates. The remainderman holds only a future interest in the fee simple, which becomes possessory at the termination of the life estate.

The owner of a life estate must not commit undue waste. The property may not be subject to permanent injury such as the cutting of timber or subjecting the property to waste, depreciation, or a land use that destroys property value. The life estate owner must pay taxes and maintain the property to preserve the value of the property for the remainderman.

OPERATION OF LAW. Life estates created by operation of law are peculiar to each state; some states provide for *homestead rights* giving limited protection of the family home from creditors. It usually requires a formal declaration on a specified form filed for record by the head of the family. State law dictates the rights held by homestead interests. The homestead laws originally protected the home from a forced sale to satisfy debtors. Maximum homestead limits may be stated in dollars or in the number of acres which are placed in the exemption. Homestead rights in Florida apply to a maximum of 160 acres on rural property. Local real estate taxes generally have priority over homestead rights.

Estates Created by Law

Estates created by operation of law result from express acts of the owner under state law. Appraisers will encounter statutorily imposed estates such as curtesy, dower, tenancy by the entireties, and community property.

CURTESY

Followed in several states, including Alabama, Arkansas, and Hawaii, curtesy typically provides a surviving husband one-third of life estate interest in real estate owned by the wife during marriage. The right requires a valid marriage and birth of a living child during marriage. The estate is terminated by divorce or death of the husband. In states providing for curtesy, husbands must sign conveyance documents to extinguish the right of curtesy.

DOWER

This is the interest of the surviving wife in land acquired by the husband during marriage. Upon the husband's death, some states provide for the division of one-third of the land to which the wife's dower is attached if she so elects. At the husband's death, the surviving wife assumes all rights and obligations of a conventional life estate tenant. A dower interest may be released by the wife joining with the husband in executing conveyance instruments. Dower estates are terminated by divorce or death of the wife or election of the wife to accept other parts of a husband's estate in lieu of the dower interest.

TENANCY BY THE ENTIRETIES

Prevailing in Florida and North Carolina, among other states, ownership by a husband and wife is treated as ownership by one person. On the death of either party, the estate is owned solely by the survivor. As tenants by the entirety, neither husband nor wife may convey property or force a property partition during the lifetime of the other spouse unless they obtain a divorce.

COMMUNITY PROPERTY

Derived from Spanish law, community property prevails in Arizona, California, Idaho, Louisiana, Nebraska, Nevada, New Mexico, Oklahoma, Texas, and Washington. These states recognize two types of property owned by married persons: *separate property* and *community property*. Separate property is owned by the husband or wife at the time of marriage, or it is acquired by either during marriage by inheritance, will, or gift. Separate property is owned independently of the other spouse.

Property acquired by either spouse during marriage becomes community property, belonging to both persons as co-owners. It is assumed that husband and wife share equally in all property acquired during marriage. Each spouse owns an undivided one-half interest of all that is earned or gained by both, regardless of the share contributed by the other spouse. To extinguish a community property interest, the husband and wife must both sign documents transferring property held as community property. No conveyances or contracts are valid without the signatures of both the husband and wife holding a community property interest.

Community property carries no survivorship rights. Each spouse may transfer his or her interest by will. The estate terminates by death, divorce, or voluntary agreement of husband and wife to divide property equally.

Less than Freehold Estates

Figure 3-2 details less than freehold estates which refer to leases that convey the right to possession, use, and enjoyment for a limited period. Note that Figure 3-2 identifies the leased fee interest of the owner, or lessor. The tenant holds the leasehold estate as the lessee, or tenant. The tenant's estate may be held in four different forms—estates for years, periodic tenancies, tenancy at will, and tenancy at sufferance.

Figure 3-2 Less Than Freehold Estates

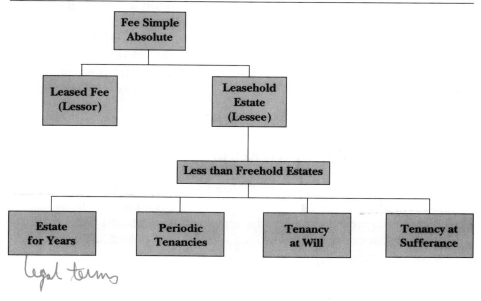

legal terms

ESTATE FOR YEARS

Leasehold estates that continue for a definite period are estates for years. The time may be highly variable: one month, one year, or, conceivably, 99 years. Under the lease agreement, the lessee or tenant has the exclusive right of possession and use provided the tenant observes lease terms.

PERIODIC TENANCIES

These leases, known as leases from year to year, continue until one of the parties of the lease gives notice of termination. Typically, parties agree to leases with weekly, monthly, or yearly rents; such tenancies may continue indefinitely. They tend to be renewed automatically unless either party gives notice of termination.

TENANCY AT WILL

An estate created lawfully with the consent of owner and tenant that may be terminated by either party constitutes a tenancy at will. Although the term is uncertain, the tenant continues in possession with the express approval of the owner. State statutes generally provide for termination if either party gives proper legal notice.

TENANCY AT SUFFERANCE

In a sense, tenancy at sufferance is a misnomer. The tenancy covers a tenant who enters the premises lawfully under an existing lease and holds over, without permission of the owner, at lease termination. In effect, the tenant has no stated rights in the real estate, since he or she continues to use the premises without the express consent of the owner. The tenancy continues until the owner either consents to the sitting tenant or takes action to repossess the premises. Because the tenant holds no interest in the premises, most states require no notice to terminate a tenancy at sufferance.

EASEMENTS AND OTHER INTERESTS

An easement is a *nonpossessory freehold interest:* the right to use land for a specific purpose. Easements are conveyed by written easement deeds. Easement rights are governed by the terms of the easement deed granting a right-of-way for construction and maintenance of power lines, pipelines, access roads, irrigation ditches, and the like.

Figure 3-3   Illustration of the Servient and Dominant Estate Created by a Right-of-Way Easement

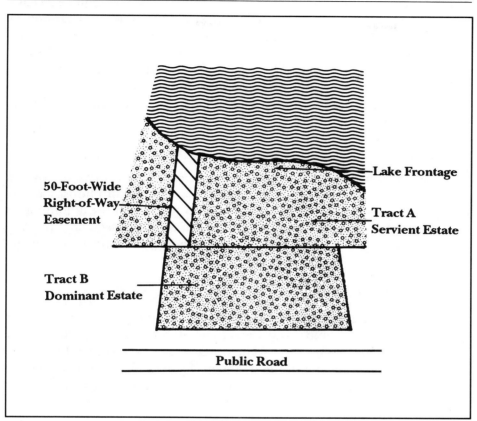

Figure 3-3 illustrates a right-of-way easement granted by A to B for access to lake frontage. In this instance, A grants an easement for the benefit of B. The person benefited by the easement holds the *dominant estate* while the person granting the easement holds the *servient estate*. An easement is said to run with the land. That is, in conveying title to C, A conveys the land subject to B's right of access over the right-of-way easement. The easement is not sold separately but is transferred with the title to the property of A.

Creating Easements

Easements are generally created by a written easement deed which describes the easement right. However, easements may be acquired in several other ways.

EASEMENT BY PRESCRIPTION

If A uses a portion of B's property for a right-of-way, A may acquire an easement without written permission of B. Such a right-of-way, acquired by "prescription," must meet requirements of state law. Generally, the right-of-way must be: hostile to the use or enjoyment by B, open and notorious, and continuing for a minimum statutory period, usually seven years. Continuous use means that property must be continually used, without interruption, over the statutory period, so as to give the owner reasonable notice of such wrongful use.

IMPLIED EASEMENTS

Suppose owners of two adjoining houses use a single driveway over a common boundary providing access to the garages of both houses. If one of the houses is sold, the driveway right-of-way partly over the adjoining lot is enforceable since the easement is *implied*. Similar easements provide access to the second story over a common stairway constructed over the boundary of two adjoining properties.

EASEMENT BY NECESSITY

If A sells adjoining land which has no access to a public road except over land of A, the buyer would acquire an easement for access by necessity over A's land. However, if there was some other means of access to the public road, however inconvenient, the easement by necessity would not be created. Easements by necessity terminate if other means of access are later available.

EASEMENTS BY CONDEMNATION

State-regulated utilities and government agencies have the right to acquire easements by condemnation. The Corps of Engineers commonly acquires land over private property for reservoirs by purchasing flowage easements. The easement right provides for the right to flood land as a normal consequence of operating flood control reservoirs. Owners who grant easements for right-of-way by condemnation are paid the market value of such rights. *Right for public use*

EASEMENTS BY RESERVATION

Owners who convey land by deed and reserve a right-of-way over the land conveyed create easements by reservation. The deed includes language to the effect that the grantor reserves the right of ingress and egress over a portion of the land conveyed.

Easement Termination

Easements may be terminated by:

1. abandonment,
2. release of the owner of the servient estate,
3. purchase, or
4. loss of purpose.

Assuming the holder of the beneficial estate acquires the servient estate, there is no further need for the easement, so the easement would be extinguished. If the purpose of an easement no longer exists, the easement terminates.

Other Interests

Appraisers face other interests in real estate such as *encroachments*. An encroachment is a building, fence, wall, or other improvement that extends over the property of another. The rights of parties affected by land encroachments vary by state laws and the facts. An encroachment would be illustrated by a building that is constructed on the wrong lot or a building that is partially constructed on neighboring parcel of land. A fence placed on land of another constitutes an encroachment. In general unless the problem of encroachment is resolved, the title remains unmarketable.

A *license* is not an interest in real property. It is merely a temporary use of private property classified as personal property. The purchase of a theater ticket temporarily permits the holder of the ticket to occupy a theater seat. The holder of a license has virtually no real property rights; the right may be revoked by the owner for any cause.

REAL ESTATE OWNERSHIP

Real estate may be owned by one individual known as an ownership in severalty. The term refers to single ownership "severed" from other real estate. While ownership may be vested in one individual who enjoys all property rights associated with ownership, there are certain differences between owning land as the sole owner and owning jointly with others—or owning under multiple ownership. The main differences relate to sharing liabilities, separating responsibility, and allocating ownership benefits.

Concurrent Ownership

Joint ownership by two or more persons, or concurrent ownership, normally assumes one of two forms: tenancy in common or joint tenancy.

TENANCY IN COMMON

Tenancy in common consists of two or more owners having an undivided interest in real estate that

1. permits ownership in *unequal shares.*
2. provides *no right of survivorship.*
3. may be created at *different points in time.*
4. includes the *right to partition* individual interests.

Under a tenancy in common, owners may hold varying shares of interest. For example, a surviving wife may inherit an apartment building as a tenant in common with other owners. An ownership may be divided by conveying a 50 percent interest to a wife with a 25 percent undivided interest to each of two children. There is no requirement that shares in a tenancy in common be equal among co-owners.

Moreover, each owner has the right to sell part or all of the tenancy in common interest or to pass the respective interest to heirs. At the death of a tenant in common, the interest of the deceased may be willed or passed to heirs under state law. Ownership shares may be merged, divided, or sold at different points in time.

In some states a tenant in common may force partition of the property to convert an individual interest to cash or to take a physically divided share of the real estate owned. If the interest is held in an apartment building, which is difficult to divide into physically separate shares, the tenant in common may force a sale to gain his or her share in money. In the case of land, appraisers may be asked to appraise property for the purpose of conveying a divided share interest to a tenant in common.

JOINT TENANCY

The *right of survivorship* is the main distinguishing feature of a joint tenancy. If A owns a joint tenancy with B, B acquires sole ownership upon the death of A. To establish this relationship, joint tenants must acquire the interest at the same time, under the same title, and with equal shares or interest.

In absence of one of these requirements, no joint tenancy is created. In contrast to tenancy in common, joint tenants always own equal shares. A joint tenancy of five ownerships would allocate a 20 percent undivided interest to each joint tenant. In addition tenants must have acquired title *at the same time under the same document.*

For this reason, it is impossible for a sole owner to convey a joint tenancy to another party. By conveying an interest back to himself or herself, he or she would violate the requirements that both joint tenants acquire title under the same document at the same time. In these circumstances the owner must transfer property to a third party (a "strawman") who in turn conveys back a joint tenancy. Under this ownership each owner has the same right of possession and with equal rights in the undivided interest.

Other Multiple Ownership

Options under multiple ownership include a wide variety of ownership forms: partnerships, corporations, real estate investment trusts, condominiums, and cooperatives. In each instance, the form of ownership is adapted to the needs of a specialized real estate investment—and to the particular requirements of owners. Fig 3-4 summarizes the available multiple ownership forms. Appraisers are frequently given appraisal assignments to determine the value of a share interest held in multiple real estate ownership.

Figure 3-4   Forms of Multiple Real Estate Ownership

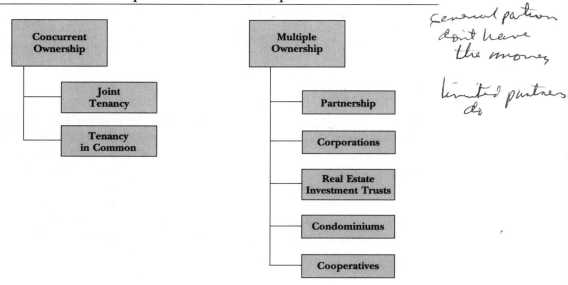

PARTNERSHIP RIGHTS IN REAL ESTATE

In most states partners share equal rights of use and possession in real estate held under partnership. A partnership interest may not be conveyed to others without consent of other partners. The partnership interest is exempt from the right of dower and curtesy and may not be partitioned among partners except to satisfy creditors. Upon death of a partner, the agreement usually provides for the transfer of a partnership interest to the remaining partners according to the value of partnership shares.

LIMITED PARTNERSHIPS

Parties may acquire title under a limited partnership which provides for *general* and *limited* partners. Two financial advantages accrue to a limited partnership: *limited liability* and *income tax advantages.* In this form of ownership, limited partners have no voice in management though they are entitled to information on financial operations. *Limited partners* can be held liable only for the amount of their capital investment. In the event of a $500,000 mortgage default, a limited partner with a $100,000 investment can be personally liable only for his or her $100,000 partnership interest.

Only the *general partner* has the right to execute deeds, mortgages, or other real estate conveyances. The general partner has responsibility for *managing* the property. In essence, the limited partner is liable for only his or her investment. Limited partners retain the limited liability of a corporation without incurring corporate net income taxes. The general partner receives a management fee for acting on behalf of the limited partnership. Tax advantages are gained by limited partners to the extent that losses and depreciation allowances are deductible against personal income of the limited partner. These deductions are subject to certain limitations.

REAL ESTATE INVESTMENT TRUSTS

Real estate investment trusts permit small investors to own small shares in professionally managed real estate. Provided that the investment trust complies with federal tax regulations, they are exempt from federal corporate net income taxes. To qualify for this exemption, they must distribute at least 90 percent of net income to shareholders.

In other respects they act like corporations; they are managed by elected trustees and function under a board of directors. Real estate investment trusts sell shares to owners who share in the income of the real estate investment trust. Hence, the real estate investment trust gives small real estate investors the same tax and economic advantages held by mutual funds that invest in stocks and bonds. Investors in real estate investment trusts gain from large-scale real estate investments and benefit from professional management associated with major real estate projects.

REAL ESTATE CORPORATIONS

Real estate corporations, chartered under state laws, extend limited financial liability of corporations to real estate owners. The developer forms a corporation allowing investors to benefit from real estate investments without endangering personal assets. Shares in the corporation may be exchanged without affecting the real estate asset. If the corporation has limited assets, lenders may require a personal pledge of assets before approving mortgages.

CONDOMINIUM OWNERSHIP

Condominium ownership, common in multiple-family dwellings, provides the advantages of multiple-family units with ownership rights common to single-family dwellings. The owner of a condominium apartment gains exclusive use of an apartment unit with an undivided interest in the *common elements*. The common elements refer to the apartment house site, the elevator, the hallway space, and all other common facilities of the project which the condominium owner shares with other owners.

In reality, the owner acquires the right to use the air space occupied by a particular apartment. Condominium owners arrange their own financing and title insurance and are free to sell their ownership in the open market. Ownership rights involve three documents: the declaration, condominium bylaws, and the management agreement.

The *condominium declaration* commits a property to condominium ownership. The declaration defines rights of individual owners with regard to condominium project maintenance and defines the responsibility of individual owners. The declaration establishes the maximum liability for individual owners for maintenance expenses and liabilities. In the usual case, liabilities and share interests are determined by the square-foot area owned in relation to the square-foot area of the entire condominium project.

The *condominium bylaws* relate to the administration of condominium affairs. Ordinarily each condominium owner has one vote. A board of directors elected by owners is vested with the right to levy and collect maintenance fees against each member and to expend funds for maintenance, repair, replacement reserves, and condominium expenses. The board of directors issues rules and regulations which must be observed by member owners.

The *management agreement* is an agreement by the board of directors that assigns daily operations to the management firm. The management firm contracts for daily maintenance, repairs, and financial services to the condominium owners. The management agreement assigns certain duties to the managing agent and provides for management compensation.

COOPERATIVE OWNERSHIP

Cooperative ownership is common for resort properties and multiple-family dwellings—for both middle-income and high-income luxury units. The cooperative is a nonprofit corporation that issues ownership shares equal in value to a given apartment unit. Cooperative owners, on issue of cooperative shares, are given a proprietary lease granting the exclusive use and occupancy of a selected apartment. Compared to condominiums, cooperative ownership has certain other major differences:

1. A cooperative project is financed with a single mortgage; a cooperative shareholder pays the prorated share of an existing mortgage on the entire project.
2. Cooperative owners have virtually unlimited liability for repair, mainte-nance, and other expenses. Each cooperative shareholder, in effect, guarantees the costs incurred by other shareholders. Condominiums, on the other hand, levy no more than a specified percentage share for expenses and other liabilities against each unit owner. Cooperative owners share joint responsibility for liabilities and any operating expenses.
3. In some cooperatives, the purchaser must resell the unit back to the cooperative at the original price. Normally there are restrictions on the right of resale and the sale price. In other respects, like condominiums, cooperative owners have equal voting rights in appointing a board of directors for management.

LAND DESCRIPTIONS

Prior to completing an appraisal assignment, appraisers verify land descriptions. Land or legal descriptions are recommended for several reasons:

1. Street addresses may be incorrect. Street addresses give no information on the land area and the property dimensions.
2. Appraisers are able to use land or legal descriptions to verify street frontages, lot depths, and land areas.
3. Land descriptions identify the correct property to be appraised. Clerical or other errors are detected by comparing the legal description with maps, deeds, mortgages, and other references.
4. A comparison of the property appraised with the land description indicates encroachments, buildings on the wrong lot, easements by prescription, and possible other title defects.

Real estate may be described by *metes and bounds, recorded subdivisions,* the *U.S. Rectangular Survey System,* and the *state plane coordinate system.* Metes and bounds descriptions are common in the 50 states. The U.S. Rectangular Survey System does not apply to the original 13 colonies, Texas, and certain northeastern states and limited other areas. Recorded subdivisions are described by lots and blocks according to local regulations.

The state plane coordinate system is highly technical and is used primarily by public utility systems and government agencies *to describe* property in spherical, or "geodetic" terms. While extremely accurate, the latter description is difficult to understand without technical training.

Metes and Bounds Descriptions

Universally used, metes and bounds descriptions identify the location and the land area by describing *boundary directions* and their *turning points.* The location is indicated by the point of beginning (POB). From the POB, the surveyor indicates the direction of the boundary line and the distance to each turning point or monument around the land described and back to the POB. A metes and bounds description should be sufficiently detailed for a competent surveyor to locate and identify the land.

The main components of the legal description consist of the *point of beginning,* the *direction of lines,* and *monuments.* The point of beginning is the position established by monuments of known positions; for example, a point 100 feet west of the intersection of 14th Avenue and Main Street or "beginning at a point 300 feet north of an iron pin representing the northeast corner of the Johnson tract." The point of beginning could refer to a natural topographical feature or a manmade structure such as a railroad right-of-way, a highway, or some other fixed point.

The direction of lines is expressed by degrees within one of the four compass quadrants. A compass quadrant is shown in Figure 3-5. Figure 3-5 shows a line drawn *north 60 degrees 20 minutes east*. To indicate direction, the surveyor first designates either a *north or south reference*. A line going in the opposite direction as shown in Figure 3-5 would read the *south 60 degrees 20 minutes west*. After the direction, the surveyor indicates the number of degrees from a north or south compass point.

Given the north or south reference, the direction must proceed either *east or west,* which identifies a quadrant and the direction within the quadrant. For example, extending the legal description "beginning at a point 100 feet east of the intersection of 14th and Main Street, north 70 degrees east 120 feet to an iron pin." By proceeding from the point of beginning to each successive direction and monument, the boundary should end or close at the POB. As the boundary changes direction, the surveyor describes each direction by compass degrees and the number of feet to the next monument, proceeding in this way back to the POB.

The term *monument* refers to an object that marks a point on the earth's surface. In original surveys, corner points were typically marked by natural objects such as trees or large stones. Today, corner monuments are established by marking points with an iron pipe or concrete marker driven into the ground.

Figure 3-5   Compass Directions for Metes and Bounds Descriptions

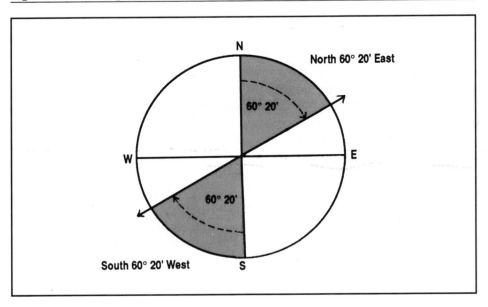

A valid metes and bounds description includes:

1. the name of the surveyor.
2. the survey date.
3. the source of the survey data.
4. the identity of the property.
5. reference to at least two durable monuments.
6. all dimensions and directions of property lines.
7. reference to a map recorded in county records.

Such a metes and bounds description that meets these criteria is shown in Figure 3-6. Usually, the map will be recorded with a *county registry of deeds* or other local office that accepts documents for public record. Generally, such maps are found in *plat books* or *deed books* open to the public and permanently filed for public reference.

Figure 3-6   An illustration of a metes and bounds land description

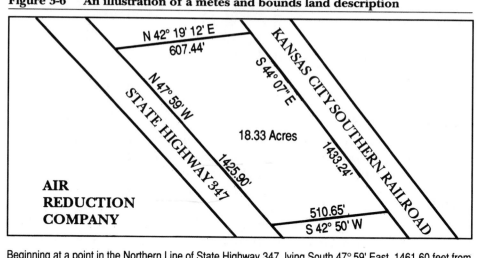

Beginning at a point in the Northern Line of State Highway 347, lying South 47° 59' East, 1461.60 feet from the West Line of the said J.S. Johnson Survey and being also the Southeast corner of that certain tract of land conveyed to Air Reduction Company by deed recorded in Volume 1389, Page 1 of the Deed Records of Jefferson County, Texas; thence with the Easterly Line of the said Air Reduction Company tract, North 42° 19' 12" East, 607.44 feet to a point for corner in the Southerly Line of the Kansas City Southern Railroad Company right-of-way; thence with the said Southerly Line of the Kansas City Southern Railroad Company right-of-way, South 44° 07' East, 1433.24 to a point for corner, said corner being also the Northwest corner of the E. I. du Pont de Nemours and Company access strip, thence with the Westerly Line of the said E. I. du Pont de Nemours and Company access strip, South 42° 50' West, 510.65 feet to a point for corner in the said Northerly Line of State Highway 347; thence with the said Northerly Line of State Highway 347; North 47° 59' West, 1425.90 feet to the Place of beginning and containing 18.33 acres of land as recorded in Deed Book 1865, Page 300, Jefferson County, Texas.

If an error in distance occurs—for example, a tract is described as north 60 degrees 20 minutes west, *300 feet* to an iron pin, and the actual distance measures *150 feet,* the *actual distance* between monuments prevails over the stated distance.

Recorded Subdivisions

For urban property, it is awkward to describe city lots and blocks by metes and bounds descriptions. It is much simpler to identify land as Lot 3, Block 4 of Innis Arden Estates, recorded in Plat Book 20, page 36, King County (Seattle), Washington. A recorded subdivision identifies the precise location of each lot and block by metes and bounds. A lot and block description that is not placed on public record is not valid.

Government Rectangular Survey System

This system, which was adopted to describe public lands, covers 92 percent of the land in the continental United States. The land identification system under rectangular survey provides for:

1. Principal Meridians and Baselines.
   The principal meridians are designated survey lines running north and south that govern land descriptions in 30 states. A baseline is associated with each principal meridian.
2. Townships and Ranges.
   Township lines run in an east-west direction at six-mile intervals from the baseline. *Ranges* divide land into six-mile-wide areas running north and south, parallel with the principal meridian. Township areas have 36 square miles.
3. Sections.
   Approximately square-mile sections are established by running parallel lines through each township from south to north and from east to west at one-mile intervals. The sections are numbered from 1 to 36, commencing with number 1 at the northeast section of a township area, proceeding west to section 6, south to section 7, east to section 12, and, alternately, to section 36 in the southeast corner.
4. Correction Lines.
   The system provides for correction lines at 24-mile intervals to account for the curvature of the earth. Correction lines are also taken in certain designated sections of a township area.

Separate principal meridians control legal descriptions in some 30 states. These are identified in Figure 3-7. For example, property descriptions in California may be described by reference to the Mt. Diablo Meridian, the San Bernardino Meridian, or the Humboldt Meridian, depending on property location. The intersection of the principal meridian and baseline is identified with a concrete monument that controls rectangular survey descriptions subject to that reference.

TOWNSHIPS AND RANGES

Range 1 West shows that land is located in a six-mile band running north and south and west of the principal meridian. Likewise, Township 3 North is in an area 12 to 18 miles north of the baseline. To describe the 36-mile area in full, the legal description would read, "Township 3 North, Range 1 West of the First Principal Meridian."

Figure 3-7 Principal Meridians and Baselines

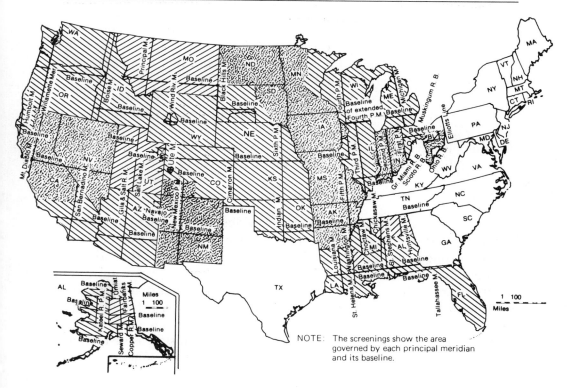

NOTE: The screenings show the area governed by each principal meridian and its baseline.

SECTIONS

Sections are square-mile areas beginning in the upper right hand corner of the township and numbered down in a serpen-tlike manner to end in Section 36. The shaded area of Figure 3-4 shows the location of Section 10, Township 3, North, Range 1, West of the First Principal Meridian. Ideally, every section measures 5,280 feet on each side (one mile), consisting of a square mile or 640 acres.

In practice, because sections are laid out on a horizontal plane without reference to the curvature of the earth, sections only approximate a square mile.

Sections may be divided into quarters of 160 acres, theoretically measuring 2,640 feet on each side. The east half of the northeast quarter of the northeast quarter consists of a 20-acre parcel measuring 660 feet by 1,320 feet. To calculate the exact number of acres, divide the total square footage by 43,560 (the number of square feet per acre).

Rectangular surveys are read backwards. For example, a survey may read, "the southwest quarter of the southwest quarter Section 1" to describe a 40-acre parcel. However, "the southeast quarter *and* southwest quarter of Section 1" describes 320 acres. Whenever the word "and" is used, it is necessary to refer back to the original section number or the last-mentioned quarter and again read backward.

Rectangular surveys frequently refer to government lots which are fractional sections. Government lots must be identified by reference to the original U.S. Rectangular Survey Maps. Because of the inaccuracy of U.S. rectangular surveys, appraisers reference the land area by the actual dimensions as indicated on surveys maps available in county offices.

State Plane Coordinate Descriptions

The state plane coordinate system provides a permanent method of identifying reference points. The method depends on a "geodetic survey" that uses spherical trigonometry to determine distances and bearings. In nontechnical terms, the state plane coordinate system relies on monuments arranged in a series of triangles, with coordinates determined precisely by *longitude and latitude*. If a physical monument is lost or destroyed, its location may be found by geodetic survey.

Grids have been developed for all 50 states. Each state is divided into zones with a maximum width of 158 miles. Each of the 111 zones is flattened mathematically with much the same effect as a flattened orange peel. Each zone is divided into a grid with a vertical Y-axis and a horizontal X-axis. Property locations are described according to their X-Y coordinates.

In short, while the system has clear advantages for measuring rights-of-way for highways, utility lines, and public lands, it has not been widely used by lay persons.

SUMMARY

Real estate refers to land and its attachments. *Real property* refers to the legal rights associated with land ownership. *Personal property* is nonreal estate property. *Fixtures* are articles, formerly personal property, installed or attached to land or buildings.

Legal estates in real estate include (1) the freehold estate or an interest in land and (2) less than freehold estates: leases which grant use and possession for a definite time.

Freehold estates may be *estates of inheritance* and *estates not of inheritance.* Estates of inheritance cover the *fee simple absolute,* which is the maximum possible ownership, or the *fee simple determinable,* which terminates on the occurrence of a known event.

Estates not of inheritance refer to *life estates,* which terminate upon the death of the person whose life measures ownership time.

Express contracts, which create life estates, are peculiar to certain states: Some states provide a *homestead right* which gives limited protection of the family home from creditors.

Legal life estates are created by express acts of the owner as required by state law. These interests include the right of curtesy, which is a right given to husbands in real estate acquired during marriage. *Dower rights* refer to the interest of the surviving wife in land acquired by the husband during the marriage. Dower and curtesy rights are released by the husband and wife executing conveyance instruments.

Tenancy by the entireties: In Florida and several other states, the state considers ownership by husband and wife as ownership by one person. On the death of either party, the estate is owned by the survivor. *Community property* recognizes two types of property owned by married persons: separate property and community property. Under community property, real estate acquired by either spouse belongs to both as co-owners. Community property does not include the right of survivorship.

Less than freehold estates refers to leases that convey the right to possession, use, and enjoyment for a limited period. The *estate for years* continues for a definite period of time. Tenants may acquire a *periodic tenancy,* which prevails until one of the parties gives termination notice. *Tenancy at will* is an estate created lawfully which may be terminated on proper notice. A *tenancy at sufferance* covers a tenant who enters the premises lawfully under an existing lease and holds over, without permission, at lease termination.

An *easement* is the right to use land for a specific purpose. Easements may be created by *prescription,* by *implied easements,* by *necessity,* by *condemnation,* or by *reservation.*

Encroachments are a fence, building, or wall that intrudes over another's property. *Licenses* are considered personal property in that they create a temporary use of private property that may be revoked by the owner for any cause.

Real estate may be held as *tenants in common* where two or more owners have an undivided interest that may be *unequal* with *no right of survivorship,* created at *different points of time* with the *right to partition* an individual interest. *Joint tenancy* requires creation at the *same time* and with *equal shares* of ownership. Joint tenants have the *right of survivorship.*

Real estate held as a *partnership* interest may not be conveyed to others without the consent of other partners. *Limited partnerships* include limited partners who have liability limited to their interest with no voice in management. *General partners* have the right to execute real estate conveyances and assume property management.

Condominium ownership provides for ownership of a condominium unit with an undivided interest in the common elements. The common elements refer to the grounds, the building sites, and other facilities shared with other unit owners.

Cooperative ownership provides for cooperative shares equal in value to the property acquired. Cooperative owners are granted a proprietary lease granting exclusive use of a selected apartment. Cooperative shareholders pay a prorated share of existing mortgages and project expenses. Cooperative owners do not have the limited liability common to condominium owners.

Land descriptions may be *metes and bounds,* in which the property is described from the *point of beginning,* and thence to a direction identified by compass quadrants to a monument. *Monuments* are turning points which are natural or manmade objects.

Recorded subdivisions allow land to be described by lots and blocks in subdivisions that are placed on public record. The *Government Rectangular Survey System* starts with a *principal meridian* and *baseline.* Property is referenced by *township* lines running east and west, and *range* lines running north and south, both at six mile intervals. Within each thirty-six square miles, land is divided into square miles called *sections.* Because of the curvature of the earth, sections only approximate one square mile.

State plane coordinate descriptions are permanent methods of identifying real estate that depend on spherical trigonometry to determine distances and bearings. Land is described according to X-Y coordinates based on longitude and latitude.

POINTS TO REMEMBER

real estate land and its attachments.

43,560 (the number of square feet per acre)

real property legal rights associated with land ownership.

fixture an article, which was formerly personal property, permanently installed or attached to land or buildings.

freehold estates an interest in land for an indefinite period.

fee simple absolute the maximum ownership in real estate that conveys title over the life of the owner. It may be inherited without restriction.

fee simple determinable an estate that terminates on the occurrence of a known event.

life estate interest an ownership that terminates upon the death of the person whose life measures the estate.

homestead right limited protection granted by selected states to protect the family home from creditors.

curtesy a life estate granted to husbands on real estate owned by the wife during marriage.

dower rights the interest of the surviving wife in land acquired by the husband during marriage.

tenancy by the entireties ownership by husband and wife treated as ownership by one person. The tenancy includes the right of survivorship.

community property a right granted by selected states that treats property acquired by either spouse during marriage as community property belonging to both persons as co-owners. Community property does not include the right of survivorship.

estate for years a leasehold estate that continues for a definite period of time.

periodic tenancies leases that continue until one of the parties of the lease gives notice of termination.

tenancy at will an estate created lawfully with the consent of owner and tenant that may be terminated by either party upon proper notice.

tenancy at sufferance a tenancy created when a tenant, who enters the premises lawfully, holds over without permission of the owner at lease termination.

dominant estate an interest of the person benefited by an easement.

servient estate the interest of a person who grants an easement.

easement by prescription an easement acquired without written permission, provided requirements of state law are met.

implied easement an easement created by the nature of a right-of-way which is implied by observation and use.

easement by necessity an easement created to allow access to a public road.

easement by condemnation a right held by state-regulated utilities and government agencies to acquire easements for right-of-way or other public use.

easements by reservation an easement created by a conveyance instrument that reserves the right to an easement.

encroachments a building, fence, wall, or other improvement that extends over the property of another.

license a temporary use of private property.

concurrent ownership joint ownership by two or more persons.

tenancy in common ownership consisting of two or more owners having an undivided interest that may be owned in unequal shares, acquired at different points of time with the right of partition.

joint tenancy ownership by two or more persons who have a unity of interest and title and who have acquired property at the same time. Joint tenancy includes the right of survivorship.

limited partnership title held as a limited partnership provides for *general* and *limited* partners. General partners assume management, while limited partners provide capital. The liability of limited partners is limited to their interest.

real estate investment trust ownership in real estate acquired by share interests that exempt owners from federal corporate net income taxes, provided the trust observes IRS requirements.

condominium ownership ownership in a unit with an individual interest in the common elements.

cooperative ownership a nonprofit corporation that issues ownership shares equal in value to a given unit. Cooperative owners acquire possession under a proprietary lease granting exclusive use and occupancy of a selected unit.

metes and bounds a method of describing land area by describing boundary directions and their turning points.

recorded subdivision a method of identifying lots and blocks in subdivisions recorded in public records. Each lot is described by a metes and bounds description.

government rectangular survey system a method of identifying land by reference to principal meridians and base lines.

townships property reference lines, under the rectangular survey system, that run east and west at six-mile intervals, north and south of the baseline.

ranges lines running north and south at six-mile intervals measured east and west from the principal meridian.

sections sections are approximately square-mile areas in a 36-square-mile township, numbered from the upper right hand corner down in a serpent-like manner to section 36.

state plane coordinate descriptions a method of identifying land by longitude and latitude that accounts for curvature of the earth.

QUESTIONS FOR REVIEW

1. In your own words, define real estate, real property, and fixtures.

2. What two forms of ownership may be assumed under estates of inheritance?

3. What interest is created under a contract for an estate not of inheritance? What variations are found under this form of ownership?

4. What are the variations among the states in providing for estates created by law?

5. What is the significance of the four types of less than freehold estates for valuation purposes? Explain thoroughly.

6. Explain the relationships between the dominant and the servient estate under a right-of-way easement.

7. Explain how easements may be created and abandoned.

8. Explain the main differences between tenancy in common and joint tenancy.

9. Contrast condominium ownership with cooperative ownership.

10. What incentives do investors have in forming limited partnerships?

11. What are the main differences between a metes and bounds description and a recorded subdivision description? Explain fully.

12. What are the main features of the U.S. Rectangular Survey System?

13. What are the advantages of a state plane coordinate legal description? Explain how you would use a state plane coordinate system in completing an appraisal assignment.

PRACTICE PROBLEMS

1. Assume that you accept an appraisal assignment from a client who gives you a street address. Explain (a) how you would identify the property to be appraised and (b) how you would determine the property rights to be appraised. In your answer, include possible suggestions to the client on identifying the property and the property rights to be appraised.

2. Suppose you are appraising a suburban residential property with ten acres. In your property inspection, you discover a dirt road across the property that apparently has been used for several years. You find no record of the access road in the legal description. Explain how you would proceed to value the property under a metes and bounds legal description.

C H A P T E R 4

Land Use Controls

After studying this chapter, you will know:

- The impact of four public rights in private property: police power, eminent domain, the right of taxation, and the power of escheat.
- Common zoning code restrictions.
- Impact of land use planning and subdivision regulations.
- The effect of environmental controls on value.
- Private land use restrictions: deeds, subdivision regulations, and other restrictions.

Private property rights are subject to the rights of others under common and statutory law. Private property may not be used in such a way as to create a nuisance or to harm neighbors. For instance, a property owner may not excavate land that endangers the support of buildings on adjoining land. Neighbors must not disturb the peace and enjoyment of other property owners. Over time, these restrictions have led to laws and regulations enacted under the *inherent powers of government.*

Appraisers weigh the impact of land use controls on market value: Does the property owner have the right to erect a television antenna on the roof? Can the owner expand the carport within 10 feet of the side boundary? Can the owner of 20 acres improve the site with 60 residential units (3 units per acre) or 200 units (10 units per acre)? While appraisers verify ownership and legal descriptions, they estimate market value in the light of land use restrictions.

The chapter divides land use controls between certain *public laws* and *private restrictions* imposed by deeds, contracts, subdivision regulations, and similar documents affecting property owners. Public controls include the many federal, state, and local environmental laws. Thus, the market value estimate incorporates judgments over the benefits of ownership associated with certain private use rights and their restrictions.

PUBLIC LAND USE CONTROLS

Government has inherent rights over private property under the right of *police power,* the *right of eminent domain,* the *right of taxation,* and the *right of escheat.* See Figure 4-1 for a brief statement of these four inherent rights.

Government, with its administrative agencies, enforces these restrictions over private property rights in the public interest. Public land use controls materially affect market value.

Figure 4-1   Public Rights Over Private Property

Public Rights	*Qualifications*
Police Power	Right to regulate private property for the public interest, convenience, and necessity
Eminent Domain	Right to take private property in the public interest upon payment of just compensation
Taxation	Right to tax private property according to constitutional and statutory law
Escheat	Right of the state to acquire title of the property of a deceased person who dies without a will or heirs

Police Power

State legislatures delegate to local governments certain rights to regulate private property. Under delegated authority, cities, counties, and other local agencies provide *zoning codes* that regulate property use; *housing codes* that affect the use and occupancy of residential property; *building codes* that ensure safe, habitable buildings; and *subdivision regulations* that apply to neighborhoods that meet minimum standards for public improvements and utilities.

Eminent Domain

The power of eminent domain refers *to the taking of private property in the public interest upon payment of just compensation.* The *federal constitution,* under the *Fifth Amendment,* states that private property shall not be taken without the payment of just compensation. Virtually every state constitution has similar provisions. The *Fourteenth Amendment* to the federal constitution, ratified in 1868, extended provisions of the *Fifth Amendment* to all states. Therefore, it is well established that private property owners are entitled to just compensation under eminent domain. Just compensation generally means market value.

Right of Taxation

Sovereign states have the inherent right of taxation. Local governments typically operate under delegated powers of the state to levy local taxes to support government. For the present purpose, this right is especially important with respect to the property tax system.

PROPERTY TAX SYSTEM

Property owners pay local property taxes according to the *assessed value* of their real estate. The assessed value is the value placed on taxable real property for property tax purposes. Given the assessed value, the annual tax is calculated from the locally imposed *tax rate* or levy. To understand how the property tax works and its possible effect on market value, assume the following facts:

Tax base: $1,000,000,000
  The tax base equals the sum of assessed values of a city, county, and other local agencies.
Required annual local budget: $10,000,000

With a proposed annual budget of $10,000,000 to operate a local agency, the agency (such as a school district) would impose a tax rate of one percent or 10 mills. A *mill* is one-tenth of a cent or $1.00 per $1,000 of assessed value.

$$\text{Tax Rate} = \frac{\text{Required Annual Budget (Tax Rate)}}{\text{Total Assessed Value (Tax Base)}}$$

$$= \frac{\$10,000,000}{\$1,000,000,000}$$

$$= .010$$

$$= 10 \text{ mills}$$

$$= \$1.00 \text{ per } \$1,000 \text{ assessment}$$

For example, assume that you are appraising a house with an estimated $200,000 market value. You know that, by regulation or law, the local assessor must assess the property at 50 percent of market value or $100,000.

If the local tax rate is 20 mills ($0.02), the estimated annual property tax equals $2,000 (0.02 x $100,000). Note that the property tax is determined by the assessed value, which is estimated by the local assessor, and the tax rate, which is determined by local government agencies. Ordinarily, the tax rate would be a *composite tax rate* consisting of the sum of tax rates separately levied by local agencies such as counties, cities, school districts, water districts, and other local agencies.

ASSESSMENT UNIFORMITY

Justice and tax fairness require the assessor to assess all property uniformly. Generally, each property must be assessed at the market value standard. Some assessors, like the Cook County Assessor of Illinois, (metropolitan Chicago), classify property and apply a different assessed value percentage to the market value of residential, commercial, and industrial property. Within each property type, assessors must assess each property uniformly.

In practice, assessors are unable to examine each property often enough to ensure ideal assessment uniformity. Because of the physical task of annually assessing every property, assessments may seriously deviate from uniformity.

Assume that the assessor must assess residential property at 40 percent of market value. If the assessor has accurately assessed a $200,000 house, the assessed value for property taxes would be $80,000. If the local tax rate is 40 mills, the annual property tax would be $3,200 ($80,000 x .04).

Suppose, however, that the assessor has erred. If the assessed value is $40,000, property taxes would be $1,600 or 50 percent of the taxes paid by the owner of a similar $200,000 house with an $80,000 assessed value. In this case, the second assessment represents an underassessment, the owner of the $80,000 assessed house pays double the property taxes of the owner of the house with a $40,000 assessed value. These inequities may pass unnoticed and continue for years, or indefinitely.

The preceding example illustrates assessment discrimination within the same property type. Assessment discrimination may also exist between owners of different property types. For example, suppose that the typical average assessed value of a house is 40 percent of market value. Suppose that in the same locality commercial real estate is assessed at 80 percent of market value. In this instance, owners of commercial property, on the average, pay double the property taxes levied against single-family-dwelling owners. In this case, the assessor has discriminated against owners of commercial property in favor of residential property owners.

As a rule, owners of new property have proportionately higher assessed values than owners of older residential property. Relatively high-priced property is generally assessed at a lower average assessment ratio relative to owners of low-priced property—a form of discrimination by property value. Owners of low-priced property pay higher effective tax rates than owners of high-priced property.

Property taxes on commercial property are the single largest expense of ownership. It follows, therefore, that property with a discriminatory, or high, assessed value has a lower net income and therefore a lower value than property with a uniform, fair assessed value. While these results depend on local market conditions, the point is that appraisers must form judgments on local property taxes as they affect market value.

POWER OF ESCHEAT

Our land tenure system provides land ownership by an individual, company, government agency, or other entity. Because of the power of escheat, all real estate is owned. If a property owner dies without a will or heirs, the title reverts to the state.

LOCAL LAND USE CONTROLS

Local land use controls include zoning ordinances, the general plan, subdivision controls, and other regulations enacted for public safety and welfare: namely, building codes, housing codes, health codes, electrical codes, and related local controls that provide for safe, habitable buildings, and land use.

Zoning Codes

Appraisers confront two main types of zoning codes: *comprehensive zoning codes* and *modern zoning practices*.

COMPREHENSIVE ZONING CODES

Comprehensive zoning codes regulate *building bulk, minimum building standards,* and *land use districts.* Building bulk is limited by zoning ordinances that provide for the maximum building height or number of stories. Washington, D.C., and Palm Springs, California, have zoning ordinances that control building bulk by restricting maximum building height. Minimum building standards are common to zoning ordinances that establish minimum building areas. These areas may be limited to, say, 600 or 1,000 square feet.

Comprehensive zoning codes divide permitted land uses into zoning districts. Most codes begin with districts identified as R1, single-family-dwelling districts. The R1 classification primarily restricts land use to single-family dwellings. Such districts establish minimum front-yard set-backs, for example, 40 feet; minimum side-yard requirements; and minimum rear-yard distances. The minimum side yard may be 10 feet, meaning that structures may not be constructed within 10 feet of the side boundaries. The rear-yard requirement may require an open space 50 feet from the rear property line. Succeeding residential districts, denoted as R2, R3, and R4, for instance, relax these restrictions and permit multiple-family residential use of various categories.

Residential districts are followed by a series of *commercial districts,* shown as C1, C2, C3, and other classifications, indicating allowable retail and commercial property uses. In some jurisdictions, residential uses are allowed in designated commercial districts.

The final classification, *industrial districts*, may be further subdivided into light, medium, heavy, or other classifications to allocate land uses among various industrial uses. Restrictions on the types of industry and their operation are common to industrial zones.

Consequently, communities that have comprehensive zones regulate building bulk and minimum building standards as part of the zoning ordinance. Under comprehensive zoning codes, zoning changes require property owners to face public hearings for approval of zoning variances. Zoning changes are allowed depending on the outcome of a hearing as a consequence of political and economic pressures—one group wins and the other loses.

Critics have held that zoning districts result in *inharmonious land uses,* especially where zoning uses become cumulative among districts, i.e., commercial use is allowed in industrial districts. Division of communities by zoning districts has led to criticisms that zoning districts are *too inflexible* and do not allow for *growth and community development.*

MODERN ZONING PRACTICES

Comprehensive zoning codes have been supplemented by zoning reforms better adapted to current needs. Among these innovations are performance zoning, development rights, and inclusionary zoning.

PERFORMANCE ZONING. Performance zoning bases land uses on performance and not land use districts. Performance zones separate land use districts by broadly different functions. Within each district, multiple uses are allowed, provided the developer observes allowable land use densities. For example, a *moderately intensive* zone may limit lot coverage for all uses to 40 percent of the land area. This means that a builder may construct a 2,000-square-foot building on a 5,000-square-foot lot (40 percent coverage). By varying the land use density, performance zoning permits a wide variety of land uses within a single zoning district.

DEVELOPMENT RIGHTS. Development rights are rights to develop vacant land for urban use according to the allowable building density. *Density* is defined according to the number of allowable dwellings per acre. Some states allow owners to sell development rights. Counties such as Montgomery County, Maryland, have designated county areas as *rural density transfer zones* and other areas as *receiving zones*. A farmer owning acreage in the rural density transfer zone may sell development rights to an owner in a receiving zone. Other states have enacted laws reserving land for exclusive agricultural use.

INCLUSIONARY ZONING. Other states, including California, require residential developers, as a condition for zoning approval, to construct a certain proportion of housing for low- or moderate-income groups.

In other cases, land owners have been awarded compensation for zoning that reserves private land for a public park. While no property may be taken, courts have allowed compensation for the exercise of police power that has the same impact as a public taking under the power of eminent domain.

IMPACT ON VALUE

Appraisers confronted with zoning restrictions must weigh their impact on value. Land may be appraised according to the most probable use under existing local zoning regulations. In other instances, development restrictions under local land use controls may seriously limit market value. Local zoning, on the other hand, may act to preserve or enhance neighborhood values. Clearly, local zoning and its administration has an important bearing on market value. To illustrate, consider the value of 27 acres zoned for RM-1 or RM-2 residential zoning. These relationships are shown in Table 4-1. Total revenues under RM-1 residential zoning total $17,280,000. In this instance, the developer can develop residential land at a density of

Table 4-1   Total Revenues Possible Under Variations in Allowable Residential Zoning Densities

	27 Acres
Total Possible Revenue Under RM-1 Zoning:	
Land values	
$10,000 per site, 8 units per acre, $80,000 per acre	$ 2,160,000
Building values	
$70,000 construction cost per unit, $560,000 per acre	$15,120,000
Total possible revenue	$17,280,000
Total Possible Revenue Under RM-2 Zoning:	
Land values	
$8,000 per site, 16 units per acre, $128,000 per acre	$ 3,456,000
Building values	
$70,000 construction cost per unit, $1,120,000 per acre	$30,240,000
Total possible revenue	$33,696,000

eight, two-bedroom dwelling units per acre. Assuming a site value of $10,000, the zoning would result in a possible revenue of $80,000 per acre from lot sales. With a construction cost of $70,000 per dwelling and eight buildings per acre, the total revenue from buildings equals $560,000 per acre. Therefore under RM-1 zoning, the developer anticipates a total possible revenue of *$17,280,000* after all units are sold on the 27 acres.

Under RM-2 zoning, which allows *16 residential units* per acre, lot sales at $8,000 per site for the smaller land area would total $3,456,000 for the 27 acres. With the same two bedroom dwellings, costing an estimated $70,000 per unit, total revenues for land and buildings would equal *$33,696,000.*

To be sure, the total revenue would be reduced by development expenses. However, the appraiser considering the value of the 27 acres would compare potential subdivision sales between RM-1 and RM-2 zoning.

In the case illustrated, acreage sales approved for RM-1 zoning were sold at an *average price of $11,000 per acre.* Land zoned for RM-2 residential zoning, comparable in most other respects, showed an *average per acre price of $30,000.* Therefore, recent land acreage sales clearly indicated that land value was related to the allowable land use density. The example shows the importance of valuing property according to the allowable land use density and other land use restrictions.

Land Use Planning

Communities that develop comprehensive, master, or general plans largely control the direction and quality of urban development. Such plans are statements of community goals that cover land use with respect to social, economic, and political objectives. General plans tentatively allocate public and private land for recreation, public, commercial, residential, and industrial use.

PURPOSE

The general or comprehensive plan coordinates public and private agencies in the continual review of land use and planning. Zoning and other land use controls then *implement* the general plan. Common observation shows that the general plan promotes the local economic base. Such plans promote tourism in Palm Springs, California, with controls on outside signs, exterior lighting, building height, and land use density.

GENERAL PLAN ADOPTION

General plans are based on surveys of physical characteristics, a study of the *economic base*—activities in which people earn their living—and *a social survey* that covers population characteristics, education, age level, household size, per capita income, and the like. The master plan leads to a tentative allocation of major land use areas. Such a plan guides public and private investments in buildings, recreation, and various property uses.

Subdivision Regulations

Local communities control residential land use density and urban development under local subdivision regulations. Such regulations ensure that new neighborhoods have streets that are uniformly wide, that are planned with respect to existing traffic patterns, and that are adapted to residential use.

APPROVAL REQUIREMENTS

Before subdivision approval, subdivisions must meet requirements concerning drainage, lot areas, street patterns, utilities, sewers, water supply, and similar features that meet or exceed local standards. These regulations ensure that land used for residential purposes and for public improvements complies with minimum local standards. The purpose of subdivision regulations, therefore, is to ensure that subdivisions conform to local regulations governing physical site requirements and utilities and that subdivided lots are suitable for residential use.

APPROVAL ADMINISTRATION

Local subdivision approval follows a complex system starting with a tentative subdivision map for review by various municipal or local offices: the fire department, water department, sewer district, school districts, and other agencies that impose minimum requirements. Approval leads to a recorded *subdivision plat.* The plat is a map filed for public record that identifies each lot and block with a metes and bounds description. The recording will be accepted if it carries an affidavit from a licensed surveyor that the survey is correct and complies with state and local laws.

    The act of recording, in most areas, publicly dedicates streets, playgrounds, public areas, and the utility system. The purchaser of a recorded subdivision lot, who benefits from compliance with minimum requirements, may secure lot dimensions from the permanently filed plat recorded in a local public office.

Regulatory Codes

Regulatory codes ensure building safety by regulating standards of construction and materials. Housing codes establish minimum housing *standards.* Various other codes dealing with minimum sewer and water systems are justified under the police power in the interest of public welfare and safety.

BUILDING CODES

Building codes are generally enforced by requiring building permits for building construction, alteration, moving, demolition and repair. Building construction is permitted only after a permit has been issued. Applicants must demonstrate that proposed construction complies with local building requirements. Inspectors must approve completed construction before occupancy. Failure to secure a permit subjects the offender to heavy fines and losses.

HOUSING CODES

Housing codes provide minimum occupancy standards. Commonly, they restrict the number of persons permitted in dwellings; they require that housing be kept in proper repair; they provide for housing maintenance and sanitary housing; and they establish minimum ventilation and lighting standards. Most housing codes require adequate protection against fire, hot and cold running water, and a heating system that complies with the local code.

Appraisers evaluate whether the property under appraisal complies with local codes. A property in violation of local codes requires an appropriate adjustment in market value if the property is appraised in an "as is" condition.

The issue is particularly relevant in appraising potential subdivision land if it is determined by a soil survey that the soil type prohibits septic tanks or that an industrial site has an unstable soil unsuitable for heavy industrial floor loads. In such cases, the impact of local code violations on market value deserves explanation.

ENVIRONMENTAL CONTROLS

While some environmental laws and regulations go back more than three generations, the more significant controls developed from the *National Environmental Policy Act of 1969*. Major environmental controls and regulations cover six areas:

> water quality and resources management,
> air quality management,
> land use management,
> wildlife management, and
> solid waste and noise control management

Add to this list current attention given *asbestos* management in public buildings and concern over radon. *Radon* is a gas that accumulates in buildings and that is formed by the decay of uranium atoms in rocks and soils. Appraisers increasingly confront the impact that environmental controls have on real estate values.

Environmental Laws

The *Clean Air Act Amendments of 1977* initiated regulations of the Environmental Protection Agency that established special requirements for communities in violation of national air-quality standards. Such standards, depending on local conditions, affect parking lots, transportation facilities, and proposed construction that increases air pollution.

Water quality programs are administered under the *Clean Water Act of 1977* as amended. The act controls land projects that cause water pollution. States must regulate water pollution from agricultural runoff and surface waters flowing from shopping center parking lots and other urban improvements.

Waste management controls and waste disposal facilities impact on surrounding properties. Virtually every urban community must deal with waste treatment and its management that affects local real estate values.

Coastal water management zones include the Great Lakes and their connecting waters, harbors, bays, and marshes. Property in coastal zones and their management area are subject to review for projects that affect population growth, economic development, industry, commerce, residential development, recreation, transportation, navigation, waste disposal, and related activities. Real appraisals in these areas must include a review of coastal zones management plans and the proposed land use plans.

ASBESTOS HAZARDS

According to the Environmental Protection Agency approximately 733,000 or 20 percent of the buildings in the United States contain asbestos materials. *Asbestos* refers to natural minerals that separate into strong and very fine fibers that are heat-resistant and extremely durable. The physical properties that allow asbestos to resist heat and decay also adversely affect human health. The microscopic fibers remain suspended in the air for long periods and can easily penetrate bodily tissue when inhaled.

Appraisers evaluating buildings suspected of asbestos contamination must consider steps to minimize exposure and their cost. Contamination leads to higher operating expenses, lower occupancy rates and, consequently, lower market values. The first task is to determine if asbestos-containing materials should be of concern to the building owner.

RADON EXPOSURE

According to the Environmental Protection Agency, indoor radon exposure ranks as the primary environmental threat of lung cancer to the

American people. From this source, lung cancer may develop over a relatively long time, i.e., about 20 years.[1] Radon exposure of a level greater than 4pCi/1 is dangerous to building occupants. This measure refers to a radon concentration in terms of picocuries per liter (pCi/1). A liter equals 1.057 quarts. A curie is a measure of radiation and a picocurie is one trillionth of a curie. If radon is suspected, the appraiser must ask for a soil test for radon contamination. Properties are ineligible for mortgages purchased by the Federal National Mortgage Association if high radon levels can only be corrected through large capital improvements or an expensive maintenance program.

In most cases, however, the cost of eliminating indoor radon exposure is relatively inexpensive. Techniques have been developed by EPA to reduce the potential liability of radon pollution.

Impact on Value

Appraisers have been advised to determine answers to the following questions in evaluating property where environmental problems may bear on market value:

1. Has the prior property owner used, stored, treated, or disposed of hazardous material?
2. Do structures contain hazardous substances?
3. If hazardous materials have been used, was the operation in compliance with government regulations?
4. Has the property been identified by government agencies as a site requiring environmental investigation?
5. Have any law suits or administrative proceedings been levied against previous owners?

While the appraiser may not be an expert in environmental matters, awareness of environmental controls allows appraisers to form the best possible judgment on environmental problems that affect market value.

PRIVATE RESTRICTIONS

Private restrictions are found in deeds, real estate contracts, subdivision regulations, and in certain other legal documents.

---

1   Kevin L. Shepherd, "Indoor Radon Rouses the Commercial Real Estate Industry," *The Journal of Real Estate Development*, Summer 1989, p. 46.

Deed Restrictions

Deed restrictions are generally placed on real estate by the seller as a condition of sale. For instance, the seller, to maintain the quality of surrounding construction, may require, as a condition of sale, that all buildings on the land conveyed must have brick exteriors or that dwellings must have a minimum area of 3,000 square feet.

Deeds may be more restrictive. Consider the seller of a house with two lots which included the restriction that no dwelling shall be constructed north of a creek that runs through the adjoining lot. Upon physically inspecting the property, most appraisers would place a separate, additional value on the adjoining lot which normally would be developed as a single-family dwelling. A review of the deed, however, indicated that the adjoining lot could not be used for a single-family dwelling. In this instance, quite clearly, the deed restriction had a direct bearing on market value.

In questionable cases, the appraiser may request legal advice. A deed restriction that reads "only buildings of standard construction may be built on the property sold" is probably unenforceable. The term "standard construction" is too indefinite to be enforceable. Further, deed restrictions must not be discriminatory, against social policy, or illegal.

Hence, appraisers make final judgments on the impact of deed restrictions that enhance property values or that so limit property use as to reduce market value.

Subdivision Restrictions

Subdivision restrictions, also called subdivision covenants, or protective covenants, seek to preserve the neighborhood, reduce property deprecia-tion and add to community amenities. Under subdivision restrictions, a developer may add controls on property use and other matters that affect the *aesthetic qualities* of the neighborhood subdivision which may not be enforceable by public ordinance.

ADVANTAGES

Subdivision covenants have the added advantage of being *more permanent* than zoning codes. Zoning codes may be changed by political pressure. Subdivision covenants may be *adapted to changing land* uses and, at the same time, preserve the character of the neighborhood. Such covenants may be changed by a majority of property owners in the subdivision.

Subdivision covenants usually include land use restrictions and archi-tectural controls. Generally, land is reserved for residential dwellings. No business or offensive activity may be permitted that causes an annoyance or nuisance to the neighborhood. In more restrictive cases, owners must park, store, or garage trailers, campers, motor homes, and similar vehicles out of sight.

Architectural control may require building plan approval by an architectural committee appointed by the developer before structures are constructed. A related issue provides for the placement of buildings on defined setback lines from streets or property boundaries. Subdividers may add restrictions that guide the appearance of the subdivision, such as prohibiting antennas, air conditioners in view of the street, and outside storage.

In some instances, landscaping must be approved by an architectural committee. Other restrictions prohibit "spite" fences on the property line and even lawn fertilizers that pollute surface waters. A miscellaneous group of covenants may control the disposition of refuse, trash, or waste materials, especially into waterways on waterfront lots. Other common restrictions cover the placement of billboards and signs. Some do not allow direct exterior lighting. Some subdivisions allow pets, provided they are not maintained for commercial purposes.

ENFORCEMENT

Covenants are enforced by the developer or lot owners who have the right to enjoin violations of recorded covenants. The appraiser judges if restrictive covenants add or detract from market value. Do restrictions preserve the subdivision environment, retard neighborhood depreciation by enhancing openness and general appearance, or minimize the loss in value from neighborhood obsolescence?

While subdivision covenants restrict property rights, it is held that property owners benefit from land use restrictions imposed uniformly on neighbors. The purchase of a lot subject to subdivision restrictions protects property owners from acts of neighbors which may limit the enjoyment of residential areas.

Other Restrictions

Private ownership restrictions, besides the limitations noted, arise from statutory law, the operation of law, and/or by contract. Recall that the appraiser makes no judgments over titles. Further, the appraiser makes no legal judgments affecting the enforceability of contracts or other matters affecting marketable title.

This does not mean, however, that appraisers should not advise clients of matters that bear on market value. Suspected liens or other restrictions that relate to market value may lead appraisers to advise clients to seek competent legal or other advice. So while appraisers do not render judgments on property restrictions such as liens, they should be aware of the consequences of other private restrictions.

Consider, for example, liens. Liens are claims of one person on the property of another held as security for a debt. Enforceable liens are recorded in public records giving notice of the debt which is secured by real estate.

For example, mechanics' liens are created by statutes that favor persons who have performed work or furnished materials in the erection or repair of a building. The right to file a mechanics' lien, is a carryover from the time when craftsmen worked on clothing, shoes, and other personal property and kept the object until paid for the work performed. Since physical possession of real estate is impossible, the law substitutes the right of others to file liens against real estate on which a worker has contributed work or materials. Such persons, with certain limitations, may look to the real estate for payment of their services.

It is generally held that a person is entitled to a mechanics' lien if he or she has improved the real estate at the request or consent of the legal owner. Generally, the amount of the lien may not be more than the value of services or materials and may attach to the owner's interest at the time of filing the lien. Hence, the buyer of a new house may be subject to a lien. An appraiser makes no judgments on the legal consequences of a lien other than to warn of its possible effect on market value.

SUMMARY

Police power is an inherent right of government to regulate private property in the public interest, safety and welfare. The right of *eminent domain* is the right of government- and public-regulated utilities to take private property in the public interest upon the payment of just compensation. Government also has the *right of taxation* and holds *the right of escheat*. The latter right permits the state to take title of a deceased person without a will or without legal heirs.

The property tax is based on the *assessed value* of real estate and the *tax rate* or *levy*. Local property tax assessors follow the *uniformity rule*: property assessments should be uniform between and among taxable properties. Assessment discrimination results if assessors over- or under-assess property. Improper assessments distort annual property taxes and the annual net income of commercial property. Since property taxes are the largest single expense for commercial real estate, discriminatory assessments materially affect market value.

Zoning codes may follow the *comprehensive zoning* code controlling building bulk, minimum building standards, and land use districts. Comprehensive zoning districts result in inharmonious land uses, especially if zoning uses become cumulative among districts. Other critics claim that zoning districts are too inflexible and do not allow for community growth. *Performance zoning* bases land use on performance and not on land use districts. Within each zoning district, multiple uses are allowed according to allowable land use densities. Other communities have established development rights. *Development rights* are the right to improve vacant land with buildings according to allowable land use densities. Some states, including California, follow *inclusionary zoning practices:* the requirement that developers reserve a certain proportion of housing for low- or moderate-income groups.

General plans, where they are required, coordinate public and private agencies; they control the direction and quality of urban development. Upon adoption of a comprehensive plan, zoning, and other land use controls, they implement the general plan. Such plans are based on a survey of physical characteristics, a study of the economic base, and social surveys.

Subdivision regulations provide that subdivisions must meet minimum local standards before approval. Approval is granted providing the subdivision developer installs the required streets, public utilities, and other regulations that ensure that land may be used as a residence. *Building codes* controlling building construction and materials provide for building safety. *Housing codes* maintain minimum occupancy standards. They restrict the number of persons legally permitted in buildings and require proper repair, housing maintenance, and sanitary housing.

Environmental controls affect land use with respect to water quality, air quality, land use management, wildlife management, solid waste, and noise control. More recently, environmental controls deal with *asbestos-contaminated buildings* and *radon* contamination. Since approximately 20 percent of buildings in the United States have asbestos contamination, asbestos surveys are often advised before making the final value estimate. The same warning applies to radon contamination, which may be easily detected and corrected.

Appraisers confronting real estate subject to environmental issues must weigh the impact of environmental problems on market value.

Deed restrictions are limitations on property use imposed by the seller as a condition of sale. *Subdivision restrictions* are added to preserve the character of the neighborhood, reduce property depreciation, and add to neighborhood amenities. Generally, such restrictions preserve the *aesthetic* qualities of the subdivision. Appraisers face other restrictions such as *mechanics' liens* that are recorded in public records to ensure payment to persons who have performed work or furnished

[handwritten marginalia] density — according to the number of allowable dwellings per acre.

$$\text{Tax Rate} = \frac{\text{Required Annual Budget (Tax Rate)}}{\text{Total Assessed Value (Tax Base)}}$$

materials in building construction or repairs. Appraisers, in reviewing property records and the title, must form judgments on private restrictions important to the market value conclusion.

POINTS TO REMEMBER

police power the right of government to regulate property in the public interest.

taxation government has the inherent right to tax private property.

escheat the power of the state to take property of a deceased person without a will or legal heirs.

tax levy the tax rate or levy imposed against real estate for property taxes.

composite tax rate a local property tax rate consisting of the sum of tax rates separately levied by local agencies.

assessment discrimination the over- or under-assessment of taxable property for property tax purposes.

comprehensive zoning codes zoning codes that regulate building bulk, minimum building standards, and land-use districts.

performance zoning local zoning ordinances that base land use on performance and not land-use districts.

development rights rights to convert vacant land to urban use according to allowable building densities.

inclusionary zoning zoning in which zoning approval requires developers to construct a certain proportion of housing for low or moderate income groups.

comprehensive (general) plans general plans coordinate public and private agencies in developing land for recreation, public, commercial, and industrial use.

subdivision regulations local regulations that ensure that subdivisions comply with traffic patterns, minimum physical requirements, and public utilities.

building codes local regulations that enforce minimum building materials and construction standards in the interest of public safety.

housing codes local regulations that maintain minimum occupancy standards and minimum quality of housing.

asbestos natural minerals that separate into strong and very fine fibers that are heat-resistant and extremely durable.

radon radioactive gas formed by the decay of uranium atoms in rocks and soils.

deed restrictions restrictions placed on land use by the seller as a condition of sale.

subdivision restrictions also called subdivision covenants, subdivision restrictions preserve the character of the neighborhood, reduce property depreciation, and increase community amenities. Usually, restrictions affect the *aesthetic* qualities of the subdivision.

mechanics' liens liens filed by persons who have performed work or furnished materials in the erection or repair of a building.

QUESTIONS FOR REVIEW

1. What type of land use controls are administered under the police power? Explain your understanding of police power.

2. What is meant by the right of eminent domain? Explain fully.

3. In appraising commercial property, what factors would you consider in estimating the effect of property taxes on market value? Give an example in support of your answer.

4. What is the purpose of the power of escheat?

5. Explain the difference between comprehensive zoning codes and zoning codes based on performance standards.

6. What is meant by development rights? Inclusionary zoning?

7. In what way do subdivision regulations relate to market value?

8. Explain the importance of regulations governing building and housing codes in estimating market value.

9. What environmental factors are subject to environmental controls?

10. Explain how you would proceed in appraising a building where you suspect asbestos hazards.

11. Why are appraisers required to consider the possibility of radon exposure?

12. What questions would you raise while appraising property that may be affected by environmental problems?

13. Explain how deed restrictions may decrease market value? Explain how deed restrictions may increase market values?

14. What is the general purpose of subdivision restrictions? Explain how subdivision restrictions may vary the market value estimate.

15. "Mechanics' liens have no influence on market value." Critically evaluate. Do you agree or disagree? Give reason for your answer.

PRACTICE PROBLEMS

1. Suppose you are requested to appraise a 40-acre site for a potential subdivision for upper-middle-income housing. The property is in a rural area subject to limited land-use controls. The current zoning is for agricultural use. What assumptions will you make on land-use controls—private or public—that you consider will give the maximum market value for subdivision purposes? Explain thoroughly.

2. Your client requests that you select an investment property that will provide a reasonably safe yield and probable capital appreciation that exceeds the expected inflation rate. You have the option of selecting property subject to highly detailed, highly restrictive public and private land-use controls, or real estate relatively free of private and public land-use controls. In a central urban area, paying particular attention to land-use controls, what environmental controls would you consider in making the final selection? Make other assumptions necessary for a realistic evaluation.

C H A P T E R 5

Real Estate Market Analysis

After studying this chapter, you will know:

- Characteristics of competitive real estate markets.
- Imperfections of real estate markets.
- Real estate market analysis techniques.
- Methods of estimating market rates of absorption.
- Real estate forecasting techniques.

Real estate appraising prequires of the appraiser a working knowledge of real estate markets and their analysis. Familiarity with *competitive markets* and *market imperfections* encountered in real estate serves as a basis of *market analysis*. Given real estate market imperfections, market analysis involves the analysis of economic conditions that closely affect real estate market performance.

Economic and demographic data support these conclusions. Finally, real estate appraisers consider *data sources that indicate the current demand and supply of real estate.* Rates of *market absorption* and data *forecasting techniques* conclude the more essential elements of real estate market analysis.

The chapter focuses on these issues, starting with a discussion of real estate market characteristics and progressing to a discussion of market analysis.

CHARACTERISTICS OF REAL ESTATE MARKETS

Real estate markets have some characteristics of *purely competitive markets.* A competitive industry or market consists of many independent firms. A competitive market in "equilibrium" is a market in which the quantity demanded equals the quantity supplied. But the competitive market ideal is considerably modified by certain real estate *market imperfections.* And while these market imperfections restrict the orderly adjustment of supply and demand, competitive forces prevail so that in the end, real estate most urgently demanded is satisfied by the market.

Real estate markets, with their many imperfections, may be judged according to the ideal, purely competitive market. Pure competition refers to markets of many buyers and sellers who trade in markets that meet competitive standards. To understand real estate markets, it is helpful to compare the purely competitive market and actual real estate markets.

Purely Competitive Markets

Under pure competition, *market prices are in equilibrium:* all buyers who wish to buy at the market price are satisfied, and all sellers who wish to sell at the market price find willing buyers. An increase in demand results in *higher prices*, which induces sellers to *increase the supply*. If the available supply exceeds the quantity buyers are willing to buy at the market price, there will be a temporary market oversupply.

The oversupply induces sellers to *lower prices*. Lower prices encourage buyers to buy more. The lower price, furthermore, decreases seller profits; some sellers are unwilling (or unable) to produce at the lower price and the *supplied quantity decreases*. Under the competitive ideal, therefore, market prices move toward equilibrium.

Such adjustments are dependent, however, on certain market conditions common to pure competition:

1. Competitive markets require many buyers and sellers, so the decision to buy or sell on the part of a single buyer or seller does not affect the price.

In an urban area, it may be claimed that there are many buyers and sellers of single-family dwellings. In reality, however, the single-family-dwelling market is highly localized. In a neighborhood of single-family dwellings, the number of buyers and sellers is sufficiently limited so that one dwelling sale tends to affect the offering and asking prices of nearby houses subsequently placed on the market.

For urban real estate submarkets, vacant land, apartment projects, retail properties, or industrial property—there are relatively few buyers and sellers for a given property; decisions of buyers and sellers tend to affect local real estate prices. The same effect may be observed for real estate having a national or international market.

These market relationships contrast to the stock market or the market for agricultural commodities, such as wheat and eggs. For example, the decision to buy one dozen Grade A large eggs does not affect the market price because of the relatively large number of buyers and sellers.

2. Buyers and sellers have perfect market knowledge.

This market ideal is approached in the market for stocks and bonds, agricultural products, and organized markets in basic industries. Buyers and sellers in the organized commodity markets may gain virtually instant price information backed by current market reports of changes in supply and demand and other factors that affect price expectations, i.e., the futures market.

In contrast, consider the relative knowledge of buyers and sellers of single-family dwellings. The average seller enters the market at infrequent periods—five or ten years or more. It is unlikely that the seller is familiar with current dwelling prices. The house buyer, in contrast, typically makes buying decisions only after reviewing dozens of dwellings for sale. To this extent, the buyer generally has superior knowledge of current dwelling prices.

The seller, in marked contrast, usually has superior knowledge of the dwelling offered for sale. After living in the dwelling, the seller has an intimate knowledge of neighborhood characteristics, the quality of construction, and condition of building equipment, among other features. These differences in market and product knowledge, between buyer and seller, interfere with market equilibrium under the purely competitive market ideal.

3. Purely competitive markets require a standardized product.

Buyers and sellers of consumer products make decisions on products that are so standardized that price comparisons may be easily made. Automobiles of a standard make with given optional features allow buyers to search for the best price among various dealers. Buyers may readily compare offering prices for standardized products. The seller in turn may calculate the projected profitability of producing a standard product at some prevailing market price.

For single-family dwellings, it is difficult for the layman to compare prices among dwellings which are unique. Each dwelling has a different location; each dwelling has construction that varies by workmanship and by quality of materials; the present condition of each house varies according to past maintenance. Clearly, houses are sufficiently differentiated so that selling prices may be distorted from purely competitive market prices.

4. Under purely competitive markets, buyers and sellers are free to enter and leave the market.

A developer of single-family dwellings with unsold houses is not able to withdraw unsold houses from the market pending a more favorable market. The cost of holding newly constructed real estate is such that developers have incentives to sell in the shortest possible time. The inability to sell newly constructed real estate leads to bankruptcy sales, real estate auctions, or other measures to sell the property below cost—a temporary market disequilibrium.

Market Adjustments

Buyers face similar market restrictions. The ability of buyers to enter the market depends on dwelling prices and the cost and availability of long-term mortgages.

Suppose, however, that an increased demand for housing creates a shortage of housing—dwelling prices increase. The time necessary to plan, finance, and construct new houses restricts the ability of suppliers to meet an increase in short-term demand. Temporary market shortages distort current prices above market prices, pending a later increase in supply.

Therefore, appraisers work in real estate markets that depart from the competitive ideal; buyers and sellers enter real estate markets that are highly imperfect. Market imperfections lead to distorted sales prices that vary from market values. Consequently, appraisers interpret real estate markets in the light of market forces. In one sense, these unique features of the real estate market require a market analysis for a market value appraisal.

REAL ESTATE MARKETS

Experienced appraisers are skilled in judging market value changes. Given a neighborhood community or metropolitan area, there are "market indicators" that identify decreasing or increasing market values. Figure 5-1 lists common indicators of market value changes.

Figure 5-1   Indications of Market Value Change

Decreasing Values	Increasing Values
Rise in vacancies	Low vacancy rates
Longer listing periods	Rising rents
Deferred property maintenance	Higher listing prices
Rising proportion of rentals (single-family dwellings)	Listing period declining
Declining rents	High level of property maintenance
Rising number of second liens, seller financing	Rising asking/selling prices
	Building permits increasing
Decreasing number of new subdivisions recorded	Increased number of new subdivisions recorded
Deed recordings down	Increased mortgage recordings
Mortgage recordings down	Increased deed recordings

Market Indicators

Market indicators reveal current changes in supply or demand. Appraisers rely on their observations of real estate market data to "indicate" current market conditions. Several of these indicators deserve added comment.

Rising vacancies in residential neighborhoods, office buildings, or shopping centers are indicative of a relative oversupply of real estate. Such vacancies may relate to a particular property type or the community in general. *Longer listing periods,* that is, an increasing interval between the time of listing and eventual sale, suggests a decreasing demand. For local neighborhoods, *deferred property maintenance* in the form of neglected landscaping, buildings in need of exterior paint, and roofs that need replacing indicate declining neighborhoods.

Appraisers determine the *proportion of dwelling rentals* that suggests owners cannot sell houses for the market value or for the amount of the outstanding mortgage. The alternative is to rent the property in the face of declining sales. Furthermore, *declining rents* show declining markets.

Turning to real estate financing, *below market financing,* meaning that sellers or lenders are willing to take liens or mortgages at less than the market interest rate, is common to depressed markets. At the same time, sellers are willing to take part of the purchase price in *second mortgages,* decreasing the need for cash among scarce buyers.

The number of building permits issued per month, sometimes classified by property types, gives current information about changes in the housing supply. A decreasing number of new subdivisions recorded, or the number of deeds recorded per month, are highly indicative of real estate activity and therefore changing values.

While these are indications of changing market value, the appraiser must document, not only the *change in real estate markets,* but the *rate of change.* Before reviewing these data sources, it is important to review the characteristics of real estate markets.

Real Estate Market Imperfections

Imperfect real estate markets arise from numerous factors, some legal and some economic. No single factor stands out above the others.

NO CENTRAL MARKET

There is no central real estate market. Real estate brokers who list houses for sale serve a market function in bringing sellers and buyers together.

Where brokers combine their listings in a multiple listing service, they provide a market for listed houses in the multiple listing area. In some metropolitan areas, offers to sell may be listed on computer retrieval systems, including listings from several multiple listing services. The same market services prevail for certain national real estate markets. For example, the Society of Industrial Realtors maintains a national listing of industrial properties for clients who list industrial property for sale through their offices.

For the most part, however, these marketing arrangements cover only a portion of all real estate bought and sold. There is no central market for real estate comparable to the stock exchange for financial investments.

LOCAL MARKETS

While there may be a national or even international demand for office buildings, shopping centers, and apartment projects, the supply of real estate and its analysis depends largely on a local market.

FIXED LOCATIONS

Because real estate is fixed in location, an oversupply of office buildings in Houston, Texas, does not offset a shortage of office buildings in Atlanta, Georgia. The fixed location means also that an investor who develops real estate locally may not compensate for a poor investment by withdrawing from the market or transferring goods to areas of market shortage.

IMPERFECT KNOWLEDGE

With few exceptions, real estate prices are difficult to determine. In some areas, such as Cook County (Chicago), Illinois, investment properties are usually conveyed to a land trust so that price information does not appear on public documents. However, Washington, Tennessee, and Pennsylvania, among other states, require a compulsory reporting of real estate prices to local or state property tax officials. With these and other exceptions, on the whole, real estate buyers, sellers, and appraisers must make personal inquiries to obtain accurate price information. There is no central place where real estate price information is public and readily available.

HIGHLY REGULATED MARKETS

Investors face added risks because of certain legal requirements not found in non-real estate investments. Buyers and sellers of real estate must observe complex local, state, and federal regulations. Local regulations deal mostly with land restrictions, while state and federal laws govern rights of parties conveying real estate and executing mortgages. Environmental compliance, local, state, and federal, introduces other regulations not encountered in non-real estate investments.

DIVISIBILITY

Real estate is highly divisible. Real estate investors and sellers may trade in partial rights in the fee interest. Rights may be conveyed under a lease, or easement, or rights may be conveyed for other specific purposes. This means that buyers and sellers face valuation issues and property-right questions that complicate market decisions.

HIGH TRANSFER COSTS

With selling and buying costs of ten percent or more of the property value, buyers and sellers cannot liquidate an investment, especially over the short-run, without capital losses—the amount of capital appreciation must equal or exceed transfer costs to avoid a loss. High transfer costs tend to lengthen the investment period in comparison to other more liquid assets such as stocks and bonds. High transfer costs discourage buyers and sellers from taking advantage of new market conditions.

PROFESSIONAL MANAGEMENT REQUIRED

Usually, an investor acquiring a major commercial property must hire a professional manager. Indeed, the quality of management often determines the success or failure of a shopping center, apartment project, or office building.

Add to these points the fact that real estate markets are highly imperfect: few buyers and sellers, imperfect market knowledge, the difficulty of entering and leaving markets, and a highly differentiated product. These market characteristics place a premium on correct market analysis.

Market Analysis

Real estate market analysis is the *collection and analysis of data to estimate current and projected real estate markets*. The data collection provides information not only on the *current* population, for example, but on population *trends*. Therefore, market analysis requires the collection of historical data showing annual changes and the degree of change.

Such data provide information on the housing market, and the projected market for projects in which investors develop for long-run yields. Some of the data collected includes *demographic data*. Demographic data refers to *population characteristics showing expansion or decline and pressures that determine these trends*. Other data relate to published economic series covering retail sales, personal income, employment and related data. Appraisers rely on other data which can be secured only from local sources and physical site surveys.

MARKET DATA RESOURCES

Appraisal clients are aware of the importance of population and its characteristics and projections. Such data are relevant in valuing residential property, shopping centers, office buildings, and even industrial property, where the occupant is dependent on employment sources. For population data, appraisers rely on reports published by the Bureau of Census.

The population census, conducted every ten years, yields data on age, sex, race, marital and work status, occupation, income, education, and migration. Publications of the Bureau of Census are supplemented by various population reports by the states and locally produced reports by county, city, and regional planning agencies. The latter reports supplement the ten-year federal census. Such data, secured over several years show percentage changes over time; they indicate comparative rates of growth and allow projections of five or ten years or more.

Retail data important to commercial appraisals, especially shopping centers, may be obtained from the Retail and Wholesale Census. Since current information is critical to commercial real estate appraising, published census data may be supplemented by annual reports of the *Sales Marketing and Management* magazine, which reports annual data in the August issue.

The magazine reports *effective buying income* by region, states, counties, major cities, and suburban areas. By reviewing the August issue, one may observe trends in local effective buying income. Effective buying income is a *measurement of the market potential indicating the ability to buy—defined as personal income less personal taxes and nontax payments*. Economists refer to this as the *disposable* or *after-tax income*. Appraisals dependent on commercial retail sales benefit from an analysis of data from this source.

For employment information, employment by source, and trends in manufacturing, appraisers refer to the *Census of Manufacturers*. Normally completed every five years, this report provides data on the number of manufacturing establishments, employment, payroll, and related data. Data are grouped by county, region, and city.

The U.S. Department of Labor publishes numerous special studies on labor market trends in the *Monthly Labor Review* showing wage rates, sources of employment, labor turnover, hourly earnings, and similar labor data. State departments of employment security and industrial development offices provide additional information on local labor costs and employment by source. Such data indicate the diversity of employment and whether the local economy is dependent on a relatively few leading industries.

REAL ESTATE SALES PRICES

Real estate appraisals rely on annual gross income and expenses for income properties and the current cost of construction for industrial and public buildings, but for properties that are frequently sold, such as single-family dwellings, apartment buildings, and office buildings, the appraiser requires a real estate sales data base. The sales data base shows price changes and provides a source for the sales comparison approach.

In most jurisdictions, sales prices are available to the public. Recorded deeds give ownership changes, but they do not indicate the property type and property characteristics important to appraisal. However, public deed records represent the main source of real estate sales filed and processed by local tax assessors and state revenue departments. The state of Pennsylvania requires county officials to submit monthly reports of real estate sales by property type. Many other jurisdictions require similar data, including the states of Washington and Tennessee, Cook County (Chicago), and certain California counties.

Other private sources regularly record detailed real estate sales information for public subscribers such as real estate appraisers, lenders, and others who rely on current real estate market data. The Appraisal Institute maintains a sales data bank of verified real estate sales from local lender files for major metropolitan areas. These housing sales, though they are derived from a limited source, are arranged for the convenience of residential appraisers.

Other sources of real estate data may be obtained from cooperating lenders and title insurance companies. Title insurance companies keep records by legal description enabling sales data to be obtained by subdivision or other geographic areas.

Virtually all appraisers rely primarily on *real estate industry sources:* information is obtained from cooperating developers, lenders, attorneys, real estate brokers, contractors, buyers and sellers, and related sources.

The more successful appraisers capitalize on the quality and completeness of their real estate sales data base.

FORECAST ANALYSIS

In appraising a projected subdivision, the appraiser bases the market value on the number of lots that may be sold annually, the number of years to sell out the subdivision, the projected prices of the lots, and subdivision development expenses.

By the same token, the value of a proposed condominium project partly relies on the length of time for the market to absorb condominium units and their estimated market value. The market value of a shopping center depends on the forecast of retail sales, expected rents, and population projections that determine total retail sales.

While such forecasts are highly subjective, remember that appraising is an art and not a science. The task of the appraiser is to make a reasonable market estimate in the light of available data. In this respect, the appraiser estimates the market rate of absorption and forecasts net income or market value.

Market Rates of Absorption

Suppose the developer employs an appraiser to estimate the market value of a 300-acre subdivision. From engineering and other data, the cost of construction may be readily calculated. But the critical problem, however, is to estimate how many years will it take to market a 300-acre subdivision and at what price.

The answer lies in surveying competing projects to determine the number of comparable lots sold in past years, their price, and their physical characteristics. A study of competing subdivision sales over the last five or ten years indicates the market rate of absorption.

The appraiser reasons that the property under valuation has certain market features that will attract buyers. The market rate of absorption, then, depends on a judgment concerning how many lots will be sold in the light of past sales and current market conditions.

While based on personal value judgments, the judgment is reached by reviewing past market performance of competing projects and estimating the rate of market absorption, according to characteristics of the property appraised relative to competing projects. With variations, this line of reasoning is typically employed by appraisers who estimate the market rates of absorption.

SUBDIVISION LOT SALES

Table 5-1 shows the projected revenue and expenses from a subdivision surrounding a 140-acre lake. The table shows actual results for the first four years. Revenue from the four years leads to a forecast of net income expected over the next seven years. Note that in the second year of operation, the developer purchased the land for $1,929,000. During the second year, revenue from lot sales totalled $2,930,000. This revenue is offset by other costs of development:

Additional land purchase	$1,577,000
Land development	3,036,000
Marketing costs	380,000
Property taxes	22,000
Overhead	334,000
	$5,349,000

Table 5-1   Forecast of Residential Lot Sales: Year 5 to Year 11

Year	Annual Revenue	Development Cost	Annual Cash Flow
		(in thousands)	
Actual			
1	--	$1,929	($1,929)
2	$2,930	5,349	(2,419)
3	4,636	5,099	(463)
4	590	4,288	(3,698)
Forecast			
5	2,622	1,866	756
6	4,809	3,186	1,623
7	3,782	1,599	2,183
8	5,001	2,179	2,822
9	5,969	1,799	4,170
10	3,922	1,369	2,553
11	4,741	1,231	3,510

Total development costs of $5,349,000 include the additional land purchase and the cost of damming a creek to create the 140-acre lake. With total lot sales of $2,930,000 and development costs of $5,349,000, the second year shows a loss of $2,419,000.

A review of Table 5-1 shows that profits are not realized until the fifth year. Beginning with the fifth year, cash flow estimates are based on a forecast of annual land sales and development costs. Note that in the ninth year expected net income peaks at $4,170,000.

SALES PROJECTIONS

Market acceptance is best indicated by the record of past lot sales over the first four years. In addition to this series, developers base revenue expectations on a series of projections related to the market for residential lots. The list of items important to this analysis includes:

population projections
    number of households
    composition of households
    family size
    family income
    age distribution
employment projections
sources of employment
building permits issued in past years for:
    single-family dwellings
    condominiums
    multiple-family residential projects
subdivisions recorded
    (number of lots)
    economic base projections

There is a direct relationship between the demand for residential lots and population projections. For this analysis, population projections are based on the number of households listed for past years. Households are reviewed according to their composition: family size, personal income, and age distribution. Since this subdivision appealed mainly to middle-income families with children in the upper-middle-income bracket, the composition of projected households assumes critical importance.

For this purpose, employment was projected by source. A study of building permits by category supplemented population and employment projections. Building permit detail depends on the local record system that classifies building permits by type of building. Land developers also review the number of past subdivisions recorded, including the number of lots. This series indicates the supply of competing subdivisions and the response of other land developers to the estimated demand.

These projections are supported further by an analysis of the economic base, the source of income to the local community. The economic base would be reviewed according to the source of employment, prospects for new industry, and prospects for manufacturing and business expansion over the marketing term.

Real Estate Forecasts

A forecast is *an estimate of future events derived from past data modified according to current conditions.* Such forecasts are important to estimating net income for new multiple-family projects, shopping centers, and related income properties. In studying past data it is implicitly assumed that past events will continue. The forecast is qualified by possible exceptions which are not predictable; for example, changes in international events, catastrophic events (earthquakes), international energy shortages, and similar events. Hence the forecaster-appraiser interprets the most current data and determines if recent changes are indicative of trends or are merely random events. In making these judgments, appraisers may rely primarily on projections based on simple regression and time series analysis.

SIMPLE REGRESSION PROJECTIONS

Simple regression is a projection method based on a relationship between two variables. Suppose the appraiser estimates the value of a proposed shopping center based on the present value of projected net income. Shopping center income is closely related to total personal income in the trade market area. By recording the personal income annually over the past 20 years, it may be shown that personal income changes each year by some arithmetic function. On the basis of this past record, the appraiser applies the arithmetic function drawn from past data and projects personal income for the investment period: ten or twenty years.

The relation between two variables shown by simple regression has several appraisal applications. Regression depends upon two variables: one is regarded as the "independent" variable and the other results in the "dependent" variable. *If the independent variable varies, it shows the value of the dependent variable.*

For example, there is generally a relationship between annual gross income and market value. By treating gross income as the independent variable, it may be determined mathematically how market value (the dependent variable) varies with a change in annual gross income. Such an analysis requires the plotting of gross incomes, the independent variable, for numerous properties with the corresponding sale price. From this relationship, it may be determined how market value changes as gross incomes vary. These relationships are shown in Figure 5-2.

The example shows a regression of the annual gross income of low rise (two-story, no elevator) apartments sold in one year in the Atlanta, Georgia, metropolitan area. From the 56 sales prices, the data indicate that as the annual gross incomes increase by one dollar, the sales price increases by $5.93. Such data are subject to further statistical analysis; they are limited to market conditions at the time of sale, and data vary by locality. The data of Figure 5-2, however, clearly shows a linear, straight line relationship (for this sample) between the independent variable, the gross income, and the sales price.

Figure 5-2   The Relation between Gross Income and Sales Price

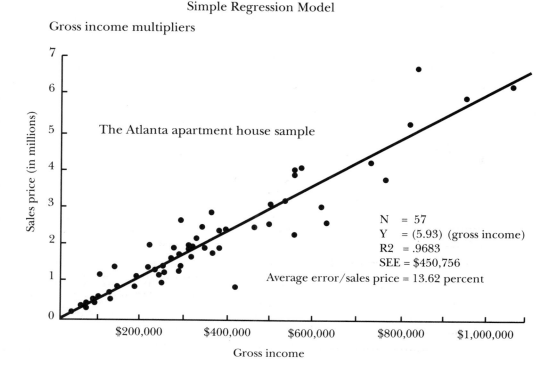

Simple Regression Model

Gross income multipliers

The Atlanta apartment house sample

N   = 57
Y   = (5.93) (gross income)
R2   = .9683
SEE = $450,756
Average error/sales price = 13.62 percent

Various other statistical tests determine the accuracy of the regression technique. In this example, *linear* or *straight line regressions* may be calculated from common computer spreadsheets or even hand calculators. The relationships described here are linear or straight line relationships. Routines are also available to adapt regression techniques for curvilinear relationships.

TIME SERIES ANALYSIS

In the time series analysis, such data are charted over successive periods to predict seasonal patterns, cyclical variations, and trends that are expressed by an arithmetic function. Such data are charted over successive years, months, weeks, or even days. By recording annual income over, say, the past five years, the series may show trends or seasonal variations. For longer periods, data may show cyclical changes.

Appraisers employ time series analysis to project income over an expected holding period. For example, income from an apartment project generally shows periodic seasonal variations and a rising or decreasing trend. Mathematically, these variations may be calculated to project future incomes.

This method differs from regression analysis in that available computer programs identify seasonal variations and changing trends that are assumed to be repeated. Time series projections are useful since they utilize computer routines that allow the appraiser to enter data and make projections based on past data. The appraiser interprets the data and makes the final projection based on judgments of current market influences.

SUMMARY

Purely competitive markets require many buyers and sellers, perfect market knowledge, standardized products, and freedom to enter and leave the market. Real estate markets may be judged with respect to certain *market indicators:* namely, rising vacancies, longer listing periods, and the increasing interval between the time of listing and sale. Such indicators suggest a decreasing demand. Deferred property maintenance indicates a declining neighborhood.

For single-family dwellings, a rising proportion of houses rented, and declining rents show lower market value trends. Below market financing and more second mortgage financing are common to a declining demand.

In comparing real estate markets with more organized markets, it may be seen that there is *no central market* for real estate. In addition, real estate is characterized by a series of local markets. A *fixed location and imperfect knowledge* among buyers and sellers are common to real estate. In addition to these recognized imperfections, real estate represents a *highly regulated market*, a market which is *divisible* into a series of property rights and interests, and a market in which high transfer costs restrict market equilibrium. Furthermore, real estate requires *professional management* to a degree not found in other types of ownership.

Market analysis is the *collection and analysis of data to estimate current and projected income or value.* In analyzing real estate markets, appraisers rely on common market data sources. Population data are published by the *Bureau of Census* and supplemented by published reports by the states and their local and regional governments. If the appraisal concerns shopping and other retail properties, appraisers obtain information on retail sales and related data from the Bureau of Census reports and annual reports of the *Sales Marketing and Management* magazine that annually publishes *effective buying income* by region, states, counties, major cities, and suburban areas. Effective buying income equals personal income, less personal tax and nontax payments (also known as disposable or after-tax income).

Employment data are published by the federal *Census of Manufacturers* on a planned cycle of five years and reports of the U.S. Department of Labor, i.e., the *Monthly Labor Review.* These data may be supplemented by reports of state departments of employment security and their various industrial development offices.

Real estate sales prices are obtained from numerous sources. In some jurisdictions, real estate prices are available from local tax assessors and state departments of revenue. Appraisers utilize certain private sources such as lenders and sales data banks supported by the *Appraisal Institute* in major metropolitan areas.

Practicing appraisers take full advantage of other real estate industry sources, including cooperating developers, lenders, attorneys, real estate brokers, contractors, and related sources.

For new projects, especially, appraisers must determine the *market rate of absorption.* The best practice recommends surveying competing projects to determine the number of properties sold or net income earned in past years. From these observations, the appraiser projects net income or other data according to the interpretation of past data and the likelihood that trends will continue as adjusted for current conditions.

Forecasts are estimates of future events. Forecasts may be based on regression projections which are based on an arithmetic relation between two variables. For example, over time, personal income of a county may increase at a constant mathematical rate that is used to make a projection over the next ten years. *Time series analysis* identifies seasonal variations and trends which are projected on the basis of past data.

POINTS TO REMEMBER

purely competitive markets a market in which the quantity demanded equals the quantity supplied.

market equilibrium a market where all buyers who wish to buy at the market price are satisfied, and all sellers who wish to sell at the market price find buyers.

market indicators economic data that show current market changes: an increasing or decreasing supply or demand.

market analysis the collection and analysis of data to estimate current and projected real estate markets.

demographic data population characteristics showing expansion or decline and pressures that determine trends.

effective buying income personal income, less personal taxes and nontax payments (disposable or after-tax income).

forecast an estimate of future events derived from past data modified according to current conditions.

simple regression a method of prediction based on a relationship between two variables that is expressed by an arithmetic function.

time series analysis data charted over successive periods to predict seasonal patterns, cyclical variations, and trends which are expressed by an arithmetic function.

QUESTIONS FOR REVIEW

1. Explain the four requirements of a purely competitive market. In the valuation of a single-family dwelling, what market indicators would you rely on to judge the local neighborhood market?

2. In the appraisal of a single-family dwelling, what market indicators would you rely on to judge the local neighborhood market?

3. What factors would you cite to support a finding of rising neighborhood residential market values?

4. What market imperfections are common to real estate?

5. What is meant by market analysis?

6. Define effective buying income. Give an example of how you would use effective buying income in an appraisal.

7. How would you establish the market rate of absorption for a new subdivision? Explain fully.

8. Define a forecast.

9. Explain how you would forecast the probable change in market value by simple regression techniques.

10. What is meant by time series analysis? Give an example of how you would use a time series projection.

PRACTICE PROBLEMS

1. For a proposed subdivision of upper middle income housing of 100 lots, your client requires an estimate of the market rate of absorption. Explain how you would proceed in completing this assignment. In your answer, identify types of data, their sources, and how you would make your final market analysis.

2. You are appraising a proposed shopping center. Your client requires a projection of gross income (rent) expected over the next ten years. Explain the data that you would collect and the basis of your forecast.

3. In the valuation of a downtown parking site, you secure a limited number of vacant downtown commercial land sales. How would you analyze these sales in light of possible market data imperfections?

C H A P T E R 6

Appraisal Mathematics

After reading this chapter, you will know:
- Six commonly used financial functions for appraisal purposes.
- How to apply the six financial functions for appraisal purposes.
- Descriptive statistics that measure appraisal data.
- Examples of descriptive statistics for appraisal purposes.

Preprogrammed calculators and computer programs may be used to calculate the six financial functions in solving appraisal problems. In employing these functions, answers show slight variations because of differences in rounding conventions and the number of calculated decimal places. Computers commonly calculate to 17 decimals. Calculators also vary in rounding techniques and the number of decimals used. Accordingly, problems solved from various calculators and computers may vary slightly from chapter solutions.

The six financial functions assume that *present goods are preferred over future goods*—the concept that future goods are discounted at some rate. See Figure 6-1. To apply the six functions, five questions must be resolved:

1. Does the problem concern future or present values?
2. What is the amount and frequency of payments?
3. Are payments made at the beginning or end of the period?
4. What is the rate of interest or discount?
5. What is the number of periods?

Each of these questions must be answered to use the six financial functions explained in this chapter.

Figure 6-1   Compounding and Discounting $100 at 12 Percent

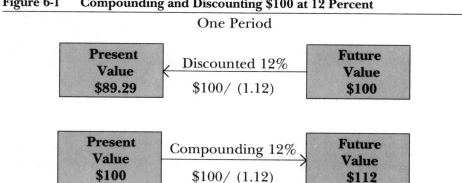

SIX FINANCIAL FUNCTIONS

The first function, the *future value factor (FVF)*, refers to the amount one dollar increases at a given interest rate over a given period, earning compound interest. This formula shows the future value, assuming an annual compound rate of increase over an investment period.

The *future value of an annuity factor (FVAF)* refers to the sum an ordinary annuity accumulates, assuming that periodic payments are invested at a given interest rate. This function gives the amount of an ordinary annuity which is the total of annual payments and interest accumulated in each period.

The *sinking fund factor (SFF)* indicates the amount that must be deposited in an interest-bearing fund to recover a given sum. Some appraisers use this function to recover an expected decrease in value or capital loss over an investment period.

The *present value factor (PVF)* gives the present value of a future sum or reversionary value. The factor is commonly used to estimate the value of property returned to the fee owner (the reversion) at the end of a lease.

On the other hand, the *present value of an annuity factor (PVAF)* refers to the present value of the right to a future income. Use this factor in calculating the present value of rental income.

Mortgage payments are given by the *installment of one factor,* sometimes called the *mortgage constant (MC)*. The factor gives the payment necessary to repay a debt of $1.00 at a given interest rate and repayment period. The mortgage constant assumes a fixed rate of interest and a given number of equal repayment periods. The following sections explain formulas for annual and monthly periods and illustrate typical appraisal problems.

Future Value Factor (FVF)

Compound interest is received on a principal sum which is increased by interest earned from preceding periods. The theory underlying compound interest is taken from alternatives facing the investor. An investor who lends $1,000 at an annual interest rate of ten percent anticipates receiving $1,000 plus $100 interest at the end of the first year. The investor then, presumably, can invest $1,100 for an additional term, earning the same market rate of interest.

Because of this alternative, investors are unwilling to lend money for longer terms unless interest is paid periodically. Though the compounding may be monthly, quarterly, or semiannually, compound interest is usually expressed as an annual rate.

FUTURE VALUE ILLUSTRATED

Common Designations
  Future value factor (FVF)
  Future value of lump sum factor
  Compound amount of one
  Amount of one
  Future value of one

Assumptions
  1. A single deposit made at the beginning of the period.
  2. Interest calculated at the end of the period.
  3. Interest paid on accumulated interest and principal.

Purpose
  To find the amount one dollar will increase at a given interest rate over
  a given period earning compound interest.

Annual Periods	*Monthly Periods*
$FVF_{i,\,n} = (1+i)^{n}$	$= (1 + i/12)^{n \times 12}$

Example: 12% annual rate, 5 annual periods

Annual Periods	*Monthly Periods*
$FVF_{12\%,\,5} = 1(1.12)^{5}$	$= (1 + .12/12)^{5 \times 12}$
$= 1.762342$	$= 1.816697$

See Table 6-1 for a tabular illustration of the compound interest
formula. The factors under the amount of one dollar per period column
of Table 6-1 show the accumulation of compound interest for one dollar.
Thus, to find the compound amount earned on $1,000 for five years at ten
percent interest, multiply the principal amount by the factor 1.610510.

Table 6-1   Future Value, 10 Percent, Five Years

Beginning	Principal (p)	10 Percent Interest Added at End of Year (i)	Compound Amount End of Year (FV)	Amount of $1 Compound Interest $FVF = (1+i)^{n}$
1	$1,000.000	$100.000	$1,100.000	1.100000
2	1,100.000	110.000	1,210.400	1.210000
3	1,210.000	121.000	1,331.000	1.331000
4	1,331.000	133.100	1,464.100	1.464100
5	1,464.000	146.400	1,610.510	1.610510

PROBLEM EXAMPLE

Assume that investor A owns property worth $100,000 which will increase in value at an annual eight percent compound rate. At the end of five years, what will be the value of A's property?

Apply the compound interest formula of $FV = P(1 + i)^n$. For the facts given, the value of the property would be equal to $146,932.80.

$$FV = \$100,000 \ (1 + .08)^5$$
$$= \$100,000 \ (1.469328)$$
$$= \$146,932.80$$

Future Value of an Annuity Factor (FVAF)

This factor is derived from the compound interest formula. The future value of an annuity refers to an annuity paid at the end of the period. In this context any periodic payment of equal amounts paid over successive periods qualifies as an annuity. The amount of an annuity is the total of annual payments and interest accumulated in each period.

An annuity of $1,000 payable for five periods is shown in Table 6-2. Note that at the end of the first period, the $1,000 annuity earns interest over four terms. Succeeding payments accumulate interest for a period one less than the preceding period. The final payment, since it is paid at the end of the fifth term, earns no interest.

Table 6-2   Future Value of an Annuity Payable for Five Periods, Compounded at 10 Percent

End of Period	Amount of Annuity	(FVF)	Accumulated Interest (i)	Amount of Annuity
1	$1,000	$(1 + .10)^4$	$ 464.100	$1,464.100
2	1,000	$(1 + .10)^3$	331.000	1,331.000
3	1,000	$(1 + .10)^2$	210.000	1,210.000
4	1,000	$(1 + .10)^1$	100.000	1,110.000
5	1,000	- -	- -	1,000.000
Total	$5,000		$1,105.100	$6,105.100

FUTURE VALUE OF AN ANNUITY FACTOR ILLUSTRATED

Common Designations
   Amount of one per period
   Accumulation of one per period
   Future value of one dollar per period

Assumptions
   1. An annual deposit (annuity) made at the end of each period.
   2. Interest earned on each deposit.

Purpose
   To find how much an annual deposit made each year accumulates as
   each deposit earns compound interest.

Annual	*Monthly*
Periods	*Periods*

$$FVAF_{i,\,n} = \frac{(1+i)^{\,n}-1}{i} \qquad\qquad = \frac{(1+i/12)^{\,n \times 12}-1}{i/12}$$

Example: 12% annual rate, 5 annual periods

Annual	*Monthly*
Periods	*Periods*

$$FVAF_{12\%,\,5} = \frac{(1.12)^5 - 1}{.12} \qquad\qquad = \frac{(1+.12/12)^{5 \times 12} - 1}{.12/12}$$

$$= \frac{1.762342 - 1}{.12} \qquad\qquad = \frac{1.816697 - 1}{.01}$$

$$= 6.352847 \qquad\qquad = 81.66967$$

Table 6-2 shows the accumulated interest and annuity over five years, which
earns interest at a ten percent annual rate. Note that the first deposit earns
interest over four periods ($464.100) while the last deposit paid at the end
of the period earns no interest ($1,000). In this way, annuity factors
indicate the accumulation of a $1.00 annuity at various interest rates and
periods.

PROBLEM EXAMPLE

At the beginning of the year a site was purchased for $100,000. Assume that property taxes of $10,000 a year were paid at the end of the year. After five years, what would be the selling price necessary to recover the investment, assuming an eight percent interest rate?

$$FVA = \frac{(1 + .08)^5 - 1}{.08} (\$10,000)$$

$$= 5.866601 (\$10,000)$$

$$= \$58,666.01$$

$$\text{Selling price} = \$100,000 + \$58,666.01$$

$$= \$158,666.01$$

An annual tax of $10,000 paid at the end of the year is equivalent to an annuity sacrificed that could have earned eight percent compounded annually. To find the accumulation of an annual payment of $10,000 earning eight percent, find the factor showing an accumulation of one dollar for five periods, which is 5.866601. Therefore, the tax sacrifice is equal to giving up a sum of $58,666.01. At the end of five years, the price must be at least $158,666.01 to recover the investment.

Sinking Fund Factor (SFF)

Sinking fund factors indicate the amount that must be deposited in an interest-bearing fund to recover a given sum. The factor showing the accumulation of one per period gives the amount that one would accumulate, provided that the annuity earned interest over the annuity period. It follows that the future value of an annuity factor is closely related to the sinking fund factor. Suppose repayment of a debt requires payment of interest and an annual sum which is to be placed in a sinking fund sufficient to repay the principal. The problem here is to find the periodic deposit required to accumulate to a given sum.

SINKING FUND ILLUSTRATED

Assumptions
  1. A deposit made at the end of each period.
  2. Each deposit earns interest at a compound rate.

Purpose
  To find the periodic deposit necessary to equal one dollar as each deposit earns a given compound interest.

$$\underset{\substack{\text{Annual} \\ \text{Periods}}}{} \qquad \underset{\substack{\text{Monthly} \\ \text{Periods}}}{}$$

$$SFF_{i,\,n} \;=\; \frac{i}{(1+i)^{\,n}-1} \;=\; \frac{i/12}{(1+i/12)^{\,n \times 12}-1}$$

Example: 12% annual rate, 5 annual periods

$$\underset{\substack{\text{Annual} \\ \text{Periods}}}{} \qquad \underset{\substack{\text{Monthly} \\ \text{Periods}}}{}$$

$$SSF_{12\%,\,5} \;=\; \frac{.12}{(1+.12)^5-1} \;=\; \frac{.12/12}{(1+.12/12)^{5 \times 12}-1}$$

$$\;=\; \frac{.12}{1.762342-1} \;=\; \frac{.01}{1.816697-1}$$

$$\;=\; .154741 \qquad\qquad \;=\; .012244$$

Table 6-3 (on page 126) shows the calculation of interest and sinking fund accumulations. At the end of the first period, $1,000 is deposited in a sinking fund that earns ten percent interest over the second period. At the end of the second period, the second $1,000 is deposited so that the sinking fund accumulates to $2,100.00. This is the amount in the sinking fund that earns interest of $210.00 at the end of the third period. By accumulating the annual deposit in the sinking fund and by accumulating interest on the sinking fund, the investor recovers $6,105.100 at the end of five years.

Table 6-3   Sinking Fund Required to Accumulate $6,105.100 over Five Periods, 10 Percent Interest

End of Period	Annual Payment	Interest	Increase in Sinking Fund	Accumulation of Sinking Fund	Declining Balance
1	$1,000	$ -------	$1,000.000	$1,000.000	$5,105.100
2	1,000	100.000	1,100.000	2,100.000	4,005.100
3	1,000	210.000	1,210.000	3,310.000	2,795.100
4	1,000	331.000	1,331.000	4,641.000	1,464.100
5	1,000	464.100	1,464.100	6,105.100	---------
Total	$5,000	$1,105.100	$6,105.100	---------	---------

PROBLEM EXAMPLE

What is the amount that must be set aside annually in a sinking fund earning eight percent, compounded annually, to recover a loss of $100,000 at the end of five years?

$$SFF = \$100,000 \; \frac{.08}{(1+.08)^5 - 1}$$

$$= \$100,000 \, (.17045645)$$

$$= \$17,045.65$$

In this case, the investor must make a deposit of $17,045.65 at the end of the year for five years to recover a loss of $100,000.

Present Value Factor (PVF)

The present value of a future sum, or a reversionary value, is also derived from the compound interest formula. Recall that:

$$FV = P(1 + i)^n$$

Hence, the sum, which gives the accumulation of principal and interest, is equal to the principal times the compound interest. To find the present value factor, solve for P.

PRESENT VALUE FACTOR ILLUSTRATED

Common Designations
> Present value of lump sum factor (PVF)
> Present value of one dollar

Assumptions
1. Present goods are more valuable than future goods.
2. Future goods are discounted in the present.

Purpose
> To find the present value of a future sum postponed for a given number of periods.

Annual Periods   *Monthly Periods*

$$PVF_{i,n} = \frac{1}{(1+i)^n} = \frac{1}{(1+i/12)^{n \times 12}}$$

Example:

Annual Periods   *Monthly Periods*

$$PVF_{12\%,5} = \frac{1}{(1+.12)^5} = \frac{1}{(1+.12/12)^{5 \times 12}}$$

$$= \frac{1}{1.762342} = \frac{1}{1.816697}$$

$$= .567427 = .550450$$

To calculate the present value of a future sum or reversion, divide the future sum by the compound amount of one dollar. Factors showing the present value of a future sum discounted at ten percent are shown below:

Present Value Factor of $1.00 (10%)

$$PVF = \frac{1}{(1+i)^n}$$

Period	
1	0.909091
2	0.826446
3	0.751315
4	0.683013
5	0.620921

Factors showing the present value of a reversion of one dollar indicate that one dollar paid at the end of five years, discounted at ten percent, has a present value of $0.620921. Put in another way, this table reveals that if $0.620921 were paid today for the right to one dollar five years from now, the investor would earn ten percent compound interest on an initial investment of $0.620921. Factors showing the present value of a future sum or reversion show the amount paid for rights to a future sum, with the assumption that the given interest rate will be earned and compounded each period.

See Table 6-4 for the derivation of present value factors. It will be noted that the present value of a future sum is a process of dividing the future sum by the compound interest factor. The discount for goods postponed to the future guarantees the investor a return on the investment and a return of the investment. The factor is used, for example, to estimate the present value of land that reverts to the owner at the end of a long-term lease.

Table 6-4   Present Value Factor, $1.00, 10 Percent

End of Period	Future Sum	Discount $(1+i)^n$	$1/(1+i)^n$	Present Value Factor (PVF)
1	$1.00	(1.10)	$\dfrac{\$1.00}{(1.10)}$	.909091
2	1.00	(1.210000)	$\dfrac{\$1.00}{1.210000}$	.826446
3	1.00	(1.331000)	$\dfrac{\$1.00}{1.331000}$	.751315
4	1.00	(1.464100)	$\dfrac{\$1.00}{1.464100}$	.683013
5	1.00	(1.610510)	$\dfrac{\$1.00}{1.610510}$	.620921

PROBLEM EXAMPLE

Suppose investor A leases an unimproved site to investor B who agrees to construct a building that would have an estimated value of $100,000 at the end of the lease. Assuming an eight percent discount rate, what would be the present value of the reversion?

$$PV = \frac{1}{(1 + .08)^5} (\$100,000)$$

$$= (.6805832) (\$100,000)$$

$$= \$68,058.32$$

Assuming an eight percent discount rate, the example indicates that $68,058.32 would be paid for the right to $100,000 postponed for five years. In paying $68,058.32, the purchaser would earn eight percent compound interest on the investment.

Present Value of an Annuity Factor (PVAF)

Factors showing the present value of an annuity give the present value of an income. In this respect, income from real property may be considered either as income received in perpetuity or income received over a given time. In the former, a land rent of $1,000 would indicate a land value, capitalized in perpetuity at ten percent, of $10,000:

$$PV = I/R$$
$$= \$1,000/.10$$
$$= \$10,000$$

By investing $10,000 in land that earns an annual rent of $1,000, ten percent would be earned on the investment. This is another way of saying that an income of $1,000 capitalized in perpetuity at a discount rate of ten percent has a present value of $10,000.

If the $1,000 income is earned for a limited period, the capitalization formula in perpetuity has little relevance. The right to $1,000 payable for five years is clearly not worth $10,000. Income for a limited period, therefore, is treated as a series of *reversions*. The present value of an income earned at the end of the year for five years is found by adding the discounted values of a future sum paid at the end of each year:

$$PVF = \frac{1}{(1.12)^1} + \frac{1}{(1.12)^2} + \frac{1}{(1.12)^3} + \frac{1}{(1.12)^4} + \frac{1}{(1.12)^5}$$

It is more convenient to calculate the present value of a future income for a limited period by the formula derived from the sum of present values of a reversion as shown below.

PRESENT VALUE OF AN ANNUITY FACTOR ILLUSTRATED

Common Designations
   Present value of an annuity factor (PVAF)
   Present value of 1 per period
   Present value of an annuity

Assumption
   A constant income paid at the end of the period over a given number of periods.

Purpose
   To find the present value of an income for a given number of periods.

Annual Periods	*Monthly Periods*
$PVAF_{i,\,n} = \dfrac{1 - \dfrac{1}{(1+i)^{\,n}}}{i}$	$= \dfrac{1 - \dfrac{1}{(1+i/12)^{\,n \times 12}}}{i/12}$

Example:

Annual Periods	*Monthly Periods*
$PVAF_{12\%,\,5} = \dfrac{1 - \dfrac{1}{(1+.12)^5}}{.12}$	$= \dfrac{1 - \dfrac{1}{(1+.12/12)^{5 \times 12}}}{.12/12}$
$= \dfrac{1 - .567427}{.12}$	$= \dfrac{1 - .550450}{.01}$
$= 3.604776$	$= 44.955038$

The present value of an income of one dollar per period, discounted at ten percent, is given below:

Period	Present Value of an Annuity of $1.00
1	0.909091
2	1.735537
3	2.486852
4	3.169865
5	3.790787

These factors show the value of an income of one dollar payable at the end of the year for five periods. It will be noted that these factors are the accumulated values of the present value factor. Hence, the present value of an income of one dollar for two years, discounted at ten percent, is $1.735537 (the sum of the reversionary values of one dollar paid at the end of year one (.909091) and year two (.826446).

To consider the earlier example again, an income of $1,000 payable at the end of the year for five years and discounted at ten percent has a present value of $3,790.787. By investing this amount, the investor recovers the initial investment and the compound interest on the annual remaining balance. The distribution of interest and repayment of principal under these assumptions is shown in Table 6-5.

Table 6-5   Present Value of an Annuity of $1,000, Five Years, 10 Percent Discount

End of Period	Annual Annuity	Interest Calculation	Interest	Principal Repayment	Declining Balance
(Beginning of Period)	-------	---------------	----------	----------	$3,790.787
1	$1,000	($3,790.787 x .10)	$379.079	$620.921	3,169.866
2	1,000	($3,169.866 x .10)	316.987	683.013	2,486.853
3	1,000	($2,486.853 x .10)	248.685	751.315	1,735.538
4	1,000	($1,735.538 x .10)	173.553	826.446	909.091
5	1,000	($ 909.091 x .10)	90.909	909.091	0.0
(Rounding Error)			-(0.001)	(0.001)	
	$5,000		$1,209.213	$3,790.787	

Table 6-5 shows the method of discounting assumed in using present value of annuity factors. In this instance the factor 3.790787 gives the present value of the right to an income of $1.00 payable over five years, discounted at ten percent. This means that over five periods, an annual payment of $1,000 will return $5,000 which amounts to recovery of the original capital and total interest of $1,209.213. Thus, in the first year, ten percent interest on a capital investment of $3,790.787 is equal to $379.079. Assuming an income of $1,000, the remainder, or $620.921, represents a partial recovery of the original capital investment.

In the succeeding period the outstanding balance, $3,169.866, earns interest of ten percent for one year or $316.987. Again, the amount remaining from the income payment of $1,000, or $683.013, is applied against capital investment so that at the end of the year only $2,486.853 remains unrecovered.

The assumption here is that part of the capital investment is returned each year and that the outstanding investment earns interest at the assumed discount rate. Factors showing the present value of an annuity of $1.00 convert the right to an income of a limited duration to capital value.

PROBLEM EXAMPLE

Suppose investor A agrees to lease a building from investor B for an annual rent of $50,000, payable at the end of the year, for four years. What is the present value of the right to the contract rent? Referring to the present value of an annuity factor, the present value would be found by the following formula. Assume a ten percent discount.

$$
\begin{aligned}
\text{PVA} &= \frac{1 - \dfrac{1}{(1.10)^4}}{.10} \ (\$50,000) \\[2em]
&= 3.169865 \ (\$50,000) \\[1em]
&= \$158,493.27
\end{aligned}
$$

The $158,493.27 represents the market value of the right to an income of $50,000 payable at the end of the year for four years, discounted at ten percent. At the end of the term, a total of $200,000 will have been collected which would constitute a return of ten percent on an initial investment of $158,493.27. The present value of the income is the sum of discounted values of each year's income.

Installment of One Factor (MC)

Installment of one or partial payment factors indicate the partial payments to amortize (repay) a loan. Amortized mortgages with constant-level payments provide that a portion of the payment constitutes interest on the outstanding principal; the remaining portion of the payment applies to repayment of principal.

Under this plan the loan principal represents the present value of a series of equal annuities or payments. If $3.79 represents the present value of the right to an income of one dollar per year for five years, assuming ten percent interest, it follows that an annual constant-level payment of $1.00 would be required to amortize a loan of $3.79 over five years, discounted at ten percent interest. Hence the installment of one is the reciprocal of the present value of an annuity factor.

INSTALLMENT OF ONE ILLUSTRATED

Common Designations

Loan constant   Installment of one dollar

Mortgage constant (annual payments)   Partial payment factor

Assumption

Payment of interest on the declining loan principal with the balance of the installment applied to reduction of the principal.

Purpose

To find the installment necessary to amortize a loan, assuming interest is paid on the declining principal.

Annual Periods

$$MC_{i,\,n} = \cfrac{i}{1 - \cfrac{1}{(1 + i)^{n}}}$$

Example:

$$MC_{12\%,\,5} = \cfrac{.12}{1 - \cfrac{1}{(1 + .12)^{5}}}$$

$$= \frac{.12}{1 - .567427}$$

$$= .277410$$

Monthly Periods

$$= \cfrac{i/12}{1 - \cfrac{1}{(1 + i/12)^{n \times 12}}}$$

$$= \cfrac{.12/12}{1 - \cfrac{1}{(1 + .12/12)^{60}}}$$

$$= \frac{.01}{1 - .550450}$$

$$= .022244$$

Table 6-6   The Amortization of $3,790.787, Five Years, 10 Percent Interest

End of Period	Installment to Amortize $1.00	Principal	Constant Annual Payment	Interest on Remaining Balance	Principal Repayment	Remaining Balance
Beginning of Period	-------	--------	-------	---------	---------	$3,790.787
1	.263797 x	$3,790.787	$1,000	$ 379.079	$ 620.921	3,169.866
2	.263797 x	3,790.787	1,000	316.987	683.013	2,486.853
3	.263797 x	3,790.787	1,000	248.685	751.315	1,735.538
4	.263797 x	3,790.787	1,000	173.554	826.446	909.091
5	.263797 x	3,790.787	1,000	90.909	909.091	0.0
(Rounding Error)				- (0.001)	(0.001)	
Total	-------	--------	$5,000	$1,209.213	$3,790.787	---------

In the preceding example it was indicated that an income of $1,000 payable for five years, discounted at ten percent, had a present value of $3,790.787. To show the relationship between the present value of an annuity factor and the installment of one, suppose that a principal of $3,790.87 is to be amortized over five periods, under a ten percent rate of interest. Table 6-6 indicates the distribution of the $1,000 annual payment.

Starting with the factor .263797, the amount to amortize one dollar, and a principal of $3,790.787, the required annual payment would be $1,000. At the end of period one, a portion of the $1,000 represents interest of $379.079 on the outstanding principal of $3,790.787. The $620.921 remaining portion of the first payment is then applied to repayment of the principal. At the beginning of the second year, $3,169.866 is the unamortized principal which, in turn, earns interest of $316.987 at the end of period two.

By deducting the principal repayment from the remaining balance at the beginning of each period, the loan is amortized or repaid over five years. The difference between the principal and the sum of payments, $5,000, constitutes total interest collected on the remaining balance. In short, the lender has purchased the right to an income of $1,000 (the annual payment) which is discounted at ten percent.

PROBLEM EXAMPLE

Investor A applies for a $100,000 loan repayable in monthly installments over 25 years. What is the monthly installment if the fixed-rate interest is ten percent? The answer is found from the installment of one formula:

$$MP \; = \; \frac{.10/12}{1 - \dfrac{1}{(1 + .10/12)^{25 \times 12}}} \; (\$100,000)$$

$$= \; \frac{.008333}{(1 - .082940)} \; (\$100,000)$$

$$= \; .009087 \; (\$100,000)$$

$$= \; \$908.70$$

Some 300 monthly payments of \$908.70 will repay the original loan of \$100,000 and earn ten percent on the remaining unpaid balance for each period. In other words, the \$100,000 face value of the mortgage represents the price paid for a monthly \$908.70 annuity over 300 months at an annual interest rate of ten percent.

STATISTICAL MEASURES

To identify typical and nontypical data, appraisers may refer to various measures or averages that measure representative sales prices, market values, and related data. A review of descriptive statistics indicates how these measures are used in appraisal assignments. Examples of descriptive statistics illustrate these statistical applications.

Averages

Descriptive statistics cover measures of central tendency, or "averages," and their scatter, or spread, around an average. Averages are measured by three common variations: the arithmetic mean, the median, and the mode.

ARITHMETIC MEAN

Averages are typical if the average selected is representative of the data measured. Averages usually refer to the arithmetic mean, which is the sum of each value divided by its number. In valuing dwellings, the appraiser may use the arithmetic mean to show the "typical" value of neighborhood houses.

For example, the total value of the seven dwelling sales in Group A listed below totals $815,000. Dividing by their number indicates the arithmetic mean, $116,429.

Sales Price

Group A	Group B
1. $ 95,000	$ 10,000
2. 100,000	50,000
3. 110,000	200,000
4. 115,000 (Median)	300,000 (Median)
5. 120,000	800,000
6. 125,000	900,000
7. 150,000	1,500,000

Total sales price	$815,000	$3,760,000
Arithmetic mean	= $815,000/7	$3,760,000/7
	= $116,429	$537,143

The arithmetic mean has certain unique qualities. *First, the arithmetic mean relies on each sale.* This latter feature may give atypical results if the number of sales is extremely small.

Suppose, for example, that the *Group A sales* above included another sale of $1,000,000. In this case, the average sale price would be $226,875 ($1,815,000/8). Note that with added sale of $1,000,000, the average value of $226,875 is not "typical" of the eight sales, though it is the arithmetic mean.

This leads to the second property of an arithmetic mean of sales prices: the *arithmetic mean is weighted by sales price.* If the eighth sale was $10,000, to cite an extremely low-valued sale, the resulting average would be $103,125 ($825,000/8). In these cases, the arithmetic mean varies significantly by the addition of one additional sale. The latter result follows because the arithmetic mean relies on every sale; the importance of each sale depends on the price and the number of sales.

For a relatively small sample the *arithmetic mean varies widely because of extreme observations.* This limitation is overcome by relatively large sales samples that give proportionately less weight to each added sale. If the arithmetic mean was calculated from 700 sales, the importance of one additional sale price would be quite nominal. Therefore, extreme prices have less significance in calculating an arithmetic mean for relatively large samples.

THE MEDIAN

Simply stated, the median represents the middle item of a series ranked according to their magnitude. In the seven Group A sales considered above, the middle item was $115,000. The representativeness of the median depends on the value of the middle item—the median is an *average of position*. That is, if the position of the middle item is not changed, sales values above and below the median are irrelevant. The value of sale 7, $150,000, could be $150,000,000, or any other value; if the position of the $115,000 sale is not changed, the median of $115,000 is unaffected. Unlike the arithmetic mean, the median is relatively unaffected by extreme values. With little or no concentration of sales around a central value, however, the median may also be "atypical."

MODE

The mode is the most frequently occurring value. An appraiser who writes that the typical neighborhood dwelling has a market value of $200,000 may be referring to the most frequently observed value, the modal average—it is the most frequently observed value—it is not necessarily the middle value (median) or the arithmetic mean.

Statisticians avoid the mode because it is not subject to statistical analysis that gives other information about averages.

Measures of Dispersion

Appraisers may indicate the variation of sales prices from the arithmetic mean or other average. In sales Groups A and B above, the arithmetic mean is $116,429 in Group A and $537,143 in Group B. Common observation shows that the $116,429 arithmetic mean Group A is more representative. Because of the dispersion or variation of the sales price of the second group, the $537,143 arithmetic mean is not representative or typical of sales in Group B. Therefore, measures of dispersion or variation often accompany measures of central tendency or average values.

In the preceding example, each sale in Groups A and B varied from the average price. For example, the $155,000 sale listed in Group B varied from the arithmetic mean by $21,429. Measures of dispersion indicate the variability, or scatter, of data around the average.

Measures of dispersion may be as important as the arithmetic mean. For the present purpose, two values help describe averages such as the average sales price: the range and the *standard deviation*.

THE RANGE

The range is the largest value minus the smallest value. In Group A, the range of sales extended from $95,000 to $150,000—a range of $55,000. The appraiser would report that neighborhood values are fairly uniform, ranging from $95,000 to $150,000 with an average (mean) value of $116,429. Range is measured by the extreme high and extreme low values.

For real estate sales, data may include questionable sales that may be distorted from market value. For this reason, in an array of several hundred or thousand sales, it is common to use the *10-90 percentile range*. After ranking sales prices in order of their value, the appraiser eliminates the lowest ten percent of the sales prices and the highest ten percent of the sales prices. Therefore, the 10-90 percentile range represents the range of sales prices after eliminating the lowest 10 percent of the sales and ten percent of the highest sales.

For other purposes, the *quartile range* provides a measure of dispersion by reporting the low-end value after eliminating the lowest 25 percent values and the high-end value after eliminating the highest 25 percent of sales. The 10-90 percentile range and the quartile range are not affected by extreme high and low values. A more satisfactory measure of variation, however, is the standard deviation.

STANDARD DEVIATION

The standard deviation rests on the proposition that the algebraic sum of the deviations above and below the arithmetic mean equals zero. The sum of the squared deviations may be derived from squaring each deviation from the arithmetic mean. The sum of squared deviations assumes the least possible value measured from the arithmetic mean. These calculations are shown in Table 6-7.

Table 6-7   Calculation of Variance from the Arithmetic Mean: Seven Sales

	Sales Price	Deviation $S - \bar{S}$	Deviation Squared $(S - \bar{S})^2$
1.	$ 95,000	−21,429	459,202,041
2.	100,000	−16,429	269,912,041
3.	110,000	−6,429	41,332,041
4.	115,000	−1,429	2,042,041
5.	120,000	3,571	12,752,041
6.	125,000	8,571	73,462,041
7.	150,000	33,571	1,127,012,041
	Total Sum of Squared Deviations		1,985,714,287
	Variance = 1,985,714,287/7 = 283,673,470		

Table 6-7 shows the array of seven Group A sales from $95,000 to $150,000. The second column is the deviation of each value from the arithmetic mean ($\bar{S}$) of $116,429. The third column shows the deviation squared. Technically, the sum of the squared deviations divided by their number is the variance of the sample of seven real estate sales. The standard deviation is derived from the square root of the variance.

Variance of the Arithmetic Mean

$$\sigma^2 = \frac{\Sigma \, (\bar{S} - S)^2}{N}$$

$$= \frac{1,985,714,287}{7}$$

$$= 283,673,470$$

Standard Deviation

$$\sigma = \sqrt{\sigma^2}$$
$$= \sqrt{283,673,470}$$
$$= \$16,482.61$$

For the seven Group B sales, the standard deviation is $16,482.61. If sales are normally distributed, meaning that one-half the sales are above and below the arithmetic mean distributed in the shape of a bell-shaped curve, two-thirds of the sales prices will be within $16,482.61 of the arithmetic mean. The standard deviation shows that the seven sales are closely concentrated around the arithmetic mean.

The sales prices of Group B, ranging from $10,000 to $1,500,000, with an arithmetic mean of $537,143, show a high standard deviation: $508,912. Both the range and the measure of standard deviation for group B sales show that property values are highly nonuniform. In this instance, the appraiser would report typical values in the neighborhood as highly variable, ranging from $10,000 to $1,500,000, with an average price of $537,143 and a standard deviation of $508,912.

Fortunately, the appraiser does not have to make these tedious calculations. Hand calculators and commonly available spreadsheets for personal computers make these calculations automatically. In these ways, the appraiser describes typical market values in terms of selected averages and measures of dispersion showing how values vary within a selected neighborhood.

SUMMARY

The six financial functions start with the *future value factor (FVF)*, which is the amount one dollar increases at a given interest rate over a given period. The *future value of an annuity factor (FVAF)* refers to the sum an ordinary annuity accumulates, assuming that periodic payments are invested at a given interest rate. The *sinking fund factor (SFF)* indicates the amount that must be deposited in an interest-bearing fund to recover a given sum. The *present value factor (PVF)* gives the present value of a future sum. The *present value of an annuity factor (PVAF)* is the factor to calculate the present value of the right to a future income. The *installment of one factor (MC)*, assuming a fixed rate of interest and a given number of equal payment periods, gives the amount necessary to repay a debt.

Descriptive statistics cover measures of central tendency and their scatter, or spread, around an average. The *arithmetic mean* is the sum of each value divided by their number. The *median average* represents the middle item of a series ranked according to their magnitude. The *mode* is the most frequently occurring value.

Measures of dispersion include the *range* defined as the difference between the largest value minus the smallest value. Variations of the range include the *10-90 percentile range* which is the difference between the value of the lowest observation less the lowest ten percent of the sample; and the value of the highest item, less the highest ten percent of the sample measured. The quartile range provides a similar measure by reporting low- and high-end values after eliminating the lowest 25 percent values and the highest 25 percent values. The latter two versions of the range are not affected by extreme high and low values.

The *standard deviation* is a measure of dispersion. Assuming a normal distribution, the standard deviation indicates that approximately two-thirds of the sample would fall within one standard deviation below the mean and one standard deviation above the mean.

POINTS TO REMEMBER

future value factor (FVF) the amount one dollar increases at a given interest rate over a given period, earning compound interest.

future value of an annuity factor (FVAF) the sum an ordinary annuity accumulates, assuming that periodic payments are invested at a given interest rate.

sinking fund factor (SFF) the amount that must be deposited in an interest-bearing fund to recover a given sum.

present value factor (PVF) the present value of a future sum or reversionary value.

present value of an annuity factor (PVAF) the present value of the right to a future income.

installment of one factor (MC) a factor that gives the payment necessary to repay a debt of one dollar at given interest rate and a given number of repayments.

descriptive statistics measures of central tendency and their dispersion.

arithmetic mean the sum of each value divided by its number.

median the middle item of a series ranked according to their magnitude.

mode the most frequently occurring value.

measures of dispersion measures that show the scatter, or variation, of items from a measure of central tendency.

range the range is the largest value less the smallest value.

10-90 percentile range the difference between the lowest value after eliminating the lower ten percent of observations and the highest value after eliminating ten percent of the highest values.

quartile range the difference between the low-end and high-end values after eliminating the lowest 25 percent values and the highest 25 percent values.

variance the sum of squared deviations from the mean, divided by their number.

standard deviation a measure of dispersion derived from the square root of the variance.

QUESTIONS FOR REVIEW

1. What is the basic assumption underlying the six financial functions?

2. Define and illustrate how the future value factor (FVF) is used in real estate appraising.

3. Define and illustrate the sinking fund factor (SFF) for appraisal purposes.

4. Define the present value factor (PVF) and illustrate your answer with a real estate appraisal application.

5. Define the present value of an annuity factor (PVAF) and show how this factor would be used in real estate valuation.

6. Define and show how appraisers may use the future value of annuity factor (FVAF).

7. Assume that you are applying for a $200,000, ten percent, 30-year mortgage. Explain the installment of one factor. Show how you could calculate monthly payments.

8. Explain the characteristics of an arithmetic mean.

9. Explain the characteristics of a median.

10. What is meant by the standard deviation? Explain the mathematics of a standard deviation.

PRACTICE PROBLEMS

1. Assume that you are buying a $200,000 dwelling. If you anticipate an increase in value at the expected inflation rate of six percent, what will be the value of your house at the end of ten years? *FV*

2. Suppose you own land worth $100,000. If you make land improvements of $10,000 per year and you expect the property to yield eight percent on your accumulated investment of $10,000 per year over ten years, what would be the value of your property at the end of ten years assuming no increase in values? *Annuity on Sinking Fund 360,758.13*

3. You anticipate buying a gravel pit for $500,000 which will be exhausted at the end of ten years. How much would you set aside annually in a sinking fund earning six percent to recover your investment over ten years? *$37,933.98*

4. You expect to invest in an income property which will have an expected value of $1,000,000 at the end of ten years. Discounted at 8 percent, what would be the present value of this property under these expectations? *Solve for PV $463,193.49*

5. How much would you pay today for the right to an income of $20,000 payable over 25 years? Use a ten percent discount rate. *Solve PV $181,540.80*

6. What are your monthly mortgage payments for a $100,000 loan, ten percent interest, 25-year term, payable monthly? *Solve for pmt $4,000.00*

7. Assume the following list of real estate sales: $200,000, $250,000, $300,000, $325,000 and $175,000. Calculate the arithmetic mean, median, and standard deviation.

add all /5 =

7.5a Cul book for deviation

250,000 median & mean

C H A P T E R   7

The Highest and Best Use

After studying this chapter, you will know:
- The concept of highest and best use.
- Techniques of estimating the highest and best use of *vacant land*.
- Techniques of estimating highest and best use of *land improved with buildings*.
- Important qualifications of the highest and best use estimate.

An appraisal is directed to a given property use. Accordingly, each appraisal report identifies the estimate of highest and best use. In appraising a single-family dwelling, the estimated highest and best use may be fairly obvious. But even here, residential neighborhoods undergoing a rapid transition in use may require a careful estimate of an assumed highest and best use. There is also the dwelling which is quite inappropriate for the neighborhood: Either it is too large and expensive—an *over improvement*—or it is too small and otherwise unsuitable—an *under improvement*. Therefore, the highest and best use assumes critical importance in appraising nonresidential property, and it may be significant in single-family dwelling appraisals.

The chapter starts with a *definition of highest and best use* with appropriate illustrations. The concept is explained for *vacant land* appraisals and for appraisals of *land improved with buildings*. The special qualifications associated with the highest and best use and factors that help determine the highest and best use close the chapter.

✓ HIGHEST AND BEST USE DEFINED

Frequently, the highest and best estimate is the most critical valuation factor. Consider 20 acres proposed for a public school fronting on a primary highway. The appraiser for the property owner held that a *motel* was the highest and best use. The $400,000 estimated market value followed from an analysis of land recently sold for *motel use*.

The appraiser for the school district claimed the highest and best use was for a *residential subdivision*. The appraiser cited recent sales of comparable land sold for *subdivisions*, which indicated a market value of *$100,000*.

In both instances, the real estate sales cited were valid, current, and comparable with respect to physical features, utilities, and location. Hence, the market value estimates of *$400,000* and *$100,000* followed from different estimates of highest and best use. In a condemnation action, the court awarded the owner $400,000 based on the highest and best use as a motel.

To resolve questions over the highest and best use and, therefore, market value, appraisers rely on the highest and best use definition, which closely follows economic concepts.

The Economic Concept

The *highest and best use* is an appraisal term derived from the economist's view that land should be devoted to that use which earns the *highest net income*. In the economic sense, the highest and best use is an estimate of the *optimum use of a scarce resource.* Consequently, a farmer would not use land for grazing sheep if wheat farming would earn a higher net income. If the farmland was near an urban center, with superior soils, income would be highest if land was used for growing vegetables on an irrigated farm.

If the land use earns the *highest possible income*, it follows that it produces the *highest land value.* Applied to urban property, the highest use is that use which brings the largest net return in money and amenities. It is implied, and quite correctly, that the highest and best use gives the highest land value and, therefore, is the most efficient land use.

Appraisal Definition

Appraisers have followed this logic with minor modifications. Generally, for appraisal purposes, it is held that the *reasonable* and *probable* use that supports the *highest present value* constitutes the highest and best use. More formally, the definition reads:

The highest and best use, reasonably probable *and* legally permissible, must prove physically possible and economically feasible. *The highest and best use results in the* highest land value.[1]

The definition requires two preconditions. First, the use must be reasonably probable and, second, legally permissible. The reasonably probable requirement eliminates uses that are only remote, speculative, and uncertain. The proposed use must be reasonably probable in the foreseeable future. A proposed use anticipated after 10, 20, or more years, in all likelihood, would not meet highest and best use requirements.

---

1 Adapted from *The Appraisal of Real Estate*, Ninth Edition (Chicago, Illinois: American Institute of Real Estate Appraisers, 1987), p. 42.

LEGALLY PERMISSIBLE

The *legally permissible* precondition requires that the proposed use complies with environmental and land use restrictions. For example, land zoned for agricultural use generally undergoes a transition to urban use near population centers. Suppose the land in question has a high potential as a regional shopping center.

Before shopping center approval, the land must be zoned for commercial use. Though agricultural use is legally permissible, the appraiser must consider possible (or probable) changes in the legal use for areas undergoing a transition in use.

PHYSICALLY POSSIBLE

Given the two preconditions, the proposed use must prove *physically possible*. This eliminates uses that, on the surface, may seem probable but not physically possible. You would not value vacant land for a potential subdivision if the soil and drainage limitations prohibited septic tanks. You would not value land for industrial use, though it was properly zoned and legally allowable, if the soil would not bear the high floor loads of industrial buildings. Therefore, appraisers must explain that the highest and best use is physically possible.

ECONOMICALLY FEASIBLE

The highest and best use must prove *economically feasible*—a restriction that deserves careful qualification. The appraiser would not value vacant land for a luxury home subdivision unless luxury home sales and other market evidence indicated that such land could be sold in a reasonable time at the current market value of luxury home sites.

Consider further a 1,000-acre cattle farm adjoining a ten-acre industrial park developed by a local government agency. The farmer claimed $1,000 per acre compensation based on industrial land prices for a required power line right-of-way. Investigation indicated that over the last ten years less than five acres of industrial land was locally developed per year. The overwhelming evidence indicated that the industrial use of *grazing land* was not economically feasible. The court awarded damages of $100 per acre for the power line right-of-way over grazing land. Economic feasibility means that the proposed use must not be remote, speculative, or uncertain.

MAXIMALLY PRODUCTIVE

The definition implies that the highest and best use must also be *maximally productive*. This means that the land must earn the highest income; the proposed highest and best use represents the *optimum use* which produces the *highest income* to the land and therefore the *highest land value*.

Highest and Best Use Premises

Some authorities describe the optimum use as the most likely use, the most profitable use, the use that produces the greatest net return, or the legal use which will result in the highest market value.

In the ultimate sense, the optimum use is that land use which results in the greatest economic return to the landowner. The estimate is based on rules of common sense; speculative uses, imaginative uses, and personal conjectures do not adequately support the finding of highest and best use. On this point, agreement has been reached on common guides to highest and best use estimates.

PRESENT ZONING

Present zoning may not denote the optimum use. For instance, land merely zoned for commercial use may not be economically suitable for commercial purposes. Finally, the estimated highest and best use depends on the local market. In the case of low density single-family dwelling zoning, the appraiser may have grounds for assuming a more intensive use—for example, duplexes or low rise apartments.

Consequently, the highest and best use may vary from present zoning, particularly where changes in zoning districts have lagged behind population shifts and trends toward more intensive land use. In these circumstances, zoning changes may be anticipated in estimating highest and best use.

SURROUNDING LAND

Surrounding land use may not indicate the highest and best use. Neighborhoods showing deferred maintenance and obsolete buildings may be undergoing a transition to lower uses. Declining commercial or residential areas and older industrial districts may recommend alternative uses in contrast to the predominating use of nearby property.

Conversely, surrounding land may have less intensive uses than other recommended uses in the face of favorable growth trends. The land use of a particular parcel may justify a higher and more intensive use than surrounding property would suggest. In other words, there may be lags in the transition from low density to higher commercial uses in expanding areas.

PRESENT USE

The present use is not always the highest and best use. Single-family dwellings at traffic intersections undergoing rapid growth may justify transition to a commercial use. Agricultural land in urban fringe areas, especially, may warrant a higher use relative to the present use.

In short, the highest and best use *maximizes the net returns* of the property under appraisal, *creates economic benefits* to the surrounding land, and results in *social benefits* to the community. Market value estimates are largely a function of land use. Future benefits of ownership depend on the land productivity in a given land use. These and other reasons for the estimated highest and best use should be fully explained.

ESTIMATING THE HIGHEST AND BEST USE

The *first* issue covers the appraisal of *vacant land*, and the *second* issue relates to an estimated temporary use, called an *interim use*, pending a more intensive use at a later date. The *third* issue covers *land with a building*. In the former case, the appraiser usually estimates net income from a proposed building that represents the optimum land use. It must be determined that the proposed building results in the *maximum net income to land.*

Vacant Land

Typically, vacant land covers agricultural land that may have a potential for an apartment building, an office building, or a neighborhood shopping center. A net income analysis would be required for each possible use to estimate the highest net income to land and the corresponding highest land value. Since the three problems require a slightly different analysis, it is convenient to demonstrate each case with separate examples.

To illustrate, three highest and best use options were selected for 8.1 acres fronting on a major access street. The street led from a downtown area to outlying suburbs. The commercial zoning permitted multiple-family, office building, or shopping center. The first two cases illustrate an *over improvement* and an *under improvement.*

An *over improvement* refers to an uneconomic building investment. That is, the estimated building cost is too high to maximize the return to the land. The *under improvement* example covers the reverse situation. The building capital is insufficient to maximize the land return.

Note that the objective is to combine the optimum building capital with land to maximize the annual return to the land. Note further that the examples are taken from a relatively small community in the Southeast. Land, building costs, and commercial rents will vary for other areas. The logic employed, however, applies universally.

MULTIPLE-FAMILY USE

The 8.1 acres was purchased for $353,000. The investor paid an additional $418,000 to adapt the site for commercial improvement. Land improvements included street curbs, land leveling, site drainage, and soil compaction. The total land cost, including land improvements, was $771,000—the final cost of the land improved and suitable for commercial buildings. Given the investment in land, the central problem then turns on the type of building that maximizes the return to the land. Table 7-1 illustrates the technique of calculating the return to the land for a proposed multiple-family dwelling.

Table 7-1   Multiple-Family Use

(Over Improvement)	
Land cost, 8.1 acres	$353,000
Land improvements	418,000
Land value (cost)	$771,000
Building cost	
160 units, 144,000 square feet	$4,320,000
Gross income	
($800/ month average rent)	$1,536,000
Less annual expenses (60 percent)	- 921,600
Net annual income	$614,400
Less income to building	
$4,320,000 x .12	- 518,400
Income to land	$96, 000
Land value	
$96,000/.10	*$960,000*

In compliance with the local zoning code, 160 apartment units of 144,000 square feet would be allowable on the 8.1 acres. Given the recommended mix of one-bedroom, two-bedroom, and three-bedroom units, it was estimated that the average monthly rent would be $800 a month providing a gross annual income of $1,536,000. Estimated operating expenses would be $921,600 providing for a net annual income of $614,400.

With a proposed building cost of $4,320,000, the investor would expect the going yield on real estate investments of ten percent in addition to an annual capital recovery of two percent of the building cost. The deduction of income to the building, $518,400, provides for an annual return of 10 percent on building capital in addition to a two percent allowance to recover the building investment over the estimated 50-year building life. This calculation gives the *annual income to the land of $96,000.*

Capitalizing the yield expected from the land at ten percent shows a land value of *$960,000.* Note that $518,400 of the $614,400 net annual income from the multiple-family project is allocated to the building, allowing $96,000 as the annual net income yield to the land. Subsequent analysis indicates that the proposed multiple-family use is an *over improvement* relative to other highest and best use options.

OFFICE BUILDING

The next option considered consisted of an office building of 50,000 square feet. In this instance, the proposed building would cost $1,500,000 which would provide an estimated annual gross income of $600,000. Deducting typical operating expenses of $360,000 indicates an annual net income of $240,000.

Again, allowing for a ten percent annual yield on the building cost ($150,000) and a two percent annual capital recovery ($30,000), $180,000 would be allocated to the building. In this case, only $60,000 remains annually for the land investment. Capitalizing the $60,000 at the ten percent market yield rate indicates a *land value of $600,000.* See Table 7-2.

However, in this case the capitalized land value is less than the actual land cost of $771,000. The data suggest that building capital of $1,500,000 is insufficient to maximize income to the land: i.e., an *under improvement.* See Table 7-2.

SHOPPING CENTER

The 8.1 acre site would be best suited for a 65,000-square-foot shopping center with adequate space for parking. For this example, the shopping

Table 7-2   Office Building

(Under Improvement)

Land cost, 8.1 acres	$353,000
Land improvements	418,000
Land value (cost)	$771,000
Building cost	
50,000 square feet, @ $30.00	$1,500,000

Gross income	$600,000
Less operating expenses	
(60 percent)	- 360,000
Net annual income	$240,000
Less income to building	
$1,500,000 x .12 =	- 180,000
Income to land	$60,000
Land value	
$60,000/ .10	*$600,000*

center building has an estimated cost of $1,959,750. Leasing commissions of $384,000 result in a total building investment of $2,343,750.

Table 7-3   Shopping Center Development

Land cost, 8.1 acres	$353,000
Land improvements	418,000
Land value (cost)	$771,000
Building cost	
(65,000 square feet)	$1,959,750
Soft costs	384,000
Total building cost	$2,343,750

Annual net income	$628,589
Less income to building	
$2,343,750 x .12	- 281,250
Income to land	$347,339
Land value	
$347,339/.10	*$3,473,390*

The estimated annual net operating income is taken from a proposed lease of 38,000 square feet to a supermarket with the balance of the annual rental income from "satellite" tenants who benefit from customers attracted by the supermarket. Annual rents are shown as net to the owner. With these allowances, the annual net operating income, $628,589, allows for a 12 percent overall annual yield on the building cost.

These allowances provide for an annual net operating income to the building of $281,250. After subtracting the estimated income to the building, *$347,339 remains for the land investment.* Capitalizing income to the land results in an estimated *land value* of *$3,473,390.* These data are summarized in Table 7-3.

If the assumptions of this problem are realized, it would indicate that the highest and best use of the 8.1 acres would be for a *shopping center.* The yield on the land greatly exceeds the estimated land yield from the office building, which appears to be an *under improvement.* The estimated land value under an office building use is considerably less than the land value under shopping center use.

The multiple-family use quite clearly represents an *over improvement.* In valuing the property, then, the appraiser would follow the example of Table 7-3 suggesting a highest and best use as a neighborhood shopping center.

Interim Use

Not all highest and best use estimates for vacant land follow the preceding rules. The appraiser may conclude that the present use as an irrigated farm represents a temporary or interim use over some limited period. At the end of the period, it is estimated that the land will adapt to a higher use, a residential subdivision, shopping center, or other urban use. An *interim use* is a temporary use prevailing until a more intensive use is economically justified.

To illustrate, suppose the appraiser values the land in its present use as an irrigated farm over the next five years with the appraisal conditioned on the highest and best use as a shopping center five years later. These estimates follow from an analysis of population trends, historical real estate sales, highway traffic counts, and similar data.

Improved Land

The appraiser faces two possibilities in appraising land improved with an existing building: the building may be adapted to a higher, *more intensive use* or the property may be appraised *as if vacant.*

Improved land – land improved with building, structures or other land developments, including leveling, drainage, curbs, paving, and the like. or "vacant.

HIGHEST AND BEST USE ESTIMATES: LAND AND BUILDING

A fairly common example relates to highest and best use of relatively large single-family dwellings, usually two stories constructed before World War I. Located on main access routes and frequently near the downtown fringe area, these older houses may be well constructed and in good physical condition; they have been adapted to restaurants and space for medical, accounting, and real estate or law offices. In this case, the appraiser proposes a building adapted to the estimated highest and best use. Table 7-4 illustrates the analysis required for the appraisal of a single-family dwelling suitable for rehabilitation to office use.

The appraiser first establishes the market value, in an as-is condition, at $300,000. The appraiser then lists the cost of adapting the building for office use. Note that the costs include updating the electrical system ($30,000), adding a central air-conditioning system ($75,000), and providing for interior partitions, doors, and redecorating ($35,000). After updating and adding new plumbing facilities at a cost of $40,000 and adding parking spaces at a cost of $12,500, the property has a total investment cost of $492,500.

The appraiser has estimated that under the proposed rehabilitation cost, net operating income from office use would total $75,000 annually. Net operating income of $75,000, expressed as a return on the invested capital of $492,500, represents a 15.23 percent overall property yield ($75,000/$492,500). These data are summarized in Table 7-4.

Table 7-4   Highest and Best Use: Improving Land

Value, as is	$300,000
Update electrical system	30,000
Add central air-conditioning and new duct work	75,000
Interior partitions, doors and redecorating	35,000
Cost of adding parking spaces	12,500
Updating and adding plumbing facilities	40,000
Total property cost, office use	$492,500
Net rental income $75,000	
$75,000/$492,500 = 15.23 percent overall property yield	

Return

Before preparing the final highest and best use estimate, the appraiser may perform a similar exercise in adapting the building to alternative uses such as a family restaurant or retail use. In short, the example shows how to estimate the highest and best use of land and buildings, assuming that the building may be adapted to an income property that maximizes the investment yield on land.

LAND AND BUILDING APPRAISED AS IF VACANT

This case covers land improved with obsolete buildings of no value. The building has no value because of its physical condition or because it is inappropriate for the site. In most respects, this case is similar to the vacant land appraisal. With existing improvements that are deemed inappropriate, the appraiser must value land according to its market value in the highest and best use *less* the cost of building demolition. These costs could be quite substantial, leading to unusually low market value estimates.

This situation is illustrated by ten acres of industrially zoned land that was improved for a mobile home park. The developer negotiated a $658,000 mortgage which, as it later developed, was more than enough to pay for the land and mobile home park improvement costs. After three years of unsuccessful operation, the owner abandoned the property, defaulting on the mortgage. The lender, to attach personal assets of the developer, required an appraisal to secure a personal judgment lien.

On analysis, data indicated that the mobile home park was not the highest and best use; the mobile home park was poorly designed (a one-half-acre cemetery was located in the center of the park); the mobile home park facilities were poorly constructed; and shade trees, which were a necessary requirement for mobile home parks in a southern climate, were lacking.

The appraiser then valued the land in its highest and best use: industrial land. The industrial land value, however, was decreased by the cost to remove underground gas, water, and sewer lines and to remove the dilapidated swimming pool and vandalized central office and recreational building. The court approved a deficiency judgment based on the first mortgage of $658,000, less the amount realized at the foreclosure sale of $68,000 (the appraised value).

In this instance, the appraiser estimated the land *as if vacant* and at its *highest and best use* for industrial use. The market value of the industrial land was decreased by the cost of placing the land in a physical condition for industrial use.

HIGHEST AND BEST USE SUPPORT

Because of the crucial importance of highest and best use estimates, appraisers document their personal value opinions. The highest and best use opinion must appear reasonable according to evidence *supported by* the appraiser. In this respect, appraisers analyze the highest and best use estimate according to *historical data, present data,* and *projected trends.* Among the factors considered in analyzing these three types of data, appraisers typically refer to:

1. Surrounding land use.
2. Existing land use.
3. Present zoning: why or why not appropriate; the probability of zoning changes.
4. Environmental laws.
5. Population trends.
6. Competing land uses. → different uses of property – Shopping Center moles
7. Automobile traffic patterns and volume.
8. The current rental market.
9. New construction.
10. Recent real estate sales.
11. Rental data.
12. Vacancy reports.

To be sure, a fairly brief statement of the highest and best use may be convincing for a single-family dwelling in a residential neighborhood. For nonresidential property, however, the highest and best use estimate must be documented by data that gives valid support for the recommended highest and best use.

SUMMARY

Economically, the highest and best use is an estimate of the *optimum use of a scarce resource.* The appraisal concept defines highest and best use, assuming that the use is reasonably *probable and legally permissible*. The highest and best use must prove *physically possible and economically feasible*. Highest and best use results in the *highest land value*.

In this regard, the highest and best use may not necessarily be the use under present zoning. Depending on the valuation problem, *zoning changes may be anticipated* in estimating highest and best use. Furthermore, *surrounding land use may not indicate the highest and best use*. Changing neighborhoods and rising or declining growth trends may recommend uses other than surrounding land use. Appraisers are not necessarily controlled by *the present use*. Property undergoing a transition in use may result in highest and best use estimates that vary from present use.

The highest and best use maximizes net returns, creates economic benefits to surrounding land, and results in social benefits.

In estimating the highest and best use, the appraiser encounters vacant land or land improved with buildings. In the former case, the highest and best use *maximizes net income to the land*. The appraiser calculates the net income to land under several options in order to estimate the optimum combination of land and buildings and maximize income to the land. The appraiser rejects those projects that represent an *over improvement* or an *under improvement*.

In some instances, an *interim use* would be advised. This is a temporary use over a limited period, pending continued growth trends in which the land adapts to a higher use.

The appraiser faces two possibilities in appraising *land with an existing building:* The building may be adapted to a higher use, or the land may be appraised *as if vacant*. In the first case, the existing building is modified to maximize income to the land. In the second case, the property will be appraised as if vacant which requires a deduction for building demolition.

In the final analysis, the appraiser *supports the estimate of highest and best use* according to historical data, projected trends and the analysis of present data.

POINTS TO REMEMBER

over improvement the allocation of excess capital to land, with the result that the return to land is below market.

under improvement the term refers to the insufficient capital to develop land, with the result that land earns a below-market yield.

highest and best use the use which is reasonably probable and legally permissible and must prove physically possible and economically feasible. The highest and best use results in the highest land value.

maximally productive the use in which land earns the highest income; the proposed highest and best use represents the optimum use that produces the highest income to land, and therefore the highest land value.

interim use a temporary use prevailing until a more intensive use is economically justified.

improved land land improved with building structures or other land developments, including leveling, drainage, curbs, paving, and the like.

QUESTIONS FOR REVIEW

1. In your own words, define the highest and best use.

2. Explain the economic concept of highest and best use.

3. What three premises are common to highest and best use estimates?

4. Explain three main benefits of highest and best use. Give examples in illustration of your answer.

5. Explain how the appraiser would estimate the highest and best use of vacant land. Explain your answer with appropriate examples.

6. Give an example of an interim use.

7. How would you estimate the highest and best use of improved land? What two alternatives are common to this appraisal problem?

8. How would you support the estimate of highest and best use?

PRACTICE PROBLEMS

1. Estimate the highest and best use for vacant land which has an estimated value of $500,000. Use a capitalization rate of 12 percent and a building recovery rate of 2.5 percent. Use the following assumptions for Proposal 1 and Proposal 2:

    Land value—$500,000.
    >   Capitalization rate—12 percent (land)
    >   Building capital recovery rate—2.5 percent.

    Proposal 1
    >   Multiple family dwelling use
    >   Building cost: $4,000,000
    >   Annual net income: $700,000

Proposal 2
   Neighborhood shopping center
   Building cost: $1,500,000
   Annual net income: $450,000

2. (a) Estimate the net return of a two-story, 4,000-square-foot single-family dwelling originally constructed in 1890 and zoned for commercial use. Estimate the net return on the property value under your estimate of highest and best use for a family restaurant, assuming the following facts:

Estimated property value as is:
   Land value $100,000
   Building value   300,000

Alteration cost:
   Alteration of kitchen $ 30,000
   Interior decorating   65,000
   Parking spaces   25,000
   Plumbing remodeling   75,000
   Electrical remodeling   45,000
                                          240,000   540,000
   Total cost $640,000

   Net annual rent $75,000

(b) Assuming a minimum rate of return with land and building investment of 10 percent and 12 percent, what minimum rent would be necessary to justify highest and best use as a restaurant?

PART 2

Approaches to Value

C H A P T E R 8

The Appraisal Process

After studying this chapter, you will know:

- The introductory elements of the appraisal process.
- The data collection and analysis routines common to real estate appraisals.
- The organization and presentation of appraisal data: general and specific.
- Reconciliation analysis for the final value estimate.

By following the required appraisal process, appraisers complete appraisals in a standard, logical format. The appraisal process applies to a broad range of properties—from vacant land and single-family dwellings to large-scale shopping centers and industrial property. To be sure, the market value evidence for individual properties varies significantly. Yet by following the accepted appraisal process, clients may easily review appraisal reports that follow a standard format. More important, the accepted appraisal process encourages appraisers to produce appraisal reports that meet professional and legal standards.

Since appraisal reports follow a well-defined organizational plan, it is convenient to explain the *introductory* section of an appraisal report. The chapter then details the second phase of the appraisal—*preliminary analysis and data collection*. The third part of the chapter covers the format followed in the *approaches to value*. The last part of the chapter deals with certain *supplemental material* usually added to an appraisal report. While appraisal detail is unique to every property, this general plan is followed for both form appraisals and narrative reports.

To appraise single-family dwellings, less data would be necessary in the second part of the report covering preliminary analysis and data collection. This part of the report deals with regional, community, and neighborhood (general) data. In appraising a multiple-building industrial plant or regional shopping center, these data would be quite detailed.

APPRAISAL REPORT INTRODUCTION

The main purpose of the introductory material is to *define the appraisal problem*. After a clear explanation of the appraisal problem, the appraisal process progresses to the next step: preliminary analysis and data collection.

Define the Problem

This part of the appraisal begins with <u>*six elements*</u> that identify the property appraised and the purpose of the appraisal: real estate identification,

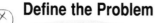

property rights, date of valuation, purpose of the appraisal, definition of value, and statement of limiting conditions. While at first glance this material may seem relatively unimportant, these elements avoid the possible misunderstanding of the property appraised or the type of value estimated.

REAL ESTATE IDENTIFICATION

The real estate appraised is identified by four criteria: the name of the legal owner, the street address, the legal description, and a general description of the location. It must not be assumed that the client or appraisal reviewer is necessarily familiar with the general property location. A typical property identification will read:

Owner: Capital Investments, Inc.
Address: 27 Chestnut Street
  Exeter, New Hampshire
Legal Description: A certain parcel of land with the buildings thereon, purporting or presumably owned in fee, situated in Exeter, County of Rockingham, and the State of New Hampshire, bounded and described as follows: Beginning at the point of intersection of the Westerly side line of Chestnut Street (formerly known as Prison Street) and the Northerly sideline of Chestnut Hill Avenue, and thence running Southwesterly along said Northerly sideline of said Chestnut Hill Avenue to the highwater mark on the Easterly side of the Squamscott River; thence turning and running Northerly along said highwater mark to land now on or formerly of one Flanigan; thence turning and running Easterly along said Flanigan land and the Southerly side-line of Jady Hill Avenue to its intersection with the Westerly sideline of Chestnut Street; and thence turning and running Southerly along said Westerly sideline of Chestnut Street to the point of beginning.
Location: The site is one block from the downtown center approximately 300 feet north of Highway 108. Exeter is 35 miles north of Boston, Massachusetts.

Frequently, appraisal reports are prepared for out-of-town lenders or clients in other states or countries. To help in the property identification, appraisers frequently accompany the written identification with a *site map*. The map shows the site under valuation with reference to local streets or other known reference points. A map that accompanies the legal description above is shown in Figure 8-1.

Figure 8-1　　Site Map: Industrial Property Appraisal

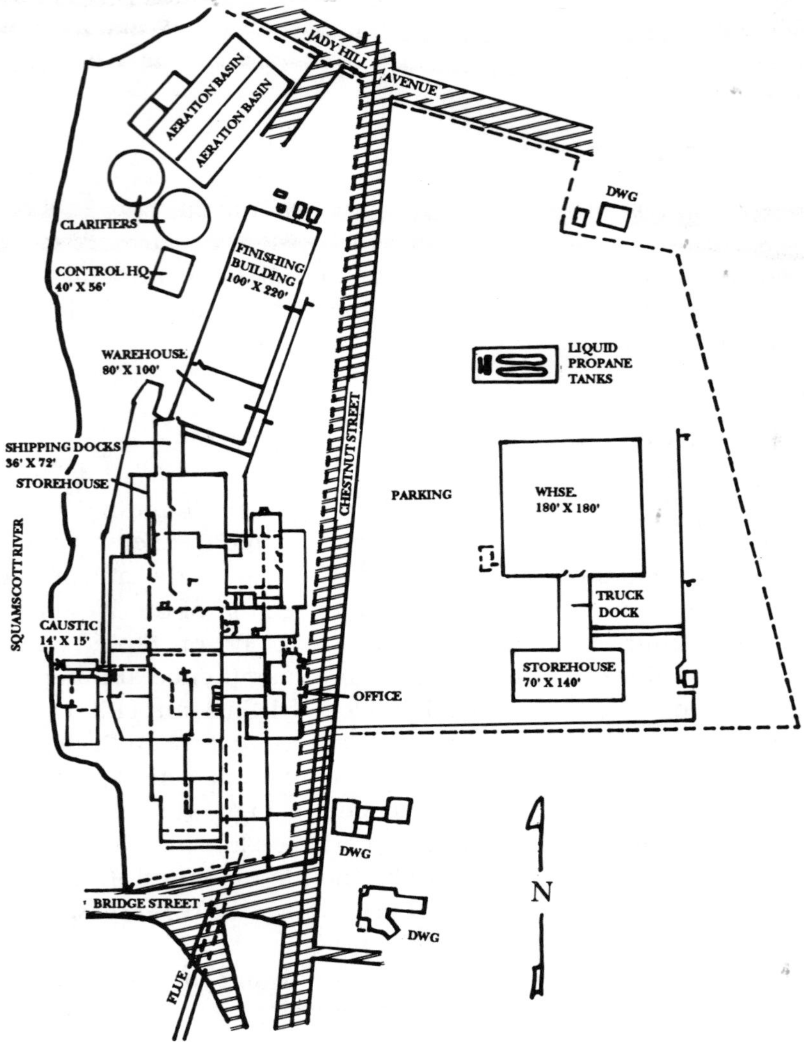

The legal description should be furnished by the client. By reviewing the legal description with property tax or surveying maps, the appraiser physically locates boundaries and monuments. The legal description enables the appraiser to verify property boundaries and the property to be appraised. The location gives the reviewer a general reference to identify the property.

PROPERTY RIGHTS

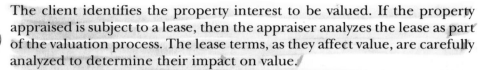

The client identifies the property interest to be valued. If the property appraised is subject to a lease, then the appraiser analyzes the lease as part of the valuation process. The lease terms, as they affect value, are carefully analyzed to determine their impact on value.

Therefore, by identifying the property rights to be valued, the appraiser limits the market value estimate to designated property interests. Given the property interest, the appraiser then refers to the appropriate documents that define the property rights under appraisal.

DATE OF VALUATION

The date of valuation has more than a casual significance. If the appraisal covers the market value as of January 15, events occurring after January 15 would not invalidate the appraisal. If additional information has occurred after the date of valuation that changes market value, the client may request an appraisal update. So the rule stands that the appraiser is not responsible for unanticipated events occurring after the date of valuation.

In other instances, the appraised value is effective only for a legally designated date. Appraisals for eminent domain are usually as of a date supplied by the client. For mortgage loan appraisals, ordinarily the date of valuation would be the *date of inspection* and not the date the report was prepared or signed. Some appraisers write the date of inspection on the reverse of photographs for verification.

PURPOSE OF THE APPRAISAL

For most appraisals, the purpose is to estimate market value. But the valuation assignment may be for special purposes, such as a value estimated for property taxes or just compensation for an eminent domain appraisal. The purpose of the appraisal affects data required for the appraisal report.

DEFINITION OF VALUE

The definition of value guides the selection of appraisal data. While most appraisals refer to market value, other appraisals require a definition of insurable value (to estimate casualty losses, for example, or to define value for other specific purposes, i.e., historical value, original cost, or value to a particular user).

LIMITING CONDITIONS

The appraiser lists limiting conditions that guide the appraisal. A common limiting condition states that "the appraiser is not compelled to give testimony in court or before administrative agencies unless arrangements are made in advance." The statement of limiting conditions indicates that the appraiser assumes that the legal description is correct, and the title is marketable.

In other cases the fee simple estate may not cover subsurface rights. The qualification that the appraisal does not cover the subsurface rights would be added to the statement of limiting conditions. Another disclaimer advises clients that data are taken from sources believed to be reliable; however "the appraiser makes no guarantee of data accuracy for information gained from third parties." See Figure 8-2 for an example of a statement of limiting conditions.

Practical Applications

The six elements of "defining the problem" are common to all appraisals. It would be difficult to complete an appraisal assignment without covering the six elements of the problem definition. It is not implied, however, that these six elements have equal importance. The time, organization, and presentation of the six elements vary considerably by the type of property appraised and the appraisal assignment.

Consider, for example, the task of appraising water rights to the Exeter River in the state of New Hampshire. A warrantee deed, originating in colonial times, conveyed water rights to a textile mill under the language that read:

> The true intent and meaning of this instrument is to convey to the said Exeter Manufacturing Company . . . all the water at all times that runs in said river . . . .

In this instance, the purpose of the appraisal was to estimate the value of all water in the river (4.0 million gallons a day, safe yield). Like other complex appraisal assignments, special importance was attached to the

Figure 8-2   Statement of Limiting Conditions

1. The Appraiser assumes no responsibility for matters of legal nature affecting the property appraised or the title thereto, nor does the Appraiser render any opinion as to the title, which is assumed to be good and marketable. The property is appraised as though under responsible ownership.

2. Any sketch in the report may show approximate dimensions and is included to assist the reader in visualizing the property. The Appraiser has made no survey of the property.

3. The Appraiser is not required to give testimony or appear in court unless arrangements have been previously made.

4. Any distribution of the valuation in the report between land and improvements applies only under the existing program of utilization. The separate valuations for land and building must not be used in conjunction with any other appraisal and are invalid if so used.

5. The Appraiser assumes that there are no hidden or unapparent conditions of the property, the subsoil, or the structures, which render it more or less valuable. The Appraiser assumes no responsibility for such conditions, or for engineering which might be required to discover such factors.

6. Information, estimates, and opinions furnished to the Appraiser, and contained in the report, were obtained from sources considered reliable and believed to be true and correct. However no responsibility for accuracy of such items furnished the Appraiser can be assumed by the Appraiser.

7. Disclosure of the contents of the appraisal report is governed by the Bylaws and Regulations of the professional appraisal organization with which the Appraiser is affiliated.

8. Neither all, nor any part of the content of the report, or copy thereof (including conclusions as to the property value, the identity of the Appraiser, professional designations, references to any professional appraisal organization, or the firm with which the Appraiser is connected), shall be used for any purposes by anyone but the client specified in the report.

9. On all appraisals, subject to satisfactory completion, repairs, or alterations, the appraisal report and value conclusion are contingent upon completion of the improvements in a workmanlike manner.

Source: Adapted from Federal National Mortgage Association, Form 1004B.

definition and explanation of value and property rights appraised. In such assignments, the appraiser proceeds according to legal advice on elements of value, evidence in the support of value, and the property rights conveyed.

convey – to deliver; to impart

Consequently, it is important to identify precisely the property under valuation. Casual references to the property to be appraised without specific descriptions of land and property rights appraised makes it difficult to adequately support the appraised value.

In other instances, the date of valuation may be subject to considerable controversy. The date of valuation must be identified to help in selecting acceptable evidence to support the market value estimate. Only when these six conditions have been identified and reported can the appraiser turn to the second step in the appraisal process: the preliminary analysis.

PRELIMINARY ANALYSIS: DATA COLLECTION

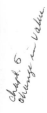

This section of the report includes *general* and *specific* data. *General data* relates to a region, city, or neighborhood. *Specific data* includes a description of the property appraised and the data that applies directly to the market value estimate.

General Data

General data applies to regions or communities and neighborhoods. For major office buildings, industrial plants, and regional shopping malls, regional data would be separately classified to show regional factors important to market value. For single-family dwellings and the smaller income properties, general data relates primarily to communities and neighborhoods.

COMMUNITY DATA

It is difficult to precisely identify relevant community data that appraisers generally use for every appraisal. In resort communities like Palm Springs, California, or Palm Beach, Florida, community factors would be selected according to their importance to the resort industry. For highly industrialized areas, such as New Britain, Connecticut (a prefabricated metal manufacturing center) or Rock Island, Illinois-Davenport, Iowa (farm implement manufacturing centers), manufacturing data deserves detailed analysis. With this qualification, as a general rule, community analysis includes data on:

Natural resources
  Climate
    Topography

    Transportation
    Water supply
    Electric power
    Natural gas
  Government services
    Utility systems
    Sewerage facilities
    Municipal services
        Police
        Fire
        Garbage collection
        Street maintenance
        Public recreation
    Schools
    Property taxes
  Social factors
    Population
    Age distribution
    Family size
    Education
    Community organizations
  Economic base
    Employment by source
    Personal income
    Retail sales by classifications
    Real estate activity
        Building permits by property type
        Deed recordings
        Mortgage recordings
        Subdivision recordings

General data collected on *natural resources* is a relative requirement. Certainly the cold climate of Fairbanks, Alaska, and the hot temperatures of Indio, California, are limiting factors for certain purposes and advantages for others. The hilly topography of Seattle, Washington, and San Francisco (with view and nonview sites) have a different impact on property values relative to the flat terrain found in Phoenix, Arizona, or southern Florida.

Similar comments apply to transportation, water supply, and electric power. Water availability and its quality are controlling valuation factors in the states of California, Florida, Arizona, and many others. Electric power rates are relatively low for hydroelectric power in the Pacific Northwest, or in North Carolina where coal-fired steam generators lead to lower power rates relative to the rates of the typical oil-fired generators of northeastern states.

Consider *government services*. In this respect, the appraiser avoids listing purely descriptive data: "There are 2,623 policemen in the police department." In commenting on police services, the appraiser would explain how the police force, with its highly trained staff and special community services, contributes to market value. In each instance, general data are described with respect to their limiting or contributing influence on property value.

Social factors refer to population, its characteristics, and trends that bear on real estate markets. Market evidence, depending on purpose of the appraisal, would be analyzed according to:

1. The present population and its characteristics.
2. Past population trends.
3. Population projections.

Current population studies are necessary to estimate the demand for real estate, not only for housing, but for retailing and for industrial real estate where industry is dependent on local labor. This section of the report would also indicate community organizations that have an indirect effect on real estate values.

The economic base is defined as the sum of all human activities followed in earning a living. For stable real estate values, the appraiser would explain the degree of employment diversification. Investment risks are reduced if employment is divided among numerous sources. In contrast, employment concentrated in a single industry increases real estate investment risks because of the possibility of large-scale unemployment resulting from a closed plant or declining industry. Single-industry communities have higher real estate investment risks.

For shopping center appraisals, this part of the report will be considerably more detailed with respect to data on personal income and retail sales by category. Here the report will show past population growth, retail sales, and personal income. These data enable the appraiser to make projections on the basis of past data and its analysis.

Table 8-1 shows the historical retail sales in a trade market area for a proposed shopping center. The trade market area consists of the geographic area served by a shopping center. The table shows the annual percentage change in retail sales each year for the preceding 20 years. From these data, a projection of retail sales was based on the annual compound growth rate of 8.1 percent experienced over this period. Current economic conditions indicated favorable prospects for this growth to continue.

Table 8-1   Historical Retail Sales: Shopping Center Trade Market Area*

Current Year to Year 20

Year	Annual Sales	Annual Percent of Change
	(in thousands)	
20	$173,411	- - -
19	178,667	3.0
18	190,797	6.8
17	200,514	5.1
16	215,076	7.3
15	253,125	17.7
14	315,301	24.6
13	342,994	8.7
12	370,587	17.5
11	416,030	12.3
10	440,562	5.9
9	490,054	11.2
8	547,711	11.8
7	616,386	12.5
6	664,327	7.8
5	683,608	2.9
4	734,092	7.4
3	728,169	(8.7)
2	824,463	10.0
(Current year)	824,463	2.9

*Annual compound rate of increase: 8.1 percent

Source: Author Survey

more general data

Note that in presenting *general data* of this type, past data show annual rates of change. These data support future prospects for real estate values and investments. Similar economic data support population, employment, and disposable income projections.

NEIGHBORHOOD DATA

Virtually all real estate is affected in some measure by neighborhood factors. Neighborhoods are local communities in which land uses are homogeneous. Neighborhood boundaries may be defined by areas that have buildings of similar size, structure, or age. Other neighborhoods are bound together by natural boundaries such as the natural terrain or water bodies—hills, mountains, rivers, lakes, or reservoirs. Manmade structures such as main traffic arteries and railroad lines effectively delineate neighborhoods.

Other neighborhoods may be indicated by the dominance of a central building such as a church, factory, or hospital. These neighborhoods usually have some binding, common characteristic such as religious preferences, common neighborhood residents, or identification with a particular school, shopping area, or similar activity.

Neighborhoods are common to appraising commercial properties, small industrial properties (distribution warehouses), apartment projects, and single-family dwellings. Though general data requirements vary according to the property type appraised, most appraisals include four general data groups: physical characteristics, social features, economic characteristics, and public services.

PHYSICAL CHARACTERISTICS. The importance of physical features depends on the property appraised. A neighborhood of $800,000 dwellings will have neighborhood characteristics and standards that do not apply to lower-priced housing subdivisions. Physical characteristics necessary to a neighborhood shopping center include surrounding land uses and highway access.

As a general rule, neighborhoods will be judged with respect to certain physical characteristics, including:

topography — *description of a particular place.*
access
physical layout
surrounding land use

Topography relates to the quality of view, storm drainage, flood plains, and cost of construction caused by steep sites or soil conditions. *Access,* especially to freeway interchanges, may be judged with respect to driving time to employment, comparison shopping, and recreation. For subdivisions, the *physical layout*—the street plan, sidewalks, lot size, street frontage, and other factors—will be part of the general data analysis. *Surrounding land uses,* ideally, should be compatible with the property appraised. A neighborhood with conflicting land uses tends to depress land values.

SOCIAL FACTORS. Social factors relate to neighborhood occupants. For residential property, occupants would be identified according to their typical age, occupation, education, and income. In this respect, the neighborhood would be judged according to how the neighborhood satisfies occupant needs. For example, the neighborhood needs of young married couples are quite different from the neighborhood needs of retirees.

ECONOMIC FEATURES. A neighborhood will be judged according to the typical employment source and personal incomes of neighborhood occupants (residential appraisals). The prevailing residential monthly rent, housing vacancies, and typical dwelling values are related data. Trends in rents, vacancies, and market values will be evaluated from a review of current data.

In single-family dwelling subdivisions, the proportion of houses rented may be indicative of declining values. For example, values would probably be declining if the appraiser reported that 25 percent or more of the houses were rented. Newly formed subdivisions and the more popular neighborhoods have a much lower proportion of rented houses.

GOVERNMENT SERVICES. These data include information on local utility rates and municipal services, such as police and fire protection, the quality of schools, and the level of local property taxes. The appraiser adds relevant information on the sewerage disposal system, natural gas and electricity rates, and other available utilities.

The government services section provides information relating to public parks and municipal recreation programs. Additional comments on special security measures, fire protection, garbage collection, street lights, traffic control, and related municipal services that contribute to stable real estate values would be noted. Land-use controls and their administration usually affect value and deserve explanation.

In short, *general features* do not relate directly to the property valued; general features cover the total environment that affects community or regional property values. Data are presented to show rising or declining value trends.

Specific Data

Specific data, *first*, includes detailed *descriptions of land and buildings.* Depending on the property appraised, sufficient detail will indicate the quality of construction, the suitability of a building design, the building plan layout, and the present building condition.

Second, specific data refers to *data acquisition* for the appraisal approaches. Data acquisition requires real estate sales data similar to the property appraised and data on the land value, the estimated cost of buildings, and property depreciation. The income approach depends on the annual gross income, expected vacancies, annual expenses, and the capitalization rate. The capitalization rate converts net annual income to market value. With these data and the appropriate capitalization rate, the appraiser estimates market value.

Figure 8-3 summarizes the data required if the three valuation approaches are followed. Not all appraisal reports include the three approaches. The cost approach, for example, would be quite irrelevant to

Figure 8-3   Specific Valuation Data

Sales Comparison Approach	Cost Approach	Income Approach
Comparable Sales Data	**Land Value** **Building** **Cost** **Depreciation**	**Gross Income** **Vacancies** **Expenses** **Capitalization Rate**

Reconciliation

Final Value Estimate

value a 20-year-old dwelling; under the income approach it would not be possible to appraise an oil refinery or a public building. For these properties, net income data are not available. If more than a single approach is used (and the appraisal report usually includes more than one approach), the appraisal process includes a "reconciliation" of appraisal approaches to value.

Highest and Best Use

At this point the appraiser includes data that supports the highest and best use estimate. The highest and best use estimate largely determines the valuation approach which will be emphasized.

Land Value Estimate

The land value would be supported here for appraisals which require a separate estimate of land value. Land characteristics, with a site map, would identify the main land elements that bear on value. The evidence of value and data analysis would precede the final estimate of land value.

APPROACHES TO VALUE

If the appraisal requires the three approaches to value, then each approach will be separately explained.

Sales Comparison Approach

The sales comparison approach refers to the *analysis of recent sales of similar property*. If the appraiser elects to estimate value from recent sales of similar property, then this part of the report details sales used in estimating market value. Each comparable sale will be described and analyzed to show how recent sales of similar property indicate market value. Individual sales will be summarized in a sales adjustment table for a form appraisal or in other written form for the narrative appraisal report.

Cost Approach

The cost approach is the estimated market value drawn from *the sum of the estimated land value and the depreciated building cost*. The market value estimate for specialized properties, such as industrial buildings and public buildings, relies mainly on the cost approach. For these properties the appraiser estimates the land value and the building cost as if new and its depreciation. For appraisal purposes, *depreciation is the loss in value from the estimated building cost as if new.* For industrial properties this phase of the report could be quite comprehensive and detailed.

Income Approach

Briefly defined, the income approach refers to the method of deriving market value by calculating *the present value of annual net income.* Investment quality properties are normally exchanged on the basis of their net income—primarily, apartments, shopping centers, and office buildings. Detailed data on gross income, vacancies, operating expenses, and capitalization rates show how the capitalization on income supports the final value estimate.

RECONCILIATION

The reconciliation summarizes the evidence of the three approaches to value; it explains how the appraiser arrives at the final estimate of value. The reconciliation provides an explanation of the weaknesses and strengths of the three approaches; it indicates how the appraiser justifies the weight given valuation evidence—cost, sales, and income data—in estimating market value. And it includes the *final value estimate.*

SUPPLEMENTAL MATERIAL

Appraisal reports require a *certificate of value.* The Appraisal Board of the state of Georgia requires an appraisal certificate that is similar in content to Figure 8-4.

Certificate of Value

First note that the certificate has a statement in which the appraiser certifies that facts in the report are true and correct. In other words, the sales and income listed are based on facts and not conjecture.

In paragraph two the appraiser references the statement of limiting conditions and indicates that his or her professional analysis and conclusions are unbiased. The appraiser does not serve as a client advocate. Significantly, paragraphs three and four indicate that the appraiser has no significant interest in the property appraised and is unbiased with respect to parties involved.

Figure 8-4   Certificate of Value

1. The statements of fact contained in this report are true and correct.
2. The reported analyses, opinions, and conclusions are limited only by the report assumptions and limiting conditions, and are my personal, unbiased professional analyses, opinions, and conclusions.
3. I have no present or prospective interest in the property that is the subject of this report, and I have no personal interest or bias with respect to the parties involved.
4. My compensation is not contingent on an action or event resulting from the analyses, opinion, and conclusions in, or the use of, this report.
5. My analyses, opinion, and conclusions were developed, and this report has been prepared, in conformity with the Uniform Standard of Professional Appraisal Practice.
6. I have made a personal inspection of the property that is the subject of this report.
7. No one provided significant professional assistance to the person signing this report.

Source: *Real Estate Appraiser Licensing and Certification Act and Rules and Regulations* (Georgia Real Estate Appraisers Board, Atlanta, Georgia, 1990), p. 48.

Departures from these general requirements are not permitted. The possible exceptions apply to paragraph three. If the appraiser has an interest or contemplated interest in the property appraised, the interest must be specified. Exceptions to paragraph six also warrant further comment. If the appraiser did not make a personal property inspection, that fact must be stated. If more than one person signs the report, the certificate must name individuals who inspected (or did not inspect) the property. Persons providing significant professional experience must be named in paragraph seven.

Exhibits

It is customary to supplement the opinion of value with maps, photographs, building plans, and other exhibits to support the value estimate. It is also customary to list appraisal qualifications at the end of the report. Qualifications are generally required to qualify the appraiser as an expert witness before government agencies and the courts.

SUMMARY

The appraisal process provides for a standard, logical appraisal report format. It adapts to a broad range of properties and applies both to form and narrative appraisal reports. The introductory part of the appraisal process *defines the appraisal problem* and provides for *general* and *specific data*.

To define the appraisal problem, six elements must be reported: identify real estate by address, legal description, and location; indicate property rights to be appraised; give the date of valuation (not necessarily the date of signature); state the purpose of the appraisal; define market value; and state the limiting conditions. The statement of limiting conditions qualifies the estimated value. In this statement the appraiser assumes a correct legal description, a marketable title, and requires additional arrangements if attendance in court is required.

The *preliminary analysis* covers *general* and *specific* data. General data relates to a region, city, or neighborhood. Specific data includes a description of the property appraised and data that applies directly to the market data.

General data refers to regional or community factors, depending on the property appraised. Community data describes *natural resources, government services, social factors,* and the *economic base* (these data help in interpreting market value for the property appraised). In reporting economic data the appraiser shows trends that support data projection.

Neighborhood data covers areas that have a homogeneous land use. Neighborhoods would be defined by common building types or by natural or manmade boundaries. General data on neighborhoods are classified according to *physical characteristics* and *social factors* on neighborhood occupants, i.e., age, occupation, education, income, and family size. *Economic features* refer to employment sources and data on typical residential monthly rents, housing vacancies, dwelling values, and related data. Past data are evaluated before judging future trends.

Neighborhoods will have varying levels of *government services* that influence market value. Utility rates, municipal services, the quality of schools, and the level of property taxes are among the items relevant to market value. Public parks, recreational programs, and special security measures further affect real estate values.

In short, general features do not relate directly to the property value; they cover the total environment that influences local or regional property values.

Specific data includes detailed descriptions of land and buildings and the data acquired for the three valuation approaches: real estate sales data, land value data, building costs (including property depreciation), and income data. The appraisal process includes a definitive statement on the highest and best use.

After the *preliminary analysis and data collection* section are completed, the appraiser considers the next step in the appraisal process: the *main approaches to value*—the sales comparison, cost, and income approaches. According to the appraisal process, the appraiser then proceeds to the *reconciliation*. Here the indicated values under the three approaches end with the *final value estimate*.

Supplemental material closes the appraisal report with the statement of limiting conditions and value. The *statement of limiting conditions* qualifies the interpretation and use of the appraisal report. Among other items, the appraiser assumes no responsibility for legal or title matters, or for the accuracy of land descriptions. Other limiting conditions narrow the interpretation of the report to stated terms and conditions.

The *certificate of value,* legally required in many jurisdictions, usually covers (as a minimum) *seven* statements that commit the appraiser to the value estimate. In essence the certificate of value attests to the fact that all data are true, that the appraiser has rendered an unbiased, personal opinion of value, and that the appraisal conforms with professional appraisal practice. Finally, the appraiser certifies that he or she inspected the property. The appraiser also certifies that compensation is not contingent on the estimated market value. The end of the report covers appraisal exhibits and lists appraisal qualifications.

POINTS TO REMEMBER

appraisal process a procedure that appraisers follow in providing appraisal reports that conform to a standard, logical format.

limiting conditions a statement of limiting conditions that the appraiser makes in estimating market value. The market value estimate is valid only to the extent that limiting conditions prevail.

economic base the sum of all human activity engaged in earning a living.

trade market area an area consisting of the geographic area served by a shopping center.

neighborhood a local community in which land uses are homogeneous.

general data a part of the preliminary analysis which includes appraisal data of a region, city, or neighborhood.

specific data data that includes a description of the property appraised and appraisal data that applies directly to the market value estimate.

sales comparison approach the estimate of value derived from recent sales of similar property.

cost approach a market value estimate derived from the sum of the estimated land value and the depreciated building cost.

income approach the estimated market value equal to the present value of an annual net income.

reconciliation evaluation of the evidence of the three approaches to value offered in support of the final estimate of value.

QUESTIONS FOR REVIEW

1. What are the main elements of the appraisal process?

2. Explain the importance of the main parts in defining the appraisal problem.

3. In the valuation of a 200-unit apartment project, what material would you include under general data? Give examples in support of your answer.

4. What specific data would be relevant to the valuation of a single-family dwelling? Explain fully.

5. Explain how you would evaluate a neighborhood for a residential appraisal. Explain thoroughly.

6. Explain the difference between specific data and general data. Give examples in support of your answer.

7. In your own words, define the three approaches to value.

8. What are the main elements included in the certificate of value? Why are these statements important to the value estimate?

9. Why is the statement of limiting conditions important to the appraisal? Explain thoroughly.

PRACTICE PROBLEMS

1. Your client asks you to estimate the market value of a neighborhood shopping center. Outline the general data requirements for this report explaining why you would include such data in your appraisal report.

2. In the valuation of a single-family dwelling, state the approaches to value you would employ. If you use more than one approach to value, explain how you would prepare the reconciliation for the final value estimate. Include in your answer the certificate of value that applies to this case.

C H A P T E R 9

Site Valuation

For Friday bring the rest of the Appraisal Report

After studying this chapter you will know:
- Important factors to consider in valuing sites.
- The comparable sales approach.
- Special valuation techniques to appraise land sites.
- Methods of valuing land for subdivisions.

The chapter is primarily limited to urban land valuation. Farm and timber land require special training for appraisal according to its agricultural productivity. Site valuation, while covering numerous land types with widely varying characteristics, follows an orderly valuation procedure. Site valuation requires a review of "value-determining" land characteristics that cover the main factors affecting market value.

The chapter covers locational characteristics in addition to certain area variables, utilities, and site improvements. These items primarily concern residential land. However, to a large extent, the same items apply to other land types. Community facilities, land use restrictions, and other general site characteristics complete the first part of the chapter.

The second part of the chapter concentrates on valuation techniques; namely, comparable sales analysis, land residual procedures, and valuation practices unique to site valuation, including ground rent capitalization and land plottage, or the assembly of small parcels of land into a larger unit. A step-by-step explanation of subdivision valuation practices completes the chapter.

SITE DESCRIPTION

The site description covers characteristics important to judging land utility. The descriptive detail supports the land value estimate. The more significant characteristics may be classified under location, area variables, utilities, site improvements, community facilities, and land use restrictions. Add to this list certain general characteristics that affect land utility.

It should be emphasized that these characteristics are not necessarily explained in order of their importance. Characteristics unique to a site may deserve greater or lesser emphasis which is not possible to anticipate.

Location Characteristics

Much of the residential land under valuation is found in the suburbs. Therefore, the distance to interchange points and driving time to main

arteries assume considerable significance. In some commuting neighborhoods, the convenience to public mass transportation is equally significant.
Residential neighborhoods must be convenient to shopping—both convenience shopping and comparison shopping, i.e., household goods and
apparel.

Some buyers place a premium on the distance to employment; the
distance to schools assumes importance if schools are an attractive neighborhood feature. The importance of location encourages appraisers to
provide a *location map* showing the site location in relation to other
community facilities.

Area Variables

The land area, dimensions, shape, and topography have a significant
impact on utility. If the residential lot is fairly *regular in shape*, it is relevant
to list the number of front feet and depth. For both measurements, there
is some locally acceptable dimension. In evaluating lot depth, it is generally
found that as the depth increases, the added increment in depth assumes
decreasing value. At some point, added lot width or added depth beyond
local standards adds little or nothing to site utility.

Sites are usually described in terms of the area, either in square feet or
acres. If the shape is *irregular,* special comments are required to explain
how the shape adds or detracts from site utility.

Topography refers to whether the lot is level, moderately sloping, or
steeply sloping. A steeply sloped lot has limited access in freezing climates.
The general preference is for a site above the street grade, gently sloping
downward to the street level. Lots below the street grade have less demand
than the lots above street grade. Topography may also affect construction
costs if foundations must be constructed on steep slopes or highly unstable
soils.

Utilities

Urban land sites are highly dependent on utilities, their availability, and
cost. Municipal water, including use restrictions and its relative cost, may
be locally quite important. The availability of public sewers rather than
septic tanks may add considerable value. Natural gas, cable television, and
electrical services—private or public systems—deserve added description.
If underground utilities are on-site, the appraiser compares their utility
with surrounding sites similarly improved.

Site Improvements

Sometimes called *off-site improvements,* this category includes improvements such as sidewalks, concrete curbs, storm sewers, and street lighting. The type of street paving and street width are equally important.

Community Facilities

Community facilities vary in importance according to neighborhoods. Some neighborhoods center around a dominant church. Schools, public libraries, playgrounds, and parks add to site utility. Outstanding public parks, playgrounds, and other outdoor facilities increase local site value. Families pay premiums for sites near water and related sports facilities. Community facilities (or their lack) that influence site values should be evaluated.

Land Use Restrictions

For virtually every site, appraisers show the extent of land use controls and their effect on values. Zoning codes frequently control housing density. For example, Exeter, New Hampshire, prohibits apartment projects of more than 12 units. Other communities, under building code regulations, restrict the number of annual residential permits. These restrictions have the effect of limiting the supply of residential sites and generally increase the market value of available sites. Environmental controls may restrict wood or coal stoves and water consumption.

Subdivision and deed restrictions tend to preserve neighborhood amenities. Restrictions on television antennas, architectural controls, and minimum building standards are cases in point. It must be explained how these controls enhance neighborhood amenities and therefore site utility.

General Site Characteristics

Surrounding land uses warrant careful explanation for newly developed areas. If sites adjoin vacant land, there is a possibility that vacant land will be improved with incompatible, inharmonious land uses. In contrast, sites that are surrounded with compatible land uses tend to maintain stable values. Depending on the site appraised, surrounding land uses justify detailed treatment, explanation, and a review of how surrounding land uses impact on the site appraised.

Property taxes partly depend on local assessment policy. Typical property tax rates and expected property taxes should be compared with similar sites to test the fairness of assessments.

Subdivision layout may follow the "grid" or "waffle iron" pattern of square lots and blocks. Contrasting subdivisions follow a curvilinear plan. The latter plan improves traffic flow, reduces the proportion of land absorbed by streets, and creates a neighborhood of contrasting but compatible buildings and sites. See Figure 9-1 for a summary of common site characteristics important to land valuation.

Figure 9-1   A Summary of Common Site Characteristics

Location	Site Improvements
Distance to main arteries	Sidewalks
Convenience to public transportation	Concrete curbs
Distance to shopping	Storm sewers
Convenience shopping	Street lighting
Comparison shopping	Other
Distance to employment	Community Facilities
Distance to schools	Churches
Other	Schools
Area Variables	Libraries
Front feet	Playgrounds
Depth	Parks
Square feet (acres)	Recreation
Shape	Other
Irregular	Land Use Restrictions
Regular	Building codes
Topography	Zoning codes
Utilities	Housing codes
Municipal water (restricted use)	Environmental controls
Sanitary sewers	Subdivision restrictions
Natural gas	Deed restrictions
Cable television	General Characteristics
Electrical (private of public)	Surrounding land uses
Underground utilities	Property taxes
	Assessed values
	Property tax rate
	Subdivision layout

VALUATION TECHNIQUES

Site appraisers use the comparable sales approach, the income approach, and certain other valuation procedures unique to land valuation. The comparable sales approach strongly supports the estimated value for sites commonly sold

Comparable Sales Approach

The comparable sales approach described here primarily concerns the narrative appraisal report. Form appraisals for residential property follow similar procedures. They are explained more fully in a succeeding chapter.

Clients can follow the valuation logic by the documentation offered for each comparable sale. Further, such documentation complies with the minimum requirements for court testimony. In these circumstances, sales detail must be shown for litigating parties and for judge and jury examination.

SALES PRESENTATION

Each sale includes minimum relevant details. The main value determining facts are listed in a sales summary table. Each sale observation is accompanied by a survey map showing site boundaries, area, and topographical features. Figure 9-2 illustrates a comparable land sale for a narrative appraisal report.

The sale is identified by the buyer and seller. The date of sale is usually the date of the sale instrument. Sale instruments are identified by the deed book, page, and county of recording. The legal description, if fairly lengthy, is referenced by the recorded plat book, page, and recording county. The land area described in acres or square feet is also shown by the location and its proximity to the property appraised. Other data includes zoning and the sales price, also shown as the price per acre (or square foot). The remarks section adds comments on how the particular sale relates to the property valued.

Thus, the comparable sales approach requires details on selected sales that relate to the property valued. After identifying sale detail, the appraiser adds a remark to each transaction showing how that particular sale leads to the final site value.

Figure 9-2   Comparable Land Site Sale: Narrative Appraisal Report

Comparable Land Sale Eight

Grantor	:	Young Women's Christian Organization of Athens, Georgia, Inc.
Grantee	:	Howard L. Dillard, David J. Dupree, John R. Green, R. McKenzie Daniel, and William S. Ellis, Jr.
Date of Sale	:	September 16, 1990
Recorded	:	Deed Book 667, Page 283-B, Clarke County, Georgia
Legal Description:		A plat recorded in Plat Book 22, Page 296, Clarke County, Georgia
Lot Area	:	52.296 acres
Location	:	This tract fronts on the west boundary of Jennings Mill Road and extends to the eastern boundary of the tract under valuation.
Zoning	:	RM-1.
Sale Price	:	$575,300; $11,000.84 per acre.
Remarks	:	This sale included abandoned buildings and the swimming pool of the former Young Women's Christian Organization camp. Development of this site will require removal of camp buildings, filling in of the swimming pool, and preservation of a small cemetery. The log cabin, a one-story lodge, has historical value. The developers plan to restore the log cabin as a recreational building. The present zoning, RM-1, allows up to ten units per acre. Development costs of the property under appraisal are believed to be somewhat lower than the cost of development of this tract because of the absence of buildings and other obsolete improvements.

CORNER INFLUENCE

For commercial and residential lots, a question arises over the value of corner lots in relation to lots in the middle of the block. For subdivisions developed before World War II, it was common practice to subdivide lots into fairly narrow widths of 40, 50, or 60 feet. With the limited side yards of inside lots, a corner lot gave added privacy. It was also true that downtown corner lots provide considerably more window-display space, and corner lots have higher pedestrian traffic. Corner influence tables have been developed that purport to establish mathematically the value added by a corner location.

In the case of residential lots, no premium may be paid for a corner location, especially if inside lots are of adequate width to provide privacy. Further, landscaping and fencing may create sufficient privacy so that inside lots have as much utility as corner lots. Others would argue that the corner lot is more costly to improve with sidewalks, streets, sewers, and storm drains. Corner lots also expose residents to additional traffic hazards. Because of these issues, corner lots should be appraised in accordance with the local market.

After citing individual sales, including remarks, the appraiser then submits a *sales summary* which lists the main features of each sale. Such a summary is shown in Table 9-1.

The sales summarized in Table 9-1 show variations from $9,492 per acre to $24,081 per acre. These price variations are largely explained by differences in zoning, locational advantages, and time of sale. An explanation of the land sales summary leads to the final value estimate. In this summary the appraiser discusses how each sale leads to the market value estimate. For some appraisals each sale will be adjusted to the property appraised,

Table 9-1   Land Sales Summary

Sale Number	Date of Sale	Number of Acres	Sale Price	Price Per Acre	Zoning
1	Dec. 20, 19__	12.708	$194,600	$15,313	RM-2
2	May 11, 19__	3.104	$ 62,900	$20,264	RM-1
3	Sep. 17, 19__	6.229	$150,000	$24,081	RM-2
4	Jun. 26, 19__	17.816	$300,000	$16,839	RG-6
5	Aug. 10, 19__	30.001	$407,600	$13,586	RM-1
6	Jul. 21, 19__	4.736	$ 84,000	$17,736	RM-2
7	Apr. 22, 19__	27.391	$260,000	$ 9,492	R-3
8	Sep. 16, 19__	52.296	$575,300	$11,001	RM-1

showing how each sale indicates value. The sales adjustment process is explained more fully in the market approach chapter and is not duplicated here.

In short, the sales comparison approach for land sites, requires presentation of sales detail explaining how each sale relates to the appraised property and a sales summary that shows how the appraiser judges each sale for the final estimate of value. The sales adjustment process represents another popular alternative.

Land Residual Techniques

The land residual technique depends on the fact that market value equals the land and the building value. Assuming further that the site is improved at its highest and best use, the land value may be derived from an improved property. In this case, net income is divided between the income allocated to the building and income allocated to the land. Given the income to the land, the land value is derived from the present value of capitalized land income.

To illustrate, assume that annual net income from land and building equals $1,000,000. If it may be shown that the building has a value of $6,000,000 and the building has an estimated economic life of 50 years, income to the building would be $720,000, based on a 12-percent capitalization rate. The annual income to the land (the land residual income) equals $280,000. Capitalized at 10 percent this would indicate a land value, under the land residual capitalization technique, of $2,800,000. These data are summarized below.

Annual net income	$1,000,000
Annual net income to building $6,000,000 x .12	- 720,000
Annual income land (residual)	$ 280,000
Land value $280,000/.10	$2,800,000

The site value, under the land residual technique, assumes that the building value may be determined fairly accurately by the estimated building cost, less building depreciation. The technique is advised if the building shows relatively little depreciation and the site is used for the highest and best use. The method is used primarily where comparable land sales are not available. If the value of land improvements is fairly low, e.g., a parking lot, the land residual technique substitutes for the sales comparison approach.

Allocation Techniques

Used primarily for residential dwellings, the technique assumes a typical relationship between land value and building value. For a neighborhood of $200,000 dwellings, presumably, there is some typical proportion between the land value and building value. Common observation discloses that buyers of residential dwellings do not pay $1,000,000 for a dwelling sited on a $10,000 lot. Conversely, it is unusual to find a $10,000 building on a $1,000,000 (waterfront view) lot.

Suppose, for example, that an appraiser establishes—by market research—that for a selected neighborhood, lot values represent approximately 20 percent of the market value of a house and lot. It follows that a $200,000 dwelling would have a land value of $40,000.

Therefore, site values may be derived from sales of improved property where a typical land/building ratio prevails. Given the prevailing land/building ratio, the land value may be estimated from the total property value, land, and buildings.

The Extraction Method

In appraising rural property, the improved property is valued according to the land value, in addition to the amount that buildings *contribute* to market value. Each building is estimated to have a "contributory value." The same reasoning is followed in valuing a house improved with a swimming pool—that is, the appraiser determines how much the swimming pool contributes to market value.

Given the market value of the property and the amount that buildings *contribute* to market value, the land value may be "extracted" by deducting the contributory value of buildings from the market value. The method tends to be more accurate when the relative contribution of the building is relatively small. Because this technique is highly subjective, other land value techniques are often preferred.

Ground Rent

Land owners may elect to lease land for 50 or more years to allow tenants to construct buildings on leased land. If the lease provides for market rent, land values may be estimated from the capitalization of net rent. To use this method, the rent must be net after property taxes, and it must be determined that the lease or contract rent equals the market rent.

With the estimated prevailing market capitalization rate, site value may be independently estimated from the ground rent. To illustrate, assume that the land earns a net annual rent (market) of $100,000 a year. If a 12-

percent capitalization rate represents the market capitalization rate, the land value equals $833,333:

$100,000/.12 = $833,333

Plottage Value

Plottage value is the added value resulting from the assembly of smaller sites. Plottage values arise from the fact that larger sites have greater utility than the sum of assembled site values, if considered as separate parcels.

Plottage values typically result from the merger of vacant residential lots into a larger site that has a higher use. While individual lots have value arising from single-family dwelling use, the larger site, for example, may be more appropriately used as a multiple-family site. In this case it is not the act of assembling smaller sites into a larger parcel that creates value—it is the *change in land use* arising from the fact that the larger, assembled site has a higher use than individual properties considered separately. This relationship is shown in Figure 9-3.

Figure 9-3   The Calculation of Plottage Value

Land Cost: Single-Family Dwelling Lots

	100'	100'	100'	100'	100'		Land Cost	
	1	2	3	4	5		Lot	Cost
150'	$15,000	$17,000	$14,000	$20,000	$19,500		1	$15,000
	6	7	8	9	10		2	17,000
150'	$19,000	$15,000	$16,000	$19,200	$16,500		3	14,000
							4	20,000
							5	19,500
							6	19,000
		500'					7	15,000
							8	16,000
		Multiple-Family Site					9	19,200
300'		150,000 square feet					10	16,500
		(3.444 acres)					Total Cost	$171,200

Market Value

Multiple-family use	
150,000 square feet, @ $3.00 per square foot	$450,000
Less cost of assembled land	171,200
Plottage value	$278,800

Figure 9-3 indicates that 10 lots were assembled at a total cost of $171,200. The lot prices vary because of the negotiated prices paid to separate owners. Given the total cost of $171,200 derived from single-family dwelling use, the ten lots have an assembled area of 150,000 square feet for multiple-family use with an estimated value of $3.00 per square foot, or $450,000. Subtracting the cost of the assembled land indicates a plottage value of *$278,800.*

Two conditions must be met to result in plottage value: sites must be available at their per parcel price for the present use and the assembled property must be usable for a higher use. It is the value of the larger parcel in a more intensive commercial use that provides for the plottage value increment—in this case, $278,800.

THE VALUATION OF SUBDIVISION LAND

Two issues stand out in appraising subdivisions: judging marketability and estimating the present value of deferred income. Judging marketability is a process of weighing relative attractiveness and amenities. The present value of deferred income depends on the number of annual lot sales and their cost of development.

Subdivision Marketability

Valuing land for potential subdivisions starts with a preliminary study of land use controls that restrict subdivision development. The proposed subdivision must conform to environmental laws and local and state land use controls.

SUBDIVISION FEATURES

In particular, land in the following categories is generally subject to restrictive land use controls:

waterfront properties
recreational areas
land near major transportation facilities
industrial projects
major residential projects

Further, the National Flood Insurance Act of 1973 governs development in areas subject to flooding. If the proposed land is affected by unduly restrictive controls, the project may not be feasible. The suitability of subdivision land is indicated by:

accessibility
adjoining land use
transportation facilities
property taxes
utility availability
subdivision requirements
land use controls

In addition, certain community facilities must serve the subdivision. A location within one mile of a school adds to residential lot value. However, a dwelling next to a school may have less value because of distracting noise during the school day.

To maximize site utility, subdivisions are convenient to churches, recreational facilities, and other community facilities. Most developers allocate a portion of the subdivision for recreation. Because of the importance of community facilities, an appraisal checklist may be used to evaluate the site. A checklist for this purpose would also include:

distance from employment (or city center)
type of surrounding developments
distance to main highways
distance to nearby thoroughfares
driving time to shopping centers
distance to airport
encroachments of incompatible land uses
sewer availability
water supply and its cost
zoning and other restrictions

First, identify each characteristic, then compare land prices in the light of these features, and finally, establish the annual land sales of competing subdivisions.

PROJECTING LOT SALES

In the appraisal of a proposed subdivision, it was estimated that the local unsold lot inventory totaled 35,999 in the market area. Over the preceding year, the four competing subdivisions had lot sales ranging from .57 per month to 2.10 per month.

Subdivision	Lot Sales per Month	Number of Months
1	.67	6
2	1.13	8
3	2.10	8
4	.57	6

Since the sales record for each subdivision covered the last year and the lot demand was increasing, it was concluded that two lot sales per month would be a reasonable sales projection.

In the valuation of a proposed waterfront subdivision on the west coast of Florida, the records of five waterfront subdivisions in the same market area indicated the annual rate of land absorption of lots similar to the subdivision appraised. While the subdivisions differed considerably in lot size, amenities, and location, the data probably furnished the best objective measure of forecasting future lot sales.

Table 9-2 shows such a comparison for a proposed subdivision on the west coast of Florida. The five subdivisions of waterfront lots are identified according to the total number of lots, the number unsold, the typical prices for inside and waterfront lots, and the age of the subdivision.

For example, some 200 lots were sold over a three-year period in the Tierra Verde subdivision—approximately 67 lots per year. By comparing the relative merits of the existing subdivision with the proposed development, some estimate of the projected sales may be made, weighed by the special advantages of the project under appraisal.

Table 9-2   Market Data of Comparable Subdivsions

Name of Subdivision	Number of Lots	Number Unsold	Typical Prices Waterfront Lots	Inside Lots	Age of Subdivision (years)
Ozona Shores	190	57	$92,500	$ 66,000	5
Fairway Estates	470	120	$123,800	$ 69,500	4
Island Estates	231	31	$115,000	$ 68,000	6
Harbor Bluffs Isle	115	95	$108,800		4
Tierra Verde	850	650	$135,000	$ 65,600	3

Present Value of Deferred Income

Given the sales projection, the next problem is to calculate the present worth of annual net income. Unlike an annuity, net income from a subdivision varies annually. Not only does the number of sales vary each year, but future lot prices change. Moreover, heavy development costs in the initial years cause fluctuations in annual net income. After adjusting for annual variations in cost, net income may be projected over the sales period. Market value results from discounting the expected net income. To illustrate, assume a subdivision of 100 lots with a cost of $13,000 per acre, three subdivided lots per acre, and development costs of $5,000 per lot. With a projection of lot sales per year, annual net income is given by deducting the expected cost of development experienced over five years. See Table 9-3. Note that in the first year a net loss is experienced. By totaling the present worth of the annual income, in this case discounted by 10 percent, the subdivision has a net profit over the five years of $737,500. These figures must be discounted to present worth. Hence, if these assumptions are realized, the investor will earn a yield of 10 percent on the project.

For an existing subdivision, project the number of lot sales per year and estimate lot prices for future years. Table 9-4 indicates the present value of a 124-lot subdivision, assuming 24 lots sold annually with an estimated ten percent price increase per year. Using a 12 percent discount factor, the subdivision has an estimated value of $1,150,000.

Table 9-3   Projected Net Income from Lot Sales

End of Period	Annual Expenses	Gross Lot Sales	Annual Net Income	Present Value (ten percent)
Year 1	$300,000	$ 250,000	($ 50,000)	($ 45,455)
Year 2	100,000	312,500	212,500	175,610
Year 3	100,000	300,000	200,000	150,260
Year 4	50,000	300,000	250,000	170,500
Year 5	50,000	175,000	125,000	77,613
Total	$600,000	$1,337,500	$737,500	$619,438

Table 9-4   The Estimated Market Value of a Subdivision of 124 Lots

Profit Statement	End of Year				
	1	2	3	4	5
Average sales price	$15,000	$16,500	$17,150	$18,865	$20,750
	x 24	x 24	x 24	x 24	x 24
Gross Income	$360,000	$396,000	$411,600	$452,760	$498,000
Less estimated expenses:					
Selling expense, 10%	$36,000	$39,600	$41,160	$45,276	$49,800
Taxes on remaining lots	9,600	7,200	4,800	2,400	- - -
Maintenance of public areas, @ $150/ lot/month	14,400	10,800	7,200	3,600	- - -
Overhead 10%	36,000	39,600	41,160	45,276	49,800
Total expenses	- 96,000	- 97,200	- 94,320	- 96,552	- 99,600
Estimated net profit	$264,000	$298,800	$317,280	$356,208	$398,400
	x .892857	x .797194	x .711780	x .635518	x .567426
Present worth, 12% discount	$235,714	$237,564	$225,834	$226,377	$226,063

Estimated market value $1,151,552
(rounded) $1,150,000

SUMMARY

In valuing sites, descriptive data should be sufficient to support the estimate of land value. Here *locational characteristics* assume major importance, such as distance to traffic interchange points, convenience to mass transportation, and convenience to shopping. Appraisal location maps show the distance to community facilities.

Residential lots are described in terms of their front feet, depth, land area, shape, and topography. If the land is irregular, special comments are required to show how the shape adds or detracts from site utility. *Topography* is usually judged according to whether the lot is level or sloping and the degree of slope. Lots below the street grade generally have less value than lots above the street grade. Lot utilities relate to the availability and cost of sewers, natural gas, cable television, and like services in comparison to competing land.

Site improvements are equally valid—sidewalks, concrete curbs, storm sewers, and street width, among other items, determine site utility. *Community facilities* that influence site values relate to schools, churches, libraries, playgrounds, parks, and other features important to the locality.

Land use restrictions have equal importance, particularly zoning codes that control housing density. Similarly, *environmental controls* that restrict the use of coal or wood stoves or domestic water deserve weight in estimating value. Sites will be judged according to how subdivisions and deed restrictions preserve neighborhood amenities. The degree of control over architecture and building standards warrants review. Certain other *general site characteristics,* including surrounding land uses, property taxes, and the subdivision layout add or detract from utility and, therefore, its value.

The *comparable sales approach* is the leading method to value sites. The listing of each comparable sale allows clients to follow the valuation logic. A *sales presentation* may be arranged to give ownership details, the legal description, the land area and other data on zoning, the sales price per unit, and comments on how a particular sale relates to the estimated value.

Corner influence and site *depth,* for residential and commercial sites, require review according to local practices and according to the market. The *sales presentation* emphasizes main differences between the property sold and the property appraised. The *sales summary* leads to the final value estimate.

Land residual techniques depend on the fact that market value equals the land and building value. Assuming the highest and best use, land value may be derived by deducting income to the building. The remaining income to the land is capitalized to derive the land value—the land residual technique.

The *allocation technique* is for residential lots. The technique assumes a typical relationship between land and building value. Given the land/building value ratio, the site value may be derived from the total property value. The *extraction technique,* highly subjective, starts with the proposition that every building has a "contributory value." Under this technique, the appraiser determines how much a building contributes to property value. Given the property value and the contributory building value, the appraiser "extracts" the land value.

For properties under lease, the appraiser may estimate the market *ground rent* and capitalize the *ground rent* at the market capitalization rate. Site value follows from the present value of the annual site rent. *Plottage value is the added value resulting from the assembly of small sites into a larger tract.* Plottage value arises from the fact that larger sites have greater utility than individual sites. Plottage values typically result from the merger of residential lots into a larger site that has a higher use. Plottage value is caused by the *change in use* arising from a higher use of the larger, assembled site.

In valuing a *subdivision,* the first task is to estimate the *market rate of absorption.* Competing subdivisions and the number of sites sold in the past are reviewed for an indication of local site values and demand. Characteristics of competing subdivisions are reviewed before *projecting lot sales* over the estimated marketing period. Given a projection of proposed lot sales, the appraiser then calculates the net income per year. The subdivision has value according to the present value of annual net income.

POINTS TO REMEMBER

location map a map showing the site location in relation to other community facilities.

off-site improvements sidewalks, streets, street width, storm sewers, street lighting, and other neighborhood facilities that serve the site under valuation.

subdivision layout the general plan of a subdivision, i.e., square lots and blocks or a curvilinear layout plan.

corner influence an increment in value assigned to a corner lot.

allocation technique a method of valuing sites by applying the prevailing land/building ratio to properties of known value.

extraction method a method of valuing sites by subtracting the building "contributory value" from the property value.

ground rent net annual rent for vacant land which may be capitalized to estimate site value.

plottage value the added value resulting from the assembly of small sites into a larger parcel. Plottage value arises from the change in use from that assigned to smaller parcels.

QUESTIONS FOR REVIEW

1. In valuing a residential lot for middle income housing, what location characteristics would you consider? Explain fully.

2. In valuing sites, what is the relative importance of area variables? Explain how a 40,000 square foot residential lot may have more value than a 100,000 square foot residential lot. Give examples in illustration of your answer.

3. In your view, how do site improvements affect value? Give examples.

4. Make a list of land use restrictions that you believe will enhance market value; make a list of land restrictions that detract from site value. Give reasons for your answer.

5. Explain how surrounding land uses may lower site values.

6. What are the minimum sale characteristics you would cite in valuing a single family dwelling site?

7. Critically evaluate site value under the *land residual* technique, the *allocation* technique and the *extraction* method. Show advantages and weaknesses of each method.

8. Explain your concept of plottage value. What is the leading explanation of plottage value? Explain thoroughly.

9. Explain how you would establish the absorption rate of a proposed subdivision.

10. Given the projected rate of absorption of a proposed subdivision, show how you would estimate market value.

PRACTICE PROBLEMS

1. You are valuing a 20-acre site for a proposed subdivision of middle income houses. You estimate that the average lot price will be $30,000 at the current market. Outline your proposal to value the subdivision including your plan to estimate the market rate of absorption, and how you would value the subdivision according to the present value of net income over the marketing period. Make other assumptions as necessary.

2. You must value a luxury home site which will be acquired by the state highway department for a right-of-way. You must present your valuation evidence in court. Indicate the evidence that you would present to defend your estimate of market value, including maps and other recommended exhibits.

C H A P T E R   1 0

Building Analysis

After reading this chapter you will know:
- Recommended techniques to judge building utility.
- Orderly methods of describing buildings.
- Methods of judging the quality of building construction.

Appraisers face three tasks in valuing buildings. First, the appraiser judges the general *building utility*. The issue here is whether the building is suited for its original purpose; alternatively the appraiser estimates the extent to which the building conforms to the estimate of highest and best use.

Given these conclusions, the appraiser then describes building features. The *building description,* described with all its components, leads to the third issue: what are the final judgments over the *quality of materials and workmanship?* After forming these judgments, the appraiser proceeds to other aspects of the valuation process. Hence, the chapter is organized around these three main issues: building utility, the building description, and the quality of construction.

JUDGING BUILDING UTILITY

Judging building utility is probably the most critical aspect of real estate appraising. The estimate of building utility affects the depreciation adjustment under the cost technique, sales adjustments necessary to the market approach, and the estimate of gross income, operating expenses, and capitalization rates common to the income approach. The building analysis adapts to the type of building under appraisal: single-family dwellings, multiple-family dwellings, commercial real estate, or industrial property. Building analysis for agricultural property is especially critical because of the rapidly changing agricultural technology.

Single-Family Dwellings

Judging the functional utility of a single-family dwelling depends on a detailed knowledge of comparable dwelling sales. Familiarity with local transactions helps the appraiser avoid problems of personal bias. The main issue is not to estimate what the value *should be* in the opinion of the appraiser, but to estimate market value according to values indicated by free negotiations between buyers and sellers.

Thus, the value is not necessarily assumed by the cost of building construction and its assumed depreciation; market value estimates and building utility are *imputed* from recent sales of like houses, preferably in the same neighborhood. To this end, single-family-dwelling utility is judged with respect to building services. In judging these services the appraiser observes the *principal of proportionality*.

A bedroom measuring 10 feet by 12 feet with limited closet space would be adequate for a two-bedroom dwelling of 720 square feet. Such a bedroom generally would be judged inadequate for a 5,000-square-foot dwelling of five bedrooms. In other words, the appraiser judges the market so that components of the dwelling and its floor plan conform to the market ideal of the "right" building proportions.

In this respect, consider the problem of judging the utility of a 20 foot by 20 foot, 400-square-foot bedroom addition to a house originally measuring 930 square feet. Such a new bedroom addition would be "out of proportion" to other building rooms.

The same conclusions follow for building equipment such as hot water heaters, heating and air conditioning systems, carports, and other building elements. Thus, a given building feature (for example, an elaborate fireplace) would be quite adequate for a 4,000-square-foot dwelling, but out of proportion for a modest 1,220-square-foot dwelling. Appraisers would refer to such an improvement as *super adequate,* i.e., "the building construction illustrates superadequacy." The principle of proportionality applies not only to the utility of the building but to other building features.

With this qualification, dwellings are judged with respect to building services, the building equipment, and building construction.

DWELLING SERVICES

Dwellings divide functionally into three areas: the sleeping area, the living area, and the service area. Bedrooms, closets, bathrooms, and dressing rooms make up the *sleeping area.* The living room, dining room, and the recreational room or family room represent the *living area. Service areas* include kitchens, laundry rooms, pantries, sewing rooms, music rooms, libraries, hobby rooms, and the like.

To serve these three functional areas, houses have a circulation system of doors, halls, stairways, guest entrances, and family or service entrances. In this respect each service area and the number of rooms and their relative size should conform to buyer and seller preferences. Therefore, a *two-bedroom* house would be quite acceptable in neighborhood A but substandard in neighborhood B, an area of *three- and four-bedroom dwellings.*

FLOOR PLAN.   Poor floor plans decrease functional utility. Appraisers frequently encounter dwellings with additional living space provided by enclosed and remodeled garages or carports, or bedrooms added to the original house. For a single-family dwelling, frequently the only alternative is to add a new bedroom by adding an addition as shown in Figure 10-1. In this illustration, while the third bedroom adds some utility, the floor plan is fairly awkward since access to the third bedroom is through a second bedroom, resulting in functional obsolescence. The floor plan illustrates functional obsolescence because, if the building were constructed new, it would not follow the floor plan of Figure 10-1.

FLOOR AREA. Since building utility and building costs are based on the square-foot floor area, floor plan measurement must follow standard practice. The square-foot floor area includes *outside dimensions of the heated living area.* On appraisal forms for single-family dwellings, this area is shown as the gross living area.

The square-foot floor area excludes the square-foot area of garages, carports, porches (open or enclosed and unheated), unheated utility space attached to the garage or carport, and open, unfinished basements

Figure 10-1   Awkward Floor Plan Resulting from Bedroom Addition

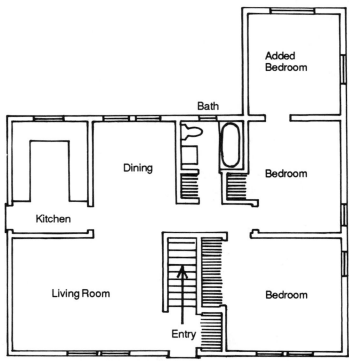

and attics. While these areas add utility, they are separately accounted for and not included in the square-foot floor area.

Figure 10-2 shows the standard method of calculating dwelling square-foot floor area. The procedure starts with the measurement of the *maximum building width and length,* outside dimensions. The court areas are subtracted from the product. In this example it will be noted that the attached garage is listed separately. Porches and patios, which contribute to value, are also listed and treated separately. Generally, appraisers provide measurements to the closest six inches or the tenth part of a foot.

If the dwelling includes a finished attic, the attic would be added to the square-foot floor area. The same point holds true for finished rooms in a split-level dwelling. For a second floor, the ground floor area is doubled.

Figure 10-2   Square-Foot Floor Area Measurements

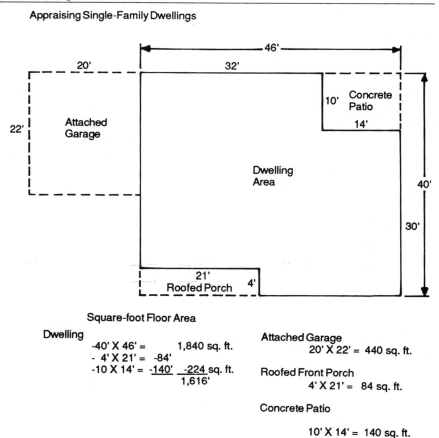

Appraising Single-Family Dwellings

Square-foot Floor Area

Dwelling
-40' X 46' =   1,840 sq. ft.
- 4' X 21' =   -84'
-10 X 14' = -140'   -224 sq. ft.
                    1,616'

Attached Garage
        20' X 22' = 440 sq. ft.

Roofed Front Porch
        4' X 21' = 84 sq. ft.

Concrete Patio

        10' X 14' = 140 sq. ft.

Basement rooms, finished after original construction, are usually not included in the ground floor but valued on a lump-sum basis according to the contribution the room makes toward market value. Added basement or attic rooms, to qualify as separate rooms, must have a minimum area of 100 square feet and a minimum clear ceiling height of seven feet.

In judging floor plans, rooms for the three main service areas must be appropriate for the house. In the kitchen, especially, the range, oven, sink, and other equipment must conform to acceptable design standards for the dwelling under valuation. Figure 10-3 illustrates the most common kitchen floor plans. Departures from these illustrations require deductions for functional obsolescence. The luxury house would have more space and the latest equipment. Older and lower-priced houses must be judged with respect to the market acceptance of equipment commonly found in the house appraised.

MECHANICAL EQUIPMENT

The mechanical equipment, for example, plumbing, kitchen appliances, laundry facilities, air conditioning, and communication and electrical systems, should be appropriate for the dwelling appraised and the neighborhood. Quite obviously, building equipment for a $500,000 luxury home would be inappropriate for a middle-income house of 1,800 square feet.

The heating and air-conditioning system should be reviewed for its capacity, present condition, and suitability for the house valued. Similarly, the plumbing, the number of bathrooms, and fixtures should meet local neighborhood standards. Other equipment such as communication systems, fire and burglar alarm systems, radio-operated garage doors, and special music, television, and telephone systems fall in these groups. These items would be judged according to their *value contribution* to the house appraised, as indicated by local market preferences.

Commercial Buildings

Judging the functional utility of commercial buildings covers a wide range of building requirements. For the present purpose attention is directed to retail and office buildings.

SHOPPING CENTERS

For shopping centers, factors that determine building utility include minimum ceiling heights. A building that does not have the required ceiling height for overhead lighting and advertising signs does not meet

Figure 10-3   Representative Kitchen Floor Plans

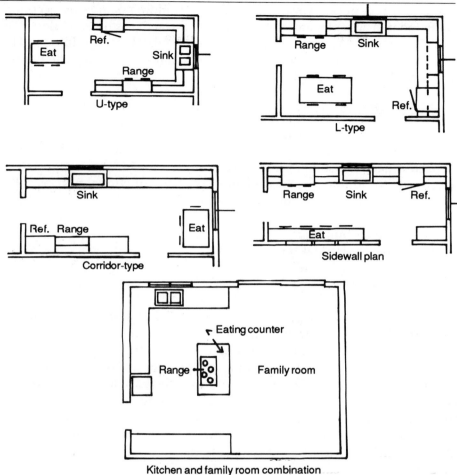

minimum retail building requirements. In other instances, retail structures may be poorly adapted to the site because buildings are below street
grade and concealed from highway traffic.

Retail buildings may have a poor building layout unless the building
conforms to common layout standards. For example, space allocated to
large-volume retailers such as supermarkets, discount drug stores, and
department stores must have the best possible access to and locations near
central parking areas. Other retail tenants with less patronage are sited in
less accessible locations—mainly, dry cleaners, restaurants, and the many
other smaller retailers.

Retail buildings follow floor plans that locate tenants to maximize customer traffic generated by the larger stores. Building plans must accommodate tenants who locate near mutually attractive stores. Unless retail buildings conform to these building layout standards, the building will lack retail utility. In short, the critical question relates to how well the building is adapted to commercial uses.

OFFICE BUILDINGS

Office buildings range from one story buildings in suburban locations to multiple-story structures in metropolitan areas. In each case the building is partitioned into smaller work spaces for professional, managerial, and clerical staff. Building utility depends upon the functional purpose of the building which generally divides into four groups:

1. Institutional buildings
2. General commercial buildings
3. Medical/dental buildings
4. Industrial office space

Institutional buildings serve commercial banks and companies that construct buildings for their own use. General commercial buildings house professional tenants and the service industries that require convenient access to transportation and customers. A prestige address is less important than the convenience to transportation. Medical/dental buildings are special-purpose buildings that combine space for medical services, supplies, pharmacies, laboratories, and other medical professions. These buildings are specially designed buildings in close proximity to hospitals. The industrially oriented building is found in organized industrial parks tenanted primarily by printers, distributors, and manufacturers who combine manufacturing with office headquarters.

Given the adaptability of the office building for a selected function, the next critical question relates to space measurement. Appraisers judge office buildings and the capitalization of net income according to two space measurements—*rentable space* and *usable square feet*. These square-foot measurements help determine building functional utility.

The building assumes value according to the space available to tenants, the largest block of contiguous space, space available for the smallest tenant, the tenant bay depth (the distance from the core wall to the windows), and the designer shape of each floor. The answer to these questions largely depends on the available rentable and usable square feet.

For appraisal purposes, office buildings include the *usable square feet,* which is the space available to tenants, not including public and service areas. Technically, the usable area is calculated by:

> *measuring to the finished surface of the office side of corridors and other permanent walls, to the center partitions that separate the office from adjoining usable areas, and to the inside finished surface of the dominant portion of the permanent outer building walls.*

This definition defines a space available to tenants in less public and service areas.

The *rentable square-foot* area includes a pro rata share of common areas such as the washrooms, corridors, and service areas for full-floor tenants. The rentable areas are found by:

> *measuring to the inside finished surface of the dominant portion of the permanent outer building walls, excluding any major vertical penetrations of the floor.*[1]

This area includes the washrooms and service areas on each floor but excludes elevator and stairway space, which are major vertical penetrations of the floor. Capitalization of the rents for an office building appraisal may be based on the usable area or rental area, provided the appraiser identifies the measurement employed. In other respects, the appraiser values an office building according to how it adapts to its particular function.

Industrial Buildings

Industrial buildings covering warehouses, multiple-story structures, and newer single-story construction must follow common industrial practices. Industrial buildings are best judged by two broad classifications: *plant layout* and *type of construction.* In the former case, buildings constructed for manufacturing generally follow a floor plan adapted to a product layout or process layout. Certain manufacturing activities are adapted to assembly operations which represent a less common but third alternative.

PRODUCT LAYOUT

Industrial buildings following a product layout scheme are adapted to assembly lines in which machinery is laid out according to a sequence of

---

1 Definitions are from the American National Standard Z65.1—1980 as quoted by Managing the Office Building, Revised Edition, (Chicago, Illinois: Institute of Real Estate Management, 1985), pp. 60–66.

operations. Equipment is arranged so that industrial processes are coordinated and organized around a single product providing for the latest automated material-handling equipment. Such buildings have certain common features:

1. They require a minimum area for material storage.
2. Traffic movement is minimized.
3. Buildings provide for the continuous flow of raw materials through the plant to the finished product.

Buildings following this plan are generally one story, with ceiling heights that permit overhead automated machinery. Floors are built for relatively heavy floor loads. The site must be level and buildings must have the widest possible clear span that gives maximum flexibility in machinery placement.

PROCESS LAYOUT

Process layout buildings are constructed for manufacturing multiple products, such as building hardware, finished metal products for an industry such as the garment industry (i.e., belt buckles, clasps, buttons, pins and the like), and the manufacture of metal hand tools. For such products, machines are grouped by processes.

For example, in prefabricated metal production, machines that perform similar operations will be arranged in functional groups. Operations that require lathes, drilling machines, planers, grinders, and metal finishing machines are a case in point.

Plants organized under this system provide for the movement of goods from operation to operation in batches or lots. Accordingly, buildings adapted to process layout will:

require space for storage at each process center.
have the largest possible floor area unrestricted by posts and columns.
have space available between process centers.
provide for maximum flexibility in regrouping of process centers.

Besides product and process layouts, buildings may be adapted to *assembly operation* for a single product. For example, airplane manufacturing requires that component parts and various types of skilled labor come to a particular product for final assembly.

Manufacturing firms, therefore, construct buildings for a particular use. Consequently, an industrial building must be considered in the light of its utility for general industrial purposes. It follows that a building designed for the original occupant may be obsolete for local industry. A building designed originally for a product layout and abandoned by the original occupant would be functionally inadequate for a process layout operation. It will be appreciated that the estimate of highest and best use assumes considerable importance in valuing industrial buildings.

TYPE OF CONSTRUCTION

Industrial buildings may be one-story or multiple-story. For other purposes, it is important to consider construction materials that are nonflammable, such as concrete, steel, aluminum, and brick. Even within these classifications, buildings show considerable variation.

One-story buildings may show various combinations of roof construction, namely sawtooth, gable, flat, and various combinations of girder-supported roofs, trusses, or column supports. For example, one-story buildings provide greater flexibility in plant layout, though they require more land area. Single-story buildings have greater floor load-bearing ability and lower construction costs per square foot.

Multiple-story buildings have certain initial advantages over one-story construction. While multiple-story buildings were common before World War I, today modern multiple-story buildings are found primarily in densely populated areas (Europe and Southeast Asia). The main advantages of multiple-story buildings may be listed in five points:

1. Multiple-story buildings conserve land.
2. With relatively high land values, it may be more economical to construct additional floors over available industrial land.
3. The protective ceilings of multiple-story buildings lower heating and air-conditioning expenses.
4. Multiple-story buildings are adapted to gravity flow, production lines, or multiple-product manufacturing.
5. Plants manufacturing by job lots may economically use multiple-story buildings because floor load requirements are low and manufacturing may be economically arranged at processing stations on various floors.

Judged according to type of construction, modern industrial buildings will provide wall and ceiling insulation, overhead sprinklers, and automated building equipment. Wood frame buildings have relatively low floor load-bearing capacities; they are limited to one or two stories and have relatively high maintenance costs. Wood-frame buildings have low initial construction costs and are less expensive to alter, expand, or remove.

BUILDING DESCRIPTIONS

The term *land improvements* may include buildings. However, this term typically refers to nonbuilding structures. In this group are included fences, sidewalks, driveways, and other on-site improvements such as concrete pipes, drainage systems, water pipes, and other utility construction. To avoid confusion, though buildings are technically "land improvements," this discussion is confined to building structures.

For appraisal purposes, buildings are described in terms of their exterior, interior, and mechanical systems. These main components are described in sufficient detail to support cost and depreciation estimates, sales adjustments, the income approach, and the highest and best use estimate. To this end, appraisers avoid describing construction trivia.

Building Exterior

Description of the building exterior supports judgments on the quality of construction and the present building condition. It may be expected that the building structure conforms to local building codes. However, poor quality materials, questionable workmanship, and lack of building code enforcement require judgments over the building exteriors for new and existing buildings.

For example, *foundations* must not show structural weaknesses. Even in new buildings, cracks in concrete or concrete block foundations may be indicative of differential settlement. Structural weaknesses stemming from poorly constructed or damaged foundations are evidenced by windows and doors that bind and by cracks in interior or exterior walls. Foundations must meet local standards governing foundation walls and supporting posts and pillars in crawl spaces under first-floor areas.

A brief description of *exterior walls,* their present condition and material, further supports the estimate of physical depreciation. Wood siding in need of paint or structural or physical deterioration of exterior surfaces would be reported in this portion of the appraisal report. The roof material and its condition adds to accurate valuation estimates.

In this analysis, the appraiser notes deficiencies in roof gutters and downspouts. In this respect, downspouts should provide for water drainage away from building foundations. Moisture from roof surfaces allowed to collect around foundation footings, leads to building settlement and moisture damage to basements or floor joists from the resulting dampness.

Building Interior

The floors, walls, and ceilings are described for each room in sufficient detail to indicate building utility and condition. For a single-family dwelling, the appraiser indicates the floor covering in the main rooms with special attention given to kitchen and bathrooms. Physical wear and tear on floor surfaces, including wall-to-wall carpeting, supports judgments over the building value in its present condition. Wall surfaces, their construction, materials, and present condition, described by room, add further to valuation accuracy. The appraiser notes differences in wall paneling (whether it is veneer or solid wood) and in interior wood trim (whether it is painted wood or metal or hardwood trim, which is more expensive). Space is provided in most common appraisal forms for these details.

Mechanical Systems

The analysis of mechanical systems varies by property type. For single-family dwellings the appraiser indicates plumbing facilities in kitchen and bathrooms. Kitchens vary according to the quality and adequacy of kitchen sinks, appliances, hot water heating systems, and the like. Unusually low or high quality items in kitchens or bathrooms would warrant additional descriptive detail. The building description covers the electrical system, including alarm systems and special electrical wiring that controls inside and outside lighting, other fixtures, communications, and entertainment equipment.

For commercial and industrial buildings, this portion of the report would be considerably more detailed, but in each instance the appraisal report would cover the building mechanical system adapted to the appraisal problem at hand. A warehouse with an automated material-handling system would deserve descriptive detail that varies from a multiple-story, rehabilitated industrial building. Similarly, luxury housing would have features especially adapted to the building structure which would not be found in other property types or less expensive housing.

In short, if the appraisal report follows the narrative style, the appraiser has more flexibility in emphasizing unique features of buildings. Though detail would vary, the narrative appraisal report would generally cover the following list:

architectural style	building equipment
building age	heating and air-conditioning
square-foot floor area	plumbing
description of floor plan	electrical wiring and fixtures
description by rooms	fireplace
basement features	energy conservation construction
exterior	wall insulation
foundation	floor and ceiling insulation
walls	double pane windows
gutters and downspouts	energy-efficient fireplaces
roof	other energy-efficient
interior	construction
floor covering and condition	site improvements
interior trim	landscaping
built-in cabinets	walks
insulation	driveway
kitchen construction	fencing
bathroom finish	drainage

Again the appraisal report would include details important to the particular appraisal report. In each instance, though varying in detail, the building description would cover the exterior, interior, and building systems. The remaining issue relates to the quality of construction.

QUALITY OF CONSTRUCTION

Building analysis would be incomplete without an evaluation of construction quality. In the building inspection, appraisers form judgments over the quality of materials and workmanship. Two buildings of identical design may have different values, according to variations in construction quality.

Building Materials

Quality materials would be evidenced by solid hardwood wall panels relative to hardwood *veneer* panels. A fireplace mantel constructed of marble or stone would be indicative of higher quality construction compared to most brick veneer fireplaces. Experienced appraisers easily note differences in the quality of plumbing fixtures, according to standard brands. They make careful comparisons of bathroom fixtures and the quality of plumbing components. Bathrooms with ceramic tile floors and walls are evidence of higher-quality construction than painted wallboard and vinyl or linoleum floors. Similarly, kitchen equipment and appliances would be classified as average or above average quality.

Workmanship

Workmanship will be evidenced in the appearance of finished kitchen cabinets, the detailed workmanship shown in door and window moldings, wall and floor finishes, and exterior construction details. Consequently, in the building inspection, besides listing building features, the appraiser forms judgments over the construction quality. The importance of this exercise relates to the comparison of real estate sales of like quality with the property appraised. The same reasoning holds in making cost comparisons. The cost per square foot applied to the property appraised must relate closely to the actual costs of constructing buildings of similar quality.

Again, care must be taken in placing too much value on over improvements. That is, a ceramic tile bathroom wall and floor may be inappropriate for a modest 1,000-square-foot building. While the ceramic tile construction may satisfy the present owner, it does not follow that for a more modest dwelling and neighborhood such *atypical* construction adds value equal to its cost.

Probably the most important element here is to insure that a dwelling in a neighborhood of luxury dwellings conforms closely to the neighborhood standard. Similarly, a house constructed in a neighborhood of average construction and materials must closely conform to surrounding property. The appraisal reviewer will judge the appraisal according to the conformity of the property under appraisal with local market preferences.

To a large degree, the quality of construction is common to building components. A builder who specializes in constructing inexpensive dwellings economizes in selecting building materials and the quality of workmanship. Inexpensive carpets would generally be associated with lower-grade lumber in the wood frame. A builder who economizes in the quality of kitchen cabinets would be expected to economize in the quality of workmanship.

At the other extreme, evidence of high-quality building materials would be associated with skilled workmanship and finer building finishing, painting, wall finishes, cabinet work, and other building components showing skilled craftsmanship. In judging construction quality, appraisers generally conclude that observed construction features control other building components. The same tendency holds for luxury buildings showing a high degree of observed craftsmanship and quality materials that generally prevails throughout the building

SUMMARY

The utility of single-family dwellings is imputed from recent sales of like houses. In judging building services, appraisers observe the principal of proportionality. For example, the square-foot area of bedrooms acceptable in a 720-square-foot dwelling would be unacceptable in a 5,000-square-foot dwelling. The same conclusions follow for other building components.

Given this qualification, *building services* are analyzed according to the *sleeping, living,* and *service areas.* Dwelling services are judged according to the floor plan and the square-foot floor area consisting of the heated area, calculated from outside dimensions. Buildings are judged according to their *mechanical equipment* which is reviewed according to how appropriate building systems are adapted to the building appraised and the neighborhood.

Buildings for shopping centers are analyzed with reference to building adaptability: minimum ceiling heights and a building layout that maximizes retail sales. For multiple-tenant buildings, floor plans maximize customer traffic generated by the larger stores.

Office buildings, ranging from one-story buildings in the suburbs to downtown multiple-story buildings, divide into four groups: *institutional buildings, general commercial buildings, medical/dental buildings,* and *industrial office space.* In each instance, office buildings are adapted for a selected function.

Building space will be analyzed according to the rentable space or the usable square feet. *Usable square feet* defines space available to tenants, less public service areas. The *rentable square-foot area* includes a pro rata share of common areas such as public rooms and service areas for full-floor tenants. Appraisers identify building measurements used for appraisal purposes.

Industrial buildings are judged according to the *plant layout* and *type of construction.* In the former case, buildings may be designed to produce a single product, i.e., assembly lines for *product layout* or a *process layout* manufacturing multiple products. A process layout requires space for storage at process centers and the largest possible floor area unrestricted by posts and columns. Certain products, such as aircraft, are adapted to assembly operations in which component parts and labor are centered around a particular product.

Industrial buildings assume utility according to the *type of construction,* whether single-story or multiple-story. Single-story buildings have greater floor load-bearing capacity and lower construction costs per square foot. Multiple-story buildings conserve land and are adapted to relatively high land values. They are adapted to job lot production and have lower heating and air-conditioning expenses. Industrial buildings classified by type of construction cover wood-frame buildings or various fire-resistant materials.

Appraisers describe buildings according to the *exterior*—the foundations, exterior walls, and roof. *Building interiors* cover detail on floors, interior walls, ceilings, and mechanical systems. The type of building determines descriptive detail of mechanical equipment.

The appraiser judges the *quality of construction* in terms of materials and workmanship. Quality judgments are less critical for middle- or lower-middle-income housing and are considerably stricter for luxury housing. The appraiser judges construction quality according to neighborhood standards and the type of building appraised.

POINTS TO REMEMBER

dwelling services the division of single-family dwellings into three functional areas—the sleeping area, the living area, and the service area.

gross living area square-foot floor area indicated by the outside dimensions of heated areas.

rentable square-foot area the square-foot area including a pro rata share of common areas such as washrooms, corridors, and service areas for full-floor tenants.

usable square feet the area for tenant use, not including public and service areas.

product layout a floor plan for industrial buildings adapted to assembly-line production, in which machinery is laid out according to a sequence of operations.

process layout an industrial building constructed for manufacturing multiple products.

QUESTIONS FOR REVIEW

1. In your view, why is the analysis of building utility important to the appraisal?

2. Explain how you would follow the principal of proportionality in judging the functional utility of a single-family dwelling.

3. What building features would you judge in evaluating dwelling services? Explain fully.

4. Give an example of how you would calculate the floor area of a single-family dwelling.

5. Contrast the mechanical equipment you would evaluate for a modern single-family dwelling of 1,000 square feet and a luxury dwelling of 5,000 square feet.

6. What factors would you consider in judging the utility of retail buildings? Explain thoroughly.

7. Explain how the functional utility of an office building depends on the functional purpose of the structure.

8. Give an example of the differences between rental space and usable space.

9. Explain the differences between industrial buildings constructed for product layout or for process layout.

10. Explain the types of manufacturing adapted to multiple-story industrial buildings; summarize the advantages of multiple-story industrial buildings.

11. Explain how you would organize a building description.

12. What factors would you consider in judging the quality of construction of a single-family dwelling? Give an example in illustration of your answer.

PRACTICE PROBLEMS

1. You accept an appraisal assignment to value a neighborhood shopping center of 68,000 square feet on an 8.1 acre site. The building is adapted to a supermarket, a discount drug store, and other tenants. What factors would you consider in evaluating the proposed commercial shopping center building? Include items you would cover in the building description and factors you would consider in judging building utility.

2. You are preparing a narrative appraisal report of a middle-income dwelling of 3,000 feet which will be taken for a highway right-of-way. In your narrative report, what factors would you consider in judging the utility of this building? Give illustrations in support of your answer.

C H A P T E R 1 1

The Cost Approach

After studying this chapter you will know:
- The procedure followed in describing buildings.
- Common applications of the cost approach.
- Methods of estimating cost.
- Sources of cost data.
- How to calculate depreciation.

The cost approach provides an estimate of market value based on the sum of the land value and the depreciated building value. Consequently, it is convenient to divide the chapter into five main parts. The chapter begins with techniques to describe buildings. Recommended applications of the cost technique are illustrated with selected cases. The chapter explains various methods of estimating building costs. This portion of the chapter ends with common sources of cost data. The chapter concludes with a discussion of recommended ways to estimate depreciation.

THE BUILDING DESCRIPTION

Building features are described in sufficient detail to justify the cost and depreciation estimates; descriptive trivia important to architects and contractors are avoided. The building description includes a general description, a review of building components, and generalization on building utility. The building description is organized to support the cost depreciation estimates.

General Description

Under this heading the appraiser describes general building features, i.e., the number of stories, the date of construction, and the main architectural features. If the appraisal covers more than one building, this portion of the report describes each building. The site plan, the building use, floor plan, and floor areas precede other building details.

Exterior

The exterior description depends on the type of building. Such a description would be highly detailed for an industrial plant. In each instance, the description includes the *foundation* which applies to residential, commercial, and industrial buildings. The exterior description includes window and door openings judged by the quality of construction and materials.

The type of roof, its architecture (shed, gable, saw-tooth, mansard, and others), and roof materials, including gutters, downspouts, and water drains, would be described to support judgments on cost and present condition. For a residential property, the building exterior is less detailed—the exterior siding, roof, and foundation.

Interior

The type of flooring, wall partitions, load-bearing members, and ceiling are explained in sufficient detail to support cost and depreciation estimates. For industrial plants, the ceiling height, column spacing, and clear floor spans are particularly important. The ceiling height relates to the utility of commercial or industrial buildings that require minimum ceiling heights. For office buildings, the interior description should be sufficiently complete to judge office building utility.

Equipment

Building equipment covers a wide range of features. The maximum electrical service and the air-conditioning and heating equipment, including the type of fuel, warrant detailed comment depending on the building type. Commercial buildings may have fire protection systems, including sprinklers (wet or dry systems) and other fire retardant construction, such as fire doors, alarm systems, and escape routes. Buildings equipped with a security system should be described showing how the system meets current requirements. Floor lighting and plumbing facilities, including their location, would be added to the building equipment description.

Utility

This part of the report allows the appraiser to summarize the general suitability of the building for its intended purpose. Limitations of the floor plan warrant special mention. For example, excessively wide corridors or, for multiple-story industrial buildings, space lost in elevator shafts and stairways deserves special comment.

Ceiling heights are described in relation to current practices or design standards. If the appraisal covers an industrial building, the adaptability of the building to modern industrial processes must be judged in the light of material handling equipment, industrial processes, and work flow. For single-family dwellings, a floor plan showing unusual room layout, room sizes, or awkward room placement would be explained.

COST-APPROACH APPRAISALS

The cost approach is frequently called the *summation method* because market value equals the sum of the depreciated building and land value. Actually, four items must be estimated under the cost approach: the building cost, site improvements costs, the depreciation allowance, and the land value. The following example shows, in short, how the market value would be estimated from these four factors:

Building cost (new)	$2,000,000
Land improvements (land leveling, paving, and landscaping)	300,000
Sum of Building + Land Improvements Costs	2,300,000
Less building depreciation	-500,000
Land & Building costs after depr	$1,800,000
Land value (estimated from comparable sales)	600,000
Market value	$2,400,000

The cost approach is a method of estimating market value from the land value and the cost of a new building, less depreciation. It is presumed that an informed purchaser would pay no more than what it would cost to produce a *substitute property* serving the same function and utility as the property appraised.

The Cost Approach Evaluated

Building #155,000
Land #18,000
Approx #173,000 Market Value

It would be reasonable to assume that a dwelling recently built for $155,000 on an $18,000 lot would have a market value approximating $173,000. In the usual case it would be unlikely for a builder to produce a house that would not sell for at least its cost of production. Similarly, buyers would be unwilling to pay more for a dwelling than the cost of building the same house new. Hence, assuming normal cost-market relationships, there is a tendency to imply that depreciated cost and value are synonymous.

Cost - depr = value

Because of the assumption that cost less depreciation tends to equal value, many hold that the cost estimate is the upper limit of value. However, on analysis, it is apparent that this conclusion rests on the assumption of perfect competition. In reality, market imperfections cause market prices to rise temporarily above the cost new. Rising short-run demand or restrictions on the supply of real estate, such as a shopping center with a location monopoly or a rising trend in a residential district, may produce market

Cost = Value

values considerably above cost. An expectation of higher rents may also justify market values that are higher than values estimated by the cost technique. In short, cost sets the upper limit of value under highly competitive conditions.

LIMITATIONS OF THE COST APPROACH

Cost of construction estimates vary because of:

1. differences in assumptions over the quality of workmanship and materials.
2. varying estimates of builder profit and overhead.
3. different degrees of builder efficiency.
4. the subjectivity of building depreciation.

Generally, cost estimates for new buildings may be verified by the cost of other similar buildings recently constructed. This advantage decreases as the age of buildings appraised increases. The more serious limitation, however, lies in the depreciation estimate. For older buildings, the degree of subjectivity in estimating depreciation seriously limits the accuracy of appraisals.

The fact remains, though, that the cost approach may be the only valuation alternative. In these circumstances, the appraiser makes the most accurate cost estimate possible, less a reasonable depreciation estimate. The depreciation allowance is based on logical reasons that support the cost approach.

ADVANTAGES OF THE COST APPROACH

The weakness of the cost approach raises serious questions on cost as a measure of market value. Indeed, the validity of sales comparisons and the income technique may render cost data irrelevant, especially for properties bought and sold on the basis of net income, such as retail buildings, apartments, office buildings, and other investment property. In estimating the market value of a single-family dwelling, heavy emphasis is placed on recent sales of similar property.

In these cases, market value, as estimated by the cost technique, may have little relevance, but it is difficult to avoid the cost technique in every instance. In fact, there are some appraisal problems for which this approach is particularly effective.

Cost-Approach Applications

The cost approach has important applications for new buildings, special purpose buildings, and certain other appraisal tasks.

NEW BUILDINGS

For a new building appropriate to the site, the cost approach provides an accurate market value estimate. Costs may be easily obtained for new buildings, since current costs of reproduction may be obtained for buildings recently constructed by local contractors. In addition, market value tends to be strongly supported by the reproduction cost, less depreciation, for buildings that represent the highest and best land use. In this case, depreciation would be nominal.

SPECIAL-PURPOSE BUILDINGS

Moreover, the cost technique is usually recommended for special-purpose buildings. Sales and income data are generally unavailable for wharves and piers, public buildings, industrial property, and buildings owned by charitable organizations such as churches. In these cases, appraisers are narrowly restricted in the choice of market value evidence; frequently, the cost approach produces the most acceptable—or only—evidence of value.

COST APPRAISALS REQUIRED

The cost technique has a wider application for certain specialized appraisals; for example, cost data are required for estimating insurable values. In appraising for proposed construction, appraisers rely heavily on the cost approach. For public buildings and large-scale industrial property such as refineries, textile plants, steel mills, or wharves and piers, the cost approach is virtually the only approach available. So although the cost approach has serious limitations, it is widely applied.

TYPES OF COST ESTIMATES

The accuracy of the cost approach depends in part on the relative proportion of land to total property value. For example, in appraising a $1,000,000 property with a land value of $900,000, the accuracy of the market value estimate rests largely on the land value estimate and not on the depreciated building cost. The converse is also true—highly refined cost data are required if the building value is relatively high compared to the land value.

Appraisal cost estimates may refer to *reproduction cost* or *replacement cost.* In either case, the appraiser estimates how much it would cost to build a new building today.

Reproduction Cost

Appraisals for insurance purposes (insurable value), appraisals for proposed building construction, and generally, appraisals for relatively new buildings require reproduction cost estimates. *Reproduction cost refers to the cost of constructing an identical building:* the building must be identical with respect to shape, structure, materials, and workmanship. It is accepted practice to derive the cost estimate from the costs of recently constructed buildings that were built in the same locality with the same materials as the building under appraisal. Cost evidence is readily available if these conditions are satisfied.

Replacement Cost

Reproduction costs would not apply to the valuation of a four-story industrial building constructed in 1890 or a dwelling built before World War II. A four-story textile mill built in 1890 would typically have solid brick walls three feet thick on the first floor, tapering to 12 inches on the fourth floor. Not only would it be virtually impossible to estimate the cost of reproducing a like building, but it is highly improbable that the building would be constructed today with the same architectural features. Modern textile mills, like other industrial buildings, are one story with relatively wide, clear roof spans of 100 feet or more and with 16-foot ceilings for automated machinery.

In these circumstances, appraisers use the *replacement cost: the cost of creating an equally desirable building that has the same utility as the property appraised.* Technically, the term has been defined as "the cost of construction at current prices of a building having utility equivalent to the building being appraised but built with modern materials and according to the current standards, design and layout."[1]

In the case of the 500,000-square-foot textile mill, the cost approach application would require a replacement cost estimate of a one-story

---

1 *The Dictionary of Real Estate Appraisal,* Second Edition, American Institute of Real Estate Appraisers, Chicago, Illinois, p. 254.

building constructed according to modern standards that would produce the same product and annual output.

For replacement cost estimates, it would be inaccurate to deduct an allowance for functional obsolescence, since the replacement cost concept corrects for losses in value from functional obsolescence. To be sure, the replacement cost estimate depends on highly personal value judgments; it is not always clear as to what type of building would serve the same utility.

Yet there is special need for a cost estimate to value properties that are not capable of being economically reproduced. For example, a single-family dwelling constructed before the Civil War would be irreplaceable in today's market, with such features as wood wainscoting, ceilings 12 feet high or more, solid brick fireplaces in almost every room, and unique exterior building trim not reproducible today. In these cases, the appraiser has only one alternative—to estimate the current cost of replacing the building with a structure that serves the same utility. If appropriate, the market or income approaches would probably yield a more accurate market value estimate.

Methods of Estimating Cost

Generally speaking, there are four methods of estimating building cost; the final method selected depends on the purpose of the appraisal, the degree of accuracy required, and the experience of the appraiser. Starting with the more detailed cost estimate, the *quantity survey,* the appraiser may also consider *unit-in-place costs,* and *unit comparisons.* In some instances, *cost manuals* that include published building costs by region and by several construction categories may be employed if local costs are unavailable. *Cost indexing* refers to the *updating of original construction costs by published cost indexes.*

THE QUANTITY SURVEY

The quantity survey is a cost estimate based on a detailed list of materials and their cost, labor costs, and contractor's overhead and profit.

HIGHLY DETAILED.   The quantity survey lists building materials that are individually priced. The amount of labor by type is estimated for each stage of construction. The contractor's overhead and profit, assuming typical management, completes the quantity survey estimate. Used by contractors in preparing bids for proposed construction, it is highly detailed and more accurate than other cost methods.

QUANTITY SURVEY EVALUATED.   Although the demonstrated accuracy of this method is certainly an advantage, there is a sizable expense involved in preparing such a detailed cost estimate—an expense that is usually unnecessary in a typical real estate appraisal. Moreover, preparation of such a cost estimate calls for considerable skill, experience, and professional knowledge of building prices, labor costs, and construction methods; few appraisers have expertise in each area. In addition, a detailed cost estimate is less important for buildings that show large-scale depreciation.

UNIT-IN-PLACE COSTS

Also known as the segregated cost method, the unit-in-place cost estimate applies to the *cost of material and labor of each building component.* Here, measurements are taken of a unit-in-place, such as a wall, a floor, or a roof. For example, the cost of a roof may be measured by the cost per *square* (an area of 100 square feet). The cost of a concrete slab floor may be expressed as the cost per square yard.

While less detailed, less time-consuming, and less expensive to estimate than the quantity survey, unit-in-place methods tend to be more accurate than unit comparisons.

UNIT COMPARISONS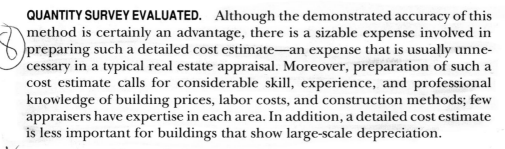

The most widely used cost estimate, unit comparison cost estimates are based on building costs per *square foot* or *cubic foot.*

Square-foot costs apply to single-family dwellings and other buildings that show fairly uniform construction standards, such as warehouses, retail stores, and office buildings. For public buildings, theatres, auditoriums, and high-rise office buildings, costs per cubic-foot are preferred because of variations in ceiling height.

ADVANTAGES.   Unit comparison cost estimates take less time to calculate and can be *easily verified.* They require *less technical knowledge* of construction practices and they are sufficiently accurate for market value appraisals. Moreover, they are *highly flexible* since square-foot or cubic-foot costs may be adjusted for the quality of building construction and materials.

COST VERIFICATION.   Market values are strongly supported by costs derived from recent construction of similar buildings constructed under typical conditions in the same locality. Costs derived from recently sold property give the strongest possible support to the cost estimate.

For instance, consider a new dwelling that recently sold for $150,000. By deducting the estimated land value (verified from recent lot sales) and the estimated value of yard improvements (including the garage or carport), it is possible to derive the square-foot building cost actually experienced in constructing comparable houses. In the following example, the $150,000 sale of a 2,700 square foot dwelling reveals a construction cost of $43.78 per square foot.

Sales price		$150,000
Less:		
Value of site	$20,000	
Sidewalks, fences, and patio	5,000	
Attached carport	4,600	- 29,600
Total cost, 2,700 square feet		$120,400
Cost per square foot, $120,400/2,700		$ 44.59

A common but less satisfactory method of verifying cost relies on authoritative opinion. The cost per square foot or cubic foot reported by contractors, architects, engineers, or others familiar with local costs sometimes supports the cost estimate. Local sources that have knowledge of new construction costs include:

architects	engineering firms
contractors	real estate developers
building suppliers	mortgage bankers
commercial banks	savings and loan associations

Information from these sources may be supplemented with construction costs published in construction cost manuals.

CONSTRUCTION COST MANUALS

Construction cost manuals are available from several companies that publish current cost data for selected cities and for different types of buildings. The manuals are useful for developing costs of unique buildings for which there are no local examples; they also serve as guides in verifying local cost estimates. Current cost multipliers, available by annual subscription, may be used to update past, original costs of construction. Some of the more popular cost manuals include:

Boeckh Building Valuation Manual, Volume I, *Residential and Agricultural,* Boeckh Division, American Appraisal Company, Milwaukee, Wisconsin.
Boeckh Building Valuation Manual, Volume II, *Commercial,* Boeckh Division, American Appraisal Company, Milwaukee, Wisconsin.

Boeckh Building Valuation Manual, Volume III, *Industrial and Institutional,* Boeckh division, American Appraisal Company, Milwaukee, Wisconsin.

Residential Cost Handbook, Marshall and Swift Publication Company, Los Angeles, California.

Marshall Valuation Service, Marshall and Swift Publication Company, Los Angeles, California.

As a basis for estimating market value, building cost manuals are subject to considerable criticism. Since the costs are based on an *average cost* for standard and typical buildings, some appraisers hold that cost manuals are inappropriate to estimate market value of a specific building in a given location. For this reason, cost manuals for market value appraisals are largely confined to estimating construction costs for the more complex, special purpose buildings.

COST INDEXING

This is a method of estimating the current cost of construction by multiplying the original cost by a cost index showing the change in construction cost from the original date of construction to the present. In this method, it is assumed that the original cost varies according to changes in a cost index that measures changes in cost over time.

Suppose, for example, that a building was built for $18.00 per square foot in 1967. If you were using a published cost manual which indicated a current cost index of 3.082, the indicated current costs would equal $55.476 per square foot today ($18.00 x. 3.082).

DEPRECIATION

For appraisal purposes, *depreciation represents a loss in value.* Under the cost approach, the loss in value represents the *difference in value between the property under appraisal and the value of a new, substitute building.* Refinements in calculating the depreciation allowance are especially important since one of the main criticisms of the cost approach lies in the highly subjective nature of depreciation estimates.

Break-down Depreciation

Depreciation estimates fall in two main categories: the *break-down methods* and *age-life methods.* Break-down depreciation methods, which calculate past depreciation, include three types of depreciation: *physical, functional obsolescence,* and *external obsolescence.*

BUILDING AGE

To measure depreciation, buildings may have an economic life and an effective age. Before illustrating these depreciation techniques, it is necessary to define building life.

BUILDING LIFE.   Building life is measured in several ways. *Actual age* is the number of years from the date of construction to the present. Properly maintained, buildings may last indefinitely. While the actual age refers to the physical life of the building, appraisers rely mainly on the *economic life— the period over which improvements contribute to market value.* So while properly maintained buildings may last indefinitely, their economic life may be considerably more limited. Because of neighborhood change, highway construction, changes in consumer preference, and many other reasons, economic life may be shorter than physical life.

The *remaining economic life,* however, is that proportion of economic life remaining as of the date of appraisal. Therefore, a motel may have an estimated economic life of 40 years and a remaining economic life of 20 years.

EFFECTIVE AGE.   Consider next a 100-year-old building that has recently been remodeled to include a new concrete foundation, new modern plumbing, and new interior lights, central air-conditioning, and modern plumbing. The dwelling may also have a remodeled kitchen with the latest appliances.

In these circumstances, the actual age may not be controlling. In this case, the appraiser would use the *effective age.* The *effective age is that age indicated by the present building condition.* Because of the extensive remodeling, the appraiser may conclude that the building has an *effective age* less than the *actual age.* In illustration, a 100-year-old building (actual age) may have an *effective age* of 20 years and a *remaining life* of 40 years.

Consider a 10-year-old building that would have an expected economic life of 50 years. Because of marked deferred maintenance, the appraiser may conclude that the effective age is 20 years relative to its actual age of 10 years. The higher effective age arises from the loss in value because of the present building condition.

PHYSICAL DEPRECIATION

The first two types of past depreciation—physical depreciation and functional obsolescence—are said to be *curable* or *incurable. Curable depreciation is depreciation that is economically feasible to correct.* The incurable forms of depreciation are not curable because of the inherent characteristics of depreciation or because of the uneconomic expense of correcting "incurable" depreciation. The following illustrations show these differences.

Physical depreciation, the *loss in value caused by physical conditions,* has three causes:

1. Wear and tear.
2. Action of the elements.
3. Catastrophic events.

Generally speaking, physical depreciation may be largely a function of age, maintenance, and intensity of use. If so, the estimation of physical depreciation is usually a matter of examining components of the building in some detail.

In valuing a single-family dwelling, depreciation will be indicated by the condition of the exterior, the interior, and the building equipment. A methodical inspection of the foundation may reveal physical depreciation in several forms—differential settlement, termite damage, moisture damage, and the like. The loss of value may also be estimated by observing the physical condition of the interior and exterior walls that need paint or other repairs. The interior floors, walls, ceilings, and building equipment (the heating, plumbing, air conditioning, and other facilities) will usually show some degree of deterioration according to the length of use, the degree of maintenance, and general wear and tear.

It is reasoned that the typical, informed buyer would offer *a price equal to the cost of a new building less the loss of value caused by physical depreciation.* Essentially then, the estimate of cost must be reduced by the amount a prudent buyer would pay and a seller would be willing to accept, given the present condition of the building. In short, the loss of value from physical causes may be found by deducting the estimated cost of correcting for observed physical depreciation. This concept leads to the *cost-to-cure method.*

CURABLE.   The assumption is that an informed buyer would pay a price equivalent to the cost new, less the cost of repairing observed defects—physical depreciation, curable. If the deficiency is economically repairable, the loss is measured by *the cost to remedy the observed physical defect.*

To illustrate, assume that the estimated physical depreciation includes the following: repainting the interior, $3,250; replacing gutters and downspouts, $875; and replacing an old kitchen sink, $400. In other words, the loss of value from physical depreciation, curable, is estimated at $4,525. These items are listed in Case 1.

It is assumed that the typical buyer would pay the cost new (including land) less $4,525—the loss in value from physical depreciation that can be economically corrected. Physical depreciation, curable, is equal to the cost of repairing physical defects that are economically feasible to correct.

Case 1

Physical Depreciation, Curable

Painting interior walls and ceilings	$ 3,250
Replacement of gutters and downspouts	875
Installation of new kitchen sink	400
Total physical depreciation, curable	$ 4,525

INCURABLE.   The treatment of incurable depreciation depends on whether, in the judgment of the appraiser, incurable depreciation covers *short-lived* or *long-lived* building components. *Short-lived building components have an economic life less than the economic life of the building*.

To illustrate, assume that plumbing fixtures have a useful life of 20 years. If the plumbing fixtures have an effective age of 10 years and would cost $5,000 new, incurable depreciation for the short-lived plumbing fixtures would equal $2,500 (10/20 x $5,000).

Therefore, to calculate incurable physical depreciation for *short-lived building components*, follow these steps:

1. Estimate the reproduction cost of building components.
2. Calculate the effective age and estimated economic life of building components.

The rate of depreciation equals the ratio of effective age to the economic life. Depreciation of the building roof, floors, plumbing fixtures, electrical fixtures, and heating and air-conditioning equipment may be calculated in this manner.

For *long-lived building components*, depreciation is calculated by taking the reproduction cost of the building less curable depreciation and incurable depreciation for short-lived components. The result is the *total depreciated cost of long-lived building components*.

The incurable physical depreciation rate for long-lived building components equals the proportion given by the *effective age divided by the economic life*. This proportion is multiplied by the reproduction cost of long-lived building components to give the incurable physical depreciation. These calculations are shown in Case 2.

Case 2

Long-Lived Incurable Physical Depreciation

Building reproduction cost		$200,000
Less reproduction cost of		
1. Curable physical components	$20,000	
2. Incurable, physical, short-lived components	30,000	- 50,000
Total reproduction cost, long-lived building components		$150,000

Assumed
  Economic life of building: 50 years
  Effective age of building: 10 years

Incurable physical depreciation, long-lived building components

Depreciation (10/50, .20 x $150,000)	$ 30,000

Case 2 indicates a reproduction cost of the building, $200,000, and a reproduction cost of *curable* physical components, $20,000, and *incurable, short-lived*, physical building components, $30,000. The total reproduction cost of long-lived building components equals $150,000.

Assuming a 50-year economic life for the building and a 10-year effective building age, the depreciation rate for *incurable physical depreciation, long-lived building components* is 20 percent. Deducting 20 percent of the total reproduction cost of long-lived building components is $30,000, the incurable physical depreciation of long-lived building components.

FUNCTIONAL OBSOLESCENCE

Functional obsolescence is the loss in value resulting from changes in design—for example, the loss in the value of a house that was built according to an obsolete architectural design. It would not be feasible to correct for losses caused by obsolete architecture. It may not be feasible to remedy defects in the floor plan—namely, an inadequate number of bedrooms, unusually small rooms, or other deficiencies that would require changes in the basic house plan.

Depreciation caused by these examples is found by *capitalizing the rental loss*—a form of functional *obsolescence, incurable*. For those items that may be economically feasible to correct, the loss in value is measured by what it would *cost to cure* the observed defects.

FUNCTIONAL OBSOLESCENCE ILLUSTRATED. Buildings lose value mainly from changes in functional utility. The utility of a building changes as the result of technological improvements, changes in design, the adoption of new materials, or other innovations that make older buildings obsolete for their original purpose. Functional obsolescence is particularly noticeable in single-family dwellings.

In appraising single-family dwellings, care must be taken to relate functional utility to a specific housing market. While the absence of central air-conditioning probably would not lower the utility of a $20,000 house, it may be considered a serious deficiency for a $150,000 residence, depending on local preferences.

In estimating the utility of single-family dwellings, certain leading features account for functional deficiencies. Although the list is not all-inclusive, the items below are characteristic of losses in value from functional obsolescence:

poorly designed kitchen cabinets	inadequate or out-of-style plumbing
awkward floor plan	
unusually small bedrooms	insufficient closet space
inadequate heating system	limited storage
inadequate hot water supply	obsolete electrical wiring
lack of insulation	poor window placement
outdated architecture	inappropriate exterior walls
inappropriate building materials	out-of-style interior walls
insufficient number of bedrooms	obsolete kitchens
obsolete kitchen fixtures	substandard floor materials

Certain qualifications are necessary to estimate functional obsolescence. For example, there is the danger of penalizing a building because it does not conform to the personal preferences of the appraiser. In reality, *functional utility must be derived from opinions of buyers and sellers active in the market*. Current design standards and minimum property requirements preferred by the typical buyer for the property in question are the true guides to functional depreciation.

Not only does functional obsolescence vary among houses in different price ranges, but it also varies by locality. While a stucco exterior would dominate in southern California, in high-rainfall areas of the Pacific Northwest or southern Florida, stucco may be quite inappropriate. Similarly, heating systems, insulation, and exterior materials would vary according to local standards and housing preferences.

CURABLE. Although functional obsolescence actually may not be corrected, its explanation indicates reasons for the depreciation deduction. It is assumed that a reasonable buyer would offer a price equal to the cost new, less the amount necessary to correct for functional deficiencies.

For instance, a single-family dwelling may show depreciation from outdated kitchen cabinets that would cost $3,000 to replace. By the same token, value may be reduced by the estimated cost of replacing an obsolete furnace. Or, for the type of house under valuation, a double carport may be typical, so that value would be reduced by the amount necessary to replace a single carport with a double carport. Case 3 shows these estimates.

Case 3

Functional Obsolescence, Curable

Replace outdated kitchen cabinets	$3,000
Install an automatic forced air furnace	3,500
Convert a single carport to a double carport	2,500
Total functional obsolescence, curable	$9,000

INCURABLE. The preferred procedure for estimating functional obsolescence incurable begins with an estimate of the *rental loss*. For example, it is assumed that a house with three bedrooms and one bath would rent for less than a comparable two-bath home, that a house with inadequate closet space would be rentable at a lower rent, or that a house with no outside storage would command a lower rent in comparison to other houses of a more acceptable design.

The appraiser converts the loss in rent to a capital value, giving an estimate of depreciation from this cause. As illustrated in Case 4, if comparable rental properties are valued under a capitalization rate of 12 percent, a rental loss of $75.00 a month would represent a capital loss of $7,500 [($75.00 X 12)/.12].

Case 4

Functional Obsolescence, Incurable
Rental loss from functional obsolescence

Loss of rent from a one-bathroom, three-bedroom house	$75 per month
Functional obsolescence, incurable [(75 x 12)/.12]	$7,500

There is also the issue of rent estimation. How can you defend a rental loss of $75 per month because the house lacks a second bathroom? In answer, it is held that these detailed calculations, however imperfect, are more accurate than unqualified, lump-sum adjustments. It is also argued that detailed depreciation estimates produce compensating errors; overestimates tend to be offset by underestimates.

EXTERNAL OBSOLESCENCE

The loss in value caused by factors other than physical or functional obsolescence may not be remedied by additions or betterments to the property appraised. Examples of external obsolescence include the effect of a commercial building that depreciates an adjoining single-family dwelling, inadequate offstreet parking for a downtown store, or neighborhood nuisances, such as smoke, dust, smells, and noise.

In these latter examples, the *loss in value is caused by forces unrelated to the property appraised.* The loss of value does not arise from deficiencies of the property valued; it arises from *external causes.* A property owner can do little to eliminate external obsolescence. Though he or she may erect fences and otherwise try to isolate the property from adjoining properties, external obsolescence may still result from factors physically unrelated to the property valued. Consequently, the loss of value from external obsolescence is especially difficult to estimate accurately.

METHODS OF ESTIMATION.   The most common way to estimate the loss in value from external obsolescence is to estimate the loss of rent. The discounted rental loss is then deducted from reproduction cost new as shown in Case 5.

Case 5

The Estimation of External Obsolescence
External Obsolescence
Monthly rental loss caused by commercial
    encroachment [($100 per month x 12) /.12] $10,000

EVALUATION.   It is assumed that the estimated rental loss can be attributed to external obsolescence. If the relationship between rents and property values is established for the property appraised, then the estimate of external obsolescence would be strongly supported.

Age-life Methods

Age-life methods of depreciation base depreciation on a *proportion of the estimated cost.* The proportion is based on the ratio of the *present age to the expected age.* Both the present and expected age are variously defined for specific purposes. If income data are not available, and if recent sales are few in number and not very comparable, age-life methods have a clear advantage.

ECONOMIC AGE-LIFE DEPRECIATION

Because of structural improvements or the installation of modern equipment, e.g., new lighting fixtures, new plumbing, or heating systems, depreciation is based on the effective age after property renovation. This method is illustrated in Case 6.

Case 6

Economic Age-life Depreciation

Replacement cost, new	$200,000
Less accrued depreciation:	
Total economic life, 50 years; effective age, 10 years; depreciation (10/50 x $200,000)	- 40,000
Replacement cost new less accrued depreciation	$160,000

Suppose a 20-year-old building has an estimated *economic life of 50 years* as determined by the quality of the original materials and construction, but because of recent remodeling, *effective* age is reduced to 10 years. In these circumstances, depreciation would be equal to a percent of the replacement cost based on the proportion of effective age to total economic life. In the example cited, depreciation is 10/50 or 20 percent of replacement cost new.

Case 7

Modified Economic Age-life Method

Replacement cost, new		$200,000
Less curable depreciation		
Physical	$ 3,500	
Functional obsolescence	5,400	- 8,900
		$191,100

(Continued from page 237)

Assumptions $191,100
   Total economic life, 50 years
   Remaining economic life, 30 years
   Effective age, 20 years
   Depreciation rate   =   effective age/economic life
                         =   20/50
                         =   40 percent

$191,100
x .40

Incurable depreciation   - 76,440

Depreciated building value $114,660
   Add land value   20,000
Market value, cost approach $134,660

MODIFIED ECONOMIC AGE-LIFE DEPRECIATION

Depreciation estimates based on this technique require the following steps:

1. Calculate the curable depreciation for *physical and functional obsolescence.*
2. Deduct the total curable depreciation from the estimated cost of construction.
3. Calculate the ratio of effective age to total economic life (effective age in years/total economic life in years).
4. Multiply the answer in (2) above times the ratio given in (3) above.

These steps for the modified age-life method are illustrated in Case 7.

SUMMARY

The cost approach results in an indicated market value equal to the *sum of the depreciated building value and the land value.* This valuation approach requires a building description, in sufficient detail, to justify cost and depreciation estimates. The building is described according to its general features, building exterior, interior, equipment, and utility.

The cost approach is limited by the difficulty of estimating the quality of workmanship and materials. The cost approach depends on assumptions over builder profit and overhead, builder efficiency, and building depreciation. *Depreciation is a loss in value.* For older buildings, the degree of subjectivity in estimating cost and depreciation seriously limits appraisal accuracy.

For the valuation of new buildings, special-purpose buildings such as public buildings, industrial property, and buildings owned by charitable organizations, the cost technique may be the sole appraisal alternative. Proposed construction, large-scale industrial property, and public buildings are appraised primarily under the cost approach.

Cost estimates may be based on the *reproduction cost*—the *cost of constructing an identical building* or the *replacement cost* which is *the cost of an equally desirable building that has the same utility as the property appraised.* (Replacement cost estimates correct for functional obsolescence.)

Estimated building cost is based upon the *quantity survey*, which is a detailed list of materials and their costs, labor costs, and contractors' overhead and profit.

Unit-in-place costs are based on the cost of material and labor of building components. Building components consist of walls (per linear foot), the cost per roof square, which is an area of 100 square feet, or of other building components. The most popular method of estimating building costs is *unit comparisons*—the cost per square foot or cubic foot. Such costs may be easily verified and take less time to calculate.

These cost estimates are preferably supported by costs derived from *recent construction* of similar buildings constructed under typical conditions in the same locality. Appraisers refer to *cost construction manuals* to estimate costs of unique buildings where there are no local examples—large-scale industrial improvements, public utilities, and the like. Construction manuals may provide a *cost index* which shows how costs have varied from some base period. Given the original cost, cost data may be updated to the current cost by cost index multipliers available from published sources.

Depreciation is the difference in value between the appraised value and the value of a new, substitute building. Appraisers rely on two methods of estimating depreciation—*break-down methods* and *age-life methods.* The break-down methods of depreciation refer to physical depreciation, functional obsolescence, and external obsolescence.

Physical depreciation equals the loss in value caused by physical conditions. *Functional obsolescence* is a loss in value resulting from changes in design. Physical depreciation may be *curable,* which is equal to the cost remedying the observed physical loss in value. *Incurable* physical depreciation consists of depreciation on short-lived building components or long-lived components.

Functional obsolescence, curable, is equal to the cost of curing functional obsolescence. For *incurable functional obsolescence,* appraisers calculate the loss in monthly rent caused by incurable functional obsolescence. Capitalizing the rental loss produces functional obsolescence, incurable.

External obsolescence is the loss in value caused by factors external to the property appraised. It is estimated by calculating the present value of the loss of rental income arising from external obsolescence.

Age-life depreciation methods may be based upon the effective age. *Effective age* is an estimate of age indicated by the present building condition. *Economic building life* equals a period over which buildings contribute to market value. Age-life methods of depreciation calculate the loss in value equal to the ratio of effective age to remaining economic life.

POINTS TO REMEMBER

summation appraisal method another term for the cost approach in which market value equals the sum of the depreciated building value and land value.

replacement cost the cost of creating an equally desirable building that has the same utility as the property appraised.

quantity survey a cost estimate based on a detailed list of materials and their cost, labor costs, and overhead and profit.

unit-in-place cost the cost of materials and labor of each building component.

unit comparisons cost estimates based on the building cost per square foot or cubic foot.

cost indexing a method of estimating the current cost of construction by multiplying original cost by a cost index showing the change in construction costs from the original date of construction to the present.

depreciation a loss in value from any cause; the loss in value is equal to the difference in value between the property under appraisal and the value of a new, substitute building.

age-life depreciation depreciation based on a proportion of the estimated cost. The proportion is based on the present age relative to the expected age. Both the present and expected age are variously defined for specific purposes.

building life building life may be *actual age*—the number of years from the date of construction to the present, or the *economic life*—the period over which improvements contribute to market value.

remaining economic life the economic life remaining at the date of appraisal.

effective age the age indicated by the present building condition.

physical depreciation the loss in value caused by physical conditions arising from wear and tear, action of elements, and catastrophic events.

physical depreciation, curable the depreciation measured by the cost of remedying the observed physical defect.

physical depreciation, incurable depreciation which is not economic to cure; incurable depreciation may apply to *short-lived* building components or *long-lived* building components.

short-lived building components building components which have an economic life less than the economic life of the building.

functional obsolescence the loss in value resulting from changes in style or design.

functional obsolescence, curable the loss in value equal to the cost of remedying functional obsolescence.

functional obsolescence, incurable the loss in value which is not feasible to correct. It is estimated by capitalizing the rental loss caused by functional obsolescence, incurable.

external obsolescence the loss in value caused by forces unrelated to the property appraised—an external cause.

QUESTIONS FOR REVIEW

1. Define the cost approach to value. How would you describe a single-family dwelling for a narrative appraisal report for the cost approach?

2. Critically evaluate the cost approach to estimate market value.

3. Give examples of buildings for which you would recommend the cost approach to value. Give reasons for your answer.

4. Give an example of how you apply the cost approach to appraise a 50-year-old industrial building.

5. What are the relative advantages of the four methods to estimate building cost? Show how you would use a cost index.

6. Give an example of how you would estimate economic age-life depreciation.

7. Define the following terms: effective age, economic life.

8. Give an example of physical depreciation, curable.

9. Give an example of physical depreciation, incurable *short-lived* building components.

10. Give an example of physical depreciation incurable for *long-lived* building components.

11. Show how you would calculate functional obsolescence, curable. Give an example in illustration of your answer.

12. Show how you would calculate functional obsolescence, incurable.

13. Define and give an example of external obsolescence in the valuation of a single-family dwelling.

PRACTICE PROBLEMS

1. To resolve an insurance claim liability dispute, you are asked to appraise a three-story, high school building constructed in 1936. The building was a total fire loss, so you must prepare an estimated market value, cost approach. Explain how you would undertake this appraisal, indicating how you would estimate building cost and building depreciation.

2. (a) You are asked to estimate market value, including the cost approach, of a proposed 100-unit motel. Explain how you would estimate market value under the cost approach.

   (b) You are requested to value a four-story industrial building of 500,000 square feet constructed in 1890. Since there are no comparable sales and you find no relevant income data, you must undertake an estimate of market value under the cost approach. Explain fully how you would estimate market value for this assignment.

C H A P T E R   1 2

The Market Approach

After studying this chapter, you will know:
- The technique of selecting comparable sales.
- Methods of refining comparable sales.
- Methods of calculating the cash equivalent value.
- Techniques of adjusting sales prices.

The market approach, known also as the market data or sales comparison approach, results in a market value estimate derived from the analysis of recent sales of properties similar to the property appraised. Selected real estate sales are referred to as *comparable sales*. Given recent sales of land and buildings that are reasonably similar to the property under valuation, and given representative sales undistorted by unusual market conditions, it is reasoned that real estate sales strongly support the market value estimate. In essence, the skilled interpretation of recent sales of like property leads to the market value estimate.

The sales comparison approach is especially useful in appraising older properties that show a high degree of depreciation. It is particularly adapted to the appraisal of single-family dwellings and it is used to value other property that is frequently sold, such as vacant land.

COMPARABLE SALES SELECTION

The selection of representative sales is critical to the market value estimate. No amount of analysis, refinement, or judgment can overcome nonrepresentative sales. Often, there is no systematic system of selection; sales may be obtained randomly from such sources as real estate brokers, county records, government agencies, or directly from buyers and sellers. However, since the sales are selected, the first step is to eliminate nonrepresentative sales.

Nonrepresentative Sales

Preferably, comparable sales represent openly negotiated sales between buyers and sellers who have reasonable knowledge of the market. Accordingly, sales that do not fall within the definition of a bona fide, free market transaction are highly suspect and must be eliminated.

It is possible to identify certain transactions that by their very nature usually include an element of coercion or duress. Nonrepresentative sales would probably fall in one of the three following groups: *government sales,* including transactions at all government levels—federal, state, and local; sales between *related parties;* and *convenience transfers.*

SALES INVOLVING GOVERNMENT OR ITS ADMINISTRATIVE AGENCIES

Government sales that should be eliminated in selecting comparable sales would include:

1. Tax sales.
2. Sheriff's sales.
3. Eminent domain sales. → *condemnation → use for general welfare. public use.*
4. Sales of surplus buildings or land.
5. Sales of partial interests—easements, leaseholds, and the like.

Sales to and from public agencies are made on a cash basis; they are frequently compulsory sales or sales showing varying degrees of duress. Generally they are poorly advertised. Since these transactions may produce price distortion, they represent poor evidence of value as interpreted under the willing buyer and seller criteria.

SALES BETWEEN RELATED PARTIES   *not good sales for market*

Sales between related parties are usually rejected for the same reasons. Sales listed below are other examples of non-bona fide transfers:

1. Sales between family members.
2. Sales to and from related corporations.
3. Sales of partial or fractional interests.

These sales are used only if they are believed representative of the market; generally they would not be regarded as representative.

TRANSFERS OF CONVENIENCE

A miscellaneous group of transfers conducted for the convenience of the parties includes:

1. Voluntary sales in lieu of foreclosure.
2. Sales by an executor.
3. Sales to or from charitable organizations. → *motive taxes*
4. Sales executed by quit claim deeds. → *says transfer in property*

Quit claim deeds transfer an *interest* held in real estate. The grantor or seller makes no warranties of title. Sales evidenced by quit claim deed are likely to be executed to correct legal title deficiencies. Under the market value standard, these sales would probably be eliminated in favor of more representative transfers. The probability is quite high that sales in these three categories would be non-bona fide and would show distorted prices.

After eliminating sales from these three groups, it can then be assumed, initially at least, that the remaining transfers are representative. The next step is to review the remaining transfers and further refine sales to verify typical values for appraisal purposes.

Sources of Comparable Sales

Usually, several sources would be contacted to secure comparable sales. It is unlikely that an appraiser will have access to all the sales information in a community; ordinarily, numerous sources must be consulted. To obtain sales data on specific property types, most appraisers would contact the following sources:

Single-family Dwellings
- Real estate brokers
- Savings and loan associations
- Subdividers
- Mortgage bankers
- Property owners
- Recorder of deeds
- Tax assessors

Commercial Property
- Life insurance companies
- Shopping center developers
- Chambers of commerce
- Downtown property owners
- Real estate brokers
- Mortgage companies
- Commercial banks

Industrial Property
- City planning departments
- State development departments
- Industrial development departments
- New industries
- Industrial real estate brokers
- Chambers of commerce
- Tax Assessor
- Public utilities

Note that sources vary by property type. Though the sources overlap, certain offices tend to have more information on single-family dwellings, for example, than on industrial property. Leads to comparable dwelling sales may be more easily obtained by making direct inquiries of neighborhood residents, but for more specialized properties, other sources are more useful. Sales of industrial property are generally secured from real estate brokers as well as from promotional departments of chambers of commerce, railroads, public utilities, and public offices—state, local and federal.

Other sales sources include various computer records. The sales data bank of the Appraisal Institute maintains a list of verified residential sales derived from local lenders in major cities. In some states and local counties, real estate conveyances are listed on computer records available to the public. Generally, these sales lists require editing to eliminate invalid transactions. Appraisers in other jurisdictions may subscribe to local sources that provide real estate sales.

Comparable Sales Verification

Sales verification requires two steps: *first*, the legal circumstances of the sale must be correct and, *second*, the sale must represent a bona fide market transaction.

LEGAL VERIFICATION

In the first instance, legal facts of the sale are best verified by *recorded* documents. Real estate conveyance instruments are normally recorded in county offices responsible for recording and filing documents of record. A warranty deed, evidencing a sale, allows appraisers to verify the name of owners and buyers, legal description, the date of sale, and the interest conveyed.

For example, a warranty deed executed on August 20 may be issued in satisfaction of a real estate contract and sale negotiated ten years earlier. The recorded instrument merely conveys the real estate title after the sale contract has been fulfilled. Though the recorded deed date is August 20 of the current year, the actual sale and the price was established at the date of the contract ten years earlier.

A warranty deed may also convey only a partial interest such as an easement. A recorded deed that applies to such a partial interest would not be a valid single-family sale.

SALES VERIFICATION

While these and other facts may be revealed by recorded documents, a more serious question arises over the sales price and negotiations leading to the sale. The sales price is best verified from the buyer or seller.

Parties to the sale may also indicate financing terms. By determining financing terms, the appraiser gains a greater understanding of concessions that may have been paid for below-market financing. Furthermore, sales may include nonreal estate property such as furniture, appliances, or personal property such as boats and trailers. These facts are usually not indicated in recorded documents.

There is also the question of buyer and seller motives. Sales in lieu of mortgage foreclosures or sales in which either the buyer or seller are acting under duress may be revealed by inquiry to buyer and seller or to other parties with special knowledge of the transaction. Other parties contributing to sales verification would be real estate agents who sold the property, attorneys, or lenders who are familiar with sale details.

Because of the complications surrounding real estate sales, appraisers do not accept sale prices from secondary sources without verifying both the facts of the sale from recorded documents and the circumstances surrounding sale negotiations.

SALES REFINEMENT

The appraisal of real estate goes beyond a mere statement of opinion. The appraisal report, though based on personal judgment, cites data supporting the value estimate. For some appraisal purposes the facts of a sale, including the interpretation of these facts, may be as significant as the value estimate. A professional appraisal report does more than report a statement of value. It includes comparable sales; it reports the facts of the sale; and it presents this information in such a way that the client may review each step of the valuation process. By following this procedure, the appraiser ensures that the opinion is based not upon hearsay but on actual facts.

Sales Price per Unit

It is difficult to generalize on real estate prices without converting prices to relative terms. By showing prices per unit, comparisons may be made between the property appraised and the property sold. Per-unit sale prices lead to judgments over sale comparability and allow price adjustment for differences between the property sold and the property appraised.

The most common units of comparison for different property types may be summarized in the following list:

Sales Price per Unit
Apartment Dwellings
      per gross square foot

per square foot of rentable space
per room
per apartment
Office Buildings
per square foot of rentable area
Shopping Centers
per square foot of leasable area
Mobile Home Parks
per mobile home pad
Motels
per room
per gross square foot
Single-family Dwellings
per square foot of heated dwelling area
building price per square foot
(sales price less land value)
Land
per square foot
per front foot
per acre

Real estate prices of apartment dwellings vary according to the number of rooms per apartment, the size of the rooms, and the square feet. Real estate apartment managers commonly report rents in prices per gross square feet of the building—the square feet of the heated building area, including upper stories.

To show variations by room and apartment size, apartment project prices are also converted to the sales price per room and per apartment. These data allow judgments over the difference in prices arising from extra features such as tennis courts, swimming pools, exercise rooms, recreational buildings, and other services. Office buildings are rented and reported according to the square feet of rentable area—the space leased to tenants. Shopping centers are judged according to the square foot price of the leasable area. The leasable area excludes public and utility areas not directly rented by tenants.

Similarly, mobile homes and motels are shown by the price per unit for mobile home pads and the price per room or per square foot. Single-family dwellings usually are shown according to the sales price of land and buildings per square foot of dwelling area. The dwelling area is defined as the outside dimensions of the enclosed, heated area. In some cases, the building price per square foot is shown after deducting the estimated land value. In the case of land, prices are shown per square foot, per front foot, or per acre. The per front foot and per square foot values relate to residential or commercial land.

Therefore, in citing real estate sales, it is relevant to report the total sales price and the relative price per unit. Since most real estate transactions are financed, the appraiser considers the effect of below-market financing on price. This calls for an estimate of the cash equivalent value.

Cash Equivalent Value

Home buyers frequently negotiate home purchases with a combination of cash payments and first- and second-mortgage financing. To promote the sale, mortgage interest rates may be "below market interest rates." Sellers or lenders may recoup below-market interest rates by increasing the sales price. In these circumstances the buyer pays a price for the real estate and the below-market interest rate financing—appraisers convert these prices (resulting from below market financing) to the cash equivalent value. *The cash equivalent value is the sale price adjusted for below-market financing.*

FINANCING TERMS

Assume a purchase price of $150,000 with a $10,000 cash down payment. Assume also that the buyer assumes the seller's $100,000, fixed rate, first mortgage, *8 percent,* for 30 years with 300 months remaining. Let us say, further, that the market interest rate is *10 percent* for first mortgages. Suppose also that the balance of $40,000 is financed by the seller who accepts a second mortgage repayable monthly over 15 years, *10 percent interest.* Assume further that the market interest rate on second-mortgage financing is *12 percent.*

In this instance the seller has accepted a below-market interest rate as a sales inducement. A mortgage of $40,000, 15 years, at a fixed interest rate of 10 percent requires a monthly payment of $429.84. For the seller, this represents an annuity repayable over the mortgage term at the mortgage contract interest rate. However, if this annuity is capitalized at the prevailing market interest rate, 12 percent, the resulting principal value is $35,814.98. This is another way of stating that the present value of the right to a monthly income of $429.84 over 15 years has a present value of $35,814.98. Likewise, the present value of the mortgage payments on the

8 percent first mortgage ($733.80) would be estimated under the market rate of 10 percent.

To calculate the cash equivalent value, you need two additional assumptions:

1. What is the expected holding period on the two mortgages?
2. Will the advantage of below-market financing be shared by the buyer and seller? If the answer is yes, then in what proportions will the buyer and seller share this advantage?

To respond to these questions, suppose it is expected that the buyer will sell in *10 years* and pay off both mortgages. In this case, the first- and second-mortgage holders have two financial rights—the right to monthly mortgage payments for 120 months and the right to the remaining balance at the end of the mortgage holding period. At this point, review the assumptions and input for this problem as they are listed in Table 12-1.

Table 12-1   Input Data for Cash-equivalent Calculations

Given: First Mortgage (below-market interest rate)

                    8 percent
                    360 months
                    $100,000
                    300 months remaining

        Second Mortgage (below-market interest rate)

                    10 percent
                    180 months
                    $40,000

Market interest rates
        First mortgage, 10 percent.
        Second mortgage, 12 percent

The holding period, 120 months.

The allocation of below-market financing benefits between buyer and seller, 50 percent.

PRESENT VALUE CALCULATIONS

In the case at hand, the buyer has negotiated two mortgages with below-market interest rates. Note further that the buyer has accepted two mortgages that have a market value less than their face value. The result is that the buyer has paid a price for favorable credit terms and a dwelling. The cash-equivalent value refers to that portion of the purchase price allocated to the dwelling.

To make this calculation, follow four main steps:

1.0 Calculate Mortgage Payments

    1.1 First Mortgage.

$$\text{MMP} = \text{MC}_{i,n} \ (\$100,000)$$

where:

    MMP = Monthly mortgage payments
      MC = Monthly mortgage constant
        i = annual mortgage interest rate
       n = term of mortgage in months

For a 360-month fixed rate mortgage of 12 percent, mortgage payments would equal:

$$
\begin{aligned}
\text{MMP} &= \text{MC}_{.08/12,\ 360} \ (\$100,000) \\
&= .007338 \ (\$100,000) \\
&= \$733.80
\end{aligned}
$$

[handwritten notes in right margin: 100,000 PV / 8 I/yr / 30 N = 360 month / solve PMT $733.76]

    1.2 Second Mortgage

$$
\begin{aligned}
\text{MMP} &= \text{MC}_{.10/12,\ 180} \ (\$40,000) \\
&= .010746 \ (\$40,000) \\
&= \$429.84
\end{aligned}
$$

2.0 Calculate Mortgage Remaining Balances

    2.1 First mortgage, remaining balance at beginning of holding period, 300 months remaining

$$\text{RMB} = \text{PVAF}_{i,n} \ (\text{MMP})$$

where:

    RMB = Remaining mortgage balance
    PVAF = Present value of an annuity factor

$$
\begin{aligned}
\text{RMB} &= \text{PVAF}_{.08/12,\ 300} \ (\$733.80) \\
&= 129.564523 \ (\$733.80) \\
&= \$95,074
\end{aligned}
$$

2.2 *First mortgage,* remaining balance at the end of the holding
 period of 120 months (180 months remaining).
 RMB $= \text{PVAF}_{.08/12, 180}$ ($733.80)
      $=$ $104.640592 ($733.80)
      $=$ $76,785

2.3 *Second mortgage,* remaining balance at end of holding period. 10 yrs
 RMB $= \text{PVAF}_{.10/12, 60}$ (MMP)
      $=$ 47.065369 ($429.84)
      $=$ $20,231

3.0 Calculate the present value of mortgages at the market rate over holding period.

 3.1 *First Mortgage*
    3.11   Present value of mortgage payments.
              PVMMP $= \text{PVAF}_{i,n}$ (MMP)
    where:
              PVMMP $=$ Present value of monthly mortgage payments
              PVMMP $= \text{PVAF}_{.10/12, 120}$ ($733.80)
                     $=$ 75.671163 ($733.80)   10 yrs
                     $=$ $55,527
    3.12   Present value of remaining balance at the end of
             holding period (180 months remaining).
              PVRMB $= \text{PVF}_{i,n}$ (RMB)
                     $= \text{PVF}_{.10/12, 180}$ ($76,785)
                     $=$ .224521 ($76,785)
                     $=$ $17,240
    3.13   Add present value of mortgage payments and
             present value of the remaining balance.
             Present value: Mortgage payments $55,527
             Present value: Remaining balance   17,240
             Market value of first mortgage $72,767

 3.2 *Second Mortgage*
    3.21   Present value of mortgage payments of second
             mortgage, market interest rate (12 percent).
              PVMMP $= \text{PVAF}_{i,n}$ (MMP)
                     $= \text{PVAF}_{.12/12, 120}$ ($429.84)
                     $=$ 69.700522 ($429.84)
                     $=$ $29,960

3.22   Calculate present value of remaining mortgage
       balance at end of holding period.
       $$\text{PVRMB} = \text{PVF}_{.12/12,\ 120} (\$20,231)$$
       $$= .302995\ (\$20,231)$$
       $$= \$6,130$$

3.23   Add present value of second mortgage payments and
       the present value of the remaining balance.

Present value, second mortgage payments	$29,960
Present value, remaining balance	6,130
Market value, second mortgage	$36,090

4.0 Calculate cash equivalent value (see Table 12-2).

With these calculations, the terms of sale and loan market values are
summarized in Table 12-2. In short, the borrower pays $145,074 consisting
of a $10,000 down payment, a first mortgage of $95,074 and a second
mortgage of $40,000. However, valued at the market interest rate, the first
and second mortgages have values of $72,767 and $36,090.

Table 12-2   Calculations for Cash-equivalent Value

Terms of Sale	
Assumed holding period	120 months
Cash	$ 10,000
Buyer assumes existing first mortgage,	
360 months, 8 percent, $733.80 payments	
per month with 300 months remaining.	
Loan balance	$ 95,074
Seller grants a second mortgage of 10 percent, $429.84	
per month for 180 months.	
Loan balance	$ 40,000
Total sales price	$145,074

Loan Market Values	
First mortgage	
($733.80 x 75.671163), 10 percent, 120 months	$ 55,527
Remaining balance ($76,785) x (0.224521)	17,240
Market value, first mortgage	$ 72,767
Second mortgage	
($429.84 x 69.700522), 12 percent, 120 months	$ 29,960
Remaining balance ($20,231) x (0.302995)	6,130
Market value, second lien	$ 36,090

Table 12-3   Cash-equivalent Analysis

Assuming seller gains 100 percent of favorable financing benefits:

	Price paid for the Dwelling (1)	Total Price (2)	Price Buyer Paid for Favorable Financing (2) - (1)
Cash	$ 10,000	$ 10,000	
First mortgage	72,767	95,074	$22,307
Second mortgage	36,090	40,000	3,910
Total	$118,857	$145,074	$26,217

Assuming buyer gains 50 percent of financing benefits:

	Price paid for the Dwelling	Total Price	Price Buyer Paid for Favorable Financing
Total	$131,965.50	$145,074	$13,108.50

Table 12-3 indicates the cash-equivalent value assuming that the seller gains the full benefit and the buyer gains 50 percent of the benefit of below-market financing. In the latter case, the buyer actually paid $131,965.50 for the dwelling and $13,108.50 for below-market financing—assuming the effect of favorable financing is shared equally by buyer and seller. In short, *the cash equivalent value is the value of below-market mortgage payments discounted at the market interest rate.*

Sales Presentation

Before sales may be analyzed, the facts of each sale must be secured and they must be presented in a logical way so that the appraisal reasoning is clearly evident. Once these facts have been obtained, the selection of sales may be refined to exclude unrepresentative sales, sales lacking comparability, or sales showing distorted prices. At the minimum, the following facts should be reported for each comparable sale cited:

1. Grantor-grantee.
2. Deed book and recording page.
3. Date of sale.
4. Legal description.
5. Source of verification.
6. Sales price (total price and unit price).
7. Terms of sale.
8. Property description.
9. Remarks.

Reporting the facts of the sale makes it fairly clear that the appraiser has investigated the market; it is also made clear that the value estimate is derived from verifiable facts. Furthermore, the client can review the same data and verify and evaluate the same material to reach the same value conclusion.

Figure 12-1 shows how these facts are arranged in the appraisal of an apartment dwelling. Usually this information is accompanied by a site diagram and a photograph. Listing the names of the buyer and the seller emphasizes the objectivity of the data. The deed book and recording page enable the client or others to verify appraisal facts. The date of sale and the legal description are items that permit the appraiser to interpret value data.

Figure 12-1   Comparable Sale: High-rise Elevator Apartment

Grantor:	Investor Equities, Inc.
Grantee:	Green, Inc. 4250 Galt Drive, Fort Lauderdale. Limited Partnership.
Date of Sale:	August 30, 19__.
Recorded:	Book 3739, Page 528, Broward County, Florida.
Legal description:	Lot 23, Block 34, Galt Ocean Mile, Addition 2, Broward County, Florida.
Lot Area:	111,600 square feet.
Location:	Site fronts on the east boundary of Galt Drive, Block 4250. Ocean and beach frontage included.
Sale price:	Total, $11,300,000; per apartment, $44,141; per rooms $11,300; per square-foot building area, $28.18.
Remarks:	Sale indicates value of a 16-story, 256-unit, apartment in the high-rise apartment area comparable to the Hallandale area. Building does not take full advantage of the ocean view. Based on a gross income of $1,426,000, the sale shows a gross income multiplier of 7.92. Building square foot area, 400,771.

The sale price is given in total and in unit prices to allow for comparison with the property under valuation. Stating the source of verification assures the reader that the data have been fully reviewed and verified. The terms of sale and a brief description of property characteristics allow the client to interpret sales evidence.

Sales Analysis

Under "Remarks," as illustrated in Figure 12-1, each sale is related to the property appraised, and the sale's relevance to the value of the property is explained. Main differences of the sale and the property appraised are described in concrete, definite terms. For example, in reporting that land sold for $25.50 per square foot, it is relevant to state how the land compares to the property appraised and how the sales price per square foot leads to the market value estimate.

It is important to remember that the analysis is not resolved by saying that the house sold is superior to the house under valuation or that the house appraised is *better* than the property sold. The point is that subjective terms such as *better, superior, inferior,* and the like must be avoided. The preferred way, and certainly a more objective way, is to give the reasons why the house sold is superior to the property appraised.

It would be better to state that the house sold has 1,200 square feet compared to the 1,000 square feet of the property under review or that the house appraised is encroached upon by a retail store. In analyzing comparable sales, the appraiser should relate characteristics of each property sold to characteristics of the property being valued. Note that no adjustment of the sales price is made at this point; this is reserved for the sales adjustments.

SALES ADJUSTMENTS

The difficulty of deriving market value from recent sales is readily apparent. Each property sold and each property appraised has different characteristics that make item-by-item comparisons difficult to evaluate. It is even more confusing if numerous sales are cited in support of the market value conclusion. These difficulties are overcome by adjusting each sale to the property appraised.

The method of adjusting sales is usually confined to one of two alternatives—*percentage adjustments* in the sales price to account for differences between the property sold and the property appraised or *dollar adjustments.*

In the latter case, main differences between the property sold and the property appraised are converted to dollars.

Percentage Adjustments

Each sale is compared to the property appraised on the basis of value-determining characteristics so that differences for each characteristic are converted into percentages.

For example, a three-bedroom house under valuation may be compared to the sale of a two-bedroom house. To account for the difference in the number of bedrooms, the price of the comparable sale may be adjusted upward 10 percent so that a $300,000 price indicates a market value of $330,000 according to this one characteristic. Other features of the comparable sale property, in turn, are compared to those of the property under valuation. Each different characteristic is given a percentage adjustment in value.

AVERAGE PERCENTAGE ADJUSTMENT

Percentage adjustments are then averaged to give an overall percentage adjustment. For example, in Table 12-4, the percentage adjustments for Sale One are multiplied together to calculate a final percentage adjustment (80.0). Sale One, which sold for $138,000, indicates a market value of $172,500 for the property appraised ($138,000/.80). Each sale is adjusted by a total adjustment factor to produce an indicated market value. Numerous sales treated in this way result in an indicated market value for the property under appraisal.

In Table 12-4, sales are judged according to the time of the sale, the characteristics of the property, and the location. Although this problem covers a single-family dwelling, other types of property may be treated in the same way. Note that each sale is compared to the *subject property, which is considered to a 100 percent base.* Each characteristic shows how much the sale price must be adjusted upward or downward, in percentage terms, in order to produce a tentative market value. That is, each sale is adjusted to indicate the *unknown market value.* Note also that percentages are *multiplied* to produce a total adjustment factor that gives an indicated market value.

SALES ADJUSTMENT PROBLEMS

The sales adjustments on Table 12-4 are multiplied using a weighted average. For example, the total percentage adjustment of Sales One is weighted by the value of each observation.

Table 12-4   Sales Summary: Percentage Adjustments of Single-family Dwelling Sales

Sales number	Price	Number of months from sales date to present	Time of sale	Rooms, floor plan	Heating, air con-ditioning	Location	Total adjust-ment factor	Indicated market value (rounded)
1	$138,000	36	85	90	110	95	80.0	$172,500
2	139,000	23	90	95	95	105	85.3	162,950
3	138,800	13	95	85	105	100	84.8	163,700
4	139,200	18	94	100	95	100	89.3	155,900
5	139,800	16	94	95	95	98	83.1	168,250
6	141,000	4	100	97	105	103	104.9	134,400
7	140,000	3	100	95	100	104	98.8	141,700
8	141,500	1	100	105	100	105	110.3	128,300
9	142,000	6	100	105	106	105	116.9	121,471
10	144,000	5	100	108	104	109	122.4	117,650

Weighted average by value   =   .85 x .90 x 1.10 x .95
                            =   .799
                            =   .800 (rounded)

The alternative is to weight percentage adjustments by number.

Weighted average by number =   .85 + .90 + 1.10 + .95
                            =   3.80 / 4
                            =   .95

The difference between weighting by value and weighting by number depends on the value of each percentage. Furthermore, if the sale price is adjusted *before* percentage adjustments, the final adjustment varies according to the *sequence of adjustments*.

Suppose for example that Sale One in Table 12-4 showing a price of $138,000 requires an adjustment for the time of sale and financing terms. That is, the *sale price itself is adjusted before adjusting* for other variables of comparability. The sale price should be adjusted for time of sale and for financing *before* making other adjustments.

Sale price		$138,000
Less:		
Time of sale		
(15 percent of $138,000)	-$20,700	
Financing terms		
(5 percent of $138,000)	6,900	-27,600
Adjusted price		$110,400
Other percentage adjustments		
Floor plan		
(sale superior to subject)		
(.10 of $110,400)	- $11,040	
Heating and air conditioning		
(sale inferior to subject)		
(.10 of $110,400)	+$11,040	
Location		
(sale superior to subject)		
(.05 of $110,400)	- $ 5,520	
Total adjustments		- $ 5,520
Indicated Market Value		$104,880

Note that the adjusted price of $104,880 is considerably less than the indicated market value of $172,500 for Sale One in Table 12-4. The large difference results because percentage adjustments were applied to the adjusted price *after* adjusting for financing and terms of sale, which were $27,600. Note also that financing terms, calling for a downward adjustment of $6,900, is not included in Table 12-4. The point is that sales adjustments lead to highly variable results depending on the method followed in applying percentage adjustments. Dollar adjustments avoid these variations.

PERCENTAGE ADJUSTMENT CRITICISMS

At first glance, percentage adjustments appear fairly precise, exact, logical, and conclusive. Yet on analysis, certain weaknesses become apparent. There is danger that the adjustment appears too precise, that an *arithmetic exercise* substitutes for *reasoned judgment*. Percentage adjustments are subject to the criticism that such tables give the appearance of an exact appraisal estimate that is not possible in practice.

A more compelling criticism is that percentage adjustments for each characteristic should not be averaged. Because it may be found that a specific item more than compensates for deficiencies in other observed characteristics, a weighted average of percentages will not always indicate market value. Unique advantages of a location may more than overcome deficiencies of a poor floor plan or a relatively poor present condition. Likewise, the quality of construction and the present condition of the property may more than compensate for locational disadvantages.

Hence, it is easy to err by attaching too much importance to percentage adjustments. The fact remains that evaluating sales involves considerable judgment—judgment that cannot be avoided by arithmetic manipulation.

Dollar Adjustments

Dollar adjustments overcome some of the problems of percentage changes. In practice, dollar changes tend to cover actual dollar differences between the property sold and the property appraised. For instance, a house of 2,100 square feet that sold for $150,000 would be adjusted downward by $3,000 in comparison to a house of only *1,950 square feet*. The $3,000 adjustment represents the value difference in dollars between the two dwellings relative to the difference in square foot area. Other differences in property characteristics may be adjusted in the same way. Some of these characteristics and their adjustments are shown in Table 12-5.

Table 12-5   Sales Summary: Dollar Adjustments of Single-family Dwelling Sale

Adjustment Item	Sale number				
	1	*2*	*3*	*4*	*5*
Floor area	-$1,600	-$3,000	-$3,000	-$2,500	-$1,800
Present condition	+3,400	+3,000	-2,500	--	-2,500
Lot area	--	+2,500	+3,500	--	-2,000
Fireplace	--	--	--	+2,500	--
Garage	+3,000	--	+1,500	--	-3,000
Landscaping	+1,000	-2,200	+3,500	--	--
Extra plumbing	--	-1,800	-1,800	+2,500	-2,200
Air conditioning	+2,800	--	+2,400	+1,600	--
Location	+5,000	--	-2,000	+3,800	--
Architectural appeal	+1,500	+1,900	-1,800	+1,000	+2,000
Time of sale	+3,600	+2,800	+1,500	--	+3,000
Total net adjustments	+$18,700	+$3,200	+$1,300	+$8,900	-$6,500
Sales price	$157,800	$162,800	$165,800	$160,400	$172,800
Indicated market value	$176,500	$166,000	$167,100	$169,300	$166,300

Market evidence expressed in dollars may be used to adjust other comparable prices. A residential lot that is 150 feet deep may sell for $2,500 more than a 125-foot-deep lot in the same neighborhood. Using this information, an appraiser could make an adjustment of $2,500 to the sales price of a lot 125 deep in comparison to a lot 150 feet deep. The appraiser's familiarity with comparable sales and the evidence of other sales included in the report may then supplement the sale analysis.

Dollar adjustments are directly related to market-value-determining factors. Square-foot cost differences in sales prices are drawn from actual experience. They do not involve the same degree of subjectivity inherent in percentage adjustments. The dollar adjustments depend on cost and sales data that can be more easily verified. By the same token, adjustments in dollars are more easily understood. The reader may make comparisons more efficiently in dollar figures than in percentages that must be converted to dollars. In short, dollar adjustments seem more logical.

Paired Sales

Appraisers may also make limited sales adjustments by employing paired sales. The paired sales adjustment requires sets of two sale properties that vary only with respect to a single value-determining characteristic. Consider three sets of paired sales of brick veneer, three-bedroom, two-bath dwellings that are similar, but located in different neighborhoods.

	Neighborhood		Percent
	A	B	Difference
Paired sales set 1	$150,000	$165,000	+ 10.0
Paired sales set 2	178,000	192,600	+ 8.2
Paired sales set 3	146,300	159,900	+ 9.3
Sum of the differences			27.5
Average paired difference (27.5/3)			+ 9.2

(Neighborhood B relative to Neighborhood A)

Given the three sets of paired sales of three-bedroom, three-bath, brick veneer houses, it would appear that average sales prices of Neighborhood B are 9.2 percent greater than the average sales prices of neighborhood A. To use paired sales analysis, the appraiser must be reasonably certain that the paired sales of the two neighborhoods are similar with respect to the main value-determining characteristics.

IMPROVING SALES ANALYSIS

By using procedures outlined in this chapter, it is relatively easy to "adjust" sales to a point at which the comparison is quite remote. Considerable importance should be attached to refinements that improve sales analysis. There is the question, for instance, of specifically what sales should be used to derive market value.

The problem can be illustrated by three dwelling sales of $130,000, $134,000, and $136,000 used in support of a $150,000 market value estimate. By clever, but questionable, adjustments, it can be reasoned that these sales support a $150,000 valuation. In like manner, arriving at a market value estimate of $25.00 per square foot for a commercial site by reference to square-foot prices of $15.00, $13.00, and $17.50 would leave a question in the minds of most reviewers. The sales prices vary too much from the market value estimate.

Ideally, appraisers would anticipate this issue by including *sales above and below* the estimated market value. Appraisers refer to this practice as sales price "bracketing." If the value conclusion leads to $200,000, it would be appropriate to analyze sales showing prices above and below this amount. In this instance, the utility of the sale properties—their advantages and limitations—would be compared to the property appraised with sales prices above and below the $200,000 market value estimate. The absence of sales that fall within these limits would probably recommend that the appraiser use other valuation approaches or suggest that the appraiser's value estimate is in error.

Overextension of Data

The deficiencies of market data or the inability or unwillingness to make a thorough market investigation may result in poor sales data that demonstrate well-known fallacies, one of which is the *overextension of data*. This means that the sales analysis is overextended because unwarranted conclusions are drawn from sales data. For illustration, suppose that a sale of a $1,000,000 downtown property includes land and a building. By deducting an estimated building value of $900,000 from the sale price, it may be reasoned that this transaction indicates a $100,000 land value, which is then used for comparison.

However, it is not always clear how a $1,000,000 transaction, which includes land and buildings, indicates a land value of $100,000. It should be pointed out, for example, that the buyer purchased a $1,000,000 property that included land and a building of certain characteristics. He did not buy a $900,000 building and a $100,000 site; rather, he paid $1,000,000 for the whole property. It would be an error to *overextend* the data by assuming facts that should be the object of investigation.

Non Sequitur

In applying the sale analysis, it would be very easy to commit a *non sequitur,* which means "it does not follow." A 50-year-old house that sold for $240,000 may not indicate a $240,000 value for the property under valuation. On investigation, the terms of sale—perhaps an unusually low down-payment or a sale from father to son—may suggest that the $240,000 sale does not indicate a $240,000 market value. The danger of committing a *non sequitur* is avoided by careful verification of sale facts and their presentation, explanation, and analysis.

Nonrepresentative Data

A more common error is to base sales analysis on *nonrepresentative data.* A sale of a residential lot 10 years ago may not be representative of current market value. A price may be distorted and nonrepresentative because of an uninformed seller. The sale of a brick veneer house 25 years old probably would be unrepresentative of the value of a single-family, frame dwelling, five years old.

Even if sales data are analyzed, adjusted, and compared on logical grounds, these analytical steps would not justify using data that are clearly nonrepresentative. In these circumstances either more sales research is required or sale comparisons must be subordinated to data that more strongly support the market value estimate, e.g., cost or income data.

SUMMARY

The market approach provides a market value estimate derived from recent sales of properties similar to the property appraised. The selection of comparable sales is critical to the market value estimate. Real estate sales, which are nonrepresentative of market sales, include *sales involving government* or its administrative agencies, *sales between related parties,* and *transfers of convenience.* Such transfers are sales in lieu of foreclosure, sales to or from charitable organizations, sales by an estate executor, and sales evidenced by quit claim deeds. In selecting comparable sales, appraisers go to industry sources such as real estate brokers, tax assessors, lenders, and buyers and sellers. Public offices are an important source of commercial property and industrial real estate sales.

Sales selected for analysis require verification—*verification of legal circumstances* and *verification of the sales price.* The legal verification depends on an examination of recorded sale documents. Sales verification requires a personal interview with parties familiar with a sales transaction. On investigation, sales are eliminated that include personal property or partial real estate interests. Unusual motives of the buyer and seller are further grounds for sales rejection. In refining sales for comparable sales analysis, sales prices are converted to per unit values. For single-family dwellings, sales prices are converted to a price per square foot while for commercial property, such as apartment houses, sales prices may be shown per gross square foot or building area, per square foot area of rentable space, the price per room, and the price per apartment. Other commercial property sales are converted to per unit values according to the type of property.

Sales financed with below-market financing require the calculation of the *cash equivalent value.* The cash equivalent value is *the sales price adjusted for below market financing.* Below-market interest rate mortgages would require calculation of the monthly mortgage payment, calculation of the remaining mortgage balance at the time of sale, calculation of the present value of mortgage payments capitalized at the market interest rate, and calculation of the remaining balance at the end of the proposed holding period and discounted at the market interest rate. These calculations give the present value of the below-market mortgage.

The next step is to estimate the benefit of below-market financing assumed by the buyer or seller. Most authorities agree that below-market financing benefits are shared between the buyer and seller. By calculating the cash equivalent value, the appraiser identifies that portion of the sales price paid for real estate and that portion paid for favorable financing.

In comparing comparable sales to the property appraised, appraisers may adjust a sale by *percentage adjustments* or *dollar adjustments.* In making percentage sale adjustments, the appraiser adjusts the sales price by a percentage according to characteristics of the comparable sale that vary from the property appraised. Features of the comparable sale that are considered superior to the property appraised call for a decrease in the sales price, which is adjusted downward by some percentage. The opposite sale adjustment is made for characteristics of the sold property which are less valuable than comparable characteristics of the appraisal property. Percentage adjustments for individual property characteristics are multiplied to provide a composite percentage adjustment. Percentage adjustments are criticized on grounds that each characteristic is given equal weight.

Adjusting sale prices by *dollar adjustments* requires that the appraiser adjust sales upward or downward to indicate the market value of the property appraised according to differences in the property sold and the property appraised. If the property appraised has a superior feature to the property sold, the indicated sale price is increased by a given dollar amount showing the indicated price for the superior feature of the property appraised. Selected negative dollar adjustments apply to features of the property appraised that are less valuable than corresponding features of the property sold. Value-determining characteristics are adjusted in this way to indicate the value of the property appraised.

In drawing inferences from comparable sales, the appraiser takes care not to *overextend data*. Overextended data refers to conclusions that are unwarranted from the sales data. A *non sequitur* means that it does not necessarily follow. A sale price of a $240,000 30-year-old brick veneer dwelling may not indicate market value of a dwelling with cedar siding, 2 years old. Sales that are *nonrepresentative* of the property appraised would also be suspect. The sale price of a brick veneer house in neighborhood A may not be representative of the value of a similar house in neighborhood B.

POINTS TO REMEMBER

comparable sales recent sales of land and buildings that are reasonably similar to the property under valuation.

nonrepresentative sales sales which are not drawn from openly negotiated sales between buyers and sellers who have reasonable knowledge of the market.

quit claim deeds deeds that convey only an interest in real estate. The seller makes no warranties of title.

cash equivalent value a sales price adjusted for below-market financing.

percentage sales adjustments percentage adjustments in the sales price to account for differences between the property sold and the property appraised.

dollar adjustments dollar adjustments in the sale price to account for differences between the property sold and the property appraised.

overextension of data drawing unwarranted conclusions from sales data.

non sequitur literally meaning "it does not follow," a non sequitur refers to a market value estimate that does not follow from the sale price.

QUESTIONS FOR REVIEW

1. Identify three main sources of nonrepresentative sales. Why are these sales considered nonrepresentative? Explain fully.

2. What comparable sales sources would you select to value a single-family dwelling? an industrial property?

3. Explain how you would verify the sale of a single-family dwelling.

4. What sales unit comparisons would you use to value a single-family dwelling, shopping center, and an apartment building?

5. What is meant by the cash equivalent value? Explain the steps you would follow in adjusting a sale for a cash equivalent value.

6. In preparing a narrative report using the market approach, explain comments you would include in the remarks section for a comparable sale to appraise a 500-unit apartment building.

7. What criticisms may be levied against percentage sales adjustments? Give reasons for your answer.

8. Give an example of dollar adjustments for at least three sales characteristics for a single-family dwelling comparable sale. Explain fully.

9. What are three main fallacies to avoid in the market approach to value?

PRACTICE PROBLEMS

1. Calculate the cash equivalent value assuming the followng financing terms:

Cash down payment, $20,000
Below-market financing
    Mortgage principal, $130,000
    Mortgage interest rate, 8.5 percent
    Mortgage term, 360 months

Assume a holding period of 10 years and a market interest rate of 11.5 percent. Show your work.

2. (a) Calculate the *dollar adjustments* for the subject property and the comparable sale below:

Date of valuation: July 15, current year.
Value per square foot: $50.
Make other assumptions as necessary.

	Subject property	Comparable sale
Sales price		$150,000
Square feet	2,000	2,300
Time of sale	current	1 year ago
Fireplace	yes	no
Enclosed attached,	garage	carport
Age	2 years	5 years
Condition	excellent	fair
Land area	150' x 250'	1 acre, (43,560 sq. ft.)

(b) For the same data, calculate the percentage adjustments (weight adjustments by their value).

C H A P T E R 1 3

The Market Approach Advanced Models

After studying this chapter, you should know:
- Characteristics of annual gross income multipliers.
- Methods of calculating annual and monthly gross income multipliers.
- The advantages and disadvantages of gross income multipliers.
- Multiple regression appraisal techniques.

The chapter begins with an explanation of gross income multipliers (GIMs). These multipliers assume a typical relationship between annual gross income and sales prices; market data generally reveals that sales prices equal some multiple of the annual gross income. Methods of refining GIMs enable the reader to use annual and monthly GIMs to supplement other indications of market value.

For the present purpose, advanced market approach models also refer to *simple* and *multiple regression appraisal models*. Regression models provide a statistical means of predicting value according to property characteristics. Given the relation between a change in property characteristics and sale prices, market value may be indicated by a computer-generated valuation formula. The chapter explains and demonstrates the more popular regression appraisal methods.

GROSS INCOME MULTIPLIERS

Appraisers and others frequently use the Gross Income Multiplier (GIM) to express the relationship between annual gross income and selling price. A property sold for $10,000,000 with a current annual gross income of $1,200,000 has a GIM of 8.3 ($10,000,000/$1,200,000). The annual gross income is actual income received in the most current year. The selling price is the price negotiated by buyer and seller before closing costs, financing charges, or real estate commissions.

Provided that it is derived from a sufficient number of comparable sales, the GIM converts gross income to an indicated value. For example, if an 8.3 GIM for multiple-family dwellings prevails generally, a similar building in the same market area with a gross income of $800,000 would have an indicated market value of $6,640,000 ($800,000 x 8.3). In short, the GIM provides a preliminary estimate of value; moreover, a GIM applied to the gross income of property to be valued supplements other appraisal approaches.

Annual Gross Income Multipliers (GIMs)

A review of GIMs of a particular period, say one year, would probably show concentration around a single value. The accuracy of GIMs, therefore, depends on the analysis of several sales of like property recently sold in the same market and their corresponding gross incomes.

There is one further point: Although a GIM is derived by dividing the selling price by gross income, it is important to realize that the *gross capitalization rate* is a *reciprocal of the GIM*. For instance, if property with an annual gross income of $600,000 sells for a price that indicates a GIM of 8, the gross capitalization rate is 12.5 percent (1/8).

DETERMINATION OF THE GIM

Observe that GIMs vary according to three factors:

1. The gross annual income.
2. The sales price.
3. The annual net operating expense ratio.

Assuming that the sales price and the gross income conform closely to the current market, an apartment dwelling showing expenses equal to 70 percent of gross income would reveal a lower gross income multiplier than similar property with expenses equal to 50 percent of gross income. Consequently, if the prevailing GIM is 8.0, an apartment project that sold for $10,000,000 with a GIM of 10 would indicate that the reported gross income was below the market rent, the property sold above the market value, or the building was operated at an unusually low operating expense ratio. One of the critical assumptions of GIM analysis is that the operating expenses of properties are similar. If not, the derived GIM is apt to be suspect.

Consider next the overall capitalization rate, which, given the gross annual income and sales price, depends on the operating expense ratio.

OVERALL CAPITALIZATION RATES

The *overall capitalization rate is the annual net income expressed as a percent of the selling price.* The point has been made that GIMs vary with the selling price, the gross income, and the net operating ratio. But what is the relationship between the GIM and overall capitalization rates?

EFFECT OF NET OPERATING EXPENSE RATIO.   In the present context, the operating expense ratio equals total annual operating expenses as a percent of reported gross annual income. To show the effect of net operating expense ratios, given the annual gross income and the selling price, assume a GIM of five. With an annual gross income of $200,000, the overall capitalization rate depends on the operating expense ratio.

Simply stated, overall capitalization rates are found by dividing the annual net income ratio by the GIM. The *annual net income ratio is the complement of the annual net operating expense ratio.* Assume a 40 percent annual net operating expense ratio. The net capitalization rate with a GIM of 5.0 percent equals 12.0 percent:

$$\text{Overall capitalization rate} \quad = \quad \frac{1 - .40}{5.0}$$
$$= \quad 12.0 \text{ percent}$$

Note that by changing net operating expense ratios for property showing a GIM of 5.0, the overall capitalization rate changes *inversely* with net operating expense ratios. At one extreme, an operating expense ratio of 80 percent results in an overall capitalization rate of 4.0 percent. As the expense ratio falls to 30 percent, the overall capitalization rate increases to 14.0 percent.

Table 13-1   The Relationship between Annual Gross Income Multipliers and the Overall Capitalization Rate

		Apartment Sales			
Gross Income	Sales Price	Annual Gross Income Multiplier	Net Income Ratio	Net Income	Overall Capitalization Rate (in percent)
$ 125,000	$ 840,000	6.72	.53	$ 66,250	7.89
600,000	5,360,000	8.93	.45	270,000	5.04
68,000	380,000	5.59	.60	40,800	10.74
430,000	3,100,000	7.21	.51	219,300	7.07
1,100,000	8,700,000	7.91	.48	528,000	6.07
98,000	580,000	5.92	.57	55,860	9.63
115,000	835,000	7.25	.50	57,500	6.89
245,000	1,550,000	6.33	.60	147,000	9.48

DERIVING OVERALL CAPITALIZATION RATES.   Given the gross income multiplier, convert net operating expense ratios to net operating income ratios. Again, the net operating income ratio is derived by subtracting the net operating expense ratio from 1. A net operating expense ratio of 47 percent may be expressed as a net operating income ratio of 53 percent (1.00-.47).

Table 13-1 shows properties with gross income multipliers ranging from 5.59 to 8.93. In this table, the net income ratio is used to indicate the overall capitalization rate. In the first example, a property with a gross annual income of $125,000 sold for $840,000. Therefore, the annual GIM is 6.72 ($840,000/$125,000). The table further indicates that, given a net operating income ratio of 53 percent, the net income is $66,250, which, expressed as a percentage of $840,000, gives an overall capitalization rate of 7.89 percent.

If the net operating income ratio is estimated for a group of properties, overall capitalization rates may be calculated from the annual GIM. To illustrate, let the following symbols represent the relevant variables:

OER   =   Annual net operating expense ratio
GIM   =   Annual gross income multiplier
R   =   Overall capitalization rate

The overall capitalization rate is given by the following formula:

$$R = \frac{(1 - OER)}{GIM}$$

If OER = .47 and GIM = 6.72, and overall capitalization rate equals 7.89 percent:

$$R = \frac{1 - .47}{6.72}$$
$$= .078869 \text{ or } 7.89 \text{ percent}$$

Hence, if a given net operating expense ratio is fairly typical for a group of properties, overall capitalization rates may be given by the GIM.

VARIATIONS IN GIMs

The reliability of GIMs depends on a fairly uniform relation between gross incomes and sales prices. If this relationship may be established within narrow limits, the prevailing GIM, *given gross income,* indicates market value. However, the GIM may be the result of distorted prices, gross incomes, or operating expense ratios. The more common factors that cause GIMs to vary deserve explanation.

VACANCY RATES.   Unusual vacancy rates change the GIM. To derive the GIM, sale prices and annual gross incomes should be compared only for properties that show "normal" vacancies. An apartment operated at a 70 percent vacancy would not give a valid GIM for appraisal purposes. Preferably, prices and gross incomes should be selected from property sales that conform to the local market and the prevailing vacancy rate.

TIME OF SALE.   Generalizations taken from past sales of more than one year are subject to changes in capitalization rates, rising gross rents, variations in operating expenses, and other factors that affect market value. If data for more than one year are used, market value estimates can be strengthened by stratifying data to show differences in GIMs by year of sale.

PROPERTY TYPES.   It would be improper to use a GIM taken from low-rise walk-up apartment sales to value high-rise elevator apartments. Too many variables are associated with gross income and prices taken from these different property types. Apply GIMs only to comparable properties.

FINANCING TERMS.   Selling prices vary because of unusual financing terms. In constructing a GIM, care must be taken to select properties sold under the usual financing terms. This does not mean that the GIM must apply to only cash sales—they are probably atypical. At the other extreme, it would be just as invalid to select a dwelling that initially rented for $750 a month and sold for $200,000 under an installment contract with no down payment. In these two examples, it is more than likely that the sales price would be distorted by the unusual terms of sale.

AGE OF PROPERTY.   Because GIMs are another way of showing the gross capitalization rate, they include provision for capital recovery on depreciable buildings. Property nearing the end of its economic life may be expected to show greater expenses for repairs and maintenance and a lower gross income. Newer properties are more likely to command higher rents than older properties that typically have higher operating expenses. It is important to compare gross incomes for properties showing the same relative degree of depreciation as the property under appraisal.

QUALITY OF INCOME.   It would be reasonable to expect similar differences between GIMs drawn from the sale of middle-income, multiple-family apartments and GIMs derived from apartments rented to low-income groups. Given the same level of gross income, GIMs may still vary because of the relative quality or risks associated with different income properties. This factor again recommends GIMs based on sales with comparable income quality.

TENANT SERVICES.   A simple comparison of gross incomes and selling prices will not account for differences in tenant services. Hence, for the highest degree of accuracy, GIMs would require the same relative level of tenant services.

   These adjustments are noted to indicate that GIMs, though useful in the general case, must be reviewed for factors that affect their value. The reasons for variation in GIMs noted here are sufficient to suggest a careful review of selling prices, gross incomes, and their related characteristics.

GIMs EVALUATED

To be sure, GIMs are not applicable to all income property appraisals. They apply only to GIMs drawn from valid market sales and their corresponding annual gross incomes. Their application requires an evaluation of GIMs.

GIM ADVANTAGES.   It is generally understood that the GIM is not a substitute for more conventional real estate appraisal approaches. With this qualification, the GIM offers four advantages for appraisal purposes:

1. *The GIM helps determine data comparability.*

   If it is established that the prevailing GIM is 6.5 and the property under review is sold for a price indicating a GIM of 4.0, the sale may be judged noncomparable. A nonconforming GIM calls for a review of the sales price, the gross income, and the operating expense data.

2. *GIMs eliminate subjectivity in estimating capital recovery.*

   In both the income and the cost approach, some allowance must be made for capital recovery or accrued depreciation. If the GIM is established for an existing property, depreciation is inherent in the price that buyers and sellers negotiate. To this extent, the GIM includes an allowance for depreciation that is independent of subjective appraisal judgments. There-fore, if the GIM covers older property of the same type and general location, it serves as a highly relevant test of other valuation approaches.

3. The GIM eliminates the need to estimate annual net operating expenses.

Some types of income-producing real estate are too highly specialized to produce meaningful expense data. Single-family dwellings (rental houses) are a case in point. If gross incomes are available for these properties, the GIM is probably more accurate than the capitalization of net income with all of its subjective detail. By eliminating the need to estimate net operating expenses, the GIM provides a considerable degree of objectivity.

4. In the final analysis, the GIM serves as a valuable supplement to other market approaches.

It helps in weighing and evaluating other market evidence. It is derived from independent prices negotiated freely in the market, and it requires a minimum of subjective analysis.

GIM DISADVANTAGES.   The merits of the GIM are not gained without certain disadvantages. Disadvantages are such that the inexperienced or poorly informed may misinterpret GIMs. The GIM has been criticized for the following reasons:

1. The GIM varies widely by outstanding differences in annual net operat-ing expense ratios.
2. The GIM does not differentiate between income properties with highly varying investment risks.
3. The GIM may result from properties that have widely different rates of capital recovery.
4. Income property is purchased for anticipated annual net income—not gross income. This is the most serious disadvantage.

Because of these disadvantages, GIMs are subject to misinterpretation by the inexperienced. The GIM is based on the assumption that:

1. Vacancy rates fall within narrow limits.
2. Annual net operating expense ratios are similar.

3. Comparable properties are drawn from similar property types and comparable neighborhoods.
4. Comparable sales are sufficiently recent to indicate local and current real estate values.
5. The property appraised by a GIM is similar to the comparable sales from which the GIM was derived.

These assumptions are probably true for rental houses, duplexes, residential apartments of 12 units or less, agricultural property, warehouses, and other properties frequently rented and sold. In short, the GIM should be interpreted in the light of other valuation approaches.

Monthly Gross Income Multipliers (MGIMs)

By convention, GIMs for single-family dwellings are taken from monthly rent–not annual rent. A dwelling that rents for $650 per month and that sold for $100,000 shows an MGIM of 153.8 ($100,000/$650). Again, the MGIM is a roundabout means of capitalizing property by gross capitalization rates. For the dwelling above, which rented for $650 a month and sold for $100,000, the gross capitalization rate equals 7.8 percent ($7,800/$100,000).

An MGIM of 100 is equivalent to capitalizing annual gross income at a gross capitalization rate of 12.0 percent. For example, assume a monthly rent of $1,000 and a monthly gross income multiplier of 100. The indicated market value would be $100,000. The resulting gross capitalization rate is 12 percent ($12,000/$100,000) based on a gross annual income of $12,000.

BASED ON AMENITIES

The MGIM measures the weight placed on services rendered by dwellings. It should be recognized that single-family dwellings are not usually built as income-producing property; they are ordinarily constructed for owner-occupants who are more concerned with the utility of the house as a dwelling. To this extent, occupants weigh dwelling livability, the pride of ownership, functional utility, and the convenience of the location. All of these factors and related factors refer to *amenities*—the *intangible benefits of home ownership*. Generally speaking, the amenities increase with market value.

In this context, a $450,000 dwelling will show a higher level of amenities than a $100,000 dwelling. But it does not follow that monthly rent increases in proportion to the increase in amenities. In fact, the contrary is usually true—MGIMs generally increase as amenities increase. This relationship has been explained by the unwillingness of rental occupants to pay for the amenities associated with owner-occupancy. It is claimed that rental occupants price services almost entirely on grounds of functional utility, while prospective buyers are willing to pay more for amenities associated with owner-occupancy.

LOCAL MGIM

Since MGIMs change as property values vary, it is highly important to develop *local multipliers* for the same property type and neighborhood. The MGIMs vary by the submarkets characteristic of residential dwellings; they are affected by neighborhood, by price ranges, by the time of sale, by architectural design, and by other aspects of the housing market. The effective use of MGIMs requires that they be derived from properties similar to the property under appraisal.

EFFECTIVE GROSS INCOME MULTIPLIERS (EGIMs)

The preceding discussion has focused on the relationship between gross income and sales prices. In trade usage, gross income multipliers are further stratified according to vacancy and bad debt allowances. In practice, the *EGIM* refers to the ratio between the effective gross income and sales price. *Effective gross income is that income after deducting an allowance for vacancies and bad debts.*

To distinguish between multipliers calculated *before* vacancy and bad debt losses, appraisers rely on the *potential gross income multiplier* (PGIM). This multiplier is based on the ratio of potential gross income to sales price. The *potential gross income is the annual gross income assuming full occupancy at the market rent.* The PGIM, therefore, is calculated before deducting vacancy and bad debt losses.

These distinctions insure that comparisons are made on a standard, uniform basis. For example, in a proposed project, if reference is made to the PGIM, calculations are based on the gross potential income. In this instance, care must be taken to insure that comparisons and the resulting analysis is based on full occupancy.

Next, consider the appraisal of an existing apartment project showing a 40 percent vacancy. In this case, the appraiser would probably refer to the *EGIM,* indicating that the gross income multiplier is derived *after* deducting vacancy and bad debts. For a property showing a current 40 percent annual vacancy, the differences between the resulting multipliers would be quite substantial. The main point is that gross income multiplier comparisons should be made between properties showing similar vacancy rates.

REGRESSION TECHNIQUES

Regression refers to the statistical association between market value and a property characteristic. For example, there is a relationship between the dwelling square-foot area and market value—that is, larger houses generally sell for more than smaller houses. In this example, the market value would be the "dependent" variable while the square-foot area would be the "independent" variable.

Two developments have encouraged appraisal techniques based on regression techniques—computer records of real estate prices and the availability of personal computers. Computer files of real estate sales that include property characteristics are increasingly maintained by financial institutions, trade associations, commercial firms, and government agencies—local, state, and federal. For instance, the states of Washington, New York, and Pennsylvania, selected counties in California and Florida, and Cook County (Chicago), Illinois, among many others, maintain computer files of real estate sales for property taxes. In most jurisdictions, computer lists of real estate sales are available to the public.

Sophisticated computers, minicomputers, and programmable calculators are increasingly available to the public. Indeed, the wide availability of personal computers makes regression techniques economical for the practicing appraiser. Personal computers and programmable calculators permit appraisers to compete with engineering, accounting, and government agencies that regularly employ advanced computer applications for real estate valuation.

Property Characteristics and Market Value

Multiple regression analysis establishes the statistical relation between selected property characteristics and market value. For example, if 200 recent single-family dwelling sales from a given community were analyzed, it would be evident that generally houses of 3,000 square feet have more value than houses of 1,000 square feet. Regression analysis may indicate the average amount that prices increase with an increase in the square-foot floor area.

It is not implied, however, that this is always the case. Sometimes a 1,000-square-foot house would be more valuable than a 3,000-square-foot house—

depending on their respective condition, location, lot area, and the quality of materials and construction, among other things. Nevertheless, with some exceptions, a fairly uniform relation between selected property characteristics and value generally prevails.

SIMPLE REGRESSION

The term *regression* refers to the relation between two variables: an *independent variable* (property characteristic) and a *dependent variable* (sales price). In a technical sense, property characteristics are regressed against sales prices to produce a valuation formula. To demonstrate, 99 real estate dwelling sales were arranged to show the relation between sales prices and the square-foot dwelling area. In this case, the sales price served as the dependent variable and the square-foot area represented the independent variable.

With one dependent property characteristic or variable, the simple regression equation may be written as:

$$Y = a + b(x)$$

where Y equals the sales price, a is a constant term, b is the coefficient (or multiplier), and x is the independent variable or square-foot area.

In this example, least-squares analysis produces a coefficient, or multiplier, of $32.67, which shows how value changes with a change in square footage. From a single regression calculation, the market value of an 1,800-square-foot dwelling would be equal to $67,900:

$$MV = \$8,131.87 + (32.67 \times 1,800)$$
$$MV = \$66,937.87$$
$$= \$67,900 \text{ (rounded)}$$

Note that the market value, with respect only to the number of square feet, is found by multiplying the coefficient, 32.67, times the square-foot floor area for the house under valuation. Adding the a constant of $8,131.87 indicates a value of $67,900 (rounded). The constant term is equal to the average value of variables left out of the equation. If the equation is perfect and there are no random or measurement errors, the constant term would be zero. Statistically, this relation describes *simple regression analysis*—the term "simple" refers to a single property characteristic.

STANDARD ERROR

In judging regression analysis, appraisers refer to the standard error which indicates the relative accuracy of a simple regression equation.

$$S_e = s/\sqrt{n}$$

where:

S_e = the standard error of the mean
s = the standard deviation of the mean
n = the number of sales

The standard error indicates the dispersion of real estate sales prices from the average sales price. For the 99 dwelling sales, the standard error is $16,357.98. This means that approximately 68 percent of the sale observations would fall plus or minus $16,357 from the average sale price of $66,011.

Appraisal accuracy is also measured by the *multiple coefficient of determination*. This statistic applies when the regression equation includes more than one independent variable or property characteristic. The multiple coefficient indicates the degree to which independent variables explain changes in the dependent variable. By convention this term squared (R^2), called the *multiple coefficient of determination, indicates the variation in the dependent variable explained by the set of independent variables.* Mathematically, the term R^2 (the correlation coefficient squared) is defined as follows:

$$R^2 = \frac{\text{variation explained by the regression equation}}{\text{total variation of the dependent variable}}$$

For example, a multiple coefficient of determination of .90, referred to as the R^2 factor, means that the significant property characteristics explain 90 percent of the variance of property value.[1] For practical appraisal use, it is desirable to refine regression models so that the R^2 factor is at least 90 percent. For the 99 sales sample, the R^2 factor is .6506, meaning that square-foot area explains only 65.06 percent of the sales price. These tests of simple regression indicate that buyers and sellers consider square footage in negotiating sales but that other property characteristics are also

---

1   For a more technical explanation, consult John Neter, William Wasserman, and Michael H. Kutner, *Applied Linear Statistical Models,* Third edition, (Richard D. Irwin, Homewood, Ill., 1990), pp. 444-46.

important. To measure the effect of other property characteristics, appraisers rely on multiple regression models.

Multiple Property Characteristics

To be sure, dwelling prices are not determined solely by their square-foot floor area. Buyers and sellers negotiate prices on the basis of many other property features. Among the more significant features considered in buying and selling are lot area, location, number of bedrooms, number of bathrooms, garages, carports, and numerous other items.

Multiple regression analysis produces a formula that predicts value given a *group* of independent variables (property characteristics). Suppose, for example, that statistical analysis revealed that the equation for market value could be written as follows:

$$\text{Market value} = a + b_1(x_1) + b_2(x_2) + b_4(x_4) + b_5(x_5) + \varepsilon$$

where

a	= a constant
$b_1 \ldots b_n$	= coefficients or multipliers
x_1	= number of square feet
x_2	= lot area in square feet
x_3	= number of bathrooms
x_4	= number of bedrooms
x_5	= date of sale (number of months from the date of sale to the date of valuation)
ε	= error term

In each case, independent variables or property characteristics are represented by the *x* term. Market value is equal to some constant value, the *a* term, plus selected property characteristics (x_1 to x_5) times their respective coefficients or multipliers.

This example follows the earlier illustration except that more than one variable is related to value. It is reasoned that values vary with changes in the selected independent variables x_1 to x_5. In each instance, least-squares analysis produces coefficients or multipliers (b_1 to b_5) that show how value changes according to variations in each of the independent variables. In practice, these independent variables may be expanded to include other characteristics that significantly affect value. The separate discussion of multiple regression analysis that follows shows how appraisals may be completed by multiple regression models.

Multiple Regression Data Requirements

Before reviewing multiple regression appraisals, it is worthwhile to empha-size several data requirements that must be met before this technique can be employed.

First, there must be a sufficient number of observations to establish a relationship between an independent variable and the sales price. For example, among 200 dwelling sales, there may be only one house that has three fireplaces. It would be unreasonable to assume a relation between houses with three fireplaces and market value if there is only one observa-tion in a sample of 200 sales. *There must be a sufficient number of comparisons to establish a relationship between a given property characteristic and sales price.*

Second, property characteristics and sales prices are assumed to be normally distributed. If the observed relationship between a variable, such as square footage, and price show a high degree of dispersion—for example, a lack of concentration around the average sale price, the multiple regression formula loses accuracy. Statistical tests are available for checking this requirement.[1]

Third, sales must represent a fairly uniform group of properties. The valuation formula would lack accuracy if sales prices of the sample varied widely—for example, from $100,000 to $1,500,000. Coefficients and sig-nificant property characteristics associated with luxury housing priced over $1,500,000 have little bearing on the value of a $100,000 house.

Fourth, sales prices must be drawn from a common market area; the resulting valuation formula should not be applied to value houses in a different market area. To cite an extreme case, a multiple regression formula drawn from real estate sales in Atlanta, Georgia, would be inappro-priate for valuing housing in Fort Lauderdale, Florida.

There is one further qualification—multiple regression techniques are inappropriate if properties are not sold in sufficient numbers to make valid statistical comparisons. As a consequence, multiple regression analysis works best for single-family dwellings, vacant land, and, in some instances, multiple-family dwellings, including rental apartments and condomini-ums. Lacking a sufficient number of recent sales of similar properties, appraisers must rely on the cost, comparable sales, or income approach.

---

1 For instance, multiple regression programs frequently print frequency distributions and histograms showing the distribution of independent variables around their respective averages.

Multiple Regression Appraisal Procedures

Like the narrative appraisal report, valuation by multiple regression analysis calls for an organized procedure. But unlike narrative appraisal reports, data requires statistical testing before the valuation formula may be used. Even then, the valuation formula is used only under very restrictive conditions. As a minimum, multiple regression procedures include six steps:

1. Define the sales sample.
2. Select property characteristics.
3. Code property characteristics.
4. Analyze multiple regression statistics.
5. Refine multiple regression data.
   a. Revise the sales sample.
   b. Revise variables.
6. Verify the valuation formula.

A brief summary of each of these steps shows how to apply this valuation technique.

DEFINE THE SALES SAMPLE

The sales sample must be sufficiently representative to produce valid results. In particular, the definition of a neighborhood—its coding, selection, and identification—and the time span over which sales are considered valid deserve special attention.

NEIGHBORHOOD SELECTION

Authorities are divided on techniques of selecting neighborhoods for sampling purposes. In one method, neighborhoods and their boundaries are defined by appraisers familiar with the community. In more sophisticated methods, neighborhoods are selected by statistical techniques programmed for computer analysis.

In the first case, neighborhoods identified by informed appraisers are numbered for computer analysis. Dwelling sales are then grouped by numbered neighborhoods. For illustration, assume that there are five neighborhoods in a given sample. The sale of a particular dwelling could occur in only one of the five neighborhoods. Letting yes = 1 and no = 0, the computer would calculate the association of each neighborhood with sales prices. With these entries, the computer would indicate the increase or decrease in value caused by location in each neighborhood, but only if a location in these neighborhoods significantly affected value.

TIME OF SALE

Within limits, time may be considered an independent variable. Although there are several methods of entering time of sale as a property characteristic, probably the most common practice is to date the sale from a base month. For example, if the appraisal is made as of January 1, each sale is judged according to the number of months from the valuation date.

Preferably, sales are taken from the preceding 12 months. However, if it is desirable to secure more sales from a given area, it is often necessary to go back an additional year. If sales are coded according to month of sale numbered from the date of valuation, regression analysis will indicate how value changes according to the month of sale.

SELECT PROPERTY CHARACTERISTICS

The main objective is to select property characteristics significant to value. Ideally, the appraiser selects *property characteristics actually considered by buyers and sellers in negotiating sales prices.* For example, buyers typically pay higher prices for larger houses than for smaller houses. The number of bedrooms, the number of bathrooms, and the size of the lot are other characteristics commonly considered. In this regard, property characteristics selected for multiple regression analysis vary from characteristics considered under the cost approach.

SIGNIFICANT PROPERTY CHARACTERISTICS

Indeed, one of the advantages of multiple regression analysis is that it requires only the more significant valuation variables. In the final analysis, appraisal experience dictates the selection of characteristics important to value, and, in making this selection, the appraiser omits much descriptive trivia common to the cost approach. Moreover, in contrast to the cost approach, the number of variables may be reduced because many building features are colinear.

COLINEARITY

Colinearity means that two property characteristics commonly occur together. For example, it is seldom necessary to enter the type of porch for a single-family dwelling, because a house built in 1936 will generally have a porch that is typical of 1936, and a two-story house recently constructed will generally have a porch that conforms to the current architectural style. It also follows that a large house will generally have larger floor joists and that a small house will have smaller floor joists. When the square-foot area is coded, many of these constructional details are automatically included.

Therefore, by listing certain property characteristics, namely, the date of construction, the type of construction, and the type of house (one-story, two-story, split-level, and the like), many other details will be automatically considered because they generally occur with the listed features. In other words, they are colinear with other property characteristics.

CODE PROPERTY CHARACTERISTICS

Coding refers to the manner in which property characteristics are listed for computer analysis. Even if the ideal set of property characteristics were properly identified, accurate appraisals would largely depend on the manner in which variables were entered for computer analysis. Moreover, after analyzing computer results, it may be determined that data must be revised to relate property characteristics more accurately to value.[1]

ANALYZE MULTIPLE REGRESSION STATISTICS

Selected variables associated with a multiple regression formula for single-family dwellings are shown in Table 13-2. The table identifies four variables and their coefficients. In this example, the computer was programmed to eliminate the *a* constant. A house in a stable neighborhood with three bathrooms, wall-to-wall carpeting, and an assessed value of $150,000 would have an estimated value of $99,961.52. These variables were the most significant of 29 variables coded for this example.

---

1   For an additional explanation of multiple regression techniques for land and income properties, consult William M. Shenkel, *Modern Real Estate Appraisals,* New York; McGraw-Hill Book Company, 1978, Chapter 15, pp. 318-470. See also Kang, Han-Bin and Alan K. Reichert, "Statistical Models for Appraising Income Properties: The Case of Apartment Buildings. Part I, " *The Real Estate Appraiser and Analyst,* Summer 1988, pp. 29-35; Part II, *The Real Estate Appraiser and Analyst,* Fall 1988, pp. 41-44; The Journal of Real Estate Research, Fall 1987, pp. 1-26; Murphy III, Lloyd T., "Determining the Appropriate Equation in Multiple Regression Analysis," *Appraisal Journal,* October 1989, pp. 489-517; Mark, Jonathan and Michael A. Goldberg, "Multiple Regression Analysis and Mass Assessment: A Review of the Issues," *The Appraisal Journal,* January 1988, pp. 89-109; Donnelly, William A., and Robert L. Andrews, "Understanding and Using Variance in Regression Based Appraisals," *The Real Estate Appraiser and Analyst,* Fall 1988, pp. 50-58; Larsen, James E. and Manferd O. Penderson, "Correcting Errors in Statistical Appraisal Equations," The Real Estate Appraiser and Analyst, Fall 1988, pp. 45-49; and Miller, Norman G. and Michael A. Sklarz, "Multiple Regression Condominium Valuation with a Touch of Behavioral Theory," *Appraisal Journal,* January 1987, pp. 108-115.

Table 13-2   Multiple Regression Coefficients for Four Significant Characteristics*

99 Dwelling Sales	
Variable	Coefficient
Stable Neighborhood	-$4,295.29
Number of Bathrooms	15.8694
Wall-to-Wall Carpeting	3,904.20
Assessed Value	.6687

*Multiple coefficient of correlation, 98.17
Average error, $6,023.52
Percent of error, $6,023.52/$66,011
              9.12 percent

$$MV = -4{,}295.29 + 15.8694\ (3) + 3{,}904.20\ (1) + .6687\ (150{,}000)$$
$$= \$99{,}961.52$$

The model accounts for 98.17 of the sale price variation and illustrates an average error based on the average sale price of $66,011 of 9.12 percent.

Before the formula is accepted for appraisal purposes, the statistical results of multiple regression must meet minimum acceptable criteria. Besides the multiple coefficient of determination (R^2), the average residual value indicates the relative accuracy of the market value estimate.

AVERAGE RESIDUAL VALUE

As a final test, multiple regression analysis includes a comparison of individual sales prices with their calculated values as determined by the multiple regression formula. The difference between the sales price and the computed value is termed the *residual*—the amount unexplained by multiple regression analysis.

SUMMARY

Gross income multipliers express the relationship between annual gross income and selling price. Provided that the GIM is derived from an adequate number of comparable sales, the GIM converts gross income to an indicated value. The *gross capitalization rate* is a reciprocal of the GIM. For example, an annual gross income of $600,000 that sells for a price indicating a GIM of 8 would indicate a gross capitalization rate of 12.5 percent. The GIM varies according to the gross annual income, the sale price, and the annual net operating expense ratio. To convert the GIM to an overall capitalization rate, divide the annual net income ratio by the GIM. Variations in gross income multipliers are caused by vacancy rates, type of sale, property type, financing terms, age of property, quality of income, and tenant services.

In evaluating the GIM, it is believed that the GIM helps determine data comparability, eliminates subjectivity in estimating capital recovery, eliminates the need to estimate the annual net operating expenses, and it serves as a supplement to other market approaches. Countering these advantages are other limitations; the GIM does not allow for differences in annual operating expenses, the GIM does not differentiate between income property with highly varying risks, and finally, income property is purchased according to anticipated annual net income—not gross income.

Monthly gross income multipliers (MGIM) indicate market value as a multiple of monthly rent—typically for single family dwellings. The MGIM is based on amenities—the intangible benefits of home ownership. The MGIM therefore is developed for residential neighborhoods covering the same property type and neighborhood.

Regression refers to the statistical association between market value and property characteristics. For example, there is a relation between dwelling square-foot area and market value. *Multiple regression analysis* is the statistical relationship between selected property characteristics and market value. *Simple regression*, in contrast, refers to the relation between two variables—the independent variable (property characteristic) and the dependent variable (sales price). Under simple regression, a property characteristic is regressed against the sale price to produce a regression coefficient or a multiplier showing the relation between a property characteristic and market value.

Regression models are tested by the *standard deviation* which indicates the relative dispersion of sales prices from the average price. *First,* multiple regression appraisals require a sufficient number of observations to establish the relationship between an independent variable and the sales price. *Second,* property characteristics and sales prices must be normally distributed. *Third,* sales selected for multiple regression must represent a fairly uniform group of properties. *Finally,* sales prices must be drawn from a common market area. Multiple regression techniques are usable for properties frequently sold in sufficient numbers to make valid statistical comparisons.

In applying multiple regression procedures, the appraiser must follow six well-defined steps—define the sales sample, select property characteristics, code property characteristics, analyze multiple regression statistics, refine multiple regression data, and verify the valuation formula.

Colinearity means that two property characteristics normally occur together. The *multiple coefficient of determination* is a measure that indicates the amount of sales price explained by the multiple regression formula. The *standard error of estimate* indicates the relative degree of accuracy. Market values fall within one standard error of the predicted value. The *average residual value* shows the average deviation between sales prices and their calculated values as determined by the multiple regression formula.

POINTS TO REMEMBER

gross income multiplier (GIM) the relation between annual gross income and selling price expressed as a ratio. Property sold for $10,000,000 with a current annual gross income of $1,200,000 illustrates a GIM of 8.3 ($10,000,000/ $1,200,000).

effective gross income multiplier (EGIM) the ratio of effective gross income, less vacancies and bad debts, to sales price.

potential gross income multiplier (PGIM) the ratio of annual gross income at full occupancy to sales price.

gross capitalization rate the reciprocal of the gross income multiplier.

overall capitalization rate the annual net income expressed as a percent of the selling price.

net operating expense ratio total annual operating expenses expressed as a percent of reported gross annual net income.

net income ratio the complement of the annual net operating expense ratio.

amenities the intangible benefits of home ownership.

monthly gross income multiplier (MGIM) the relationship between monthly gross income and sales price.

simple regression analysis the statistical association between market value and a property characteristic; the relationship between an independent variable (property characteristic) and a dependent variable (sales price).

standard deviation statistical measures showing the relative dispersion of sales prices from the average sales price.

multiple regression analysis the statistical technique of predicting market value from a group of independent variables or property characteristics.

colinearity the tendency of two property characteristics to occur together.

multiple coefficient of determination (R^2) a statistical measure that indicates the variation in the dependent variable explained by a set of independent variables.

standard error of estimate a statistical measure that indicates that the predicted value would fall within 68 percent of the cases.

residual value the amount of variance unexplained by multiple regression analysis.

QUESTIONS FOR REVIEW

1. Explain thoroughly the GIM and the monthly GIM.

2. Explain the main determinants of a GIM.

3. Give an example showing how the overall capitalization rate may be calculated from the GIM.

4. Show how the monthly gross income multiplier is actually a method of appraising by the gross capitalization rate.

5. Discuss the main factors that cause variations in GIMs.

6. Critically evaluate GIMs.

7. What are the assumptions basic to using the GIMs for appraisals?

8. What types of properties would you recommend for appraisal by means of the GIM? Give reasons for your answer.

9. Explain what is meant by simple regression techniques.

10. What are main requirements that must be met to undertake a multiple regression appraisal?

11. What procedures would you follow in completing a multiple regression appraisal? Explain fully.

12. Explain how you would analyze a multiple regression model.

13. What property characteristics would you consider significant in predicting market value of single-family dwellings? Explain fully.

PRACTICE PROBLEMS

1. From a local source such as a multiple listing service, compare the sales prices and the reported gross income for five sales of income property. Explain the variation in gross income multipliers observed in your sample.

2. Secure from local real estate sources five sales of income properties of different types, i.e., shopping centers and apartment houses. Compare gross income with each sales price. Explain why gross income multipliers for your sample properties vary.

3. Calculate the overall capitalization rate assuming an operating expense ratio of 40 percent and a gross income multiplier of 6.5.

4. From local interviews or recent property sales, identify monthly gross income multipliers for low- or middle-income housing in your community. If possible, base your conclusions on actual rental properties that have recently been sold.

5. (a) Give an example of how you would calculate the overall capitalization rate from the GIM.
   (b) Explain why the GIM may give erroneous results. Explain thoroughly.

6. Suppose you elect to develop a multiple regression valuation formula for a large neighborhood of single family dwellings. Explain how you would proceed in designing the multiple regression program and determining the appraisal accuracy of the resulting multiple regression formula.

C H A P T E R   1 4

Real Estate Finance

After reading this chapter you will know:
- The legal foundations of real estate mortgages.
- Financial rights of lenders and borrowers.
- Financing under trust deeds.
- Various mortgage repayment plans.
- Federal housing administration mortgage terms.
- Terms of veterans administration guaranteed loans.

Appraisers interpret financing terms to qualify real estate sales. The market value estimate presumes that the property will be sold under typical purchasing terms, including prevailing financing plans. Therefore, it seems relevant to review mortgage instruments, repayment plans, foreclosure procedures, and the special features of FHA and Veterans Administration loans that may bear on real estate markets and market value estimates. Following these concepts, the chapter deals with contractual aspects of mortgages–mainly, financial rights of lenders and borrowers. Trust deeds are reviewed since many states substitute trust deeds for mortgages. In all states, trust deeds and mortgages vary by the repayment plans, reviewed in the next portion of the chapter. The chapter includes a summary of loans insured by the Federal Housing Administration and guaranteed by the Veterans Administration.

MORTGAGE AGREEMENTS

Simply stated, *mortgages pledge a real estate interest as security for a debt.* A *borrower,* who grants a mortgage pledge, is the *mortgagor.* The *lender* granting the loan represents the *mortgagee.* Usually the interest secured is the title of the fee owner. However, partial interests may be mortgaged, such as a landowner's leased fee interest or a tenant's leasehold interest. Virtually any interest may be pledged as security for a debt. In this respect, however, the states vary in the way in which a real estate interest secures the debt.

Mortgage Instruments

Mortgages developed under English common law originating from feudal practices of the twelfth century. As initially conceived, the borrower conveyed an interest in property to the lender. States that continue to treat mortgages as conveyances are known as *title theory* states. Certain other states, known as *lien theory* states, vest title in the borrower and define mortgages as a lien. A few states follow an *intermediate theory.*

TITLE THEORY STATES

Mortgages in these states transfer title from the borrower to the lender. Such mortgages generally stipulate that the borrower or mortgagor remains in possession, as long as the borrower is not in default. Upon payment of the mortgage, title reverts to the borrower. If the borrower defaults on the mortgage, possession of the land passes to the lender.

Suppose A borrows from lender B in a title state. The mortgage given by A to B will state that if A makes the required payments, the mortgage will be void. However, even if title reverts to lender B in a title state, B must still follow foreclosure procedures.

LIEN THEORY STATES

Most states define mortgages as a lien. Under this concept, the borrower retains legal title to the mortgaged property and transfers only a security interest to the lender. The mortgage does not entitle the lender to possession. The borrower retains the right of possession incident to the title until the borrower defaults.

INTERMEDIATE THEORY STATES

A few states follow the intermediate theory. Here the mortgage granted by borrower A to lender B constitutes a lien. On default by A, title passes to lender B, who then forecloses. In most instances, the rights and duties of parties to a mortgage do not depend on the location of title. However, because of the differences in title concepts, legal remedies must conform to state requirements. The main difference between lien, title, or intermediate states lies in the method of foreclosure.

Promissory Note

The promissory note (in some states, a bond) is the borrower's personal promise to repay a debt. The note is accompanied by a mortgage or similar instrument that pledges real estate as additional security. Thus, the lender acquires the personal promise of the borrower to repay the loan and holds the mortgage as additional security.

Financial Rights of the Lender-Mortgagee

State legislation considerably modifies rights of the borrower and lender. Not only must the mortgage conform to state laws, but it must conform to certain federal laws. Critically important to lenders are clauses that cover:

1. The right of acceleration.
2. Due on sale clauses.
3. Escrow provisions.
4. Other considerations.

ACCELERATION CLAUSES

Suppose the borrower defaults on a mortgage payment of $710.92 for a mortgage of $60,000 which has a remaining balance of $59,878.61. Technically the borrower is in default on only the delinquent monthly payment of $710.92. Without an acceleration clause, the lender must initiate foreclosure procedures to recover each delinquent installment of $710.92.

The acceleration clause avoids such a procedure. On default, the acceleration clause gives the lender the right to demand full payment of the remaining balance of $59,878.61. To enforce this clause the lender must observe mortgage terms and state law.

It should be added that the borrower-mortgagor would be in default for failure to perform any duty required of the mortgage. Besides failure to make monthly payments, the next most frequent cause of foreclosure would be nonpayment of property taxes or the lapse of fire insurance. While the lender would have the right to initiate foreclosure procedures if the borrower makes late payments, in practice lenders would not foreclose unless the loan was 60 to 90 days delinquent.

DUE ON SALE CLAUSES

Due on sale clauses give lenders the right to payment of the debt on sale. A typical clause would read:

> *If all or any part of the property or any interest in it is sold or transferred without the lender's prior written consent, lender may, at its option, require immediate payment in full of all sums secured by this security instrument.*

Two reasons justify due on sale clauses. First, the clause protects lenders from uncreditworthy buyers who might assume an existing mortgage. Since the lender has loaned money on the personal qualifications of the borrower, it is reasoned that the borrower cannot escape the obligation unless the party assuming the loan has equal or better credit. So, before the original buyer is released from the loan, the lender may require that the proposed purchaser be qualified in the same way as the original borrower.

Second, due on sale clauses are effective in terminating below-market interest rate loans. Suppose, for example, that the borrower purchased a dwelling for $17,500 down and borrowed $167,500 under an 8.5 percent interest rate mortgage. If the property is sold five years later and the current market interest rate is 12 percent, a due on sale clause permits the lender to cancel the existing 8.5 percent interest loan and negotiate a new mortgage at the 12 percent rate.

Formerly some state-chartered financial institutions were prohibited from enforcing due on sale clauses by state law. However, the Garn-St. Germain Depository Institutions Act of 1982 allows all lenders to enforce due on sale clauses. As it stands, the federal law supersedes state laws that prohibit enforcement of due on sale clauses.

If, however, the loan is *assumable,* buyers may continue an existing loan by purchasing subject to an existing mortgage or assuming an existing mortgage. A buyer who assumes and agrees to pay the mortgage expresses an intent to assume personally the mortgage debt; thus, if the mortgage is foreclosed and the proceeds of the sale are insufficient to satisfy the debt, the lender may hold the assuming party personally responsible. However, state laws vary on this point.

The distinction between buying subject to and assuming an existing loan affects payments of a deficiency under a foreclosure sale. If A sells a $200,000 dwelling subject to a $160,000 mortgage, the buyer merely acknowledges the mortgage. If the new buyer fails to make payments, the lender forecloses. Suppose, however, that the foreclosure sale results in a deficiency of $20,000. In this case, the seller-lender must assume the deficiency—the buyer only loses his or her paid-up equity. Unless released by the lender, the original borrower remains personally liable for the deficiency under the promissory note.

ESCROW PROVISIONS

Mortgages require that the borrower insure the property mortgaged against loss by fire or other hazards. In addition, the borrower agrees to pay all taxes and assessments. To meet these requirements, mortgages allow for escrow funds which are paid monthly according to the escrow clause:

> *Borrowers shall pay one-twelfth of yearly taxes and assessments and hazard insurance premiums.*

Such mortgage clauses might also include leasehold payments or ground rents and mortgage insurance premiums. The lender makes reasonable estimates of these charges to calculate the required monthly escrow deposit. Any excess of escrow funds above actual taxes or insurance premiums are paid or credited to the borrower. Similarly the borrower must promptly pay deficiencies if the escrow payments have been under-estimated.

The *Real Estate Settlement Procedures Act of 1974,* as amended, prohibits lenders from establishing escrow accounts for property taxes, insurance, and other charges for more than the amount needed to make payments plus two months' deposits. Besides the federal regulation, nine states require lenders to pay interest on escrow accounts. In some states such as Illinois, borrowers may pledge a savings account as collateral in lieu of an escrow account.

DEFICIENCY JUDGMENTS

In most jurisdictions, the lender may secure a judgment against the assets of the borrower equal to the difference between the mortgage loan and proceeds of the foreclosure sale. In states allowing for this procedure, the courts would award a judgment for the unpaid loan balance.

However, this remedy may not be effective. In most cases a defaulted borrower would not have assets to make up the deficiency; otherwise, they would have been used to prevent the foreclosure. A deficiency judgment is uncollectible against a borrower who has no assets. Moreover, the deficiency judgment is not effective against the dishonest debtor who conceals assets or avoids payments by not owning real estate in his or her name.

In addition, some deficiency judgments do not apply to trust deeds. They are prohibited in loans insured by the Federal Housing Administration and by several states for seller-financed mortgages. Because of these limitations, lenders depend on borrower's equity in the loan and the mortgage insurance as loan security.

OTHER LEGAL CONSIDERATIONS.

Since the mortgage pledges real estate as security for a debt, mortgages usually require that the borrower keep the property in good repair. Mortgage clauses prohibit the borrower from permitting property impairment or deterioration. To enforce the mortgage, the lender reserves the right to make reasonable entries and inspections of the property after giving prior notice to the borrower.

Lenders who originate mortgages reserve the right to assign mortgages to others. Since the mortgage is personal property, the transfer may be made without the borrower's consent.

Financial Rights of the Borrower-Mortgagor

While the borrower has the right of possession, even in states that transfer title of mortgaged property to the lender, certain other rights modify mortgage agreements. Some of these financial rights are subject to negotiation and, in some cases, they are unique to specific types of mortgages. The more important topics relate to prepayment privileges, the right of redemption, and the right to a mortgage release upon satisfaction of the debt.

PREPAYMENT PRIVILEGES

Suppose a lender grants a mortgage of $200,000, with a fixed interest rate of 10 percent repayable over 360 months. Over the life of the loan the lender would collect total interest of $431,850 (360 monthly mortgage payments of $1,755.14, less the $200,000 principal). In this sense the mortgage may be viewed as an enforceable contract that entitles the lender to a total cumulative return of $431,850 on invested capital of $200,000. Providing that the mortgage interest rate is at the market level or above, the lender has no incentive to accept prepayments. If the mortgage interest rate is above the market rate, a borrower with prepayment privileges may negotiate a new loan at a lower interest rate and prepay the original loan.

Unless the promissory note provides that the note may be paid in full before maturity, the borrower may prepay only if the lender grants this privilege. Some lenders levy *prepayment penalties* if the loan is prepaid before maturity.

The lender, however, may face restrictions on prepayment fees. Generally if the borrower prepays, it is common to decrease prepayment penalties as the maturity of the loan increases. However, loans guaranteed by the Veterans Administration may be prepaid at any time without penalty. Further, if the loan is to be sold to the Federal Home Loan Mortgage Corporation or the Federal National Mortgage Association, prepayment penalties are prohibited. Likewise, mortgages providing for variable interest rates over the mortgage term allow prepayments without penalty.

THE EQUITY OF REDEMPTION

The lender has the right to foreclose if the borrower breaches any of the covenants or promises stated in the mortgage. Yet the borrower has the right to redeem the property and prevent foreclosure by paying the full amount of the debt including interest and expenses incurred by the lender. This right is expressed as the equity of redemption. Thus, the borrower has the right to have any foreclosure proceedings discontinued at any time before the foreclosure sale provided, however, that the borrower cures all breaches of any mortgage agreements and pays all reasonable expenses incurred by the lender in enforcing the mortgage, including legal fees.

STATUTORY RIGHT OF REDEMPTION

Some states give the borrower *additional time to redeem the property after the foreclosure sale* which is called the *statutory right of redemption.* While the equity of redemption ends with foreclosure, the statutory right starts only after the equity of redemption has terminated. Unlike equitable redemption, the property may be redeemed by paying the foreclosure sale price (more or less than the loan) plus interest at the rate specified in the redemption statute.

Typically, states providing for this right limit the statutory period to six months or one year after the foreclosure sale. In essence, the statutory right of redemption gives the purchaser at a foreclosure sale a conditional title. The title will not be absolute until expiration of the redemption period. Parties with the right to redemption would be unlikely to redeem unless the value of the property increases over the foreclosure sale price. Though the statutory period of redemption gives the borrower time to refinance and redeem, purchasers of foreclosed property will not secure clear title until expiration of the statutory redemption period. Figure 14-1 illustrates the difference between the two types of equity of redemption.

Figure 14-1   Borrower Rights of Redemption

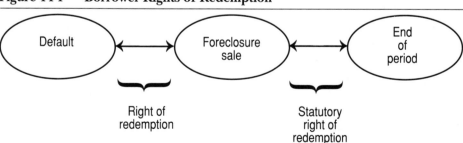

MORTGAGE RELEASE

Payment of the debt releases the borrower from the lender's interest in the property. At this time the borrower has the right to have the public record cleared of the lender's interest in the mortgaged property. To clear public records, the lender must execute an instrument that releases the borrower's property from the mortgage. Recording of this release form clears the borrower's title. In lien theory states payment of the debt extinguishes the lien. Here the borrower should be given the canceled note in evidence of the payment. In other instances, the release would be accomplished by recorded instruments or notation and recordation of the repayment on the recorded mortgage. In some cases the public recorder makes an entry of satisfaction on the margin of the recorded mortgage. In addition the insurance company should be notified and given evidence of the mortgage satisfaction.

TRUST DEEDS

Trust deeds are written instruments in which a borrower (trustor) transfers a real estate title to a trustee who holds title in trust for a lender (the beneficiary) as security for a loan. The deed contains a clause giving the trustee power of sale if the borrower defaults. In some states the instrument is referred to as a deed of trust or a trust deed mortgage. While functionally the trust deed is similar to a mortgage and promissory note, trust deeds avoid the more time-consuming mortgage foreclosure procedures.

Figure 14-2 illustrates the three-party relationships established by the trust deed. For trust deeds, like mortgage instruments, the borrower executes a promissory note. To secure the loan the lender appoints a trustee who holds title under the trust deed. However the trustee has only an interest in the trustor's property which is necessary to fulfill responsibilities to the trust deed beneficiary or lender. The title is held only in the sense that it secures repayment of the loan. Though the trust deed is held by the trustee, the borrower essentially holds the full legal title to the property. The borrower can still sell the property, borrow additional funds, lease the property, or use the property in any manner not inconsistent with the rights of the lender-beneficiary.

Figure 14-2   Parties to a Trust Deed

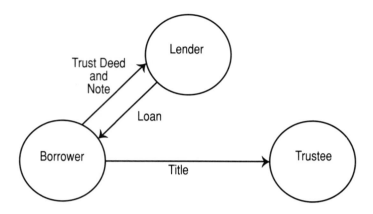

Trust Deed Procedures

In general, terms of the trust deed closely parallel mortgage clauses. Over the duration of the loan, the borrower makes payments to the beneficiary according to the promissory note. Terms of the trust deed require that the borrower pay taxes and insurance and maintain the property as stated in the trust deed. While these procedures are similar to mortgage terms, the administration of a defaulted loan varies under a trust deed.

Defaults under a Trust Deed

If the debt is delinquent, the beneficiary notifies the trustee of the default and requests sale of the property to satisfy the debt. The promissory note and the trust deed will be delivered to the trustee with this request. The trustee then records the notice of default. The recording must be done in a certain minimum time before issuing a notice of the sale—for example, 90 days in California.

Following the 90-day or other statutory period, the trustee executes a notice of sale which includes a property description and the time, place, and reason for the sale. Most statutes require that notice of the sale must be printed in a newspaper of general circulation for a stated minimum number of times. After these statutory requirements are met, the property will be placed on sale at a specified location in the county in which the property is located. The highest bidder will receive a trustee's deed. This process may be completed in a minimum of three months and 22 days in the state of California.

MORTGAGES CLASSIFIED BY REPAYMENT PLANS

Lenders and borrowers may select from a wide range of repayment plans. Generally, borrowers prefer amortized mortgages. Amortized mortgages provide for partial payment of principal with each mortgage payment. Amortized mortgages, therefore, include monthly payments that cover partial payment of principal and interest payments on the remaining mortgage balance. If the mortgage is held to maturity, monthly payments provide for "amortization," or repayment of mortgage principal.

Most amortized mortgages fall under fixed interest rate, level payment mortgages; variable interest rate mortgages; term mortgages; variable payment amortization; and balloon mortgages. These various mortgages may be modified by mortgage "buydowns" that reduce monthly mortgage payments.

Fixed Interest Rate, Level Payment Mortgages

In this case, the mortgage payments are constant, the amount accruing to principal and interest varies with each payment, and interest is calculated against the remaining balance. For instance, a $175,000 mortgage at 10 percent interest per annum for 25 years would require a monthly payment of $1,590.23. In the first payment, $1,458.33 would be paid to interest, while the balance of the payment ($131.90) would retire principal. The interest of $1,458.33 represents the first month's interest on $175,000 (.10/12 x $175,000). Since the interest is calculated on the remaining balance, interest payments decrease over the life of the mortgage while principal payments slowly increase. The amortization schedule for the first 12 months of this loan is shown in Table 14-1. Note that over the 12 months, principal payments increase from $131.90 to $144.50. The level payment loan allocates a greater proportion of each payment to interest during the early years of the loan.

Table 14-1   Monthly Amortization of a Level Payment Mortgage of $175,000, 10 percent interest, 25-year term*

Number of of Months	Principal Payments	Interest Payments	Remaining Balance	Percent of Principal
1	$131.90	$1,458.33	$174,868.10	99.9
2	133.00	1,457.23	174,735.10	99.8
3	134.10	1,456.13	174,601.00	99.8
4	135.22	1,455.01	174,465.78	99.7
5	136.35	1,453.88	174,329.43	99.6
6	137.48	1,452.75	174,191.95	99.5
7	138.63	1,451.60	174,053.32	99.5
8	139.79	1,450.44	173,913.53	99.4
9	140.95	1,449.28	173,772.58	99.3
10	142.13	1,448.10	173,630.45	99.2
11	143.31	1,446.92	173,487.14	99.1
12	144.50	1,445.73	173,342.64	99.1

*Monthly Payments are $1,590.23; total interest for 12 months: $17,425.40.

Variable Interest Rate Mortgages (VRM)

The distinguishing feature of a VRM mortgage is that interest rates may be adjusted periodically to an index. The VRM shifts the risk of interest rate changes from the lender to the borrower. By assuming this risk, the borrower is initially given a slightly lower interest rate than the rate prevailing for fixed-rate mortgages.

Lenders have many options to offer prospective borrowers. The options are limited by federal regulations affecting savings institutions and the Office of the Comptroller of Currency that regulates VRMs for national banks. The states have also enacted laws that govern VRMs for state-chartered lenders.

These various regulatory authorities allow lenders to vary three main features common to VRMs:

1. *Frequency of the interest rate change.* National banks with a federal charter may change mortgage rates no more than every six months. Savings associations operating with federal charters have no such restrictions.

2. *Magnitude of the rate change.* National banks are restricted to a maximum change of one percentage point in six months. Federal savings and loan associations have no maximum limits.

3. *Interest rate index.* National banks may adjust mortgage contract rates for previously occupied homes to changes in three- or six-month Treasury Bill rates. Savings associations may choose any index that can be verified and that is beyond lender control.

Term Mortgages

Term mortgages do not amortize the principal. They are interest-only loans. Ordinarily, term mortgages are confined to borrowers with excellent credit; such mortgages are generally limited to relatively short periods of three to five years.

For instance, suppose a borrower executes a $100,000 mortgage with a three-year maturity and a 12 percent interest rate. The parties may agree to an annual interest of $1,200 payable monthly, quarterly, semiannually, or annually. At the end of three years, the principal of $100,000 would be due.

If the $100,000 principal is not paid on the due date, the borrower's only remedy is to refinance or renew the mortgage for another three years.

Variable Payment Amortization

Under this plan, which is less commonly used, the amortization calls for a *constant payment to principal.* Here the lender and borrower agree to a fixed amount that is applied to principal. With agreement on this point, mortgage payments may be calculated, given the annual interest rate and the frequency of payment. Assuming a principal repayment of $1,000 per year to retire a $10,000 loan and an annual interest rate of 12 percent, the first payment of $2,200 ($1,200, interest; $1,000, principal payment) decreases to $1,120 at the end of the 10th year. In this example, principal repayments would total $10,000, and interest would amount to $6,600. These figures are summarized in Table 14-2.

Under this plan, the payments are relatively large during the early years of the mortgage compared to those in the final years. Because of this feature, the variable payment mortgage is not very common.

Table 14-2   Amortization under a Variable Payment, $10,000 Mortgage, 12 percent interest

End of Year	Principal Repayment (constant)	Annual Interest	Annual Mortgage Payment	Remaining Balance
1	$ 1,000	$ 1,200	$ 2,200	$9,000
2	1,000	1,080	2,080	8,000
3	1,000	960	1,960	7,000
4	1,000	840	1,840	6,000
5	1,000	720	1,720	5,000
6	1,000	600	1,600	4,000
7	1,000	480	1,480	3,000
8	1,000	360	1,360	2,000
9	1,000	240	1,240	1,000
10	1,000	120	1,120	0
Total	$10,000	$ 6,600	$16,600	

Balloon Mortgages

To illustrate, assume that payments on a $40,000 loan are based on a 20-year term for only $20,000 with a lump-sum payment for the balance of the mortgage due at the end of 10 years. In effect, the loan represents a 10-year mortgage with a lump-sum payment of the remaining principal at the date of maturity. The amortization schedule is drawn for less than the principal. In practice, the lump-sum payment, referred to as a balloon payment, is seldom made at maturity since the partial amortization increases equity and qualifies the property for refinancing under a fully amortized mortgage.

The effect of the balloon mortgage is to reduce monthly payments without reducing interest rates and without extending loan terms beyond legal maximum limits. A borrower, who has excellent credit and is expected to have an increasing income over the life of the mortgage, will be attracted to this loan. Frequently, the plan is used for borrowers approaching retirement age.

Mortgage Buydowns

Buydowns make high-market interest rate mortgages more affordable. With a buydown the borrower pays lower than market interest rates.

Mortgage buydowns are *payments to the lender by the seller, builder, or buyer to reduce the mortgage interest rate and, therefore, monthly payments.*

Assume that a dwelling may be financed with a 12 percent, fixed-rate mortgage of $90,000, 30 years. Under these terms the borrower must make monthly mortgage payments of $925.74. Applying a 25 percent mortgage payment-to-income ratio, the borrower would require a monthly income of $3,702.96 ($925.74 x 4) or almost $45,000 per year.

To lower monthly payments, the builder might advertise the house with financing available at a 9 percent, fixed-rate interest, repayable over 360 months. The monthly payments of $724.14 on a $90,000 loan would qualify buyers earning not less than $34,750 annually. If the lender accepted these terms, mortgage payments would be $201.60 less than the market interest rate of 12 percent ($925.74-$724.14).

If the lender considers the average mortgage to be outstanding for 12 years or 144 months, the lender faces a loss of $201.60 over 144 months which has a present worth of $15,349.25.

$$\text{Loss} = \text{PVAF}_{.12/12} \, 144 \, (\$201.60)$$
$$= 76.137157(\$201.60)$$
$$= \$15,349.25$$

Therefore, for the lender to accept a 12 percent yield on a fixed-rate mortgage, the builder would "buydown" the mortgage by paying the lender the present worth of the monthly loss or $15,349.25. If the dwelling was initially priced at $100,000, it would now be advertised for $115,500 which would require that the buyer pay $25,500 down with a $90,000 first mortgage, at nine percent interest.

In short, the buyer trades off the lower monthly payments by paying a higher price for the dwelling. The buyer hopes that price inflation over the ownership period will eventually recoup the higher-than-market price. In this case, the buyer purchases a dwelling which includes a $15,500 payment for the right to below-market financing. It should be noted that not only builders but other sellers may offer the same terms.

Mortgage Discounts

Lender approval of a $100,000 mortgage, nine percent interest, for 30 years does not necessarily mean that the borrower will have $100,000 to apply toward a purchase. This is because lenders engage in mortgage discounting. While loan repayment would be calculated on a $100,000 principal, a lender who discounts the mortgage by two points (two percentage points) would advance only $98,000. Mortgage discounting is the process of *increasing the mortgage interest rate without increasing loan payments.* The borrower would make mortgage payments on the basis of a $100,000 principal though the borrower was actually loaned only $98,000.

To calculate the effective interest rate, it is commonly presumed that the mortgage will be repaid at the end of year 12. If the loan is repaid at an earlier date, the yield increases. In the above example the effective interest rate is found by following three steps:

Assume that a lender offers a mortgage of $100,000, nine percent interest, 25 years with a two-point discount. Further assume a holding period of 12 years. The first two steps require calculation of the monthly mortgage payments and the remaining balance at the end of the holding period.

$$\text{MMP} = \text{MMC}_{i/12,(n \times 12)} (P)$$

Where:

MMP = the monthly mortgage payments
MMC = the monthly mortgage constant
i = the annual mortgage interest rate
n = the mortgage term in years
P = mortgage principal
    $= \text{MMC}_{.0075,300} (\$100,000)$
    $= .008392\ (\$100,000)$
    $= \$839.20$
RmB = $\text{MPVAF}_{.0075,156}\ (\$839.20)$
    $= 91.770018\ (\$839.20)$
    $= \$77,013.4$

Where:
RmB = remaining mortgage balance
MPVAF = monthly present value of an annuity factor

Under the assumed terms, the lender has the right to $839.20 over 144 months and the right to the remaining balance of $77,013.40 at the end of 144 months. For this financial benefit the lender has paid $98,000.

$$\$98,000 = \text{MPVAF}_{?,n} (\text{MMP}) + \text{MPVF}_{?,n} (\text{RmB})$$
$$= \text{MPVAF}_{?,144}\ (\$839.20) + \text{MPVF}_{?,144}\ (\$77,013.40)$$
$$= 9.300\ \text{percent}$$

Where:

n   = The expected holding period in months
MMP   = Monthly mortgage payments
MPVF   = Monthly present value factor
?   = Unknown effective interest rate

   The effective interest will be given by solving for the unknown effective interest that equates the present value of mortgage payments and the present value of the remaining balance to $98,000. Iterative computer routines make successive changes in the interest rate to show an effective yield of 9.3 percent.

   This calculation is sensitive to the assumed holding period. If, in fact, the mortgage is repaid in seven years, the effective yield increases to 9.408 percent. The yield increases because the discount is now repaid over a shorter period with a consequent higher yield.

FEDERAL HOUSING ADMINISTRATION INSURED MORTGAGES

As an agency of the Department of Housing and Urban Development (HUD), the Federal Housing Administration (FHA) insures mortgages on one- to four-family dwellings. In addition, FHA provides mortgage insurance for multiple- and single-family housing, such as condominiums and cooperatives. Other programs provide subsidies to special groups such as low- and moderate-income families.

Mortgage Terms

The present discussion covers mortgage terms common to FHA-insured mortgages on unsubsidized mortgages for one- to four-family dwellings.

NO DUE ON SALE CLAUSES

FHA-insured loans are assumable. Currently, buyers may assume existing FHA loans without penalty. However, unless the new buyer is qualified by FHA, the original borrower remains liable for the FHA mortgage. Only if the new borrower is qualified by FHA will the original borrower be released from liability for the original mortgage.

PREPAYMENT PRIVILEGES

FHA borrowers can prepay loans without penalty. If the FHA borrower has a fixed-rate mortgage with an above-current market interest rate, the mortgage may be refinanced at a lower interest rate. Under a conventional mortgage, the monthly savings resulting from refinancing may be offset by prepayment charges equal to two percent (or more) of the mortgage principal.

MORTGAGE INSURANCE PREMIUMS (MIP)

FHA-insured loans require a lump sum payment of MIP. Unless paid in cash, the MIP may be paid under one of two plans.

1. If the loan is less than the maximum allowable, the borrower adds the MIP to the loan.
2. If the loan equals the maximum allowable loan, the borrower must finance the MIP according to the permissible loan-to-value ratio.

For loans repaid before maturity, FHA refunds the unused MIP.

The MIP depends on the loan-to-value ratio and the mortgage term. Table 14-3 indicates that premium rates vary from 2.344 percent to 3.8 percent of the principal. Assume, for example, that a borrower negotiates a loan of $67,500, equal to 97 percent of the FHA-appraised value. Since the loan is for the maximum allowable principal, the proportion of the MIP financed is less than 100 percent but more than 95 percent, the correct premium would be 3.793 percent of the loan or $2,560 (.03793 x $67,500). Ninety-five percent of the $2,560 premium ($2,432) would be added to the loan principal and the down payment would be increased by five percent of the required MIP or $128. In 1991, the premiums of Table 14-3 were increased by .5 percent.

Table 14-3   Mortgage Insurance Premium (MIP) Rates*

Percent of MIP Financed	Payment Terms in Years			
	Less than 18	18-22	23-25	over 25
100	.02400	.03000	.03600	.03800
95	.02397	.02996	.03594	.03793
90	.02394	.02991	.03587	.03786
85	.02391	.02987	.03581	.03778
80	.02389	.02982	.03574	.03771
0	.02344	.02913	.03475	.03661

*Add an additional premium of .5 percent (.005) to the above premiums.

MINIMUM PROPERTY STANDARDS

FHA loans require an FHA appraisal by staff or designated appraisers. Not only is the loan subject to an FHA appraisal, but the property securing the loan must conform to FHA minimum property standards. The loan security must have workable plumbing, heating, and electrical systems; the building must be structurally sound with adequate roofing, exterior siding, and foundations. The property should not be subject to flooding, erosion, or other hazardous conditions that endanger occupant health and safety.

LOAN-TO-VALUE RATIO

Loan ceilings vary by geographic regions. For illustration, consider a maximum loan of $101,250 on a single-family dwelling and a sales price of $100,000. The insured loan would be based on loan-to-value ratios of 97 percent on the first $25,000 and 97 percent on the balance of $75,000. Cash required at closing would include the down payment, closing costs, and the first month's escrow deposit. The escrow deposit would equal the first month's cost of annual property taxes and hazard insurance.

However, if the buyer purchases a dwelling for $125,000, the FHA insured loan would be limited to the maximum of $101,500. The buyer would have to pay the difference between the purchase price and the maximum allowable loan.

Loan Forbearance

If loan default occurs under circumstances beyond the borrower's control, FHA loans give borrowers *special forbearance privileges*. Forbearance privileges apply to *temporary delinquencies* caused by temporary unemployment and illnesses or injuries which will not be permanently disabling. FHA regulations prescribe forms and procedures to follow for delinquencies of more than 30 days.

Lenders must make a reasonable effort to personally interview delinquent borrowers before the loan is 90 days delinquent. Depending on causes of the delinquency, the loan may extend 10 years beyond the maturity date to reduce payments. In other instances, lenders are allowed to increase principal to include past-due payments. Forbearance may be extended up to 36 months maximum with agency approval. Special forbearance privileges apply to delinquent borrowers currently in military service.

VETERANS ADMINISTRATION GUARANTEED LOANS

Eligible veterans may have loans guaranteed by the VA. Eligibility requires at least 90 days of active duty during dates prescribed by the VA. Moreover, veterans may restore eligibility if a property previously guaranteed has been sold and the loan has been repaid.

Maximum Loans

The maximum VA loan is $144,000. On loans of less than $45,000, the VA guarantee is limited to 50 percent of the loan. The maximum loan the VA guarantees to the lender is currently $36,000 or 40 percent of the loan, whichever is less.

The reasonable value is estimated by the VA or a VA-designated appraiser. The law requires that the loan may not exceed the reasonable value. If the purchase price exceeds the reasonable value, the veteran must certify that he or she has paid the excess in cash. While the VA does not impose loan ceilings, secondary market agencies such as GNMA or FNMA impose maximum loan to guarantee ratios.

Loan Terms

The VA does not require a down payment. Down payments are negotiated between the veteran and the private lender. Because of the guarantee, the lender could make a $144,000, no down payment loan which, in effect, would be a 75 percent loan ($108,000/$144,000). The lender may not charge origination fees in excess of one percent of the loan. If the mortgage loan is discounted by the lender so that the one percent origination fee is exceeded, the points must be paid by the seller.

Closing costs may not be included in the loan but must be paid in cash at the time of closing. The lender must observe VA maximum limits for charging appraisal fees, recording charges, credit reports, insurance, surveys, and related charges. The VA imposes a maximum term of 30 years and 32 days which allows for the first payment not later than 60 days after closing and an even 360 payments.

VA loans have no prepayment penalties. Further, VA loans can be assumed by nonveteran purchasers without VA or private lender approval. Only nominal assumption fees may be charged for changing records. However, without a VA release of liability, the original borrower remains liable for the loan. The release of liability must be signed by the new purchaser and approved by the VA. The VA grants the release if the purchaser qualifies for the loan on the same terms extended to veterans.

SUMMARY

Mortgages are instruments that pledge real estate as security for a debt. Under a mortgage the borrower is the *mortgagor* and the lender represents the *mortgagee*. Mortgages issued in *title theory states* provide for the transfer of title from the borrower to the lender. The mortgage stipulates that borrowers remain in possession as long as the borrower is not in default. In *lien theory states* the borrower holds title subject to a mortgage lien. On mortgage default the lender forecloses and takes possession as security for the debt. In each instance, mortgages are based on a debt or a *promissory note* (or "bond" in some states), which is a personal promise to repay the loan.

Lenders have the right to exercise the *acceleration clause,* which gives the lender the right to declare the remaining balance due on borrower default of a mortgage payment. *Due on sale clauses* give lenders the right to payment of the debt on sale.

A buyer who *assumes* an existing loan expresses the intent to personally assume the mortgage debt. However, a buyer who buys a dwelling *subject to* an existing loan merely acknowledges the mortgage debt without assuming personal liability for mortgage repayment. Mortgages may provide for escrow provisions which require monthly payments to lenders for payment of annual property taxes, insurance premiums, and other charges levied on an annual basis.

In some states, mortgage lenders have the right to a *deficiency judgment,* which is a lien against personal assets of the borrower equal to the difference between the outstanding mortgage principal and proceeds of a foreclosure sale. Lenders have the additional right to assign mortgages to others without borrower approval.

Mortgages may give borrowers the right to repay the debt before maturity without penalty. More commonly, lenders under conventional loans require *prepayment penalties* for loans repaid before maturity, especially over the early years of the mortgage.

Mortgages provide for the *equity of redemption,* which is the right to prevent foreclosure by paying the full amount of the debt including interest due and expenses. This right must be exercised prior to foreclosure sale. In a few states the borrower has an additional right—the *statutory right of redemption.* This is the right to redeem the property after foreclosure sale, typically limited to one year or less after the foreclosure sale. On payment of the mortgage, borrowers are entitled to a mortgage release or mortgage cancellation.

Trust deeds are instruments in which borrowers transfer real estate title to a trustee who holds title in trust for a lender as loan security. The trustee is granted the power of sale if the borrower defaults on the loan.

Amortized mortgages are loans in which monthly mortgage payments include partial payment of principal and interest on the remaining mortgage balance. Amortized mortgages with fixed interest rates provide for level monthly payments. *Variable interest rate mortgages* (VRM) allow lenders to adjust the mortgage interest rate periodically according to an index. The effect of the VRM mortgage is to shift the risk of interest rate changes from lenders to borrowers. VRM mortgages vary according to the frequency of interest rate changes, the allowable magnitude of rate changes, and the interest rate index selected for determining mortgage interest rates.

Term mortgages do not amortize the mortgage principal. The borrower pays only interest over the mortgage term. At the end of the mortgage, the total principal is due. *Variable payment amortization* provides for a constant payment of the principal. The mortgage payment decreases according to the declining interest paid on the remaining balance. These mortgages provide relatively large payments during the early years of the mortgage. *Balloon mortgages* are usually based on partial amortization payments with a balloon or lump sum payment required at a specified date.

Borrowers may purchase property with lower monthly payments under a *mortgage buydown*. Under these plans the seller pays cash to the lender who decreases the mortgage payment in return for the cash payment that increases the effective mortgage yield. In other instances borrowers may purchase subject to *mortgage discounts*. Mortgage discounts have the effect of increasing mortgage yields without increasing loan payments. A one point discount is equivalent to one percent of the mortgage principal.

Mortgages insured by the Federal Housing Administration prohibit due on sale clauses. Further, FHA borrowers can prepay loans without penalty. FHA-insured loans require a lump sum payment of mortgage insurance premiums which may be financed with the mortgage principal. Mortgage loans under FHA terms cover property that meets minimum property standards and conforms to prevailing loan-to-value ratios of FHA-insured mortgages. FHA borrowers gain from loan forbearance which applies to temporary delinquencies. Veterans Administration guaranteed loans are based on the reasonable value as required by the Veterans Administration. Loans must conform to statutory loan-to-value ratios. Given these loan guarantees, lenders may not require a down payment. Origination fees and other loan costs must comply with maximum limits established by the Veterans Administration.

POINTS TO REMEMBER

mortgage a pledge of a real estate interest as security for a debt.

title theory states states in which mortgages transfer title from the borrower to the lender.

lien theory states states that treat mortgages as a lien on the title.

intermediate lien theory states states which establish mortgages as liens on the borrower's title. On default, the title passes to the lender.

promissory note a personal promise to repay a debt.

right of acceleration a clause that gives the lender the right to demand full payment of the remaining mortgage balance.

due on sale clauses the right of the lender to payment of a debt on sale or transfer of real estate.

loan assumption a real estate purchase in which the buyer assumes an existing mortgage and agrees to repay the debt personally.

subject to refers to borrowers who buy real estate subject to an existing mortgage but who do not personally assume responsibility for the unpaid debt.

escrow funds funds collected monthly by the lender to pay yearly taxes, hazard insurance premiums, and monthly mortgage insurance premiums.

mortgage assignment the right of the lender to transfer the mortgage to others without the borrower's consent.

prepayment privileges the right to prepay the mortgage before the due date.

equity of redemption the right of the borrower to redeem the mortgage before foreclosure by paying the full amount of the debt, including interest and expenses of the lender.

statutory right of redemption the right of the borrower to redeem the property by paying the foreclosure sales price plus interest and expenses after the foreclosure sale.

mortgage release the right of the borrower to have the public record cleared of the lender's interest in mortgaged property.

trust deeds written instruments in which a borrower transfers title to a trustee who holds title in trust for a lender as security for a loan.

deficiency judgment a personal judgment granted if proceeds of a foreclosure sale do not satisfy the mortgage debt.

amortized mortgages mortgages that provide for monthly payments that cover partial payment of principal and interest payments on the remaining mortgage balance.

variable interest rate mortgages mortgages that vary interest rates according to changes in an interest index. Mortgage payments vary according to the frequency of the interest rate changes and the magnitude of the allowable rate change.

term mortgages mortgages that do not amortize the principal. Payments cover interest only.

variable payment amortization mortgages that cover a fixed payment to principal. Under this plan, mortgage payments are relatively large during the earlier years of the mortgage.

balloon mortgages mortgages that require a lump sum payment at the date of maturity.

mortgage buydowns payments to the lender by the seller, builder, or buyer to reduce mortgage interest rates and, therefore, monthly payments.

mortgage discount a discount required by the lender to increase the effective mortgage interest rate. A one-point mortgage discount equals a one-percent reduction in the mortgage principal.

FHA insured mortgages mortgages insured by the Federal Housing Administration.

minimum property standards minimum property requirements for FHA-insured mortgages.

loan forbearance special forbearance privileges prevailing under FHA-insured mortgages for temporary mortgage delinquencies.

Veterans Administration guaranteed loan loans that are guaranteed by the Veterans Administration for eligible veterans.

QUESTIONS FOR REVIEW

1. What is a mortgage? Describe fully.

2. Explain the difference between mortgages held under title theory states and lien theory states.

3. Explain your understanding of four financial rights of a lender. Give examples in illustration of your answer.

4. Give an example showing the difference between a mortgage assumed by a buyer and a dwelling purchase subject to an existing mortgage.

5. What rights are normally associated with the borrower-mortgagor?

6. Explain how a trust deed accomplishes the same purpose as a mortgage.

7. Contrast the difference between a fixed interest, level payment mortgage, and a variable interest rate mortgage.

8. Define the following terms:

   term mortgages
   variable payment amortization
   balloon mortgages

9. Give an example of a mortgage buydown. What are the advantages and disadvantages of a mortgage buydown to the buyer?

10. What is the purpose of a mortgage discount? Explain thoroughly.

11. What elements of an FHA insured mortgage benefit borrowers?

12. What are the distinguishing features of a loan guaranteed by the Veterans Administration? Explain thoroughly.

PRACTICE PROBLEMS

1. Calculate total interest paid over the life of a $100,000 mortgage, eight percent interest, payable over 360 months. Make a similar calculation for the same mortgage, but assume a 12 percent interest rate. With this 50 percent increase in the interest rate, does the total interest increase proportionately? Why or why not?

2. Assume a mortgage principal of $100,000 and an eight percent interest rate with payments over 180 months. Calculate total interest paid over the 180 months. Make a similar calculation for the same mortgage but assume a mortgage interest rate of 12 percent. Did the total interest paid increase by the same proportion as in question 1? Why or why not?

C H A P T E R   1 5

The Income Approach

After studying this chapter, you will know:
- The advantages of the income approach.
- The main variables of the income approach.
- Methods of estimating annual gross incomes and expenses.
- Direct capitalization and residual capitalization techniques.

After explaining advantages of the income approach, the chapter shows how to estimate values using the three main variables: annual gross income, annual operating expenses, and residual methods of capitalization.

In the income approach, market value is assumed equal to the present value of anticipated annual net income. In this respect it may be said that income-producing real estate is purchased to acquire rights to future benefits that are measured by the annual net income.

JUSTIFICATION OF THE INCOME APPROACH

The preceding discussion leads to the income approach rationale—market value is largely a function of the present value of anticipated annual net income. Ideally, if annual gross incomes, expenses, and the capitalization rate have been estimated with reasonable accuracy, market value closely agrees with buyer and seller opinion.

Main Advantages

Lenders rely on the income technique since mortgage payments are highly dependent on annual net income. Hence, because of the relationship between mortgage security and annual net income, the income approach is required to support loans on income property.

The income approach avoids the difficulty of estimating costs and depreciation. To this extent, the income technique appears more objective, accurate, and acceptable than the cost technique. Moreover, under the income approach, market value estimates do not depend on separate land and building values. For this reason, the income approach is generally preferred to value older income property.

In addition, the income approach eliminates the adjustment of real estate sales to compensate for differences between the properties sold and the property appraised. Finally, the income approach relies on the strongest possible logic: market value is a function of anticipated annual net income and its conversion to present value.

Variables of the Income Approach

The income approach depends on four variables:

1. *The estimate of annual gross income.* Annual gross income refers to the *anticipated* income which may not agree with *present* or *past* income.
2. *An estimate of annual expenses.* Expenses listed in accounting statements must be supplemented by estimated costs that do not appear on annual accounting statements.
3. *The capitalization rate.* This item is the most critical variable, for small errors in capitalization rates are magnified when annual net income is converted to capital value.
4. *The method of capitalization.* Different methods of capitalization produce different market values. The capitalization method depends on assumptions about capital recovery, the remaining building life, and the discounting process.

If the income approach conforms to the market, the market value estimate closely agrees with prices negotiated between informed buyers and sellers.

ESTIMATING GROSS INCOMES

The income technique requires an estimate of the *annual gross income* and the *effective gross income.* The former refers to the *annual income that would be earned if the property were fully occupied.* Effective gross income refers to *annual gross income less annual vacancies and bad debts.*

A 100-unit apartment building with all apartments renting for $800 a month (the market rent) would have a potential annual gross income of $960,000. The annual gross income must be reduced to allow for vacancies, bad debts, and collection losses.

In apartments, especially, vacancies occur as a result of normal tenant turnover and changes in the supply and demand of competing housing. While an apartment project may show no current vacancies, it is customary to deduct a vacancy allowance; newer, competitive apartments will result in later vacancies. Similar reasoning applies to other types of income property.

Stabilizing Annual Gross Income

The capitalization process requires a projection of future net income. Before deducting expenses from annual effective gross income, some reasonably accurate method must be found to predict annual gross income.

GROSS INCOME VARIATION

Future annual gross income varies considerably over a building life. Government programs, monetary policy, demand and supply, and unpredictable events affect annual gross income. A variation in governmental expenditures may result in an increase or decrease in the demand for local housing and other urban real estate; similarly, a change in the interest rate may affect the ability to finance private construction, industrial plants, commercial buildings, and apartment projects and dwellings. Some properties, such as food-processing plants and resort properties, are closely affected by changes in the weather.

Annual gross income generally declines over the building life. Older properties increasingly face competition from more modern, better-located properties. At the same time, as population increases, the better locations experience rising values and higher rents. Locations that are difficult to duplicate, such as water-front sites, downtown office sites, and established industrial districts, tend to show rising annual gross income, provided that zoning and other land use controls preserve and enhance property values.

INTERPRETING PAST INCOME

In estimating future net income, appraisers interpret past data. If past gross incomes are available, weight must be given to preceding years; here practice varies widely. Some appraisers use *average gross incomes* to stabilize future income, arguing that higher-than-normal rents should not be used to estimate future income. For example, an average annual net income over the past three years may be used as a "stabilized income." But in using averages, equal weight is given each year, with the consequence that more recent years—and probably the most important years—are not given the importance they deserve.

Interpretation of Supplementary Data

Estimating gross incomes by past experience, however refined the method may be, is based on historical data that may have only a remote relationship to future income. Furthermore, rents tend to lag behind changes in capital value, especially for commercial stores under long-term leases. It may be found that current gross income results not from current rent but from *contract* rent negotiated in earlier years under substantially different market conditions. Contract rent refers to rent determined by a written lease.

Consequently, appraisers frequently rely on supporting (nonincome) data. For example, recent population growth and associated data that show a growing demand for housing might be used to estimate future apartment rents. Similarly, a steadily increasing per capita income—the result of a new industry—may justify an optimistic prediction of shopping center gross income.

In fact, current developments that affect economic growth and future prospects are an important element in stabilizing gross income estimates. So while past experience is an important guide to income expectations, these expectations may be revised in the light of current economic developments that lead to higher rent, and therefore, higher property values.

Comparable Rental Data

Annual gross incomes are defended in the same way that recent sales support market value. For income property, annual gross income is supported by current rents for similar properties. In projecting future income estimates, some consideration may be given to local trends. Hence, annual gross income estimates depend on the interpretation of local trends and past rental data.

JUDGING PRESENT RENTS

In projecting gross incomes, care must be taken not to rely entirely on present rents. In the *first* issue, the property may not be devoted to its optimum use. It would be incorrect to base an appraisal on the annual net income from a mobile home park when the site would be more suitable for retail and office use, and it would be inappropriate to base a projected annual gross income on an apartment project if the site would be more suitable for a shopping center. Hence, the first precaution is to relate the annual gross income estimate to the estimated rent earned from the highest and best use.

The *second* issue is to critically evaluate the annual gross income paid by a particular tenant. In commercial real estate, concessions may be granted for nonmonetary reasons. A store may be leased on a very favorable basis to a preferred tenant because of the pedestrian traffic generated by the tenant. Similarly, a corporation with a preferred credit and national status may be able to negotiate an unusually favorable rent on the basis of the income security offered the owner. As a general rule, the gross income estimate relates to the typical tenant and not to a particular property use or a tenant who has negotiated an unusually favorable rent.

COMPENSATING FOR UNCERTAIN INCOME

If there is a question about the certainty of annual net income, buyers tend to pay less for the rights to annual, but fairly uncertain, net income. In other words, uncertain net income would be capitalized at a relatively high rate. The real problem is to judge the relative risk and equate the capitalization rate with the rate earned from competing investments with similar degrees of risk and income characteristics.

ESTIMATING ANNUAL OPERATING EXPENSES

Generally, three sources are available to estimate expenses: the *owner's statement of actual expenses, expenses of similar properties,* and *published expenses reported by trade associations.* Owner expense statements may include only out-of-pocket expenses or they may include items deductible for net income taxes but unrelated to annual net operating income. It is also quite probable that operating expenses of comparable properties will require considerable adjustment for estimating expenses of the property appraised. Published expenses cover widely dissimilar properties in different locations; therefore, average operating expenses taken from these sources may serve only as general guides. In addition, there is the problem of stabilizing expenses.

Revising Accounting Records

Ordinarily, certain operating expenses must be *added* to expense records prepared for the owner. Certain others must be *deleted* and still others must be *stabilized.* It is unlikely that an accounting statement of annual operating expenses will be acceptable for appraisal purposes without these revisions.

ADDING OMITTED EXPENSES

Expenses most commonly omitted and which need to be added include:

1. Anticipated annual repair expenses.
2. Annual replacement reserves for equipment and furniture.
3. Management expenses.
4. Redecorating and other maintenance expenses.

These omissions may occur for several reasons. The owner may have postponed needed repairs. For an owner-operated property, the owner may not have incurred a cash outlay for management expenses. The reasons for adding these expenses deserve further explanation.

REPAIR EXPENSES.   If repairs have not been paid in the current year, they will not appear on the owner's income statement. Yet certain repairs are inevitable over the building life. Periodically, the exterior and interior will require repainting, a new roof will be needed, and repairs must be made to other building components.

Therefore, appraisers estimate the *average annual cost of repairs.* Although in any one year actual repairs may be above or below the estimated annual amount, some reasonable allowance must be made for annual building repairs. The annual amount depends on the type of construction, present condition, and building use.

EQUIPMENT REPLACEMENT COSTS.   In an apartment building, refrigerators, washers, dryers, ovens, and range tops require periodic replacement. Again, if such fixtures are not replaced during the past year, their cost will not appear on accounting statements. However, if a refrigerator, which has a replacement cost of $650, must be replaced in 10 years, the average annual cost of that refrigerator would be $65. For an apartment complex project with 100 refrigerators that cost $650 each and that have a 10-year life, the annual replacement cost would be $6,500 as shown below.

($650 x 100)/10 = $6,500

The reserve for replacements represents the average annual cost of personal property such as appliances, lobby furniture, and other short-lived items that need frequent replacement. The reserve for replacements is really not a reserve in the accounting sense but is merely a means of recording the annual average cost of replacing building equipment.

VACANCY AND BAD DEBTS.   Appraisers reduce the gross income by an annual allowance for vacancies and bad debts to calculate *effective gross income.* Annual expenses are then deducted from the effective gross income.

A property fully occupied during the year will show no allowance for vacancies on an annual accounting statement. Accordingly, appraisers must revise such a statement to include a normal, expected vacancy over the early years of the building life. A property fully occupied eventually competes with new buildings. Changes in locational preferences and newer store buildings, offices, and apartments cause vacancies to increase in the older properties. Consequently, each appraisal shows the annual gross income estimated as if the property were fully occupied, less an allowance for anticipated vacancies and bad debts.

MANAGEMENT EXPENSES.   Management expenses are added for properties which are owner operated. If the owner contributes his or her labor to the enterprise, the accounting statement will show no cash entry for this expense. However, management is a required expense in operating properties, and since it is assumed that a prudent buyer may opt to hire management, management expenses should be added.

Practices vary in estimating annual management expenses. For some properties, management fees are a percentage of annual gross income. For instance, management expenses of four percent of effective gross income are fairly typical for a luxury apartment project, but seven percent for a low-income apartment project. Other property managers charge management fees per apartment unit or per square foot. The best practice is to base management fees on local management expenses of like property.

REDECORATING EXPENSES.   Suppose the current income statement shows no redecorating, rehabilitation, or remodeling expenses. As a practical matter, rental property requires periodic redecoration. Redecorating expense is partly determined by property type. For example, a luxury, high-rise apartment building in Fort Lauderdale, Florida, may require redecoration of the lobby every three years. Appraisal judgment must be exercised in reporting the average annual redecorating costs of similar properties. Failure to include this allowance results in an overstatement of annual net income and a distorted market value.

DELETING IMPROPER EXPENSES

A review of owner-operated accounting statements typically reveals deductions unrelated to income property operation:

1. Personal business expenses.
2. Additions and betterments.
3. State and federal net income taxes.
4. Owner salary or drawing accounts.
5. Mortgage payments (including interest and principal).

Recall that for appraisal purposes, annual net income must be independent of financing and the personal relationship of the owner to the business. The final statement reports annual net operating income on a uniform basis.

PERSONAL BUSINESS EXPENSES.   A property owner may deduct certain personal business expenses to determine taxable net income. Attendance at out-of-town trade meetings or business functions may qualify as a federal net income tax deduction. If these expenses do not directly relate to operating real estate, however, they should be omitted.

ADDITIONS AND BETTERMENTS.   Real estate brokers and laymen, inexperienced in accounting rules and income tax laws, may consider additions and betterments as expenses of operation. In actuality, such expenditures are additions to capital; for instance, the construction of a new garage or carport for an apartment project would probably be classified as an addition to capital (subject to an additional depreciation deduction) and not as an annual operating expense. Capital improvements are not shown as annual operating expenses.

STATE AND FEDERAL NET INCOME TAXES.   Net income taxes relate to the personal income of an individual or corporation. In valuing an income-producing asset, annual net income should be calculated *before* net income taxes. Chapter 15 shows how income taxes are deducted to calculate cash flow—the amount remaining after income taxes and mortgage payments.

OWNER SALARY OR DRAWING ACCOUNTS.   Suppose a property owner opens a drawing account or deducts a personal salary. Usually these deductions are not accepted as typical annual operating expenses. The best technique is to omit personal payments to the owner and to substitute the prevailing annual expenses for janitorial, custodial, or resident management services. The intent should be to deduct typical annual operating expenses in earning annual net income.

MORTGAGE PAYMENTS.   Mortgage payments vary according to loan terms. Since there is so much variation in mortgages of individual properties, it would be improper to list mortgage payments as an operating expense. To be sure, mortgage payments are deducted to show cash flow, and interest is a deductible item for state and federal net income taxes; nonetheless, neither principal nor interest payments can appropriately be considered annual expenses of operation. Mortgage payments listed on an income statement should be omitted.

STABILIZING EXPENSES

Since the object is to forecast annual net income, it is necessary to stabilize expenses. Stabilizing means that expenses of the past year must be adjusted upward or downward to account for anticipated future expenses. In the face of a probable increase in expenses over the early years of the property life, certain expenses may require an upward adjustment. Alternatively, extraordinary expenses may have taken place because of inclement weather or unusual operating problems and must be decreased.

Property taxes normally account for the largest single annual expense and, consequently, they require a critical review. If a property revaluation program is proposed or underway, it may be anticipated that property taxes will increase over succeeding years. Direct inquiry to local agencies is the best source of information to stabilize property taxes.

Table 15-1 reveals average operating expenses for 31 elevator apartment buildings in Chicago surveyed by the Institute of Real Estate Management. Although expenses do not include depreciation or replacements, total expenses equal 55.3 percent of gross possible income (GPI). Property taxes (14.5 percent of GPI) followed by maintenance expenses (9.1 percent of GPI) are the two leading expense items. The average net operating income of 34.1 percent of GPI must be sufficient to pay debt service, replacements, capital recovery, and a return on the investment.

Table 15-1   Median Income and Operating Expenses: 31 Elevator Apartments, Chicago, Illinois*

Item	Per Square Foot	Percent of Gross Possible Income	Per Room
Gross Possible			
Rents	$8.50	98.5	$1,818.02
Vacancies	- .59	- 6.6	- 118.56
Total Rent			
Collected	$7.95	91.6	$1,647.77
Other Income	.14	1.5	29.21
Gross Possible			
Income	$8.86	100.0	$1,867.26
Total Collections	$8.09	93.4	$1,675.86

Note: Table 15-1 is continued on the next page.

Table 15-1   (Continued)

Item	Per Square Foot	Percent of Gross Possible Income	Per Room
Expenses			
Supplies	$ .06	.5	$ 11.00
Heating Fuel	.22	2.7	47.21
Electricity	.23	2.7	46.26
Water/Sewer	.13	1.4	30.53
Gas	.09	1.4	24.59
Building			
Services	$ .08	1.0	$ 21.12
Other Operating	.13	1.5	37.71
Total Operating			
Expenses	$1.13	12.6	$ 267.26
Security	$ .22	2.6	$ 44.55
Grounds			
Maintenance	.05	.4	10.73
Maintenance–			
Repairs	.47	5.4	118.26
Painting/			
Decorating	.21	2.3	55.86
Total Maintenance	.95	9.1	$ 210.35
Real Estate Taxes	1.23	14.5	$ 266.13
Other Tax/Free/			
Permit	.01	.1	1.03
Insurance	.26	2.5	55.35
Total Tax-			
Insurance	$1.55	17.8	$ 309.82
Recreational/			
Amenities	.01	.1	2.31
Other Payroll	.59	6.6	135.10
Total Expenses	-$5.15	- 55.3	-$1,135.50
Net Operating			
Income	$3.25	34.1	$ 692.81

* Totals may not add correctly because not all apartments surveyed submitted entries for every category.

Source: *Income/Expense Analysis: Conventional Apartments,* (Chicago, Illinois: Institute of Real Estate Management, 1989), p. 45. See current reports for later data.

Types of Expenses

For accuracy, annual expenses should be considered in two categories—fixed expenses and variable expenses. *Fixed expenses* do not vary with the occupancy rate. For example, property taxes must be paid each year whether the property is 50 percent occupied or 100 percent occupied. *Variable expenses* vary according to the occupancy rate.

FIXED EXPENSES

The following expenses are usually fixed expenses:

insurance
property taxes
depreciation on fixtures and furniture (replacement reserves)
contract services (window washing, ground maintenance, elevator contracts, janitorial services)

The annual depreciation on fixtures and furniture is listed as a replacement reserve; it is included under fixed expenses to show that the cost of personal property must be recovered over the life of the asset. If maintenance services are furnished under annual contracts, they represent expenses unrelated to income and are classified as fixed expenses.

Fixed expenses continue independently of property use. A 160-unit motel in Pennsylvania, for example, found that business did not justify the operation of all 160 units. Shortly after opening they closed down 40 units to save variable expenses. However, the fixed expenses as listed above continued for the 40 units that produced no gross income.

VARIABLE EXPENSES

Expenses that change with occupancy rates are fairly limited:

utilities (water, heating fuel, electricity)
repairs
supplies
management expenses (estimated as a proportion of effective gross income)

In the case of the 160-unit motel, if gross income from the last 40 units did not cover variable expenses, it would be more economic to discontinue their operation. If annual net income does not equal or exceed variable expenses, it is more economic to abandon the property—which explains the abandonment of substandard apartment buildings in New York City, Chicago, and Washington, D.C.

Sources of Expense Data

It is advisable to judge annual expenses from two common sources: the expense records of similar properties operating under typical management and published expense surveys.

LOCAL EXPENSE DATA

A review of expenses incurred by similar properties in the same location gives the best possible support to estimated expenses. However, the appraiser must take care to *analyze expenses of like properties.* It would be inappropriate to refer to the annual expenses per square foot of a regional shopping center that had 500,000 square feet of rentable area if one were appraising a neighborhood shopping center with 100,000 square feet of rentable area. Similarly, it would be unacceptable to cite annual expenses per unit for a 10-story, 25-year-old apartment building to support an appraisal of a new, 100-unit, garden-court apartment.

There is the additional problem of showing expenses under typical management. A corporation that owns and operates 10 shopping centers gains from purchasing supplies and services in quantity and from certain economies experienced under a central management. In this case, the annual expenses for a single shopping center would show below-normal expenses because of the unusual efficiency of a large-scale operation. For help in judging the comparability of expense data, appraisers refer to published expense data.

PUBLISHED EXPENSE DATA

Expenses published by national organizations are not always drawn from representative properties. They do not always account for the expenses experienced in a particular community. Frequently their data apply to selected properties that may not be typical of the property under appraisal. Yet these sources furnish guides that can help the appraiser interpret local data. Among the publications available are:

Dollars & Cents of Shopping Centers. Urban Land Institute, Washington, D.C., published every two years.
Income/Expense Analysis: Conventional Apartments. Institute of Real Estate Management, Chicago, Illinois, published annually.

Trends in the Hotel-Motel Business. Annual Review, Pannell, Kerr, Forster, Accountants and Consultants, Atlanta, Georgia.

Expense Analysis: Condominiums Cooperatives and PUDs. Institute of Real Estate Management, Chicago, Illinois, published annually.

Downtown and Suburban Office Building Experience Exchange Report. Building Owners and Managers Association International, Washington, D.C., published annually.

Income/Expense Analysis: Suburban Office Buildings. Institute of Real Estate Management, Chicago, Illinois, published annually.

Expense data published by the Urban Land Institute show operating income and expenses of shopping centers by type of center and by geographic area. Similarly, income and expenses for conventional apartments published by the Institute of Real Estate Management show operating expenses by type of apartment, regions, age groups, and cities. The Building Owners and Managers Association International supplies similar data for office buildings.

CAPITALIZATION RATES

The estimation of capitalization rates generally centers on three techniques: the band of investment, the market comparison method, debt coverage ratios, and other yield comparisons.

Band-of-investment Method

Appraisers rely heavily on the band-of-investment method to estimate capitalization rates. In essence, the method weights the yield earned by the lender and owner of the equity interest. In this method, the term of the mortgage must be known in addition to the loan-to-value ratio and mortgage interest rate. To illustrate, assume typical financing under a 75 percent mortgage at an annual 9 1/2 percent interest rate with a 25-year mortgage term. The appraiser weights the resulting annual mortgage constant by the loan-to-value ratio.

Therefore, to estimate the overall (market) capitalization rate, first calculate the annual mortgage constant by multiplying the monthly mortgage installment factor by 12 (months). The annual mortgage constant of .104844 applies to a typical first mortgage, with a 75 percent loan-to-value ratio, 25-year term, and 9 1/2 percent annual interest, payable monthly:

$$AMC = MMC_{i/12,\ n \times 12} (12)$$

where:

AMC = Annual mortgage constant
MMC = Monthly mortgage constant (or monthly installment of one dollar)
i   = Annual interest rate
n   = Mortgage term in years

Therefore:

$$
\begin{aligned}
AMC &= MMC_{.095/12,\ 25 \times 12} (12) \\
&= 008737\ (12) \\
&= .104844
\end{aligned}
$$

Given the yield on equity, the appraiser calculates the weighted average, which is the *overall capitalization rate:*

Share Interest	Weight		Yield	Weighted Yield
1st mortgage	.75	x	.104844	= .078633
Equity	.25	x	.2	= .05
			Overall capitalization rate	= .128633
				12.8633%

The 12.8633 percent overall capitalization rate accounts for all net operating income. Here it is assumed that after paying the annual debt service, the remaining income reverts to the equity owner who owns a 25 percent share interest.

Suppose, for example, the annual net income was $128,633. Under direct capitalization, the market value equals $1,000,000

$$
\begin{aligned}
MV &= \$128,633/.128633 \\
&= \$1,000,000
\end{aligned}
$$

Under the given assumptions, an investor paying $1,000,000 for the property would receive an annual yield of $128,633. The overall capitalization rate equals the sum of the *weighted* yield earned on equity and the *weighted* yield earned by the lender.

Market Comparison Method

The appraiser using this method should ascertain that the sales selected are comparable with respect to location, property characteristics, and time of sale. For certain types of investments, these data are often available from lenders and investors. In this case, the overall capitalization rate (R) will be indicated by relating net operating income to the sales price. With an annual net income of $105,000 and a sales price of $1,000,000, the indicated overall capitalization rate (R) would be 10.5 percent.

$$R = NOI/SP$$
$$= \$105,000/\$1,000,000$$
$$= 10.5 \text{ percent}$$

The appraiser would select property sales that compare favorably with the annual net operating income of the actual property being appraised. Further refinement of the market comparison techniques were discussed in Chapter 13 under gross income multipliers.

Debt Coverage Ratios

The debt coverage ratio shows the relationship of net operating income to annual debt service. The ratio is derived under the formula:

$$DCR = NOI / DS$$

where:

$$NOI = \text{Net operating income}$$
$$DS = \text{Annual debt service}$$

Lenders who rely on this ratio may restrict the maximum loan so that the debt coverage ratio does not fall below some minimum value, such as 125 percent. In practical application, the debt coverage ratio helps indicate the overall capitalization rate given the loan to value ratio and the annual mortgage constant.

Consider a property that sold for $3,000,000, financed under an 80-percent mortgage of $2,400,000, 11-percent interest rate, for 25 years. The monthly installment factor equals .00980, resulting in an annual mortgage constant of .11761 (.00980 x 12). Assume further that the annual net income equals $352,840.65. With this information, the appraiser calculates the overall capitalization rate under the formula:

OR   =   DCR (LVR) (MC)

where:

OR   =   Overall capitalization rate
DCR   =   Debt coverage ratio
LVR   =   Loan-to-value ratio
MC   =   Annual mortgage constant

Therefore:

OR   =   1.25 (.80) (.11761)
      =   .11761
      =   11.76 percent (rounded)

In this hypothetical case, the overall capitalization rate equals the mortgage constant. With a debt coverage ratio of 125 percent, the overall capitalization is 11.76 percent. Therefore, given the net operating income and mortgage terms, the overall capitalization rate is given by the debt coverage ratio.

Other Yield Comparisons

For some property types, band of investment data and market comparison are not available. The appraisal of leasehold interests, leased fees, and special purpose property, such as coal mines, quarries, hotels, and commercial land are so unique that the estimated capitalization rate depends mostly on yields earned from investments with similar risks.

Under this type of analysis, it is reasoned that the estimated yield on the real estate appraised must bear some relationship to yields earned in other ventures. For example, Table 15-2 compares yields and interest rates on selected investments. Note that yields range from 4.03 percent for stocks to over 10 percent for home mortgages. It should be noted that the yield on stocks includes dividend yields only; capital gains are not shown. Generally, yields measure the investor assessment of risks and future expectations. These data help appraisers select capitalization rates by analyzing yields on non-real estate assets so that yields estimated for real estate will attract capital at competitive yields.

Table 15-2   Yields and Interest Rates on Selected Investments

Investment	Rate in Percent
Prime commercial paper	7.81
Prime banker's acceptance, 3 months	8.02
Federal Fund's Rate	8.26
U. S. Government securities	
3-month treasury bills	
Secondary market	7.29
Auction rate	7.32
12 months	7.25
Three year	8.33
State and local government, Aaa	7.40
Corporate, Aaa seasoned	9.63
Corporate, Baa seasoned	10.76
High-grade municipal bonds, (Standard and Poor's)	7.35
Home mortgages	
FHA-insured, new	10.24
Conventional, new	10.18
Corporate bonds (Moody's Investors)	
Industrials (all industries), Aa	9.56
Public utilities, Aa	9.58
Stocks	
Preferred (Standard and Poor's, 10 stocks)	9.13
Composite (500 stocks)	4.03

Source: Data are compiled from various issues of the *Federal Reserve Bulletin, Economic Indicators,* and *Standard and Poor's Statistical Service.* Data were reported at the end of 1990.

CAPITALIZATION TECHNIQUES

The capitalization of income from real property must be treated in a special way. The special treatment is required because real estate annual net income is calculated before depreciation. Consequently, the capitalization of net income from buildings must allow for a *return* on capital and the *recovery* of capital. To allow for capital recovery of buildings, annual net income must be allocated between land and buildings on the assumption that land does not depreciate.

To allocate income between land and buildings, two methods are used: the *land residual* and *building residual* techniques of capitalization. A third method, the *property residual* technique, largely eliminates the problem of allocating income between land and buildings. *Direct capitalization* avoids these issues by converting annual net income from land *and* buildings *directly* to value.

Direct Capitalization

Direct capitalization converts annual net income to value under the formula:

MV = NOI/R
    = $1,000,000/.12
    = $8,333,333
    = $8,300,000 (rounded)

where:

MV   = Market value
NOI = Annual net income
R   = Overall capitalization rate

The estimated market value of $8,300,000 represents the present value of $1,000,000 capitalized in perpetuity. The overall capitalization or discount rate is taken from the market, based on a comparison of annual net incomes and sales prices (NOI/SP) of like property. Therefore, it follows that the overall capitalization rate includes an allowance for capital recovery and a yield on the investment. If direct capitalization is not supported by market evidence, appraisers may turn to residual capitalization to allow specific allowances for capital recovery and a return on capital.

Land Residual Capitalization

The appraiser begins by estimating the building value independently of the annual net income. The unknown factor is the land value, which is estimated from the income allocated to land. The sum of land and building values represents the market value estimate. Therefore, under the land residual method there are two factors that must be estimated independently: the building value and the remaining life of the building.

CAPITALIZATION TECHNIQUE

In the land residual method, the *building value is estimated from cost less depreciation*. With the other given factors, namely the rate of return on capital and the economic life of the building, the amount of annual net income to be allocated to the building is calculated. The residual income is then assigned to the land and capitalized to give the land value. The land and building values are added to derive market value. This technique is shown in Case 1.

Case 1

Land Residual

Annual net income	$ 1,000,000
Income allocated to building	
$5,000,000 (.08 + .02)	- 500,000
Income allocated to land	$ 500,000
Land value	
$500,000/.08	$ 6,250,000
Add building value	$ 5,000,000
Estimated market value.	$11,250,000

Given the estimated net income of $1,000,000 (before depreciation on building), a rate of return of 8 percent, and a remaining building life of 50 years ($1/50 = .02$), the income allocated to a $5,000,000 building would be $500,000 (.08 + .02). Although the total property, land and building, produces an annual net income of $1,000,000, it is presumed that an investor would be entitled to an annual 8 percent return—which is the market rate—or $400,000 on the building value of $5,000,000. In addition, the investor would probably expect to receive $100,000 each year for 50 years to recover the building cost. The recapture provision is based on the assumption that the investor would be satisfied with a *return of capital* in annual increments of $100,000 for 50 years.

The land residual is the annual net income allocated to land. Assuming the same capitalization rate of 8 percent, land value would be $6,250,000. Adding the $6,250,000 land value to the building value of $5,000,000 produces a market value estimate of $11,250,000, land residual.

In short, the land residual, capitalization technique calls for seven steps.

1. Estimate building value from local construction costs, i.e., 100,000 square feet at $50 per square foot = $5,000,000.

2. Estimate the economic life of the building (for example, 50·years).
3. Calculate the capitalization rate:
   a. Return on capital: 8 percent
   b. Return of capital:
      i. Divide the economic life of the building into 1.0 (for example, 1/50 = 2.0 percent).
      ii. The overall capitalization rate equals the return on capital and the recovery of capital (8 percent + 2 percent = 10 percent).
4. Calculate the income allocated to the building ($5,000,000 x 10 percent = $500,000).
5. Subtract income allocated to the building from the annual net income ($1,000,000 - $500,000 = $500,000).
6. Capitalize income to land ($500,000/.08 = $6,250,000).
7. Add land value to the building value to arrive at market value:

   $ 6,250,000   Land value
   +   5,000,000   Building value
   $ 11,250,000   Estimated market value

RECOMMENDED USE

Because of certain inherent deficiencies, the land residual technique is restricted to special cases. For the most part, it is used to value:

1. New buildings for which building costs may be determined fairly accurately.
2. Buildings that show relatively little depreciation.
3. Buildings in which comparable land sales are not available.
4. Buildings that represent the highest and best use.
5. Property in which the building value is relatively low in comparison to the land value.

It should be appreciated that in using this capitalization technique for new buildings, the chance of error is minimized since replacement costs of new buildings are easily verified. Moreover, if buildings show substantial depreciation, the residual income allocated to land may be under- or over-estimated if the estimate of building depreciation is incorrect. Errors in the income allocated to land are magnified when the land residual technique is used.

It should also be noted that distortions in market value result if the income is derived from a land use that is no longer appropriate. For example, market value would not be indicated by the capitalization of income from a two-story downtown loft building if the highest and best use recommends a modern office building. The determination of the highest and best use is essential to the land residual technique.

Some of these errors may be minimized if buildings or land improvements are of relatively low value, e.g., parking lots. Here the value of land improvements is relatively low compared to the vacant land value. In addition, for highly developed areas, such as downtown districts where there are few, if any, vacant land sales, land values may be estimated by using the costs of a hypothetical building; this method, however, is highly subjective.

Building Residual Capitalization

This method begins with an estimate of the land value and the economic life of the building. The initial unknown factor is the building value—the residual. See Case 2.

Case 2

Building Residual

Net income	$ 1,500,000
Income allocated to land	
$8,000,000 x .08.	- 640,000
Income allocated to building	$ 860,000
Building value	
$860,000/(.08 + .02)	$ 8,600,000
Add land value.	$ 8,000,000
Estimated market value	$16,600,000

CAPITALIZATION TECHNIQUE

Note that this technique starts with an allocation of the annual net income to the land. The land value of $8,000,000 is estimated by the market approach. With an 8 percent capitalization rate, annual net income of $640,000 is allocated to the land ($8,000,000 x .08). The residual net income of $860,000 is capitalized by the overall capitalization rate, which includes an 8 percent return and a 2 percent allowance for capital recovery: $860,000/(.08 + .02). The land and building values are added to obtain the market value estimate of $16,600,000.

To use the building residual, follow these steps:

1. Estimate market value of the land from comparable land sales.
2. Estimate the capitalization rate (for example, 8 percent).

3. Calculate the annual return to land ($8,000,000 x .08 = $640,000).
4. Subtract the annual return to land from the annual net income ($1,500,000 - $640,000 = $860,000).
5. Estimate the economic life of the building (for example, 50 years).
6. Estimate the overall capitalization rate.
   .08 Return of capital
   <u>.02</u> Recovery of capital (1/50 = .02)
   .10 Overall capitalization rate
7. Calculate the value of the building ($860,000/.10 = $8,600,000).
8. Add the land value and the building value to obtain market value ($8,000,000 + $8,600,000 = $16,600,000).

This method avoids certain deficiencies of the land residual method. In the building residual technique, the building value is estimated from net income; this eliminates the problem of estimating building replacement costs. The case for building residual capitalization is strengthened further if land values are strongly supported by comparable sales. If building value constitutes a high proportion of total value, the building residual method probably gives the most reliable answer. It should be noted that these capitalization techniques illustrate "straight line" capital recovery methods. Other methods based on annuity factors are also used.

RECOMMENDED USE

The building residual is preferred for valuing income property in which:

1. Buildings show substantial depreciation.
2. Land may be accurately estimated from recent sales.
3. Land represents a relatively small proportion of the total property value.

If buildings are substantially depreciated, capitalizing by the building residual technique leads to a more accurate estimate of value. It is generally assumed that land value can be more accurately estimated from the market. Furthermore, errors in estimating land value tend to be reduced if the land represents a relatively small proportion of the total property value.

Property Residual Capitalization

In this method, annual net income is treated as if it were earned from the whole property over the economic life of the building. At the end of the building life, it is assumed that the building has no value. Following the assumption that land is not depreciable and that land values are unchanged, the present value of land is estimated at the end of the building life. Presumably the land remains available for use after the building has been economically "used up." This procedure is comparable to finding the present value of a future sum. Case 3 illustrates the property residual method.

Case 3

Property Residual Method

Net income	$ 8,000,000
Present worth of income	
$8,000,000 x 12.233485 (present value of an annuity factor, 8%, 50 years)	$97,867,880
Land reversion	
$5,000,000 x .021321 (present value factor, 50 years, 8%)	106,605
Estimated market value	$97,974,485
(rounded)	$98,000,000

CAPITALIZATION TECHNIQUE

In this case the net income from land and buildings, $8,000,000, is discounted at 8 percent over 50 years. The value of $97,867,880 represents the present value of the right to an income of $8,000,000 earned over 50 years and discounted at 8 percent. At the end of 50 years, it is assumed that the building is exhausted and that only the land remains. With a land value of $5,000,000, what is the present worth of the land at the end of 50 years assuming no change in value and a capitalization rate of 8 percent? Multiplying by the present value factor, 50 years, at 8 percent, shows that the present value of the land is $106,605. Under the property residual method, the market value is estimated at $98,000,000, rounded.

Note that the present value of the land under the property residual method ($106,605) represents less than one percent of the market value. Although future land values are uncertain, errors in the land value estimate are reduced as the discount period increases.

The property residual requires the following procedure:

1. Estimate the annual net operating income.
2. Estimate the remaining economic life of the building.
3. Select the appropriate capitalization rate.

4. Determine the present value of an annuity factor for a period equal to the remaining economic life of the building at the selected capitalization rate.
5. Multiply the net income by the selected present value of an annuity factor.
6. Multiply the land value by the present value factor for a period equal to the remaining economic life of the building.
7. Add the present value of the net income produced in (5) above to the present value of the land value in (6) above.

RECOMMENDED USE

Generally speaking, the property residual technique is used to value older buildings when it is difficult to value buildings independently from the land. Specifically, this technique would be used in the following cases:

1. The property residual is preferred for valuing old buildings, when virtually all the value is in the land.
2. The property residual is recommended if the annual income assumes characteristics of an annuity, i.e., for the valuation of property subject to a lease.
3. The property residual technique is especially appropriate to value highly depreciated buildings, especially if land or building values are difficult to estimate.

Like the land and building residual techniques, the property residual technique accounts for the *recovery of* capital and a *return on* capital.

The land residual, building residual, and property residual techniques give identical answers if the same capitalization rate, economic life, and net operating income are assumed. Although the answers are the same, the technique selected depends on the available data and the appraisal problem.

SUMMARY

Under the income approach, it is assumed that market value is the present value of annual net income. The income approach is frequently required to estimate the maximum mortgage loan. The method avoids the subjective costs and depreciation estimates of the cost approach. Besides this advantage, the income approach eliminates adjustments common to comparable sales.

The income approach is based on the estimated annual gross income, vacancy and bad debts, annual operating expenses, the capitalization rate, and the method of capitalization. *Annual gross income* is defined as the annual income that would be earned if the property were fully occupied. *Effective gross income* refers to annual gross income less annual vacancies and bad debts.

The annual gross income is supported by an analysis of comparable rental data—the *market rent* earned by comparable properties. In the case of an uncertain gross income, appraisers estimate the prevailing market rent and capitalize the annual net income by a capitalization rate that provides for risk and uncertainty.

Annual operating expenses may be derived from the owner's statement of actual expenses, expenses of similar properties, or expenses published by trade associations. In analyzing accounting records, appraisers typically *add* expenses commonly omitted; they omit inappropriate expenses and they *stabilize* expenses.

For some purposes, appraisers analyze expenses according to whether they are fixed or variable. *Fixed expenses* do not vary by the occupancy rate. Insurance, property taxes, depreciation on fixtures and furniture, and certain contract services fall in this category. *Variable expenses* change with occupancy rates which include utilities, repairs, supplies, and management expenses calculated as a percent of effective gross income.

Appraisers estimate capitalization rates by following the *band-of-investment method,* by the market comparison method, or by deriving capitalization rates from a comparison of yields earned on non-real estate assets. The band of investment represents a weighted average of yields earned on mortgages and the equity interest. The *market comparison method* results in the overall capitalization rate taken from the relationship between the annual net operating income and the sales prices of representative properties. Alternatively, appraisers analyze yields on non-real estate assets to estimate the capitalization rate for income property.

Given the appropriate capitalization rate, appraisers rely on *direct capitalization,* which gives value by dividing annual net operating income by the *overall capitalization rate.* The overall capitalization rate includes an allowance for capital recovery and investment yield.

Land residual capitalization starts with an independent building value estimated from the cost approach; income is then allocated to the building. The remaining income, or residual income, applies to the land. The present value of land follows from capitalization of income allocated to land. Land residual capitalization is used for new buildings showing little depreciation. The method is preferred if comparable land sales are not available, buildings represent the highest and best use, and the building value is relatively low compared to the land value.

Building residual capitalization begins with an estimate of the land value and economic life of the building. Income is allocated to the land with the residual income applied to the building. The income to the building is capitalized by the yield rate on the building investment, in addition to an allowance for capital recovery. The capital recovery allowance is based on the reciprocal of the building life. The land value, derived from comparable sales, is added to the capitalized building value to estimate market value.

Building residual capitalization applies to properties in which buildings show substantial depreciation; to properties where land values may be accurately estimated from recent sales; and to cases in which the land represents a relatively small proportion of total property value.

The *property residual technique* capitalizes income from the total property over the economic building life. Assuming the building has no value at the end of its economic life, the remaining land value is converted to present value. The present value of land postponed to the end of the building life is added to the present value of annual net income.

The property residual method is preferred for valuing old buildings when virtually all value is assigned to the land. The property residual method is preferred if the annual net income assumes characteristics of an annuity, i.e., property subject to a lease.

POINTS TO REMEMBER

annual gross income annual gross income that would be earned if the property were fully occupied.

effective gross income annual gross income less annual vacancies and bad debts.

contract rent rent determined by a lease

replacement cost of equipment the annual cost of replacing equipment according to its replacement cost and economic life.

reserve for replacement the average annual cost of replacing personal property.

vacancy and bad debts an allowance deducted from annual gross income which gives the effective gross income.

fixed expenses expenses that do not vary with the occupancy rate.

variable expenses expenses that vary according to the occupancy rate.

band-of-investment a method of estimating capitalization rates by calculating the weighted average of mortgage yields and the yield on the equity interest.

debt coverage ratio the annual net operating income divided by the annual debt service.

land residual capitalization capitalization by allocating income to the building and capitalizing the remaining income to the land. The sum of the building value and land value equals the estimated market value.

building residual capitalization a method of allocating income to land and capitalizing the remaining income to the building. The sum of the building value and land value equals the estimated market value.

property residual capitalization capitalizing annual net income to the property and adding the present value of land at the end of the building economic life.

QUESTIONS FOR REVIEW

1. Summarize in your own words the main advantages of the income approach.

2. Explain the main variables of the income approach.

3. Explain how you would estimate annual gross income for a 200-unit apartment project.

4. Critically evaluate three sources to estimate expenses of a shopping center.

5. Explain three steps you would take to revise an owner's income and operating expense statement for an apartment project.

6. Give three examples each of fixed and variable expenses for a 500-unit apartment project.

7. Calculate the capitalization rate assuming: a first mortgage loan-to-value ratio of 80 percent, a fixed rate mortgage interest of 10 percent, a 30 year term, and a yield on equity of 20 percent. Show your work.

8. Explain how you would estimate market value, using land residual capitalization, for a downtown retail building. When would you recommend this capitalization technique?

9. Explain circumstances in which you would rely on building residual capitalization.

10. Contrast direct capitalization with property residual capitalization.

PRACTICE PROBLEMS

1. To appraise a 500-unit apartment project, you are given an owner's income statement as listed below. Assuming the following facts, reconstruct the operating statement for appraisal purposes. Average rent per unit, $600 per month. Replacement costs per unit: refrigerator, $450 (12-year life); carpets, $800 (10-year life); range top and oven, $500 (15-year life). Make other assumptions as necessary to complete this problem.

Gross income:		$3,240,000
Annual expenses:		
Personal net income taxes	$324,000	
Owner drawing account	100,000	
Mortgage interest	189,561	
Insurance	20,250	- 688,811
Annual income		$2,606,189

2. Estimate market value using the land residual technique given the following facts: annual net income, $1,000,000; building replacement cost, $4,000,000; return on capital, 10 percent; estimated building life, 40 years.

3. Estimate market value using the building residual technique given the following facts: land value, $3,000,000; return on capital, 10 percent; estimated building life, 50 years; annual net income, $5,000,000.

4. Estimate market value under the property residual method, given the following facts: annual net ncome, $1,000,000; estimated building life, 33 years; estimated land value, $4,000,000; return on capital, 10 percent.

PART 3

Valuation Practices

C H A P T E R 1 6

Cash Flow Estimates

After you have finished reading this chapter you will know:
- The purpose of discounted cash-flow appraisal models.
- Variations in before-tax cash-flow models.
- Discounted after-tax cash-flow valuation estimates.
- Financial ratios important to cash-flow analysis.
- Assumptions common to discounted cash-flow appraisals.

Before- and after-tax cash-flow models, while illustrating common valuation techniques, are based on certain assumptions that affect the final value estimate. In practice, however, before- and after-tax cash-flow models vary according to future expectations of owner benefits, i.e., annual cash flow and capital appreciation or depreciation.

Consequently, the *first* task of this chapter is to show how to adapt before- and after-tax cash-flow models to market expectations. The *second* task is to show how to analyze cash-flow models according to selected financial ratios. Financial ratios generated from cash-flow models help in judging relative degrees of risk and valuation accuracy. An understanding of these two tasks leads to more accurate appraisals.

BEFORE-TAX CASH-FLOW MODEL

Before-tax cash-flow models include the present value of net annual income less the annual mortgage interest and principal payments, and the present value of sales proceeds. Sales proceeds refer to the projected sales price less the remaining mortgage balance. Before-tax cash-flow models are also known as pre-tax cash-flow models.

It is held that before-tax cash-flow models conform to real estate markets in which real estate financing has an important bearing on real estate values. In this respect, the before-tax cash-flow model varies markedly from the rigid assumptions of the residual income appraisal models and direct capitalization in perpetuity. Before covering before-tax cash-flow variations, the assumptions underlying before-tax cash flow deserve review.

Basic Before-Tax Cash-Flow Model

The before-tax cash-flow valuation model, presumably, follows investor behavior, developers, and others that regularly finance and trade in income properties. In this model it is implicitly understood that real estate investments are financed.

Because of this assumption, it is held that real estate valuation should include typical financial terms. Following this reasoning, the valuation partly turns on financial variables—mortgage interest, the mortgage term, and the loan-to-value ratio. In practice, financing terms provide monthly mortgage payments that are less than the monthly net operating income, providing for a positive annual before-tax cash flow. For the present purpose, monthly mortgage payments are converted to *annual debt service*—the total annual mortgage payments, including interest and principal. The result gives the annual before-tax cash flow.

This simplistic model, however, is complicated by variable mortgage interest rates, mortgages convertible to an equity interest, and other financial agreements. Further, for some investment properties, the valuation model must consider negative annual cash flows.

Before investors used the before-tax cash flow, it was implicitly assumed that appraisers estimated market value over the *economic building life*. The economic building life is that time period in which the building has no value. For example, a hotel building may have no economic property value after 25 years because the location is no longer suitable for a hotel, the hotel building is obsolete according to current hotel designs, or the current market would not support hotel use.

Accordingly, under the conventional residual income appraisal, net annual income would be capitalized over 25 years—the economic life of the hotel. However, the before-tax cash-flow model, according to cash-flow advocates, conforms to investor behavior in which investments are held over relatively short periods, say five, ten, or fifteen years. Hence, annual before-tax income should be capitalized *over the investment holding period*. Shorter periods of ownership are discouraged by relatively high transfer costs that make short period investments uneconomic. In contrast, investments over the longer term postpone opportunities for capital appreciation. While the before-tax cash-flow model is not dependent on a given ownership term, in practice the model normally applies to a period shorter than the economic life.

Early valuation models assumed supply and demand equilibrium, i.e., real estate assumed value solely with respect to annual net income. Under a growth economy, cash-flow proponents observed that investors invest in real estate assets not only for the annual cash flow, but for *capital gains*. Conversely, assuming unfavorable expectations, the cash-flow model may incorporate possible *capital losses*. In other words, the valuation, or proposed investment, partly depends on projected capital gains or losses which are incorporated in the before-tax cash-flow appraisal model.

Investors consider yields on the equity interest or down payment—not the total property value. The yield on the equity interest is also called the *cash-on-cash return* and *the equity dividend rate*. Again, this represents another departure from the conventional valuation model. Equity yield consists of two parts: the annual cash flow earned on the *equity interest*—the actual interest held by the investor—and the before-tax sales proceeds. The equity interest equals the difference between the market value and the mortgage principal. For a new property, the equity interest would be the down payment or required cash, given the mortgage principal. *Sales proceeds are defined as the projected sale price less the remaining mortgage balance at the time of sale.* Therefore, the before-tax cash-flow model depends on the yield on the equity interest and not the total property value.

Valuation Formula

The before-tax cash-flow model produces a capitalization rate that, given net operating income, gives a market value which provides the *required yield rate* on equity. Assume, for example, that the proposed investor requires a *15 percent* yield on equity. Further, assume certain other conditions that might prevail in the market:

1. Mortgage terms: 30 years, 10 percent, $17,482,834
2. Principal (75 percent loan-to-value ratio)
3. Anticipated appreciation: 20 percent over 5 years
4. Annual net operating income: $1,935,000
5. Holding period: 5 years

For the present, assume that a discount rate of 15 percent, 5 years (.083010) applies to the net income of $1,935,000 giving a value of $23,310,000. In this instance, the factor, .083010, represents the overall capitalization rate.[1]

MV   =   NOI / R

MV   = $ 1,935,000
               ─────────────
                 .083010

      = $23,310,445
      = $23,310,000 (rounded)

---

1 Calculations are the result of a computer program that calculates to 16 decimals. Only the first six decimals are shown. Cumulative rounding errors resulting from hand calculators give slightly different answers. For a review of financial factors, see Chapter 6.

This model says that to realize a 15 percent yield, given other assumptions as listed, a valuation of $23,310,000 would allow for a 15 percent yield on the equity interest. The calculation to find this answer is given by the Ellwood formula:[1]

R = Y - MC [+dep (SSF)] or [-App (SSF)]

where:

R   = overall capitalization rate
Y   = yield rate
M   = loan-to-value ratio
C   = the mortgage coefficient factor to account for mortgage principal payments
dep = depreciation over the holding period, 5 years
App = appreciation over the holding period, 5 years
SSF = sinking fund factor at the yield rate over the holding period

The C factor would be found under the formula:

C   = $[Y + (S_p - 1)/(S_m - 1) (SSF)] - f$

where:

S_p = Monthly compound amount of one over the *holding period* at the mortgage interest rate
S_m = Monthly compound amount of one over the *mortgage term* at the mortgage interest rate
SSF = Annual sinking fund factor at the yield rate over the holding period
f   = The annual mortgage constant (monthly installment of 1 x 12)

The formula provides an overall capitalization rate which produces a value such that the investor would realize a 15 percent yield on equity. This procedure may be demonstrated by adopting the same assumptions given earlier. The capitalization rate would be given by first solving for C.[2]

_____

1 See L.W. Ellwood, *Ellwood Tables for Real Estate Appraising and Financing*, fourth edition, Cambridge, Massachusetts: Ballinger Publishing Company, 1977, pp. 79-102.
2 See Chapter 6 for the financial factors used in this chapter.

C = .15 + (1.645309 - 1)/(19.837399 - 1)(.148316) - (.008776 x 12)
  = .15 + (.034257)(.148316) - (.105312)
  = .155081 - .105312
  = .049769

With C given, the overall capitalization rate then equals:

R = .15 - (.75 x .049769) - (.20 x .148316)
  = .15 - (.037327) - (.029663)
  = .083010

This figure may be verified by applying the same variables to the format shown in Table 16-1. If this procedure is followed, the mortgage principal would equal $17,482,834, which would produce an *annual debt service* of $1,841,152. In this instance, the present worth of income to equity totals $314,593 while the sales proceeds equal $11,088,059 or, after discounting, $5,512,728. Given the loan-to-value ratio and other mortgage terms, the present worth of the equity interest equals $23,310,445 or $23,310,000 rounded.

Table 16-1   Before-Tax Cash-Flow Model: Constant Income Projection

Net operating income	$ 1,935,000	
Less annual mortgage requirement	-1,841,152	
(.75 of $23,310,445 x .105312)		
Annual income to equity	$ 93,848	
Present value of annual income to equity		
$93,848 x 3.352155 (present value of annuity factor)		$ 314,593
Present value of sales proceeds		
Sales price	$27,972,534	
Less mortgage balance	-16,884,475	
Sales Proceeds	$11,088,059	
$11,088,059 x .497177		
(present value factor, 5 years, 15%)		5,512,728
Value of equity interest		$ 5,827,321
Add original mortgage		17,482,834
Property value to realize a 15% yield		$23,310,155
Rounding error		290
		$23,310,445

Before-tax Cash-flow Options

The example of Table 16-1 assumes a constant income over the projection period. Furthermore, the net operating income of $1,935,000 provides only for a debt-coverage ratio of 105 percent ($1,935,000/$1,841,152). The *debt-coverage ratio equals the annual net operating income, divided by the annual debt service.* For added security, lenders typically prefer a debt-coverage ratio of 125 percent or more. Table 16-2 provides a before-tax cash value with the same variables of Table 16-1 except that the model substitutes the required debt-coverage ratio, 125 percent for the loan-to-value ratio.

REQUIRED DEBT-COVERAGE RATIO

The model shows a before-tax cash value of $22,159,579. In this instance, under the same assumptions, the original mortgage is reduced to $14,699,656, which allows for an annual debt service of $1,548,050, resulting in the minimum debt-coverage ratio of 125 percent, $1,935,000/$1,548,050. Note that the value of the equity interest, $7,459,923, equals the sum of the present value of annual income to equity of $1,297,116 and the present value of the sales proceeds of $6,162,807. In this instance, the

Table 16-2   Before-Tax Cash Flow With A Debt-Coverage Ratio of 125 Percent

Net operating income	$ 1,935,000	
Less annual mortgage requirement	-1,548,050	
($14,699,656 x .105312)		
Annual income to equity	$ 386,950	
Present value of annual income to equity		
$386,950 x 3.352155 (present value of annuity factor)		$ 1,297,116
Present value of sales proceeds		
Sales price	$26,591,692	
Less mortgage balance	-14,196,093	
Sales proceeds	$12,395,599	
$12,395,599 x .497177		
(present value factor, 5 years, 15%)		6,162,807
Value of equity interest		$ 7,459,923
Add original mortgage		14,699,656
Property value to realize a 15% yield		$22,159,579

developer needs a larger initial equity of $7,459,923 and the lender reduces the loan to $14,699,656.

SECOND-LIEN FINANCING

Suppose that an investor finances an income property under a 75-percent mortgage of $18,848,454, 10-percent interest, 360 months, and a 20-percent second mortgage (a principal of $5,026,255), 12 percent interest, 300 months. See Table 16-3.

Given the annual net operating income of $1,935,000, the property shows a *negative cash flow* of $685,157. If the investor expects that the property will appreciate 20 percent over five years and the investor requires a 15 percent equity yield, the value of the equity interest would equal $1,256,565, indicating a property value of $25,131,274.

Table 16-3   Before-Tax Negative Cash Flow With Secondary Financing

Net operating income		$1,935,000	
Less 1st mortgage payments	$ 1,984,904		
Less 2nd mortgage payments	635,253	-2,620,157	
Annual income to equity		$ - 685,157	
Present value of income to equity			$ -2,296,752
($ 685,157 x 3.352155)			
Present value of sales proceeds			
Sales price		$30,157,527	
Less 1st mortgage balance	- $18,202,767		
Less 2nd mortgage balance	- 4,807,774	- 23,010,541	
Sales proceeds		$7,146,986	
Present value of sales proceeds			
$7,146,986 deferred 5 years x .497177			3,553,317
(present value factor, 5 years, 15%)			
Value of equity interest			$ 1,256,565
Add first mortgage			18,848,454
Add second mortgage			5,026,255
Property value to realize a 15% yield			$25,131,274

Note that the present value of income to equity has a negative value of $2,296,752. However, the estimated sales price of $30,157,527, after repayment of the remaining balances on the first and second mortgages, shows a present value of $7,146,986, which, discounted by the 15 percent yield, equals $3,553,317. In this case, the favorable expectations for capital gain more than offset the present value of negative cash flow.

NET INCOME: COMPOUND RATE OF INCREASE

These first before-tax cash-flow examples assumed a constant annual cash flow. While each model required an assumption of the expected sales price at the end of the holding period, the first two models varied by financing terms. Tables 16-2 and 16-3 valued the discounted before-tax cash flow according to the assumption of a debt coverage ratio and secondary financing.

Appraisers have the further option of assuming a varying annual net income. Table 16-4 gives an estimate of the present value of a net operating income of $1,935,000, which increases at a *six-percent compound rate* per year over the five years. Other assumptions of this model are:

1. Mortgage interest rate, 10 percent
2. Mortgage term, 360 months
3. Loan-to-value ratio, 70 percent
4. Required yield on equity, 15 percent
5. Proposed investment cost, $20,000,000
6. Projected sale price, $24,000,000

Table 16-4   Before-Tax Cash Flow Assuming a Six Percent Compound Rate of Increase in Annual Net Income

	Year 1	Year 2	Year 3	Year 4	Year 5
Net Income	$1,935,000	$2,051,100	$2,174,166	$2,304,616	$2,442,892
Debt Service	-1,474,320	-1,474, 320	-1,474,320	-1,474,320	-1,474,320
Cash Flow	$ 460,680	$ 576,780	$ 699,846	$ 830,296	$ 968,572
Discount Rate	.869565	.756144	.657516	.571753	.497177
Discounted	$ 400,591	$ 436,128	$ 460,160	$ 474,724	$ 481,551
Cumulative	$ 400,591	$ 836,719	$1,296,879	$1,771,604	$2,253,155

The discounted value of annual tax cash flow over the holding period totals $2,253,155. See Table 16-4. The example shows that annual net income increases annually at a six percent compound rate. Given the mortgage terms, a principal of $14,000,000, and a projected sale of $24,000,000, the value of the equity interest totals $7,463,369. With a mortgage of $14,000,000, the investor could pay $21,463,369 to realize a 15 percent yield on equity. These data are summarized in Table 16-5.

NET INCOME: CONSTANT DOLLAR INCREASE

An alternative option provides for an annual before-tax cash flow assuming a *constant annual dollar increase* in net income. To illustrate, assume the annual net income for year one, $1,935,000. While initially increasing by 6 percent, or $116,100 in year two, the annual income increases each year by the same constant amount. By further assuming other variables of the preceding illustration, the discounted annual before-tax cash flow, over five years, equals $2,214,764. These calculations are shown in Table 16-6. With the same assumptions for the projected sales proceeds and financing terms, Table 16-7 shows a discounted before-tax cash flow of $21,424,978.

Therefore, given the assumptions of yield, holding period, and financing terms, the estimated discounted before-tax cash flow varies according

Table 16-5   Discounted Before-Tax Cash-Flow Assuming An Annual Six Percent Compound Rate Of Increase In Net Income

Discounted annual cash flow		$ 2,253,155
Present value of sales proceeds		
Sales price	$24,000,000	
Less mortgage balance	- 13,520,405	
Sales proceeds	$10,479,595	
$10,479,595 x .497177		5,210,214
(present value factor, 5 years, 15%)		
Value of equity interest		$ 7,463,369
Add original mortgage		14,000,000
Property value to realize a 15% yield		$21,463,369

Table 16-6   Annual Before-Tax Cash Flow Assuming A Constant Annual Dollar Increase In Net Income ($116,100)

	Year 1	Year 2	Year 3	Year 4	Year 5
Net Income	$1,935,000	$2,051,100	$2,167,200	$2,283,300	$2,399,400
Debt Service	- 1,474,320	- 1,474,320	- 1,474,320	- 1,474,320	- 1,474,320
Cash Flow	$ 400,680	$ 576,780	$ 692,880	$ 808,980	$ 925,080
Discount Rate	.869565	.756144	.657516	.571753	.497177
Discounted	$ 400,591	$ 436,128	$ 455,580	$ 462,537	$ 459,928
Cumulative	$ 400,591	$ 836,719	$1,292,299	$ 1,754,836	$2,214,764

Table 16-7   Discounted Before-Tax Cash Flow Assuming A Constant Dollar Increase In Annual Net Income ($116,100)

Discounted annual cash flow		$ 2,214,764
Present value of sales proceeds		
Sales price	$24,000,000	
Less mortgage balance	13,520,405	
Sales proceeds	$10,479,595	
$10,479,595 x .497177		5,210,214
(Present value factor, 5 years, 15%)		
Value of equity interest		$ 7,424,978
Add original mortgage		14,000,000
Property value to realize a 15% yield		$21,424,978

to alternative assumptions adopted by the appraiser. Assumptions regarding annual before-tax cash flow are:

1. Constant annual net income
2. Compound rate of increase in annual net income
3. Constant dollar amount of annual increase in net income
4. Projected annual net income
5. Projected sales price

The capital value of before-tax cash flow may be expected to vary according to assumptions over the sales price and future net income.

By adopting a constant income, compound rate of increase, or a constant dollar increase in net income, the appraiser employs *deductive reasoning* in estimating cash flow. Deductive reasoning refers to reasoning from the general case to the specific case. Here the appraiser-analyst establishes the general principle of a 20 percent capital appreciation and other variables which are then applied to a specific investment. If, however, a cash-flow projection is based on past data (a forecast), the before-tax cash-flow model then follows the reasoning that past net income patterns will be followed in the future. While these calculations in the last analysis are based on subjective, personal evaluations, they must agree with reasonable expectations of the market. The degree of reasonableness may be tested with respect to cash-flow financial ratios.

AFTER-TAX CASH-FLOW MODELS

After-tax cash-flow models rest primarily on the variables common to before-tax cash-flow models. However, after-tax cash-flow models report *cash flow after payment of corporate or personal income taxes.*

Accordingly, cash flow and sales proceeds then vary according to certain tax variables:

1. Capital recovery allowances on buildings
2. Income tax rates
3. Capital gain taxation
4. Treatment of tax losses

Given the variations in annual after-tax cash flow and sales proceeds as a result of these additional tax factors, it is difficult to judge appropriate financial results. Consequently, appraisers analyze discounted after-tax cash flow according to selected financial ratios, i.e., financial ratios help in judging the effect of before-tax cash-flow assumptions. Financial ratios also help determine the required yield, given investment risks.

The analysis of after-tax cash-flow ratios assumes critical importance among lenders since financing terms frequently give lenders a share in the equity interest. For an income property, investors—including pension funds, insurance companies, and other sources of real estate capital—acquire equity shares in return for project financing. Because lenders no longer take a passive interest in merely acting as suppliers of credit, their equity shares encourage additional performance analysis that helps judge before-tax cash flow and its relative risk.

Income Tax Variables

Annual after-tax cash flow equals net operating income, less *annual debt service* and *income taxes*. Its estimation, therefore, requires calculation of *annual taxable income*. Taxable income represents annual *net operating income* less mortgage interest and the capital recovery allowance. The capital recovery allowance depends on the property use.

CAPITAL RECOVERY ALLOWANCES

Investors may recover the building cost at a constant annual rate, depending on whether the building is an income residential property (apartment) or other commercial property. Therefore, for an apartment building valued at $10,000,000, the depreciation basis will have an annual tax deduction after the first year of $363,600 over 27.5 years [$10,000,000 (.03636)]. The annual depreciation allowance for the first year depends on the month in which the building is placed in service. See Table 16-8. For a commercial building of the same value, the annual depreciation deduction after the first year would be $317,500, based on a recovery period of *31.5 years*. Depreciation rates are based on *straight-line rates*. This means that annual depreciation rates are uniform over the building-recovery period, i.e., 1 / 31.5 of $10,000,000 per year. The annual depreciation rates for residential and nonresidential property are shown in Table 16-8.

Table 16-8   **Straight-Line Annual Capital Recovery Rates For Residential And Nonresidential Real Estate**

	Month Placed in Service										
Years	1	2	3	4	5	6	7	8	9	11	12
	27.5-year Residential Real Property										
1	.03485	.03182	.02879	.02576	.02273	.0197	.01667	.01364	.0	.0455	.01520
2-27	.03636	.03636	.03636	.03636	.03636	.03636	.03636	.03636	.0	.03636	.03636
	31.5-year Nonresidential Real Property										
1	.03042	.02778	.02513	.02249	.01984	.01720	.01455	.01190	.0	.0397	.0132
2-31	.03175	.03175	.03175	.03175	.03175	.03175	.03175	.03175	.0	.03175	.01375

Source: Internal Revenue Service, *Depreciation*, Pamphlet 512 (Washington, D.C.: U.S. Department of Treasury, 1988)

INCOME TAX RATES

Given the taxable income, which varies by the annual capital recovery and mortgage interest deductions, cash flow will vary according to the annual income tax rate. For corporations earning an annual taxable income over $335,000, the current tax rate is 34 percent. Table 16-9 summarizes the taxable income for individuals married and filing jointly, or single persons. For the examples given in this chapter, it is assumed that the investor is subject to a marginal income tax rate of 28 percent. If the investment is held by a corporation, use the corporate tax rate of 34 percent.

CAPITAL GAINS TAXATION

Sales proceeds are calculated after deducting the remaining mortgage balance and the capital gains tax. The capital gains tax is based on the sales price, less the *adjusted cost basis*. For example, assume a sales price at the end of five years of $22,000,000. For a commercial building (nonresidential) with an original cost of $18,000,000, the adjusted cost basis would be $18,000,000, less the accumulated depreciation taken over the five years of $1,889,040 (building cost, $12,000,000).

	Depreciation Rate	Annual Depreciation	Cumulative Depreciation
First year	.03042	$365,040	$ 365,040
Years 2-5	.03175	$381,000	1,524,000
Total depreciation, 5 years			$1,889,040

Table 16-9   Personal Income Tax Rates Under The Revenue Reconciliation Act of 1990 As Amended

Taxable Income (Unadjusted for inflation)	Tax Rate
Married filing jointly	
$0 - $32,450	15%
$32,451 - $78,400	28
Over $78,400	31
Single	
$0 - $19,450	15%
$19,451 - $47,050	28
Over $47,050	31

The example assumes the building is placed in service in January. Therefore, the taxable gain would be equal to the sales price, $22,000,000, less the adjusted cost basis of $16,110,960 ($22,000,000 - $1,889,040) or $5,889,040. Assuming a tax rate of 28 percent, the capital gains tax would be $1,648,931. The reported capital gain would then reflect the following calculations:

Sales price		$22,000,000
Less the adjusted cost basis		
Cost	$18,000,000	
Less depreciation taken	- 1,889,040	- 16,110,960
Taxable gain		$ 5,889,040
Capital gains tax, 28%		$ 1,648,931

TREATMENT OF TAX LOSSES

Tax legislation classifies income as passive or nonpassive. Generally, *passive income* relates to income earned from a trade or business in which the taxpayer does not *materially participate,* i.e., an investor holding a limited partnership interest in a shopping center does not materially participate in that activity. Hence, income and losses from the limited partnership interest would be a passive source of income.

The importance of the passive definition relates to the deduction of losses on passive investments. Given these general rules, taxpayers may *deduct losses from passive* activities only against income from other passive activities. For the most part, losses from passive activity are not deductible from income from nonpassive activities. The law provides, however, that losses may be carried forward indefinitely and used to offset passive income realized by taxpayers in later years.

The rules defining the treatment of tax losses on rental real estate are subject to many exceptions and are largely dependent on a case-by-case analysis. The law further grants tax incentives to investors in low-income rental housing. Tax credits are allowable for preferential depreciation, five-year amortization of rehabilitation expenditures, and special treatment of construction interest expenses and taxes.

With these qualifications, it is presumed that after-tax cash-flow estimates represent income from passive sources. Therefore, losses reported in the models in this chapter are presumed to be not deductible from salaried (nonpassive) income. For real estate properties showing tax losses, the counsel of tax accountants and attorneys would generally be required.

Discounted After-tax Cash-flow Model

The formula for this model states that the discounted after-tax cash flow provides first for the annual net income, less income taxes, and annual debt service over the holding period, discounted by the yield rate. The second term discounts the sale price, less the capital gains tax and less the remaining mortgage balance at the end of the holding period.

This model may be illustrated by assuming the variables necessary to the model:

Mortgage principal, $15,000,000

Mortgage interest rate, 10

Mortgage terms (months), 360

Building value, $12,000,000

Building life (years), 31.5

Building in service, January (first year)

Effective gross income, $4,000,000

Annual operating expense, $2,065,000

Personal income tax rate, 28 percent

Holding period in years, 5

Annual discount rate, 15 percent

Original cost, $18,000,000

Projected selling price, $22,000,000

The illustration covers an office building showing an annual gross income of $4,000,000, with annual operating expenses of $2,065,000. The model further assumes an income tax rate of 28 percent and an annual discount rate or yield rate of 15 percent. Assuming an original cost of $18,000,000 with a proposed property selling price of $22,000,000, the model calculates the discounted after-tax cash flow. The discounted after-tax cash-flow estimate leads to the calculation of selected financial ratios. The discounted cash flow over five years is shown in Table 16-10.

Note that for the first year, the taxable income is $73,665. Assuming a tax rate of 28 percent, the tax liability equals $20,626. The model starts with the net operating income, which is assumed as unchanging for the five years of $1,935,000. Deducting the annual taxes and mortgage payments

Table 16-10   Annual Discounted After-Tax Cash Flow

	Year 1	Year 2	Year 3	Year 4	Year 5
Net operating income	$1,935,000	$1,935,000	$1,935,000	$1,935,000	$1,935,000
Less mortgage interest	- 1,496,295	- 1,487,565	- 1,477,920	- 1,467,270	- 1,455,495
Less depreciation	- 365,040	- 381,000	- 381,000	- 381,000	- 381,000
Taxable income	$ 73,665	$ 66,435	$ 76,080	$ 86,730	$ 98,505
Income taxes (28% tax rate)	20,626	18,602	21,302	24,284	27,581
Net operating income	$1,935,000	$1,935,000	$1,935,000	$1,935,000	$1,935,000
Deduct taxes	- 20,626	- 18,602	- 21,302	- 24,284	- 27,581
Less mortgage payment	- 1,579,680	- 1,579,680	- 1,579,680	- 1,579,680	- 1,579,680
After-tax cash flow	$ 334,694	$ 336,718	$ 334,018	$ 331,036	$ 327,739
Present value factor, 15%	0.869565	0.756144	0.657516	0.571753	0.497177
Discounted after-tax cash flow	$ 291,038	$ 254,607	$ 219,622	$ 189,270	$ 162,944
Cumulative after-tax cash flow	$ 291,038	$ 545,645	$ 765,267	$ 954,537	$1,117,481

over the year gives an after-tax cash flow in the first year of $334,694. Because the income tax deduction decreases each year, the taxable income increases, giving a higher income tax deduction each year, or a declining after-tax cash flow. The discounted after-tax cash flow for each year is shown in Table 16-10; it varies from $291,038 to $162,944 for the fifth year. The cumulative value of discounted after-tax cash flow totals $1,117,481 over five years.

After-tax sales proceeds and the discounted after-tax cash flow are listed in Table 16-11. Given the sale price of $22,000,000, the model starts with an original cost of $18,000,000, less the total depreciation taken over the five years, or $1,889,040. After deducting the adjusted cost basis, the capital gains tax is calculated on a taxable gain of $5,889,040, resulting in a capital gains tax of 28 percent, or $1,648,931.

Table 16-11   Discounted After-Tax Cash Flow

Sales price		$22,000,000
Less adjusted cost basis		
Cost	$18,000,000	
Less depreciation	- 1,889,040	- 16,110,960
Taxable gain		$ 5,889,040
Capital gains tax (28%)		$ 1,648,931
Sales price		$22,000,000
Less capital gains tax	$ - 1,648,931	
Less remaining mortgage balance	- 14,486,145	- 16,135,076
After-tax sales proceeds		$ 5,864,924
Present value of sales proceeds		
$5,864,924 x .497177 (PVF, 15%, 5 years)		$ 2,915,905
Discounted after-tax-cash flow		
Present value of after tax cash flow		$ 1,117,481
Add discounted after-tax sales proceeds		2,915,905
Discounted after-tax cash flow		$ 4,033,386
Add mortgage principal		$15,000,000
Estimated market value		$19,033,386

Therefore, the after-tax sales proceeds equals $5,864,924, which is the sale price, less capital gains taxes and less the remaining mortgage balance at the end of the fifth year. The present worth of sales proceeds, discounted at 15 percent, equals $2,915,905, which, with the present value of the annual after-tax cash flow, makes for a total after-tax cash flow of *$4,033,386.*

The property value, based on this analysis, equals the discounted after-tax cash flow of $4,033,386 plus the $15,000,000 mortgage or *$19,033,386.* These calculations follow the formula for the discounted after-tax cash-flow model. The question then arises as to whether the estimated cash-flow value of $19,033,386 conforms to the market. Are the variables adopted for this analysis in agreement with general market experience? Selected financial ratios give insights on the reliability of the discounted cash-flow value.

FINANCIAL RATIOS

It is convenient to analyze financial ratios in four main groups—mortgage ratios, cash-flow measures, operating ratios, and yields.

Mortgage Ratios

The two main ratios, here printed as additional output by a computer cash-flow model, indicate a possible erroneous net income or atypical mortgage terms.

DEBT-COVERAGE RATIO

The debt-coverage ratio equals the net operating income, divided by annual debt service. In the present case, the debt coverage ratio equals 122.49 percent.

$$
\begin{aligned}
\text{DCR} \;&=\; \text{NOI} \,/\, \text{DS} \\
&=\; \$1,935,000 \,/\, \$1,579,860 \\
&=\; 122.49 \text{ percent}
\end{aligned}
$$

Assuming that a debt ratio of 125 percent is a normal market expectation, the model indicates that the debt-coverage ratio approximately meets market standards. On its face, the debt-coverage ratio confirms other variables that validate the discounted after-tax cash flow. A relatively *low* debt-coverage ratio, say 105 percent, would indicate the possibility of a below-market annual net operating income, a relatively high loan-to-value ratio, or a relatively high annual debt service.

LOAN-TO-VALUE RATIO

The $15,000,000 mortgage given for this problem is based on the original cost of $18,000,000. The resulting loan-to-value ratio of 83.33 percent conforms to accepted financing terms. The loan-to-value ratio in this instance is calculated as:

$$
\begin{aligned}
LTV &= \text{Mortgage principal / Original cost} \\
&= \$15,000,000 \ / \ \$18,000,000 \\
&= 83.33 \text{ percent}
\end{aligned}
$$

An unusual loan-to-value ratio, i.e., below 50 percent or a loan-to-value ratio that exceeds 100 percent, would be indicative of an incorrect mortgage principal or an original cost that is distorted either upward or downward; hence, a review of the loan-to-value ratio shows two elements that may be in error—the mortgage principal or the original cost, or both. These ratios may be further tested by additional financial ratios.

Cash-flow Measures

The net present value and the profitability index provide relative measures to evaluate after-tax cash flow. These ratios must meet investor requirements in view of the perceived investment risk and yields on alternative investments.

NET PRESENT VALUE

The proposed investment should have a positive net present value. Although it is not a ratio, it is the basis for calculating the following ratio or profitability index. Because the net present value is defined as the discounted after-tax cash flow, less the equity interest, it must be positive before the investment is deemed profitable. The net present value would be given by:

$$
\begin{aligned}
NPV &= DATCF - E \\
&= \$4,033,386 - \$3,000,000 \\
&= \$1,033,386
\end{aligned}
$$

A negative net present value would suggest that the yield rate is distorted upward, the mortgage terms are unreasonable, the net operating income is understated, or the original cost is too high. The general rule is that the net present value must be positive to justify a proposed investment.

PROFITABILITY INDEX

The profitability index converts the net present value to a relative term. The profitability index should be over 1.0 to indicate a positive net present value. The profitability index is a means of rating alternative investments showing a positive net present value. The profitability index for the present problem is calculated by dividing the discounted after-tax cash flow by the equity:

$$
\begin{aligned}
PI &= DATCF / E \\
&= \$4,033,386 / \$3,000,000 \\
&= 1.34
\end{aligned}
$$

The profitability index shows that the present value exceeds the equity interest by 34 percent. This figure assumes that if the assumptions of the problem are realized under the given discount rate, mortgage terms, and holding period, the net present value is 1.34 times the value of the original equity of $3,000,000. A profitability index greater than 1.0 indicates a favorable investment.

Operating Ratios

Two ratios test the validity of operating expenses and mortgage terms. The two ratios cited below assume that some typical relationship generally prevails between these variables.

BREAK-EVEN POINT

The break-even point indicates the relative risk assumed by the lender and investor. Calculate the break-even point by adding debt service and annual operating expenses and dividing their sum by gross income. In the present case the break-even point equals 91.1 percent:

$$
\begin{aligned}
BEP &= (DS + EXP) / EGI \\
&= \frac{(\$1,579,680 + \$2,065,000)}{\$4,000,000} \times 100 \\
&= 91.1 \text{ percent}
\end{aligned}
$$

Note that the annual debt service and operating expenses total $3,644,680. To put it differently, the effective gross income could decrease by $355,320 before effective gross income would be less than debt service and annual expenses. In this instance, if the gross income declines by more than 8.9 percent ($355,320/$4,000,000), the investor would have insufficient funds to pay annual debt service and operating expenses.

NET OPERATING RATIO

For a given property type and real estate market area, there is a common operating ratio prevailing for investment properties. The *net operating ratio refers to the net operating income expressed as a percent of gross income.* The typical operating ratio may be identified from comparable properties in the same market or by reference to published income and expense detail circulated by real estate trade associations. These sources are identified in Chapter 15. The net operating ratio for the example of Table 16-10 is 48.4 percent:

$$
\begin{aligned}
NOR &= (GI - EXP) \; / \; EGI \\
&= \frac{(\$4,000,000 - \$2,065,000)}{\$4,000,000} \times 100 \\
&= 48.4 \text{ percent}
\end{aligned}
$$

An operating ratio that falls considerably below local market experience, for example, 25 percent, would suggest that estimated operating expenses have been understated or that the gross income has been overstated. In other words, the net operating ratio allows the asset manager to judge the accuracy of gross income and operating expenses.

Yields

Yield analysis permits managers to compare yields between alternative investments. The three yields considered here include the overall capitalization rate, the return on equity, and the internal rate of return.

OVERALL CAPITALIZATION RATE

Recall that the overall rate of return includes capital recovery and a yield on the property investment. Because net operating income for real estate excludes building depreciation, capital recovery is provided by the overall capitalization rate:

$$
\begin{aligned}
OR &= NOI \; / \; MV \\
&= \$1,935,000 \; / \; \$18,000,000 \times 100 \\
&= 10.75 \text{ percent}
\end{aligned}
$$

The overall rate of return is easily calculated, readily compared to like property, commonly understood and frequently used. Unusual overall capitalization rates encourage further investigation of gross income and operating expenses.

RETURN ON EQUITY

The return on equity relates the net operating income to the value of the equity. Based on first-year results, the return on equity for the present example equals 64.5 percent:

$$\text{ROE} = \text{NOI} / \text{E}$$
$$= \$1,935,000 / \$3,000,000 \ (100)$$
$$= 64.50 \text{ percent}$$

The cash-on-cash return is more appropriate to analyze before-tax cash flow. The income assumptions and the after-tax sales proceeds introduce other variables that affect investment decisions. The return on equity, therefore, should be interpreted in the light of other financial ratios. An unusually low return on equity would indicate a below-market net income and unusual financing terms.

INTERNAL RATE OF RETURN (IRR)

Institutional investors—for example pension funds, real estate investment trusts, insurance companies, and others—rely heavily on the internal rate of return. The IRR refers to that *yield rate which equates the discounted after-tax cash flow with the equity interest.* The IRR allows investors to compare the projected IRR with the required rate of return. The expectation would be that, given the element of risk, the discounted cash flow would result in an IRR that meets investor requirements. If a project shows an internal rate of return of less than a required minimum IRR of 15 percent, it would not qualify for investment or development. Alternatively, if several investments conform to other investment objectives, that investment which earns the highest rate of return may be selected.

The IRR is calculated under the formula:

$$E = \sum_{t=1}^{n} \frac{CF_t}{(1 + i)^t} + \frac{NSP}{(1 + i)^n}$$

where:

E = Equity
CF_t = Annual after-tax cash flow in year t
NSP = After-tax sales proceeds
n = Holding period in years

For the preceding problem, substituting the following values for the five years gives an internal rate of return of 23.18 percent:

$$\$3,000,000 = \frac{\$334,694}{(1 + i)^1} + \frac{\$336,718}{(1 + i)^2} + \frac{\$334,018}{(1 + i)^3} +$$

$$\frac{\$331,036}{(1 + i)^4} + \frac{\$327,739}{(1 + i)^5} + \frac{\$5,864,924}{(1 + i)^5}$$

$$= 23.18 \text{ percent}$$

Programmable calculators and computer spreadsheets solve for i given the annual cash flow, after-tax sales proceeds, and the holding period. In this case, with an equity of $3,000,000, the internal rate of return would be 23.18 percent.

The best investment, however, is not necessarily indicated by the highest IRR. While the IRR indicates the highest percentage yield, it does not include the investment base from which the IRR is calculated. A 30 percent IRR earned on a $100,000 equity may be less desirable than an IRR of 15 percent earned on an equity investment of $3,000,000. Moreover, if negative cash flows are reported over the holding period, the internal rate of return gives ambiguous results. The conclusion follows that the internal rate of return must be judged with respect to the net present value and related financial ratios.

SUMMARY

Before-tax cash-flow models assume that typical real estate investments are financed, that investors invest over relatively short periods, and that investors consider capital appreciation or depreciation in weighing investment yields. The before-tax cash-flow models implicitly assume, moreover, that investors look to yields on equity and not on the total property value. Therefore, the before-tax cash-flow model depends on the present value of annual cash flow on equity and the present value of sales proceeds.

The before-tax cash-flow model results in a market value which will provide the *required* yield rate. Before-tax cash-flow options include models that insure a minimum *debt-coverage ratio.*

Before-tax cash-flow models may also value projects that earn the required yield given *second-lien financing.* Further, before-tax cash-flow models may be adapted to annual income that increases at a compound annual rate or a constant annual dollar amount. In addition, investors may calculate before-tax cash flow using forecasted net operating income. A statistical forecast may be more realistic than a model that predicts net operating income by a mathematical function.

After-tax cash-flow models are based on the annual after-tax cash flow and the after-tax sales proceeds. This requires the assumption of building *depreciation rates, income tax rates, capital gains taxes,* and *the treatment of tax losses.* The income tax variables require the assumption of straight-line capital recovery rates for depreciable buildings, 27.5 years for residential income property, or 31.5 years for commercial buildings. *Taxable income,* then, is based on the net operating income, less mortgage interest and less the depreciation allowance.

In calculating the *after-tax sales proceeds,* the taxable capital gain equals the projected sales price less the *adjusted cost basis.* The adjusted cost basis is given by the acquisition cost of the real estate, less the accumulated depreciation taken over the holding period. The *capital gains tax,* calculated at ordinary income tax rates, is applied against the sales price less the adjusted cost basis.

The final calculation for after-tax sales proceeds equals the present value of the sales price, less the capital gains tax and the remaining mortgage balance. The final answer, the discounted after-tax cash flow, equals the present value of annual after-tax cash flow, plus the discounted value of after-tax sales proceeds. Adding the given mortgage principal results in an estimated property value.

Before- and after-tax cash-flow models may be analyzed according to selected *financial ratios.* Financial ratios should fall within reasonable limits. Financial ratios that vary significantly from accepted investment standards, allow asset managers to re-examine investment and financing relationships to judge investment prospects. The *debt-coverage ratio* (annual operating income divided by annual debt service) indicates the degree of risk assumed by lenders and investors. The *loan-to-value ratio* has equal importance. An unusually low loan-to-value ratio indicates conservative financing or a questionable market value estimate. The re-evaluation of these other ratios gives insight into reasons for an atypical loan to value ratio.

Proposed investments should have a positive *net present value.* The net present value equals discounted after-tax cash flow, less the equity interest. A negative net present value suggests a questionable discount rate, unusual mortgage terms, or a distorted estimate of annual net operating income or projected sales price. Similarly, the *profitability index* converts the net present value to a relative term. Generally, a profitability index of less than 1.0 would be grounds for rejecting the investment.

The *break-even point* provides information on the relative risk assumed by lenders and investors. Annual debt service added to annual operating expenses, divided by the gross income, gives the break-even point expressed as a percentage. For a given investment property, there is a typical *net operating ratio,* the net operating income expressed as a percent of gross income. Typical net operating income ratios are provided by similar investment properties in the same market area or in published reports of income and operating expenses for apartments, office buildings, shopping centers, and hotels.

Finally, the *overall capitalization rate* shows the net return on the total property value. The *return on equity*, in contrast, also known as the cash-on-cash return, relates net operating income to the equity value. This ratio applies primarily to before-tax cash-flow analysis. The income tax variables in the after-tax cash-flow model make this return less important.

The *internal rate of return (IRR)*, which equates the discounted after-tax cash flow with the equity, allows investors to compare the projected internal rate of return with the required rate of return. The required rate of return is interpreted in the light of other financial ratios. Given the favorable comparison of other financial ratios, the preferred investment would show the highest internal rate of return. Investors, however, may focus on net present value and other investment measures to reach investment decisions. For investments that show negative annual returns, the internal rate of return gives ambiguous results.

POINTS TO REMEMBER

economic building life the time in which a building has no economic value.

equity dividend rate the yield on the equity interest. It is also called the cash-on-cash return.

required yield rate the yield required by a typical real estate investor.

annual debt service the monthly mortgage payment times 12. Annual debt service includes the total annual mortgage interest and principal payments.

second-lien financing financing that includes a mortgage loan subordinate to the first mortgage.

deductive reasoning the process of reasoning from the general case to the specific case.

taxable capital gains the sale price, less the adjusted cost basis.

adjusted cost basis the original cost, less accumulated depreciation taken over the investment holding period.

loan-to-value ratio the mortgage loan expressed as a percent of the estimated market value.

net present value discounted after-tax cash flow, less the equity interest.

profitability index discounted after-tax cash flow divided by the equity.

break-even point the sum of the annual debt service and annual operating expenses divided by the annual gross income.

return on equity the annual net operating income divided by the value of the equity.

internal rate of return (IRR) the yield rate which equates discounted after-tax cash flow with the equity interest.

QUESTIONS FOR REVIEW

1. Explain the assumptions underlying before-tax cash-flow models.

2. Explain the meaning of the variables included in the before-tax cash-flow valuation formula.

3. In considering the before-tax cash-flow options, explain options that you would recommend for a particular before-tax cash-flow valuation. Give reasons for your answer.

4. Explain the main differences between before- and after-tax cash-flow models.

5. Explain the differences between the formula to calculate discounted after-tax cash flow and the internal rate of return. Explain thoroughly.

6. Explain the main steps to calculate the discounted after-tax sales proceeds.

7. What is the significance of financial ratios for a discounted after-tax cash-flow?

8. Show how you would interpret net present value and the profitability index in judging an income property appraisal.

9. Explain how you would use the break-even point and the net operating ratio to judge the accuracy of an income appraisal.

10. What precautions would you follow in interpreting the internal rate of return?

PRACTICE PROBLEMS

1. Using a hand calculator or computer routine, calculate the discounted after-tax cash-flow model assuming the following variables:

Effective gross income, $2,800,000	Holding period, 5 years
Annual operating income expenses, $800,000	Personal income tax rate,
Mortgage terms	28 percent
12 percent interest rate	Discount rate, 15 percent
25-year term	Building value, $10,000,000
80 percent loan-to-value ratio	Original cost, $15,000,000
Expected sales price, $20,000,000	Building life, 31.5 years

2. For practice problem 1, calculate the:

Debt-coverage ratio	Net operating ratio	Profitability index
Break-even point	Cash on cash	Overall capitalization rate
Return on equity	Net present value	Internal rate of return

On the basis of these ratios, would you consider this an accurate indication of market value? Why or why not? Give reasons for your answer.

C H A P T E R   1 7

Lease Valuation

After reading this chapter you will know:
- Financial rights of parties to a lease.
- Techniques to value the leased fee.
- Techniques to value the leasehold interest.
- How to analyze lease terms that bear on market value.

The valuation of leased estates deals with the financial rights of the owner leasing the property (the *lessor*) and the financial rights of the tenant (the *lessee*). After describing these financial rights, the chapter shows how to value the *leased fee* with its most common variations. The leased fee is the interest held by the lessor. This material is followed by illustrations of techniques to value the *leasehold interest*—the interest held by the tenant-lessee.

The balance of the chapter covers variations in leases that require special appraisal techniques—methods of valuing leases with varying rent terms and with tenant improvements. The chapter closes with an illustration of the valuation of a neighborhood shopping center developed under a combination of 20-year and short-term leases.

FINANCIAL RIGHTS

Recall that tenants acquire exclusive rights of use over time. In return, tenants pay rent and perform other duties as stated in the lease. In effect, use-rights granted tenants are paid in installments as the property is used, i.e., the lease conveys property rights over time.

Contrast leases with purchase of the fee simple estate; here buyers acquire exclusive rights of ownership in perpetuity. The buyer pays a price or lump sum which is the present value of future property rights. Thus, in large measure, the election to lease depends on the financial advantages of a lease.

Considered in this manner, the lease creates certain financial rights unique to the owner and tenant. Technically, rights are assigned to the owner, who holds the *leased fee estate,* and to the tenant who holds the *leasehold* interest. That is, the lease divides the fee simple, or freehold, estate into the two property interests as shown in Figure 17-1. Assuming the same capitalization rate, the value of the fee simple estate equals the sum of the leased-fee interest and the leasehold interest. Valued separately, the fee simple estate would be valued according to the market rent.

Figure 17-1   The Appraisal of Owner and Tenant Interests

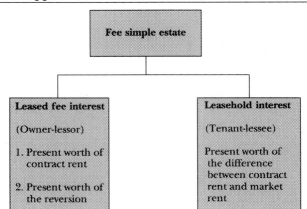

Lessor Rights

Figure 17-1 shows that the lessor, the holder of the leased fee interest, has the right to:

1. The contract rent, and

2. The reversion, or the present value of the leased property at the end of the lease.

The right to the contract rent has a present value, depending on the length of the lease and the discount rate. *Contract rent* refers to the rent required under the lease. The reversionary value is the present value of the leased premises at the end of the lease. At that time, the lessor acquires the exclusive right of ownership common to the fee simple estate. The reversionary value is equivalent to the value of a postponed sum.

Suppose that a potential warehouse site has a value of $2,000,000. The fee owner may not have the capital or ability to improve the land with an appropriate industrial warehouse, but a national corporation may be willing to lease the land with the object of building a modern warehouse. If the owner leases this land for 25 years at an annual rent of $120,000 for construction of a tenant-constructed building, the fee owner, now the lessor, has the right to collect an annual rent of $120,000 and the right to the exclusive ownership of the building and land at the end of 25 years.

The value of the lessor interest, then, equals the present value of $120,000 annual rent payable over 25 years and the present value of the reversionary interest postponed 25 years. Such a lease is called a *net ground lease*. Note that the lessor gains the present value of the right to the land at the end of 25 years, in addition to the value of the building postponed 25 years. Since the building is attached to the land, both the land and the building revert to the lessor at the date of lease termination.

Lessee Rights

The tenant has an incentive to enter into the lease since:

The lease, in effect, represents a 100 percent, 25-year loan equal to the land value of $2,000,000.
The tenant gains from the income tax deductibility of land rent.
The building may be depreciated over the life of the lease, 25 years.

In addition, if the building is financed under a long-term mortgage, the tenant gains the advantage of the income tax deductibility of mortgage interest. In short, the tenant, or lessee, enters the lease with the prospect of benefiting from the income tax deduction of rent, mortgage interest, and in some cases, property taxes. The lessee also has the exclusive right to use the property over the lease term. The value of the leasehold interest is subject to capital appreciation, or depreciation, like other property interests.

MARKET VALUATION

Given the local real estate market, market values of properties subject to lease are largely determined by the lease. The lease may deal with many variations in rental payments. In this respect, the appraiser judges the effect of escalation clauses, minimum rents, overage rents, price index adjustments, step-rate leases, common area charges, and leases calling for tenant-constructed buildings. The lease also imposes on tenants certain other duties that bear on market value, such as leases that require minimum investments in buildings or other improvements at certain intervals over the lease. There is also the effect of lease options on lease valuation.

It is first deemed appropriate to show how to value a fixed-rent lease. With an understanding of lease appraisals, rental terms are varied to show how various lease and rental terms affect value. A case study shows how complex rent variations may be incorporated into lease valuation models.

Leased Fee

In the simplest case, the value of the leased fee depends on four variables: the contract rent, the due date of rent payments, the reversionary value, and the rate of discount. The due date controls the number of periods for valuation—typically, monthly, quarterly, semiannually, or annually. Rent is usually payable at the beginning of the rental period.

The reversionary value constitutes the present value of property as it reverts to the lessor at lease termination. The rate of discount or capitalization rate that converts rent to present value is derived from an analysis of risk, the relative certainty of rents, and yields earned on alternative investments. More than one rate of discount may be used to value various payments required by a lease.

Questions may be raised over the present value of the reversion. It would be difficult, for example, to support a projection of property values at the end of a 25-year lease. Current practice favors the acceptance of current value or the capitalized value of rent projected at the end of the lease. It will be appreciated that the error in estimating reversionary values tends to be compensated by the lower discounted values as the lease term increases. While the present value estimate is not absolute, it provides an effective means to estimate market value.

BEGINNING-OF-PERIOD PAYMENTS

The formula for the present value of an annuity factor assumes end-of-year payments; however, rents are typically paid at the beginning of the period. Calculators and computer programs provide options for payments at the end of the period or at the beginning of the period. The point is illustrated by a net ground lease that provides for annual rent payments on January 1 covering the calendar year. With this example, assume an annual net ground rent of $100,000 over 25 years capitalized at 10 percent.

Assumptions
25-year ground lease, payable for the calendar year, $100,000 annual rent, 10 percent discount.

End-of-year payments

$$
\begin{aligned}
MV &= PVAF_{10,\ 25}\ (\$100,000) \\
&= 9.077040\ (\$100,000) \\
&= \$907,704
\end{aligned}
$$

Beginning-of-year payments

$$\begin{aligned} MV &= PVAF_{10,\ 25}\ (\$100{,}000)\,(1.10) \\ &= 9.07704\ (\$100{,}000)\,(1.10) \\ &= \$998{,}474 \end{aligned}$$

Under end-of-year payments the present value of rental income totals $907,704. The present value increases to $998,474 with beginning-of-year payments. For beginning-of-period payments, the general rule is to correct the present value factor by multiplying by the *base*. The base in this instance is the interest rate for the first period plus 1, or in this case 1.10. For monthly rent payable in advance, the base would be $1 + .10/12$. Pocket calculators and computer programs provide automatic calculation for beginning-of-year payments, making it unnecessary to multiply end-of-period factors by the base.

GRADUATED LEASES

Graduated leases assume many forms. Initially, owners may grant rent concessions over the early years while the property is undergoing development, i.e., $20,000 monthly for the first three years and $30,000 monthly for the remaining lease term. In other cases, 20-year shopping center leases may require an acceleration of common area charges (the expense of maintaining common areas allocated to tenants) graduated upward over each five-year interval. Other leases may provide fixed rents graduated over the lease term.

To value a lease fee with graduated rents, treat each graduated rent separately. Consider the following lease:

Lease term, 15 years
Rent, payable monthly at the beginning of the month
Discount rate, 11.5 percent
Monthly rent:
    First five years, $10,000
    Second five years, $15,000
    Third five years, $20,000
Estimated reversionary value, $1,500,000

See Table 17-1.

Table 17-1   Valuation of a Graduated Lease

Present Value of Rental Income
(PVAF = Beginning period payments; PVF = End of year payments)

First Five Years
$$PV = \$10{,}000 \; PVAF_{60, \, .115/12}$$
$$= \$459{,}056$$

Second Five Years
$$PV = \$15{,}000 \; PVAF_{60, \, .115/12} \; PVF_{5, \, .115}$$
$$= \$688{,}584 \; PVF_{5, \, .115}$$
$$= \$399{,}561$$

Third Five Years
$$PV = \$20{,}000 \; PVAF_{60, \, .115/12} \; PV\,F_{10, \, .115}$$
$$= \$918{,}112 \; PVF_{10, \, .115}$$
$$= \$309{,}134$$

Present Value of Reversion
$$PV = \$1{,}500{,}000 \; PVF_{15, \, .115}$$
$$= \$293{,}068$$

Present Value of Leased Fee
  Value of Rent

First five years	$459,056	
Second five years	$399,561	
Third five years	$309,134	
		$1,167,751
Value of Reversion		293,068
	Leased Fee Value	$1,460,819
	(rounded)	$1,460,800

Note that the annual present value of an annuity factor is converted to a monthly factor to account for the monthly rent of $10,000, payable over five years. For the first five years, the beginning of the year payment is accounted for by multiplying the end of the year annuity factor by the base of 1.01. The present value of a monthly rent, payable at the beginning of the month, of $10,000 over 60 months equals $459,056.

The second five years follows the same algorithm except that the market value equals the present value of the rent *postponed* for five years, at the 11.5 percent discount rate. The monthly rent of $15,000 paid over the next five years has a present value of *$399,561.* For monthly rent earned over the third five years, $20,000, the income is *postponed for 10 years* giving a present value of $309,134. Adding the present value of rent for the three five-year periods and the present value of the reversion of $293,068 gives the leased fee value, $1,460,819.

SUBLEASES

Commercial leases may be granted for terms to 99 years. Leases for office buildings and shopping centers, constructed on leased land including industrial projects, are frequently negotiated for 55 years or more. It is unlikely that the original parties will continue their ownership over such long periods. Moreover, for some developments, the original tenant, the lessee, anticipates subleases. In a sublease, which creates a new estate, the original lessee remains responsible to the lessor. See Figure 17-2. Subleases are also known as sandwich leases. If A leases to B and B subsequently leases to C, B holds the "sandwich" lease.

Figure 17-2   Diagram of a Sublease Interest

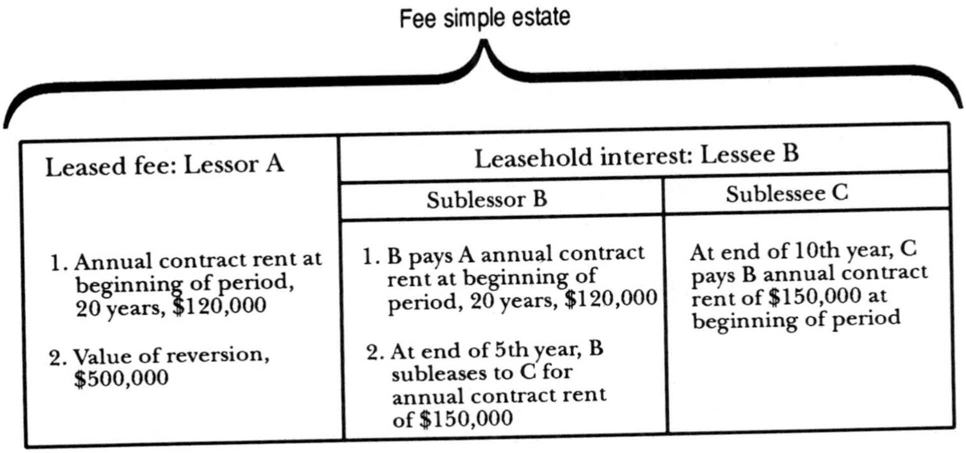

Fee simple estate

Leased fee: Lessor A	Leasehold interest: Lessee B	
	Sublessor B	Sublessee C
1. Annual contract rent at beginning of period, 20 years, $120,000	1. B pays A annual contract rent at beginning of period, 20 years, $120,000	At end of 10th year, C pays B annual contract rent of $150,000 at beginning of period
2. Value of reversion, $500,000	2. At end of 5th year, B subleases to C for annual contract rent of $150,000	

In the case of a ground lease, A may lease to B over a relatively long term of 20 years, while B then subleases building space to subtenants for relatively short periods of three, five, ten, or fifteen years. To illustrate the value of a sublease assume that:

1. A leases to B for an annual contract rent of $120,000, 20 years, payable at the beginning of the year.

2. The value of the reversion is $5,000,000.

3. The value of all lease interests is capitalized at 9 percent.

4. At the end of the *fifth year*, B leases to C for an annual contract rent of $150,000, 15 years, payable at the beginning of the year.

5. The estates of A and B are valued at the end of the 10th year with 10 years remaining in the lease.

In the multiple-lease valuation problems, it is advisable to diagram the circumstances of each lease. The valuation problem is illustrated in Figure 17-3. Note that when B subleased to C, a new estate was created.

Figure 17-3   An Illustration of a Sublease Appraisal

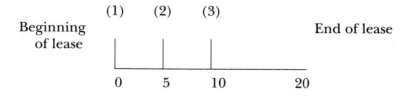

Point (1) A leases to B for 20 years.

Point (2) B leases to C at the end of the fifth year.

Point (3) Date of valuation, end of tenth year, 10 years remaining.

In valuing the leased fee held by lessor A, the contract rent is discounted by the present value of an annuity factor for 10 years, indicating the value of the leased fee, $2,841,484. The value of the leasehold interest held by lessee B equals the *difference between the contract rent received from C, less the contract rent paid to A*. The difference of $30,000 is converted to present value by the present value of an annuity factor, 10 years, 9 percent, times the base to account for rental payments in advance—$209,857. These data are summarized in Table 17-2.

Table 17-2   Value of Subleasehold Interest

1. Value of leased fee (Lessor A)

    (a) Present value of contract rent

         $PV\ AF_{.09,\ 10}\ 1.09\ =\ \$120{,}000 \times 6.417658(1.09)$ $ 839,430

    (b) Present value of the reversion

         $PVF_{.09,\ 10}\ =\ \$5{,}00{,}000 \times .422411$ $2,112,054

    (c) Valued of leased fee
         $2,841,484

2. Value of leasehold interest (lessee B)

    (a) Present value of rental income

Contract rent received from C	$150,000
Less contract rent paid to A	- 120,000
	$ 30,000

    (b) $PVAF_{.09,\ 10}\ 1.09\ =\ \$30{,}000 \times 6.417658(1.09)$ $ 209,857

Leasehold Interests

It is usually presumed that leases initially provide for the highest market rent. At the beginning of the lease, contract rent is usually equal to market or economic rent. As a result, the value of the leased fee approaches the fee simple estate value; the leasehold interest value is nominal since contract and market rent (also referred to as "market rental value") are equivalent.

To illustrate, assume that the market value of vacant land is $1,000,000. If a prospective lessee offers to lease the vacant land for *20 years* at a fixed rent of $100,000 a year, the owner would receive a rent equal to a 10 percent return on the $1,000,000 investment, assuming the tenant agrees to pay annual property taxes.

TENANT BENEFITS

The tenant benefits in proportion to the amount that market rent exceeds contract rent. Suppose that over the first 12 years of the lease, rent increases at an average annual compound rate of 6 percent. At the end of the twelfth year, market rent more than doubles (an increase of 101.2 percent).

Figure 17-4 illustrates how the leasehold interest owner benefits from a rising market rent. Using these data, the market rent would be $201,220 compared to the contract rent of $100,000. The leasehold interest value would be equal to the present value of $101,220 over the remaining eight years of the lease. Calculations of the leasehold interest value of $560,000 are shown in Table 17-3.

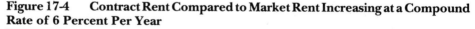

Figure 17-4   Contract Rent Compared to Market Rent Increasing at a Compound Rate of 6 Percent Per Year

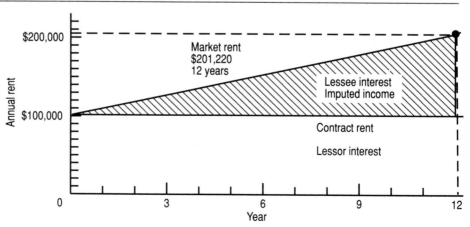

Table 17-3   Value of the Leasehold Interest

Market rent	$201,220
Contract rent	- 100,000
Imputed income	$101,220
Present worth of $101,220 x 5.534819	
$(PVAF_{8, .09})$	$560,234
Value of leasehold interest (rounded)	$560,000

While the illustration assumes a discount rate of 9 percent, the discount rate would vary according to prospects for a rising or stable market rent. The nature of the lease and the risks inherent in earning future market rent determine the discount rate for valuing the leasehold interest. Ordinarily the discount rate for the leasehold interest would be higher than the discount rate for the leased fee interest.

TENANT IMPROVEMENTS

To carry Table 17-3 one step further, let us say that the tenant constructs a building with an economic life of 20 years, and at the end of the 12th year the buildings have a remaining life of eight years. On the date of valuation—end of the twelfth year—the market value of tenant improvements is estimated as $500,000. In this case, the leasehold interest would have a market value of $1,060,000. See Table 17-4.

Table 17-4   The Valuation of a Leasehold Interest with Tenant Improvements

1. Present worth of imputed income	
Market rent	$ 201,220
Contract rent	- 100,000
Imputed income	$ 101,220
$PVAF_{8, .09}$ = $101,220 x 5.534819	$ 560,234
2. Market value of tenant improvements	500,000
3. Value of leasehold interest	$ 1,060,234
(rounded)	$ 1,060,000

MARKET RENT VARIATION

Owners and tenants negotiate according to future expectations. Over a long-term lease, anticipated variations in market rent encourage various rental adjustment clauses. If parties to a lease anticipate price changes, they would probably agree on CPI rental adjustments. Besides changes in the price level, market rent variations may result from:

changes in the utility of the given location
management efficiency
changing property characteristics

Because of these rent variations, discount rates to value leasehold interests vary widely. The final discount rate depends on appraisal judgments over the risk and "quality" of expected market rent. The more common ways to vary rent include:

percentage rents
reappraisal leases
index leases
escalation clauses

An explanation of these rent clauses indicates how appraisers discount rents under various rent agreements.

PERCENTAGE RENTS.   Percentage rents, in part, base the rent on a specified percentage of tenant gross sales. Accordingly, they are restricted to tenants who sell products and who maintain adequate records. These rents are poorly adapted to the smaller merchant where enforcement of percentage provisions would be difficult.

Generally, percentage rents are accompanied by a minimum rent. The minimum rent gives the developer-owner a required rate of return to justify the initial investment. The developer-owner negotiates for a minimum rent at least sufficient to pay expenses and service debt. The percentage rent, which is also referred to as overage rent, usually applies after reaching a minimum sales volume. Under favorable leases, the minimum rent or percentage rent may result in *excess rent*. Excess rent is rent that exceeds market rent. Usually excess rent is discounted separately at a higher capitalization rate than the rate applied to minimum or market rent.

Percentage rents vary according to the sales markup and inventory turn-over. For example, a supermarket in a neighborhood shopping center would typically pay a percentage rent of one percent of gross sales—a low markup, high-volume sales business. At the other extreme, a regional shopping center may grant a lease to an arcade amusement store of 12 percent of receipts or charge an ice-cream parlor or a cookie shop percentage rents of 10 or 12 percent of sales—a low sales volume, high markup retail business.

Regional shopping centers are dominated by major or key tenants such as a full-line department store, a junior department store, or a similar dominant retailer. The Urban Land Institute compiles median values for sales per square foot, percentage rents, tenant charges, and other expenses for shopping centers. Table 17-5 summarizes data for U.S. regional shopping centers.

Table 17-5 Percentage Rent and Related Terms Per Square Foot: Regional Shopping Centers (General Merchandise)

Tenant	Sales	Median Value Percentage Rate	Rent	Tenant Charges	Property Taxes
Department Store	$134.37	2.00	$2.60	$ .25	$ .29
Junior Department Store	103.21	2.50	3.95	.55	.64
Variety Store	92.18	4.00	4.13	1.01	.62
Discount Department Store	105.28	2.00	3.63	.15	---
Catalog Store	141.77	1.50	3.64	.89	.29

Source: *Dollars and Cents of Shopping Centers, 1990,* (Washington, D.C.: Urban Land Institute, 1990), p. 92.

Note that there is a typical (median) volume of sales and percentage rents prevailing for shopping centers. Table 17-5 indicates that department stores pay a median percentage rent of two percent of retail sales. Their median rent, including percentage rents, is $2.60 per square foot compared to over $3.95 per square foot collected from junior department and catalog stores. Table 17-5 also summarizes typical tenant charges levied to maintain parking and other common areas, in addition to property taxes and insurance. Similar data are available for other types of shopping centers and tenants.

It should be pointed out that the total rent per square foot is usually calculated according to minimum rent, percentage rent over a given sales volume, and common area charges levied against each tenant for parking space, public relations, and other functions.

Because percentage rent, or overage rent, is less certain than minimum rent, appraisers discount percentage rent at higher capitalization rates. Assume that shopping center rents are derived from the three following sources:

Tenant charges	$ 35,000
Minimum Rent	150,000
	$185,000
Overage or percentage rent	60,000

Present value
Minimum rent
$185,000 / .10 $1,850,000
Percentage rents
$60,000 / .12   500,000
Estimated market value $2,350,000

If the appraiser capitalizes over the lease term, present value-of-annuity factors substitute for direct capitalization. The example shows that rent from less uncertain sources is discounted with higher rates.

REAPPRAISAL LEASES.   Long-term leases (over 15 years and up to 99 years) may require periodic reappraisals to establish the fair market rent. Some lenders approve reappraisal leases only if the reappraisal occurs after mortgage payments have been completed. Typically, the owner and lessor select qualified appraisers, with a third appraiser selected by the two appointed appraisers. The rent is usually based on a stated percentage of the appraised value. For example, an industrial lease of 30 years calling for reappraisal every five years provides in part:

> *...that the lessor and the lessees (the lessees acting as one party) shall each select an appraiser and give notice thereof to the other party. In the event of failure on the part of either and lessor or the lessees to select an appraiser...the party who has named an appraiser shall have the right to apply to the superior court requesting selection and appointment of an appraiser to represent the party so failing to appoint an appraiser. The two appraisers thus appointed shall select and appoint a third appraiser and give notice thereof to the lessor and lessees.*

Failure of the two appraisers to appoint a third appraiser gives either party the right to request the superior court to appoint a third appraiser.

While reappraisal leases theoretically seem fair, practice reveals that appraisers selected by either owner or tenant may be biased in favor of their clients. Since the reappraisal is undertaken at infrequent intervals, the rent changes are usually substantial; as a consequence, agreement may not be reached on the final appraisal for rental adjustment. Observers have noted that reappraisal leases frequently encourage expensive court litigation.

In these cases, the appraiser estimates the most "reasonably probable" rent to value leases that contain reappraisal rental clauses.

INDEX LEASES.   With the assumption that the declining value of the dollar is indicated by a selected price index, leases may adjust rents according to changes in a selected price index. Suppose for example that the Consumer Price Index had been selected to adjust leases at the end of the base month, March of each year. For this purpose the rental adjustment would be based on the Consumer Price Index at the beginning of the base month.

If the lease began March 1989, the base index would be 122.3, the Consumer Price Index for that month. This figure would be the denominator divided into the price index of the adjustment month. If the lease required an adjustment at the end of March 1990, the 1990 rent would be increased by multiplying the base month rent by 1.05 percent (122.3/116.5). The presumption is that the declining value of the dollar would vary according to the selected price index.

Alternatively, index leases may specify the formula for a Consumer Price Index (CPI) lease as follows:

1. CPI current year minus CPI base year = absolute CPI increase.
2. CPI increase divided by CPI base year = percentage increase in CPI (if 2 percent or more compute additional rent).
3. Minimum fixed rent multiplied by CPI percentage increase = current adjusted rent.

In this calculation the percentage increase in the Consumer Price Index applies only if the increase is two percent or more.

The rental adjustment clause tied to an index suffers from one common fault—the declining value of the dollar may not correlate with expected changes in net operating income. Hence, appraisers would generally project income independently of expected changes in the price level. It should be noted that if the appraiser discounts expected annual net operating income by the *market rate of discount* (overall capitalization rate), the market expectation of inflation is automatically accounted for in the market discount rate.

ESCALATION CLAUSES.   Escalation clauses variously cover such items as real estate taxes, utility expenses, and certain other costs. Escalation clauses adjust rents for increases in selected or total annual operating expenses. While escalator clauses may take many forms, a clause adapted for this purpose is illustrated by the lease of a Chicago office building.

> *The tenant shall pay to the landlord as additional rent for the current tax, calendar, or fiscal year (as the case might be) during the term of this lease the sum of:*
> *a. the tenant's proportionate share of any increase in:*
> > *1. the lienable charges against the real property subject to this lease for any tax year over and above the lienable charges in the base year as hereafter defined and/or;*
> > *2. the cost of operating the premises for any calendar or fiscal year over and above such cost in the base year and/or;*
> *b. an amount computed to reflect an increase of two percent or more in the annual average Consumer Price Index Urban (CPIU) over the index as it exists in the base year, such increase being applied to the Minimum Fixed Rent as set forth in paragraph 4 of this lease, annualized to reflect the rent for the current year.*

Note that the rent is adjusted according to changes in property taxes/operating expenses, or an increase of two percent or more in the annual

Consumer Price Index. The tenant's proportionate share is defined as follows:

Tenant's Proportionate Share (TPS) is expressed as a percentage computed by dividing the space demised or used by the Tenant by the total rentable space of the building of which the demised space is a part.

Base Year is the calendar year in which the lease is executed except that in new construction, the base year shall be the calendar year in which the land and building is fully assessed and at least partially occupied for the first time.

Formula 1: *Increase of Lienable Charges*
Current Taxes minus taxes for base year multiplied by TPS = Current Rent

Formula 2: *Increase of Operating Cost*
Current Costs minus costs in base year multiplied by TPS = Current Rent

In short, the tenant's proportionate share of rent will be increased according to annual changes in operating costs or lienable charges. Though this formula does not adjust for changes in the purchasing power of the dollar, it protects the owner from disproportionate increases in operating costs.

The escalation clause should maintain the ratio of net operating income to expenses as of the date of the lease. This approach is preferred since certain expenses are highly variable; for example, utility costs may hinge on variations in the weather, while wages and the cost of supplies may show unpredictable changes.

Given the base year, an escalation clause that preserves the ratio of net operating income and expenses would state:

The rent for each leasehold year after the first leasehold year shall be increased by a percentage of the original rent equal to the percentage of said excess in operating expenses for the fiscal year ending immediately prior to the commencement of such leasehold year, over the amount of operating expenses for any fiscal year exceeding operating expenses for the base year by one percent, then the rent for the following leasehold year shall be increased by one percent.

The escalation clause defines operating expenses to include:

payroll costs
personal property and real estate taxes
special assessments

The lease states the number of employees by category for purposes of calculating changes in payroll expenses.

Escalation rent clauses simplify the discount process. In this case the appraiser deals with a constant annual yield on invested capital. The escalation clause shifts the risk of rising expenses to the tenant and should be considered in selecting the capitalization rate.

In practice, leases that shift net operating expenses, in part or in total, are called *net, net leases*. The difference between net or net, net leases (or even net, net, net leases) depends on local practice. Leases in which the landlord assumes all net operating expenses are known as *gross leases*.

A NEIGHBORHOOD SHOPPING CENTER: A CASE STUDY

To illustrate the valuation of a leased fee interest, a neighborhood shopping center development was selected covering 8.1 acres. The developer proposed a shopping center building of 65,000 square feet. The leased fee valuation was calculated after the developer secured a 20-year lease with a national supermarket chain for 38,200 square feet and a 20-year lease to a national discount drugstore for 8,468 square feet. On the strength of these firm commitments, the remaining 18,332 square feet assumed value according to the potential for leasing the remaining space to small or satellite tenants.

The problem then focused on the value of the lease to the national supermarket chain, the lease to the discount drug store, relatively short-term leases to satellite tenants over 20 years, and the reversionary value at the end of 20 years.

Valuation of the Supermarket Lease

The supermarket lease provided for a minimum annual rent of $227,290 for the first 10 years, payable monthly in advance, and a minimum annual rent of $244,480 for the following 10 years. The lease provided an overage rent of one percent of retail sales, payable annually, in addition to tenant charges of $4,730 for the first five years, $9,550 for the next five years, and $13,370 for the remaining 10 years.

A discount rate of nine percent was considered appropriate for this lease. The overage rent was based on projected retail sales in a feasibility report prepared by the supermarket chain showing annual gross sales of $8,411,052. From this base figure, the annual growth rate of retail sales was estimated at seven percent, compounded annually based upon a time series analysis of other demographic data.

Operating expenses of 90 cents per square foot, excepting property taxes which the tenant agreed to pay, were derived from local data. The 90 cents per square foot estimate closely agreed with current reports of comparable shopping centers surveyed by the Urban Land Institute. It was assumed that expenses would increase at a compound rate of six percent consistent with economic trends over the last 20 years. Based on these assumptions, retail sales increased to the point that overage rent was payable in the seventeenth year. See Table 17-6.

Table 17-6   The Present Value of Contract Rent: Supermarket Lease

Year	Rent	Less Expenses	Net Income	Present Value*	Total	Rent / Sq. Ft.	Sales / Sq. Ft.
1	$233,020	$20,205	$212,815	$202,794	$ 202,794	$6.10	$220.18
2	233,020	21,417	211,603	184,345	387,139	6.10	235.60
3	233,020	22,702	210,318	167,512	554,651	6.10	252.09
4	233,020	24,064	208,956	152,154	706,805	6.10	269.74
5	233,020	25,508	207,512	138,144	844,949	6.10	288.62
6	236,840	27,039	209,801	127,690	972,639	6.20	308.82
7	236,840	28,661	208,179	115,836	1,088,475	6.20	330.44
8	236,840	30,381	206,459	105,027	1,193,503	6.20	353.57
9	236,840	32,203	204,637	95,172	1,288,675	6.20	378.32
10	236,840	34,136	202,704	86,188	1,374,863	6.20	404.80
11	257,850	36,184	221,666	86,168	1,461,031	6.75	433.14
12	257,850	38,355	219,495	78,006	1,539,037	6.75	463.46
13	257,850	40,656	217,194	70,569	1,609,605	6.75	495.90
14	257,850	43,096	214,754	63,792	1,673,397	6.75	530.61
15	257,850	45,681	212,169	57,619	1,731,016	6.75	567.75
16	257,850	48,422	209,428	51,997	1,783,013	6.75	607.50
17	271,220	51,327	219,893	49,913	1,833,646	7.10	650.02
18	284,590	54,407	230,183	47,768	1,884,070	7.45	695.52
19	297,960	57,672	240,288	45,588	1,932,875	7.80	744.21
20	311,330	61,132	250,198	43,397	1,979,295	8.15	796.30

Present Value of Supermarket Lease Income: $1,979,295

*Data are discounted monthly at 9 percent. Thus, net income from the first year equals:

$212,815 / 12 $(PVAF_{12, .09/12})$

Net income for the second year equals:

$211,603 / 12 $(PVAF_{12, .09/12})$ (PV $(PVF_{2, .09/12}$ monthly) compounding

Overage rent for the seventeenth to the twentieth year is discounted at 12 percent.

Table 17-6 shows that the annual rent per square foot ranged from $6.10 in the first year to $8.15 in the twentieth year, including tenant charges. The first-year sales per square foot are consistent with local experience of $220.18 and published data. With annual sales growth at seven percent per year, the overage rent was not effective until the beginning of the seventeenth year. The value of the contract rent equals $1,979,295.

Valuation of the Discount Drugstore Lease

The discount drugstore agreed to pay $7.50 per square foot or $63,500 annually over 20 years, the minimum rent. The discount drugstore also agreed to pay an overage rent of two percent of retail sales. First-year retail sales were estimated as $153.14 per square foot. Retail sales were projected at an annual growth rate of seven percent to calculate the overage rent. In this case, overage rent was payable in the fifteenth year. The total value of the lease income including overage rent and minimum rent was estimated as $627,296. The discount drugstore lease's value is detailed in Table 17-7.

Table 17-7   The Present Value of Contract Rent: Discount Drugstore Lease

Year	Rent	Present Value	Cumulative Total	Rent/Sq. Ft	Sales/Sq. Ft.
1	$63,500	$62,527	$ 62,527	$7.50	$153.14
2	63,500	57,165	119,692	7.50	163.86
3	63,500	52,262	171,954	7.50	175.33
4	63,500	47,780	219,734	7.50	187.60
5	63,500	43,682	263,416	7.50	200.74
6	63,500	39,936	303,352	7.50	214.79
7	63,500	36,511	339,863	7.50	229.82
8	63,500	33,380	373,243	7.50	245.91
9	63,500	30,517	403,760	7.50	263.12
10	63,500	27,900	431,660	7.50	281.54
11	63,500	25,507	457,167	7.50	301.25
12	63,500	23,320	480,487	7.50	322.34
13	63,500	21,320	501,806	7.50	344.90
14	63,500	19,491	521,397	7.50	369.04
15	66,876	19,520	540,034	7.50	394.88
16	71,558	19,580	558,326	7.50	422.52
17	76,567	19,257	576,186	7.50	452.09
18	81,926	18,718	593,627	7.50	483.74
19	87,661	18,088	610,660	7.50	517.60
20	93,797	17,447	627,296	7.50	553.83

Present Value of Discount Drugstore Lease Income: $627,296

Satellite Lease Valuation

The remaining area was to be leased to satellite or local tenants at an estimated minimum annual rent of $9.00 per square foot, comparable to local rents for similar space. Operating expenses of $1.35 per square foot were taken from local experience and consistent with published reports. An annual vacancy rate of five percent was estimated over the 20-year term for leases, which were typically three to five years. In this case, net rent per square foot ranged from $8.80 to $31.17. The present value of leases to the satellite tenants totaled $2,384,883. See Table 17-8.

Table 17-8   The Present Value of Contract Rent: Satellite Leases

Year	Rent	Less Expenses	Net Income	Present Value	Total	Rent/Sq. Ft.
1	$161,277	$ 6,980	$154,297	$147,031	$ 147,031	$ 8.80
2	172,248	7,399	164,850	143,615	290,646	9.40
3	183,988	7,842	176,146	140,295	430,941	10.04
4	196,550	8,313	188,237	137,067	568,008	10.72
5	209,990	8,812	201,179	133,928	701,936	11.45
6	224,372	9,340	215,032	130,873	832,809	12.24
7	239,760	9,901	229,859	127,900	960,709	13.08
8	256,226	10,495	245,731	125,005	1,085,714	13.98
9	273,844	11,125	262,719	122,185	1,207,899	14.94
10	292,696	11,792	280,903	119,438	1,327,337	15.97
11	312,867	12,500	300,367	116,761	1,444,097	17.07
12	334,450	13,250	321,200	114,151	1,558,248	18.24
13	357,543	14,045	343,499	111,606	1,669,855	19.50
14	382,254	14,887	367,366	109,125	1,778,979	20.85
15	408,694	15,781	392,913	106,704	1,885,683	22.29
16	436,985	16,727	420,257	104,341	1,990,024	23.84
17	467,256	17,731	449,525	102,036	2,092,061	25.49
18	499,646	18,795	480,851	99,786	2,191,847	27.26
19	534,304	19,923	514,381	97,590	2,289,437	29.15
20	571,387	21,118	550,270	95,445	2,384,883	31.17

Present Value of SatelliteTenant Lease Income: $2,384,883

The present value of the leased fee, less the cost of development is shown in Table 17-9. The present value of lease income is $4,991,474. The reversionary value was calculated by capitalizing the total rent in the final year of the lease, $646,184, at nine percent to produce a reversionary value of $7,179,821. The present value of this sum postponed 20 years, discounted at nine percent, equals $1,281,102. The value of the leased fee interest, therefore, is $6,272,576.

Table 17-9   Value of Leased Fee Interest Less Development Costs

Present value of net lease income		
Supermarket lease	$1,979,295	
Discount drug store lease	627,296	
Satellite leases	2,384,883	
Total present value, net lease income		$4,991,474
Present value of reversion, 20 years		
(Market value, postponed 20 years)		
Total net rent, 20th year	$ 646,184	
Property value, 20 years	7,179,821	
Present value		$1,281,102
Value of total leased fee interest		$6,272,576
Less total investment costs		
Land costs	$ 353,000	
Land improvements	418,000	
Building construction	1,959,750	
Total soft costs	384,000	
Total investment cost		- 3,114,750
Leased fee interest		$3,157,826

Subtracting the total investment costs of $3,114,750 results in a net value of the leased fee interest of $3,157,826. Note that the total development cost of $3,114,750 included the original land cost of $353,000, land improvement costs of $418,000, the building cost of $1,959,750, and soft costs of $384,000.

SUMMARY

The valuation of leases includes the valuation of the *leased fee estate*, which is the interest held by the *lessor*. If the estate of the tenant is under valuation, the appraiser estimates the value of the *leasehold interest* held by the *tenant-lessee*. As owner of the leased fee estate, the tenant has the right to the contract rent and the right to the reversion—the present value of the leased property at the end of the lease. The value of the leased fee estate equals *the present value of annual income and the present value of the reversion* which is postponed to the end of the lease. The value of the tenant-lessee interest equals the *present value of the difference between market rent and contract rent.* The contract rent is the rent provided by the lease, while the market rent is the prevailing rent at the time of lease valuation. Valuation routines for leased estates are valued to account for beginning-of-year payments.

Graduated leases that provide for rents that vary over the lease term require the valuation of rent for each graduated period. The right to a specific rent over the lease is converted to present value by present value factors, since rent earned over the graduated period is postponed to the time of graduation.

Subleases are separate estates that are valued separately from the leased fee and leasehold interest. A tenant who holds a subleased estate has an interest equal to the present value of the difference between the rent received and rent paid to the original lessor.

Variations in rent terms justify projections in net income and require special attention to the selection of capitalization rates. Among the rent variations considered are *percentage rents, reappraisal rent clauses, index leases,* and *escalation clauses.* The valuation of shopping centers requires separate capitalization of net income derived from major tenants and satellite tenants.

POINTS TO REMEMBER

lessor an owner who leases real estate.

leased fee estate the interest held by the lessor.

leasehold interest the interest held by the tenant-lessee.

lessee the tenant who holds the leasehold estate.

net ground lease a lease covering land only leased to tenants who construct buildings on leased land.

reversionary value the present value of property reverting to the lessor at lease termination.

graduated leases leases in which rents are varied at stated intervals over the lease.

subleases a lease in which the lessee leases to a third party. The lessee remains responsible to the original lessor.

overage rents rents that exceed the minimum rent.

percentage rents rents based on a specified percentage of tenant gross sales; also known as overage rents.

excess rent rent that exceeds market rent.

net leases leases that shift part or all net operating expenses to tenants.

gross leases leases in which the landlord assumes all net operating expenses.

reappraisal leases leases that base rent on periodic reappraisals to establish the fair market rent.

index leases leases that adjust rent according to changes in the selected price index.

escalation clauses clauses that adjust rents for increases in selected expenses or total annual operating expenses.

base year the calendar year in which the lease is executed.

QUESTIONS FOR REVIEW

1. Explain the financial rights of the lessee and lessor under a long-term lease. Give an example in illustration of your answer.

2. Give an example of methods of estimating the leased fee value and the leasehold estate value under a fixed rent lease. Give an example showing how you would value a leased fee estate under a graduated lease.

3. Explain how you would value a leased fee estate providing for end-of-year payments. In your answer show the necessary adjustments for monthly and annual rents.

4. Describe the general procedure in valuing the leased fee under a graduated rent schedule.

5. Give an example showing how you would value a subleased fee estate.

6. Give an example showing how you would value a retail lease providing for a monthly minimum rent and an "overage" rent.

PRACTICE PROBLEMS

1. For a proposed neighborhood shopping center, develop your own model showing how you would calculate the value of the leased fee over 20 years. In your model, treat the leased fee of the key or major tenant separately from the valuation of satellite leases. Explain how you would support the variables necessary to this calculation.

2. Value the leased fee estate under the following assumptions.

   a. A leases to B for a term of 20 years payable at the beginning of the month under the rent schedule as follows:

      Annual rent:
      First 5 years, $120,000
      Next 5 years, $180,000
      Next 10 years, $220,000

   b. At the end of the eighth year, B leases to C for $280,000 annually for 12 years, rent payable monthly at the beginning of the month; value the reversion at $5,000,000. Use a discount rate of 10 percent. Value the estates of A and B at the end of eight years.

C H A P T E R 1 8

Valuation of Partial Interests

After reading this chapter you will know:
- Valuation techniques for eminent domain purposes.
- Techniques to value easements.
- Methods of valuing condominium interests.
- The valuation of other special-purpose interests.

The right of eminent domain is granted to the government, its administrative agencies, and public utilities subject to public utility regulation. Special eminent domain appraisal procedures conform to eminent domain law. In some instances, these procedures are governed by statutes that cover the taking of private property for government purposes. Similarly, the valuation of easements—the right to use property for a special purpose—requires valuation techniques that conform to the law and good valuation practices. Condominium interests, including timeshare interests, are also governed by legal rights acquired by condominium owners. The appraisal of development rights and preservation easements closes the chapter.

THE RIGHT OF EMINENT DOMAIN

When government agencies or regulated public utilities take property under eminent domain, private property owners are entitled to "just compensation." Most courts consider just compensation equivalent to market value. Though qualifying adjectives are encountered, such as fair-market value, leading decisions define just compensation as value in the usual context adopted for valuation purposes. In addition, just compensation may be warranted if only part of the property is taken, a partial interest is acquired, or no part of the property is taken. Thus, just compensation may arise under three circumstances:

1. *The taking of the whole property.*

Construction of a new highway may require the acquisition of a house and lot. If the whole property is taken, just compensation requires an estimate of market value of the house and lot.

2. Partial takings.

Construction of a highway through an 80-acre orchard would require an estimate of damages for the land taken. The location of the new highway may cause a loss in value to that part of the orchard remaining after the taking. If the relation of the highway to the orchard is such that continued orchard use is uneconomic or less efficient, the owner would be entitled to recover damages to the land remaining after the taking. Such damages are referred to as *severance damages.* Severance damages have been defined as the loss in value to the property remaining after a public taking. The part left after the public taking is called the *remainder.*

3. No part of the property taken for public improvement.

Property owners in the vicinity of a highway or an airport may suffer damages because of the loss of value caused by the public improvement. In this case, just compensation refers to *consequential damages,* i.e., the loss in value of a parcel, no portion of which is acquired or taken, resulting from the public improvement.

For a partial property interest, the preceding examples assumed that title was taken in fee. For many purposes, it is unnecessary to acquire the fee simple interest. The construction of electric power transmission lines, pipelines, and the right to flood private land usually involve taking an *easement,* the right to use private property for a particular purpose. In these instances, the estimate of just compensation applies only to the easement rights acquired.

Noncompensable Damages

Though property owners may be compensated for property rights acquired, they may suffer economic losses which are legally not compensable. On this point, it is possible only to offer broad generalizations since jurisdictions vary in the interpretation of compensable losses. A representative list of damages which are not compensable covers:

1. Moving costs (unless allowed by statute)
2. Loss of business profits
3. Loss of good will
4. Circuitry of travel
5. Inability to duplicate property taken

MOVING COSTS

Historically, courts have denied compensation for the cost of moving personal property on grounds that damages occurred to the owner and not to the property taken. It has been reasoned that the owner's necessity of moving personal property is unrelated to the property taken, and, therefore, such costs have been held not compensable.

Federal legislation and the laws of some states authorize limited moving costs as part of just compensation. Under special laws, federal agencies may pay moving expenses as indicated below:

1. Actual reasonable moving expenses for family, business, farm operations, or other personal property
2. Actual direct losses of tangible personal property as a result of moving or discontinuing a business or farm operation, but not to exceed an amount equal to the reasonable expenses that would have been required to relocate such property, as determined by the head of the agency
3. Actual reasonable expenses in searching for a replacement business or farm

Generally, maximum dollar moving expenses prevail for household, business, and farm moving expenses.

NONCOMPENSABLE LOSSES SUBJECTIVE

Loss of business profits may be incurred by interruption of a business during construction or by the loss of profits by relocating to a less profitable location. Similarly, loss of good will resulting from a shift in neighborhoods required by a relocating business falls in the same category. It would be difficult to objectively determine losses occurring from this source.

Construction of new highways, especially limited access highways, may deny direct access to the highway which had existed before the taking. The inconvenience of a more indirect route, provided a reasonable substitute route is available, defeats a claim for just compensation. Again, the final test lies in the market value of the property affected after the taking. The mere change in access routes, in itself, does not justify compensation.

Valuation Procedures

The appraisal procedure varies somewhat according to whether the taking relates to the taking of the *whole property* or a *partial taking*. A third type of appraisal covers *consequential damages* in which no part of the property is taken. If the taking covers the fee simple interest of the whole property, the appraisal follows the appraisal process common to estimating market value.

For a partial taking and consequential damages, legal interpretation of compensable and noncompensable items would be required. The appraisal of easements introduces additional techniques of valuation. In the estimation of just compensation for eminent domain, special rules apply to virtually all cases, with respect to the date of valuation and the estimate of highest and best use. The four main valuation problems are summarized in Figure 18-1.

Figure 18-1   The Four Main Problems in Eminent Domain

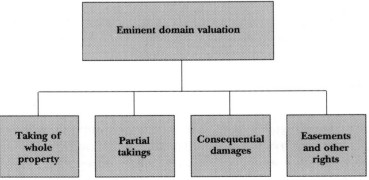

DATE OF VALUATION

The planning and construction of a public project may take several years. After announcing a pending condemnation, the actual taking of private property may be delayed for months or years. As a consequence, the date of appraisal assumes particular importance. At the time of project announcement, land values may be rising or declining. If the time of taking is not prescribed by statute, a legal interpretation of the date of valuation is advised.

HIGHEST AND BEST USE

Consider the appraisal of a farm taken for public purposes in an area undergoing transition to subdivisions. The valuation requires a judgment over whether the present use, farming, should prevail (with a $2,000-per-acre value) or whether the land should be appraised as subdivision land (with a $15,000-per-acre value).

In submitting proof of the highest and best use, three tests have been suggested: (1) Is the land *legally available* for the estimated highest and best use? Zoning and other land use controls should allow the assumed highest and best use. (2) Is the land *physically adapted* to the proposed highest and best use? (3) Is there a *present demand* for land for the highest and best use in the reasonable future? Generally, the courts have held that just compensation may be based not only on the current use but also on uses to which land may be currently adapted. The usual instruction is that property must be appraised and valued in view of all available uses.

It is fairly clear that mere physical adaptability of the property to a particular use is not enough to establish demand. The taking of farmland for an airport does not mean that the farm has potential value as industrial property without showing proof of demand for this purpose.

Partial Takings

The valuation of partial takings raises questions over severance damages and the value of the part taken. The valuation of severance damages follows strict legal requirements.

SEVERANCE DAMAGES

In a partial taking, payments for the part taken may not compensate the owner for losses to the remaining property. If 50 percent of a residential lot, measuring 50 feet by 100 feet, is taken for a street right-of-way, the remaining portion may be virtually valueless, since the area would be too small for a dwelling. To include severance damages in the estimate of just compensation, certain legal requirements must be met.

First, since severance damages arise only if part of an ownership is taken, there must be a *direct physical relationship* between the property taken and the property remaining. Mere common ownership of two separate parcels, unrelated physically, for example, lots one and two, probably would not justify severance damages, since the taking of one parcel would cause no damages to the other.

A *second* requirement deals with the *unity of use.* It would be invalid to assign severance damages to a 20-acre pasture for the taking of a one-acre service station site included in the same 20-acre pasture owned by the same person. Furthermore, the unity of use must be actual and not planned, remote, or speculative. Documentation of unity of use must support the claim for severance damages.

Third, there must be *unity of ownership.* The taking of parcel A owned solely by a husband will not create severance damages on the adjoining parcel B owned separately by his wife. For severance damages to occur, the remainder must be under the same ownership as the part taken.

CAUSES OF SEVERANCE DAMAGES

Severance damages occur if the taking changes the *intensity of use.* Because of a partial taking, a potential shopping center site may revert to an apartment house site—a less intensive use. The highest and best use of an irrigated farm may change to a pasture use after the taking; the smaller area and division of the site may not justify continued irrigated farming. Generally, if the taking changes the highest and best use to a lower use, severance damages would be indicated.

The remaining property may show severance damages because of an *uneconomic shape.* Long, narrow triangular shapes are difficult to use. An irregular shape increases costs of construction and fencing, often resulting in unusable land areas. In these circumstances, payment for the actual land taken and loss in value to the remainder seems justified.

If the taking results in an *uneconomic size,* an additional basis for severance damages would be warranted. In some circumstances, a land area too small for economic use would warrant severance damages equal to the value of the whole property, though only portions of an ownership would be taken. Relatively small remainders characterized by odd shapes, irregular boundaries, and separation from other sites have virtually no use or any economic value. In such cases, just compensation includes severance damages that approach the value of the whole property.

ESTIMATING SEVERANCE DAMAGES

In part, the method of valuation turns on the nature of the property appraised. In part, the procedure followed depends on legal requirements. Most jurisdictions, however, would accept one of two methods of valuation:

1. Appraise the property *before and after* the taking. The difference is just compensation. This procedure is termed the "before-and-after rule."
2. Value the part taken and estimate damages to the remainder by estimating the value of the remainder before and after the taking.

BEFORE-AND-AFTER RULE.   Figure 18-2 illustrates a five-acre parcel in which the taking covers a triangular area of 2.5 acres. Assume that before the taking, the five-acre parcel had a value of $10,000 per acre, or $50,000, and that the remainder had an estimated value of $2,000 per acre, estimated from comparable sales. The estimate of just compensation, $45,000, would include $20,000 severance damages.

Figure 18-2   A Partial Taking Showing Severance Damages

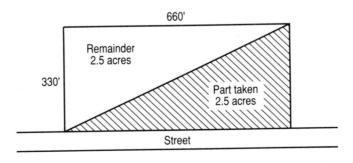

Value before taking (5 acres @ $10,000)	$ 50,000
Value after taking (2.5 acres @ $2,000)	- 5,000
Estimate of just compensation	$ 45,000
Less value of part taken (2.5 acres @ $10,000)	- 25,000
Severance Damages	$ 20,000

The main support for the before-and-after rule lies in its claimed accuracy. If value is estimated by customary appraisal methods, just compensation equals the sacrifice resulting from the taking.

The principal disadvantage stems from the lack of appropriate sales to value the remainder. Frequently, parcels of uneconomic size and irregular shape have no counterpart in the market. Usually, comparable sales require substantial adjustments, based on personal value judgments, to show the loss in value for irregular shape, small size, or change in use.

VALUE OF THE PART TAKEN AND DAMAGES TO THE REMAINDER.   Referring again to Figure 18-2, the same estimate of just compensation may be found under a different procedure. Under this method, just compensation would be calculated as:

Value of part taken (2.5 acres @ $10,000)	$ 25,000
Damages to the remainder (severance damages)	
(2.5 acres @ $8,000)	20,000
Estimate of just compensation	$ 45,000

Critics have pointed out that the estimate of damages to the part taken may be fairly unrealistic under this procedure. The method assumes that the value of the whole property can be apportioned between the part taken and the remainder. In the end, the method adopted must conform to legal requirements.

VALUE OF THE PART TAKEN

Because the part taken represents such a small portion of the whole of the property before the taking, severance damages are unlikely. Widening of a highway that adjoins farms or timberland of large acreage are cases in point.

BEFORE-AND-AFTER RULE IMPRACTICAL.   In these cases, clearly it is impractical to value the property before and after the taking. There would seem little point in appraising a 3,000-acre farm to estimate the value of 25 feet adjoining the highway which was being widened. Timber tracts would be very expensive to value if only a 25-foot strip bordering the existing highway were taken. The problem is resolved by valuing only the part taken, assuming that the land taken has a per-unit value equivalent to the larger parcel.

"BACK-LAND" THEORY.   In valuing the part taken without reference to the before-and-after value, consider the taking of a strip of land for highway widening. Under certain circumstances, the additional frontage taken is assumed to have the value of the rear portion of the property. These circumstances are shown in Figure 18-3.

Figure 18-3   A Partial Taking Illustrating The "Back-Land" Theory

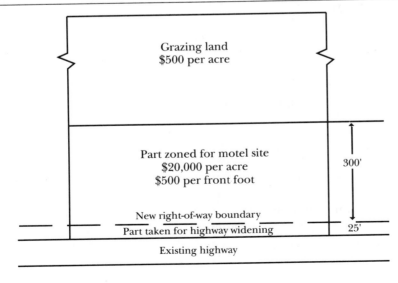

The example assumes that the intensity of the use remains unchanged, that the zoning code allows the highest and best use, that access rights are not altered, that the topography does not limit land use, and that trees are not affected. Though the front portion generally has a higher per-unit value than the rear portion, the "back-land" theory requires that the more valuable front land be appraised according to the lower value of the back land. The effect of the taking merely causes land use to move back 25 feet.

Consequential Damages

Consequential damages may be equivalent to severance damages, depending again on state statutes and local practices. The more common meaning of consequential damages refers to *the loss in value to property no part of which was taken for eminent domain purposes.* They are termed consequential because the damage occurs as a consequence of the public taking. Though allowance for consequential damages differs between jurisdictions, consequential damages are generally caused by:

a change in grade
noise caused by the public facility
a change in access

To qualify for consequential damages, also known as proximity damages, it must be shown that the market value is affected by public taking.

CHANGE IN GRADE

On the first point, it is generally held that new construction which materially changes the level of the street causes consequential damages. If a property formerly on an access road, no part of which is taken, depreciates in value because of the grade change, the abutting owner generally may recover consequential damages.

NOISE

By the same token, if it can be shown that market value after the taking decreases as a direct result of noise, consequential damages may result. The appraisal must show that the airport or traffic adversely affects market value. Usually, the mere showing of noise, by itself, would not support consequential damages. Direct evidence of a lower market value after the taking would be required.

CHANGE IN ACCESS

The construction of limited access highways creates dead-end streets, restricts right-of-way access of abutting property, and results in an indirect, inconvenient access to a main highway. If a property is "landlocked," consequential damages may result, since use of the property is seriously handicapped. Some of the conditions that cause consequential damages arising from restricted access cover:

the probable use of the property
the manner in which access is restricted by the taking
other means of access
topography
location of a building in relation to the public construction

The mere inconvenience of access or circuitry of travel which does not affect market value would not result in consequential damages. On the other hand, vacated streets and cul-de-sacs caused by the construction of limited-access highways may warrant consequential damages.

VALUATION OF EASEMENTS

Easements, which are the right to use part of the property of another for a special purpose, include a variety of appraisal problems. A list of the more common easements suggests the high degree of appraisal specialization required:

1. **Air rights** The right to use air space above the land surface
2. **Avigation easements** The right to use air space above the glide path extending from airport runways
3. **Flowage easements** The right to flood private property for flood control or water reservoirs
4. **Pipeline easements** Easements for the construction, operation, patrol, maintenance, and replacement of pipelines across private property
5. **Electric transmission line easements** The right to construct, operate, and maintain electric transmission lines over private property

The valuation of these easement rights, in contrast to a partial taking, requires an estimate of a partial interest in real estate. In some instances, the partial interest for an easement may be virtually equal to the value of the fee simple estate. Methods of appraising the more common easements show how the appraisal process adapts to these special valuation problems.

Air Rights

Air rights refer to the right to possess and use air space, considered part of the real property ownership. Air rights are acquired over highways for the construction of restaurants and motels, and frequently they are acquired over the space above railroads.

The appraisal starts with the estimation of additional costs of development associated with buildings constructed on the basis of air rights. Some of the additional costs include added costs of construction to support the "deck" that substitutes for the surface; the loss of a basement for heating, air conditioning, and elevator equipment; the cost of insulating buildings from noise, vibration, and air pollution caused by the surface use; and the possible increased cost of access over the ground facility.

Given these added costs, the development of air space is feasible *if the cost of constructing the deck, substituting for the surface area, is less than the price of comparable land.* Added costs of developing air rights are partly offset by the savings realized by avoiding excavation and demolition costs associated with surface construction.

The value of air rights is estimated by adding the cost of the deck forming the first floor to the cost of the maximum building area permitted under the zoning code. This cost is compared to the cost of a similar building plus land. The ratio of both costs reduced to the cost per square foot of building area provides a ratio that gives the approximate value of air rights relative to the fee value of vacant land. In other respects, the appraisal follows other accepted elements of the income approach.

Avigation Easements

Generally speaking, aircraft have the right to air space 1,000 feet over the highest obstruction. The right to use air space may be further regulated by local zoning regulations, for example, that prohibit construction of buildings over 45 feet high. In order to allow aircraft to fly below 1,000 feet, public agencies may acquire avigation easements over the inclined glide path to an airport runway. The value of avigation easements depends on how the easement restricts the highest and best use.

Like other appraisals, value follows from the estimate of the highest and best use for an avigation easement above 100 feet of the surface. For agricultural land, the avigation easement has a relatively low value. On the other hand, an avigation easement 100 feet above the surface of potential industrial land would lower the intensity of land use, imparting considerable value to the avigation easement.

Flowage Easements

Some agencies, such as the Corps of Engineers and the Bureau of Reclamation, acquire the right to flood land. Flowage easements give the property owner the right to use land not inconsistent with the flowage easement. Generally, the easement restricts the right to construct permanent buildings on land subject to a flowage easement.

The value of the bundle of rights included in the flowage easement depends on the frequency of flooding, the length of time land is flooded, and the time of year in which flooding occurs. In addition, the highest and best use before the flooding affects the easement value; more intensive land uses will show higher flowage easement values. Flowage easements over pasture land would be less costly than flowage easements over potential commercial land.

Pipeline Easements

Easements for pipelines grant the right to construct, operate, patrol, maintain, replace, or remove a pipeline across a legally described parcel of land. Pipelines, which are usually 30 inches below the surface, may provide for pipes up to 36 inches in diameter. The required right of way is not limited to the width of the pipeline but provides sufficient space for construction, maintenance, and patrol. An installed pipeline is not visible from the surface.

As in other property acquisitions, the valuation is directed to the rights acquired. The pipeline easement may include land-use restrictions and may provide for surface installations. After the before-the-taking value is estimated, the next critical problem is to estimate the value of the property with the pipeline in place. Restrictions of the pipeline easement may affect location of buildings in such a way that the best potential use may revert to agricultural or other low density use. If the pipeline is 30 inches below the surface, usually dry land farming, grazing, and row crop agriculture are not affected.

Easements for Electric Transmission Lines

Here the right-of-way easement describes the right to erect, construct, maintain, and operate an electric transmission line over a 100-foot or even a 300-foot right-of-way. The easement restricts the use of the property by barring buildings and trees within the right of way. The taking authority reserves the right to cut "fall trees" that may grow outside the easement area if there is danger that fall trees may damage the line.

The value of an easement depends on the degree to which the transmission line changes property use. If the construction of the line interferes with ordinary farming practice, the value of the easement right would be increased because of the lowered farm efficiency. For example, transmission lines through orchards may interfere with aerial spraying or require the removal of producing trees. In these cases, the change in use may result in a value equivalent to the fee value.

Appraisers generally estimate the value of the easement by *estimating the value of the property before the taking and the value after the taking*. Transmission lines that cross commercial, industrial, or other land uses may depreciate land to a point approaching fee value. In these instances, a study of comparable land sales, with and without transmission lines, constitutes the best approach to value.

CONDOMINIUMS

The main problems encountered in appraising condominiums concern the valuation of a new condominium project, the appraisal of individual condominium units, and condominiums offered as timesharing units. Recall that a condominium refers to an ownership interest and not a particular property type.

Condominium Interests

Condominium owners have *a fee interest in a designated space and an undivided interest in common elements*. Defined by state statute, the designated portion describes a cubic-foot area, usually representing a residential unit, office, or other space. *Common elements include land and other improvements with use-rights shared with others*, i.e., recreation buildings, parking space, swimming pool, hallways, elevators, and the like. For residential property, separate ownership of a condominium unit may be represented by an apartment in a high-rise elevator building, a town-house, or a detached housing unit. Property rights of a condominium, illustrated in Figure 18-4, depend on the declaration, corporate bylaws, and the management agreement.

Figure 18-4   Establishment of Condominium Interests

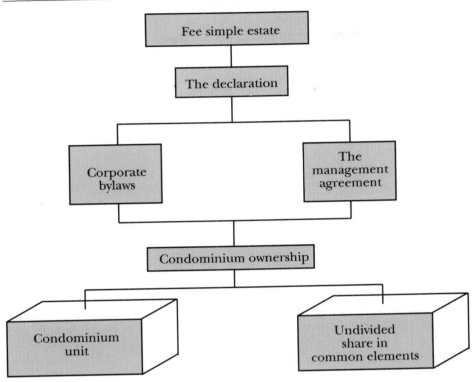

DECLARATION

The declaration, also known as the master deed, creates the condominium entity. Recorded as a deed or other conveyance instrument, the declaration permanently identifies each condominium unit and sets the *pro rata* interest of unit owners in common elements.

The market value of a condominium consists of the value of the condominium unit and its associated undivided interest in common elements. Moreover, the *pro rata* interest in the common elements limits the liability of unit owners for operating and management expenses.

Though statutes vary, usually the liability of unit owners is allocated according to the proportionate square-foot area of each condominium unit. For example, if a two-bedroom apartment has an undivided share in the common elements equal to its proportionate square-foot area of 3.433

percent, the unit owner would be liable for 3.433 percent of maintenance charges, property taxes, and other operating liabilities of the condominium association. A condominium project with different floor plans allocated the share in common elements for each unit according to the following schedule:

Type of Unit	Percentage ownership of common elements
A Unit, 1 bedroom, 1 bathroom	3.433
B Unit, 1 bedroom, 1 1/2 bathrooms	3.951
C Unit, 2 bedrooms, 2 bathrooms	4.585

The value of the common elements would ordinarily be allocated to condominium units on the basis of the undivided share as indicated in the declaration.

CONDOMINIUM BYLAWS

As an operating organization, the bylaws establish management rules and ownership authority. The bylaws define voting rights, establish a system of electing a board of directors, and list powers and duties of the board. The bylaws provide for membership meetings and selection of officers and make provisions for bylaw amendments.

In this document the board is given all the powers and duties of the association, including the right to levy and collect maintenance, repair, and other operating expenses. The board may elect to manage the project or delegate management duties to a professional manager under the management agreement.

MANAGEMENT AGREEMENT

Especially critical to the newly developed project, the management agreement defines duties of the manager. For new projects, the developer reserves the right to manage the property until a specified number of units is sold. If this number is unreasonable and the agreement provides for relatively high management fees, the value of condominium units may be depreciated.

The manager, as required by agreement, must make contractual payments on behalf of condominium owners and maintain records for audit by the board. To a large degree, the strict enforcement of condominium rules increases the amenities associated with condominiums.

Appraisal of Single Condominium Units

Some lenders estimate the value of individual units by appraising the entire project and allocating a proportionate share of market value to individual units on the basis of the undivided share interest. This technique could be quite time-consuming, since the appraisal would require an estimate of value for all units and for the common elements. In a more active condominium market, sufficient data may justify sales comparisons of individual condominium unit sales.

Condominium unit sales require different types of sales adjustments. Clearly, the sale of a one-bedroom condominium unit in project A, even in the same neighborhood, may not be comparable to the appraisal of a one-bedroom condominium unit in project B. Given a sufficient number of recent comparable sales and sales taken from different projects, factors deserving sales analysis would include:

management efficiency
rights of owners in comparable units
location
square-foot area
exposure of the condominium unit in the condominium complex, i.e.,
     view, corner location, and the floor level

Because unit-owner rights vary between projects, comparable sales analysis would involve a comparison of rights granted under various declarations, bylaws, house rules, and management agreements. To correct for variations in square-foot area of the unit, experience recommends adjustment of condominium unit prices according to the price per square foot of condominium unit living area.

These problems are minimized if comparisons of sales are confined to a single project which includes the subject appraisal. Because of the physical, legal, and economic factors that vary between condominium projects, condominium unit sales among projects other than the project of the property appraised are less preferred.

Timesharing Interests

Timesharing, also called resort timesharing, interval ownership, or timesharing vacation, is relatively simple. The timeshare owner pays for a condominium or hotel unit for a given time and shares proportionately in the annual operating and maintenance costs of the timeshare project. Timesharing usually requires a minimum time purchase of one week.

The ownership is frequently referred to as an extension of the condominium concept. While a condominium building is divided into individual units, each condominium unit may be further divided into 52 weeks under a timeshare arrangement. Under timesharing, each week can be owned or leased by different individuals. Hence, a single project could have several thousand owners.

There are primarily two variations in timesharing—timeshare ownership and right-to-use timesharing.

TIMESHARE OWNERSHIP

Timeshare ownership, or *interval ownership,* consists of an undivided fee simple interest conveyed to each purchaser as a tenant-in-common. A tenant-in-common interest may be willed—it has no right of survivorship—and it may represent unequal shares which may be rented and sold at any time. Timesharing rights depend on *declaration covenants* in which timeshare owners agree to limit property use to *specific time periods* each year. Subsequent purchasers are bound by these provisions.

In a sense, interval ownership is an extension of the condominium concept which provides one deed for each condominium unit. The interval ownership adds a time element to the condominium interest. The purchaser buys an interest for a specific time period each year, usually in one-week intervals.

The number of years that interval ownership prevails depends on the estimated economic life of the building, for example, 50 or 60 years. At the end of the specified years, the original tenancy for years lapses and the *reversionary* or *remainder interest* is converted to a tenancy-in-common. At this time, the owners can elect to continue as tenants-in-common, renew the interval ownership tenancy, or sell the property and distribute the assets.

RIGHT-TO-USE TIMESHARING

The right-to-use plan may assume three forms: a *lease, license,* or *club membership.* In contrast to the interval ownership, *the right-to-use form does not include ownership*; ownership reverts to the developer after the use period expires.

The timeshare *right-to-use lease* constitutes a prepaid lease in which the purchaser has the right to occupy a particular unit for a specific period each year over a designated number of years. The purchaser is given all the privileges of a tenant, who must comply with the lease. The developer and tenant are subject to landlord-tenant laws of the state or country of jurisdiction.

Under the *vacation license*, the developer transfers a "license" to a buyer for use of a specific unit for a designated period each year for a given number of years. As a license, the ownership is not considered an interest in real property, though it may be subject to state timesharing laws.

The *club membership* form is established by a corporation created to own or lease the resort project. The buyer receives a *certificate of membership* in the club entitling the use of a unit for a designated period of time each year. The articles of incorporation and bylaws determine rights and duties of the members, including the right to use recreational facilities. The length of membership may extend, typically, 10 to 20 years. At the end of the membership, the certificate may be resold to the original purchaser or another party. *Club membership conveys no interest in real property.*

VALUATION OF OTHER PROPERTY INTERESTS

The right of eminent domain has extended to special-purpose rights associated with protecting the environment. The main instrument of importance here covers the valuation of development rights and preservation easements. Their growing importance promises to make these special-purpose valuations more frequent.

Appraisal of Development Rights

A system of development rights attempts to preserve environmental qualities. The system requires that a municipality designate a reserved area as open space, prohibiting development in a designated area. The residential development potential in the *restricted area* is transferred by the owner to an *unrestricted area* where development is approved and feasible. In this way, owners of land in the restricted area are permitted to sell development rights to others for development on unrestricted land.

This requires an appraisal of the development right, i.e., the right that permits an owner to build or develop land. Suppose, for example, that the area reserved as open space has utility for agricultural use. Since residential subdivision development is restricted in this area, the value of development rights would tend to be equal to *the difference in value between land used for a subdivision and land used for agricultural purposes.*

In defining the right of development as a property right and placing a value on this right, authorities avoid depreciating property values (without compensation) by exercise of the police power. Currently, a property owner would suffer economic loss if potential subdivision land is restricted to an agricultural use. By transferring development rights from one designated area to another, the right of eminent domain substitutes for police power to the end that community objectives are satisfied while compensating owners for loss of development rights.

Preservation Easements

The owner of property subject to a preservation easement gives up the right to modify a structure, use a historically significant structure, or use land in a way that is harmful to the preservation of the site. As in other takings, the preferred valuation procedure follows the before-and-after rule.

In estimating the value before the easement, appraisers consider only the net benefit of development. If a subdivision conforms to the highest and best use of the land, the net expected cash flow over the development period must be discounted to the present. Terms of the easement dictate the after-easement valuation. In both instances, sales and leases support estimated values.

SUMMARY

Appraisals for eminent domain require estimates of value for taking of the whole property, a partial taking, and appraisals in which no part of the property is taken for public improvements. The estimate of compensation normally does not cover noncompensable damages, i.e., moving costs (unless allowed by statute), loss of profits, loss of good will, noise and traffic fumes, circuitry of travel, and inability to duplicate property taken.

The valuation of just compensation starts with identification of the date of valuation. In this assignment, the highest and best use estimate is critical, i.e., the land must be legally available for the estimated highest and best use, physically adapted for the proposed use, and there must be a proven demand for the land appraised.

In partial takings, estimates of compensation may apply to *severance damages*— payment for damages to the property remaining after the property taking. Severance damages apply if there is a *direct relationship* to the property remaining and the property taken, a *unity of use* and a *unity of ownership* between the property taken and the property remaining. Severance damages arise because of a change in the intensity of use, an uneconomic shape, or an uneconomic size. Appraisers follow the before-and-after rule in estimating severance damages. The "back-land" theory holds that additional frontage taken assumes the value of the rear portion of the property.

Consequential damages depend on state statutes and local practices. *Consequential damages equal the loss in value no part of which was taken for eminent domain purposes.*

The valuation of easements includes easements for *air rights, avigation easements, flowage easements, pipeline easements,* and *electric transmission lines.* The appraisal of air rights requires an estimate of additional costs to support the "deck" that substitutes for the surface, the loss of basement areas, and the cost of insulating the building from surface uses. Air rights are feasible if the cost of constructing the deck substituting for the surface area is less than the price of comparable land. *Avigation easements* are valued by estimating the highest and best use for the avigation easement above the surface. *Flowage easements* cover the right to use the property before the flowage easement. The loss in value depends on the frequency in which flooding occurs, the length of time the land is flooded, and the time of year flooding occurs.

Pipeline easements cover the valuation of land use restricted by the pipeline easement. Restrictions cover the placement of buildings and the possible use over the pipeline easement. The value of easements for *electric transmission lines* depends on the degree to which the transmission line changes property use. The value of the easement depends on the value before the taking based on comparable sales and the value of the property after the taking.

The valuation of *condominium interests* includes the market value of a condominium unit and the undivided interest in common elements. In this appraisal assignment the appraiser refers to the *declaration,* which creates the condominium entity; *condominium bylaws,* which establish management rules and authority; and the *management agreement,* which defines manager duties.

Timesharing interests include *interval ownerships* consisting of undivided fee simple interests, giving owners the right to use a unit for a specific time. The *right-to-use* timesharing covers *leases, licenses,* or *club memberships.* Right-to-use timesharing, based on licenses or club memberships, convey no real estate interest. The valuation of other timesharing interests depends on the comparable sales of like properties. In these appraisals, particular attention is drawn to legal provisions that govern timesharing rights by state or by country of origin.

Development rights are valued according to the difference in value for agricultural use and the value as developed for urban use. *Preservation easement* values are based on the value before the easement, less the value of the property with the easement.

POINTS TO REMEMBER

right of eminent domain the right of government and regulated public utilities to take property in the public interest.

back-land theory the concept in which frontage taken for a right-of-way is assumed to have the value of the rear portion of the property.

air rights the right to use air space above the land surface.

avigation easements the right to use air space above the glide path extending from airport runways.

flowage easements the right to flood private property for flood control or water reservoirs.

pipeline easements an easement for the construction, operation, patrol, maintenance, and replacement of pipelines across private property.

electric transmission line easements the right to erect, construct, operate, and maintain electric transmission lines over private property.

condominium interest a fee interest in a condominium unit and an undivided interest in common elements. Common elements include land and other improvements with use-rights shared with other condominium owners.

declaration the instrument that creates a condominium entity.

condominium bylaws regulations that establish management rules and condominium authority.

management agreement an agreement defining duties of the manager to condominium owners.

timesharing interest an ownership of a condominium or a hotel unit for a given time.

interval ownership an undivided fee simple interest to each purchaser of a condominium as a tenant-in-common.

right-to-use timesharing the right to a timeshare interest governed by a lease, license, or club membership.

preservation easements an easement right in which the property owner gives up the right to modify structures, to use an historically significant structure, or to use land in a way that is harmful to the preservation of the site.

QUESTIONS FOR REVIEW

1. Explain the differences between three main valuation problems encountered in estimating just compensation.

2. What is meant by noncompensable damages? Give examples in illustration of your answer.

3. Explain rules governing the highest and best use estimate for eminent domain valuation.

4. Show how you would estimate severance damages.

5. What is meant by the "back-land" theory?

6. What is meant by consequential damages? Give an example of consequential damages to a single-family dwelling resulting from a right-of-way taking.

7. Explain how you would value an air rights easement.

8. What factors would you consider in valuing an easement for an electric transmission line?

9. Show how you would value a condominium unit for an existing project.

10. Explain the difference between an interval timeshare ownership and a right-to-use timeshare interest.

11. How do appraisers value development rights?

12. What determines the value of a preservation easement?

PRACTICE PROBLEMS

1. Estimate just compensation, including severance damages, for a partial taking assuming:

   Value before taking: 10 acres @ $20,000
   Value after taking: 5 acres @ $5,000
   Value of part taken: 5 acres @ $20,000

2. (a) Give an example showing how you would value an easement for a 300-foot-wide electric distribution transmission line over irrigated farmland.

   (b) Indicate how you would value the various forms of timeshare interests.

C H A P T E R   1 9

Appraisal Review

After reading this chapter you will know:
- Techniques to review appraisal reports for technical detail.
- Methods of reviewing appraisal reports for compliance with administrative requirements.
- Procedures to review appraisal reports for logical reasoning.
- Elements of the appraisal review certificate.

The chapter starts with an explanation of the appraisal review function: its need, purpose, and objectives. Procedures determining whether the appraisal meets administrative and legal requirements follow. The chapter then deals with the most important aspect of the review process—appraisal logic and common logic errors. The chapter closes with uniform standards that control the appraisal review process.

APPRAISAL REVIEW PROCESS

Virtually every appraisal is subject to review. If the appraisal report is prepared for a private client, the appraisal will be reviewed with respect to how the appraiser estimated market value. Strictly speaking, if the appraisal report is prepared for an institution or government agency, the appraisal report is not acceptable until it has been reviewed by a technically qualified reviewer. In the latter case, after review, the appraisal report constitutes the basis for financial decisions.

Before the appraisal report receives the benefit of a technical examination, the market value estimate does not have the sanction of the reviewing institution. In this sense, the review appraiser represents the employer and assumes responsibility for appraisal acceptance. The technical review may be justified solely on grounds that the review serves as a basis for some later administrative decision.

The appraisal report may be subject to more than one review. The supervising appraiser may sign a residential appraisal report (Fannie Mae form 1004) as a review appraiser. In this role, the "certified" appraiser reviews appraisal data entered by an "appraisal trainee" who is not certified. In other instances, the review may follow a more formal agency review. Fannie Mae form 2000, a *Residential Appraisal Field Review Report,* includes a review of original appraisal data. The review appraiser, in this instance, follows a specified review procedure. The Federal National Mortgage Association staff member makes a further examination and, on approval, signs the review as the "Review Underwriter."

In the final analysis, the reviewer gives the appraisal report the effective weight of two qualified opinions. A favorable review creates confidence in the final estimate of market value; an unfavorable review recommends further appraisal analysis.

Review Functions

At the outset, it is worthwhile to note the main function of the reviewer:

review technical details
ensure compliance with administrative requirements
determine the validity of appraisal logic

While these functions would appear all inclusive, they do not include the basic valuation responsibility—it is the appraiser who signs the certificate of value; the market value estimate is the opinion of the appraiser and *not* the opinion of the reviewer. In performing these three functions, the reviewer testifies that the appraisal information is technically correct, that the appraisal report meets administrative and minimum procedural requirements, and that the conclusion of value follows accepted appraisal logic.

If the reviewer accepts the appraisal report, judged on the three functions above, it follows that others may rely on the opinion of value. A more detailed explanation of these review functions illustrates the critical role of an appraisal reviewer.

TECHNICAL COMPLIANCE

As a technician, the appraisal reviewer ensures that the appraisal detail is true and correct. A residential lot that measures 80 feet by 125 feet must have a reported 10,000 square-foot area. Likewise, a one-half-acre lot should have approximately 21,780 square feet.

More important, the square-foot area of the heated living space of a single-family dwelling must follow standard measurement practices. A dwelling diagram and floor plan should provide outside dimensions so that the review appraiser may review the accuracy of the square-foot area. In this respect, the house area would not include the enclosed garage space. Further, the square-foot area should show the basement and upper floors separately.

Other issues relate to the legal description and other factual data. The legal description should be compatible with the site plan and reported street frontages and other lot dimensions. In short, the review appraiser examines the appraisal report for discrepancies in dates, measurements and reported distances that are not consistent with appraisal report detail. In this examination the review appraiser tests the report for its completeness—there should be no voids or omissions that the appraisal assignment requires.

ADMINISTRATIVE REQUIREMENTS

While these functions are fairly broad, the authority of the review appraiser is fairly limited. Though the person reviewing the appraisal report has an administrative function, the reviewer has no authority to change the appraiser's opinion of value. The appraisal must stand on its own merits—either it is satisfactory and meets current administrative needs, or it must be rejected. While the appraisal may be returned for correction or suggested revisions, authority for review does not include the right to change the market value opinion.

Moreover, if the appraisal is reviewed by a technically qualified reviewer, the same conclusion applies. If the reviewer changes the opinion of value, the reviewer assumes the role of a joint appraiser and should sign the appraisal report jointly with the appraiser, subject to a third-party review. With these qualifications, the reviewer then reviews the appraisal according to acceptable appraisal logic.

Appraisal Logic

Assume that the appraisal report meets all administrative requirements, and that the appraisal complies with federal and state Uniform Standards of Professional Appraisal Practice. The reviewer faces the main question: Does the market value estimate follow from the facts presented? In this phase of the review process, the reviewer examines appraisal logic.

Logic has been defined as the study of a *consistent set of beliefs*. Beliefs are said to be consistent if they are compatible with each other. To the reviewer, the market value estimate is valid if *there is no possible situation in which valuation data are true and the estimated market value is not true*. In other words, the market value estimate would be valid, since the valuation evidence is said to determine the value conclusion.

Applied to a single-family dwelling, under the market data approach, the appraiser infers value from characteristics of the property sold. In this exercise, the central issue is whether the appraiser has used deductive or inductive logic.

DEDUCTIVE LOGIC

Appraisers who employ deductive logic first establish a general principle. This general principle is then applied to a specific property to estimate market value. The method is commonly employed to value property under the income approach; for instance, the appraiser may establish, as a general principle, a 12 percent capitalization rate. The capitalization rate is then applied to a specific property. Under deductive logic, the appraiser has reasoned from a *general principle* to a *specific case*.

The reviewer then must decide whether deductive logic is appropriate. The test of the valuation conclusion rests on the experience of the appraiser and his or her other appraisal qualifications. In the former example, in questions over the capitalization rate, it is held that a 12 percent capitalization rate is valid because of the authority and reputation of the appraiser. While logically correct, the danger of deductive logic is that the appraiser may follow the principle of *ipse dixit*—it is so because I say it is so. Inductive reasoning avoids this limitation of deductive logic.

INDUCTIVE LOGIC

An appraiser who depends on inductive reasoning makes repeated observations of the market. From repeated observations of *specific cases* (comparable sales), the appraiser proceeds to the general case: the market value estimate. In contrast to deductive reasoning, which proceeds from the *general case* to the specific case, inductive logic starts with numerous specific cases leading to the main conclusion or the general case. Like deductive reasoning, inductive logic is subject to certain appraisal logic errors.

COMMON APPRAISAL ERRORS

Before outlining errors in reasoning or logic errors, attention is directed to errors frequently reported by appraisal reviewers. Some errors seem deliberate, some are accidental, and some result from negligence or carelessness.

It will be appreciated, however, that honest errors are to be expected; indeed, an apparent error may be an honest difference of opinion. Appraising is an art and not an exact science. The complexity of real estate valuation often leaves considerable room for varying valuation opinions. In illustration, is a downturn in housing sales and values in the month of October merely a seasonal, temporary occurrence, or is it a turning point indicative of a change in long-term trends in value?

To answer these questions, the reviewer determines if the appraiser has employed the available and appropriate evidence to render an accurate and reasonable market value estimate. A review of the more frequently occurring errors precedes a discussion of appraisal logic.

Frequently Encountered Appraisal Errors

Appraisal errors may arise from incorrect appraisal data, invalid appraisal techniques, and general appraisal inadequacies.

COMPARABLE SALES ANALYSIS

Field inspections have disclosed cases in which the appraiser has cited erroneous real estate sales that, on the face, do not support the value conclusion. For example, sales prices of $150,000 to $175,000 may be cited to support a valuation of $165,000. A field review, however, may disclose that while the sales prices seem valid, the sales are taken from *dissimilar neighborhoods* or the *physical characteristics* of the property are quite unlike the property appraised. In these instances. it is quite clear that the appraiser has selected sales prices that are comparable to the presumed market value, but which cover properties that are physically or otherwise dissimilar.

A related problem concerns real estate sales that are not sufficiently current to support the market value estimate. Preferably for single-family dwellings, comparable sales should have occurred during the last three months. Dwelling sales of over two years would probably be invalid.

Other real estate appraisers have mistakenly used *listing prices* or *construction costs* as indicative of market value. Listing prices and construction costs may not necessarily be indicative of current market value.

Moreover, in making sales adjustments, appraisal adjustments may not be consistent within the same appraisal report. The appraiser may adjust sales for the same item, i.e., fireplaces or attached garages in an inconsistent, unexplained manner. In other instances, the adjustments may have been excessive. Clearly, selection of a $200,000 sale which is adjusted to the point of supporting a $125,000 market value would be invalid. A valid appraisal avoids sales adjustments which appear excessive.

Experienced reviewers recommend comparable sales that are *higher and lower in price* than the estimated market value. Such "bracketing" of the market value estimate enables the appraiser to establish a value range and estimate market value within acceptable upper and lower limits of value.

Comparable sales that have not been personally inspected by the appraiser may result in misleading sales adjustments. Consider the adjustment of a comparable sale for a detached garage which the property appraised lacked. An adjustment of $1,200 was deducted from the sales price for a detached garage. On a field inspection, it was found that the detached garage was a 10-foot by 20-foot, wood-frame building, 1920 construction, used as a storage building, and clearly of nominal value. The sales adjustment of $1,200 was not warranted to appraise a dwelling of less than 10 years of age. It was readily apparent that the appraiser had not seen this comparable sale.

Comparable sales adjustments should be based on market analysis. Sales adjustments are not entirely based on the unsupported and subjective opinions of the appraiser. Sales adjustments must bear some relation to how property features are viewed by buyers and sellers.

NEIGHBORHOOD ANALYSIS

Questionable appraisal reports may lack relevant information on neighborhood trends. It is difficult to make an intelligent review if the appraiser has not analyzed both positive and negative features of neighborhoods. The same comments apply to the site improvements and comparable sales.

OTHER ERRORS

Photographs that are lacking or that do not adequately show the property appraised or sold are other sources of complaint. Faulty or missing information is another common appraisal error. While the appraisal report lists an estimated market value, it is not always clear that the property is *marketable* under current market conditions. Loss of a major industry, a declining local economy, or a particular value feature of the property—or its location—may make the property unmarketable. Appraisal clients are entitled to know if the property appraised has limited marketability.

Logic Errors

Typically, the review appraiser does not examine the property appraised. In most cases, the reviewer approves the report on the evidence submitted by the appraiser and the soundness of the value conclusion. In this aspect of the review process, the reviewer confronts six common appraisal logic errors.

INCONSISTENT CONCLUSIONS

If the market value estimate, based on the given facts is not true, the appraisal conclusion is inconsistent, and therefore invalid. For example, the reviewer notes that in judging the neighborhood, the appraiser has rated employment stability, property compatibility, and protection from detrimental conditions as fair or poor. However, the appraiser has not deducted a depreciation allowance for external obsolescence.

In the valuation of a single-family dwelling, the appraiser has weighed plumbing, kitchen cabinets, and equipment as fair or poor because of out-of-style or out-of-date equipment or design, but no allowance for these items is deducted under functional obsolescence. In both instances, the sales comparison fails to allow for these limitations.

To cite another example, the building sketch of a single-family dwelling shows an odd floor plan of an owner-built and -designed dwelling, yet no allowance is made under functional utility adjustments in the sales comparison method. In analyzing comparable sales, dwelling prices per square foot range from $50 to $75 per square foot. The appraiser's conclusion of $115 per square foot is inconsistent with the data cited. Therefore, on the appraisal record above, the value conclusion is not consistent with the appraisal evidence.

AMBIGUOUS CONCLUSIONS

An appraisal is ambiguous if more than one value estimate follows from the appraisal evidence. For instance, the reviewer notes that the comparable sales listed for a single-family dwelling are sold with below-market financing. However, the market value estimate of $150,000 has been estimated without adjusting comparable sales for below-market financing. A cursory review would indicate a market value estimate of $130,000 if the appraiser had adjusted sales for below-market financing.

According to evidence of the appraisal report, two value conclusions may be indicated—the market-value estimate without below-market financing adjustments ($150,000) and a $130,000 market estimate *with* below-market financing. The appraiser has committed an ambiguous logic error.

In other instances, the appraiser may be uncertain over the final value estimate. An appraiser who reports a market-value estimate of $200,000 under single-family dwelling zoning and $500,000 if commercial zoning is granted has committed an ambiguous appraisal error.

There is only one market-value estimate. The client is entitled to the market-value estimate based on the appraiser's opinion of value under current market conditions and under the most probable outcome.

MISLEADING CONCLUSIONS

An appraiser who states in the appraisal report that lot sales currently range from $8,000 to $10,000 per lot, when in fact no lots have sold for more than $5,000 per acre, has made a misleading conclusion. Personal knowledge of the review appraiser or a field inspection may disclose misleading conclusions.

OVEREXTENSION DATA

The market-value estimate would be overextended if conclusions are unwarranted, based on the available appraisal data. The appraiser may submit convincing evidence showing that a dwelling of 2,500 square feet has a market value of $60 per square foot. It does not necessarily follow, however, that a dwelling of 4,000 square feet has a value of $60 per square foot. Similar appraisal errors are commonly found in the valuation of land where front-foot or square-foot values are indiscriminately applied to noncomparable sites.

NON SEQUITUR ERRORS

The appraiser may submit evidence that the capitalization rate to value a 100-unit apartment project, 12 percent, would be equally valid to capitalize annual net income from a duplex dwelling. However, it does not follow that the capitalization rate appropriate to value a 100-unit apartment applies to the valuation of a duplex. Further, it does not follow that a single-family dwelling that sold for $200,000 or $60 a square foot in *neighborhood A* indicates a market value of $60 per square foot in *neighborhood B*. It does not follow that the sale of a 30-year-old house indicates the value of a 5-year-old house. Non sequitur errors are common to the market approach to value.

NONREPRESENTATIVE ERRORS

This error source was encountered by a review appraiser of a federal agency that approved a market-value estimate of $125,000 for a single-family dwelling. The real estate agency selling the property claimed the property had a market value of $160,000 and submitted comparable sales that presumably supported a $160,000 market value.

The property appraised covered a two-story, wood-frame dwelling, 30 years old, with aluminum siding. In a field review it was disclosed that the appraiser cited three single-family dwelling sales in comparable neighborhoods of two-story, wood-frame buildings over 20 years of age. These sales supported a $125,000 market value.

The real estate agency, submitting the appeal, based the $160,000 conclusion on three sales of one-story, brick-veneer houses of less than five years of age sold in the same neighborhood. In this case, the review appraiser concluded that sales of five-year-old, one-story, brick-veneer houses were not representative of the property appraised. The original appraisal report was accepted.

Especially in comparable sales analysis, the sales selected should be reasonably representative of the property appraised. The same judgment holds true in the income approach where rental data, operating expenses, and capitalization rates must be drawn from the same property type in comparable locations. Likewise, cost data must be taken from recent construction costs of comparable properties. An appraisal report based on the valuation evidence drawn from nonrepresentative properties invalidates the value conclusion.

UNIFORM REVIEW STANDARDS

The Appraisal Standards Board of the Appraisal Foundation has published Standard 3, which governs review appraisals. Standard 3 is an integral part of the *Uniform Standards of Professional Appraisal Practice* adopted by the Appraisal Foundation. Like individual appraisers, the review appraiser must observe published standards and uniform review appraisal practices. According to Standard 3, the review appraiser must form an opinion:

as to the adequacy and appropriateness of the report being reviewed and must clearly disclose the nature of the review process undertaken.

In observance of this standard, the review appraiser may prepare a review report or submit a signed review check-list which is attached to the appraisal report reviewed. Also acceptable are signatures of the reviewer, or stamps attesting to the review. A stamp or signature must refer to an available file that clearly outlines and details the review process followed.

Standards Rule 3: Review Requirements

Standard 3 follows two rules: Standards Rule 3-1 and Standards Rule 3-2.

STANDARDS RULE 3-1

Under Standards Rule 3-1, the review appraiser is directed to identify facts of the appraisal. The rule specifically requires identification of:

1. The appraisal report under review.
2. The real estate appraised.
3. The real property interest appraised.
4. The effective date of the review opinion and the date of the review.
5. The extent of the review process undertaken.

Standards Rule 3-1 requires that review opinions specifically cover:

1. Completeness of the report.
2. The adequacy and relevance of the data, including data adjustments.
3. The appropriateness of appraisal methods with reasons why the review appraiser disagrees with appraisal techniques employed.
4. The reviewer's judgment on whether the appraisal conclusion is appropriate and reasonable. Reviewers must give reasons on why they disagree with appraisal opinions.

It should be noted that Standards Rule 3-1 apparently allows the review appraiser to offer an opinion of value that varies from the appraiser's estimate of value. Such a departure from review procedures is allowed providing that the review appraiser satisfies requirements of Standard 1 that governs the appraisal process; the review appraiser identifies and adds additional appraisal data that leads to a different estimate of value; and the reviewer identifies and explains all assumptions and limitations that lead to a different opinion of value.

Compliance with the latter requirements, in effect, results in a separate appraisal report. To satisfy the requirements of Standard 1, essentially, the review appraiser must submit a separate appraisal report. Quite clearly, this remedy would be a fairly limited option.

STANDARDS RULE 3-2

Under this standard, the reviewer must explain the review procedure. The review appraiser is required to disclose the nature of the review process. Information required under Standard 3-1 must be summarized with any opinions or required conclusions. In observing this standard, the reviewer must provide all information relevant to the review. Moreover, Standard 3-2 requires a signed certificate of review.

REVIEW CERTIFICATION

The required, signed review certificate contains language that conforms to Figure 19-1. In completing the certificate of review, it may be seen that the review appraiser executes a certificate comparable to the certificate required for appraisers. In other words, the review process conforms to the same standards of practice enforced against real estate appraisers.

Figure 19-1   Appraisal Review Certificate

To the best of my knowledge and belief, I certify that:

1. The facts and data that I have used in my review are true and correct.
2. My opinions and conclusions are limited only by the stated assumptions and limiting conditions.
3. Opinions expressed in this report represent my personal unbiased, professional analysis.
4. I have no present or contemplated interest in the property appraised in this report.
5. I have no personal interest or bias against property owners or appraisers involved in this case.
6. My fee is not dependent on my analysis, opinions, or conclusions.
7. My conclusions were prepared in compliance with *The Uniform Standards of Professional Appraisal Practice.*
8. I have (not) inspected the property under appraisal subject to this review.
9. With the exception of individuals named below, no other individuals provided professional assistance in completing this appraisal review.

Figure 19-1 shows the content of a suggested Review Certificate in which the review appraiser certifies that facts and data as used are true and correct. Like the appraiser, the reviewer must certify that the conclusions of the reviewer are unbiased opinions based on the reviewer's professional analysis. Here the reviewer states that the conclusions are limited only by assumptions and limiting conditions stated in the review report.

Other parts of the certificate require the review appraiser to certify that he or she has no present or prospective interest in the property appraised. Further, it is certified that the reviewer holds no bias against parties involved in the property reviewed. Moreover, the reviewer must certify that compensation is not contingent on the review. By stating that the review complies with the Uniform Standards of Professional Appraisal Practice, the review appraiser can be held responsible for noncompliance with published uniform standards. The reviewer completes the certificate by indicating whether the property has been inspected by the reviewer; the reviewer identifies individuals who may have provided professional review assistance.

Review Checklist

The Chapter Appendix provides a suggested checklist for compliance with Standard 3. The checklist provides a review of *Standards Rule 3-1, appraisal data, the valuation approach,* and *Standards Rule 3-2.*

THE APPRAISAL PROCESS

The suggested checklist covers points encountered in the appraisal process: the appraiser reviews the adequacy of the report with respect to the real estate description, property interest, and the purpose and intended use of the appraisal report. Other minimum requirements of the appraisal, such as limiting conditions, appraisal date, and the value defined, are other steps in the appraisal process covered by the review.

In this respect, the checklist requires close observance of the appraisal process. For instance, if the appraiser has based the market value estimate on the most probable price, this fact must be indicated. Cash equivalency value and various legal restrictions, if found, must be considered in the valuation. The treatment of fractional interests and personal property is covered in this part of the checklist.

VALUATION APPROACH

This portion of the checklist covers the land valuation: land use regulations, their probable modification, and possible changes in the highest and best use should be covered in the report and are subject to a checklist review.

The next part of the checklist covers the cost approach while two checklist items relate to the comparable sales approach. The income approach is reviewed by questions on comparable rental data, operating expense data, and capitalization rates. The reviewer, according to the checklist, critically evaluates rent, expenses, and lease terms in applying the income approach.

In valuing the leased fee or leasehold estate, lease terms must be considered. The issue of assemblage and the appraisal of partial interests is covered by the next checklist item. On- or off-site improvements and the three main forms of depreciation require reviewer attention in the checklist that follows.

The last two items cover new construction. The reviewer considers whether proposed improvements have been valued at the time of completion. Other appraisal evidence for new construction, as indicated by the review checklist, must be estimated at the time of project completion.

SUMMARY

Appraisal reports that comply with Uniform Standards of Professional Appraisal Practice, technically, are not valid until the appraisal report has been reviewed according to Uniform Standards of Review. An appraisal reviewer, conforming to Uniform Review Standards, must sign appraisal reports as a reviewer or submit an Appraisal Review Certificate. By following these steps, the reviewer assures third parties that the appraisal meets minimum standards, that the appraisal complies with Uniform Professional Appraisal practice, and that the appraiser has applied acceptable appraisal logic.

In reviewing for technical matters, the reviewer examines the report for clerical errors or other discrepancies that lead to questionable value conclusions. Third parties may accept reviewed appraisal reports knowing that the appraisal does not have substantial errors, or an accumulation of errors, that would render the appraisal report unacceptable.

To guide the appraisal review for administrative requirements, the review appraiser utilizes a checklist that methodically traces the appraisal process through each required step of the Uniform Standard of Professional Appraisal Practice.

The checklist shows compliance, or noncompliance, with the appraisal process. Reviewers must also review each approach to market value as indicated by the checklist in the chapter appendix.

In short, the review appraiser follows a checklist covering those elements of the appraisal critical to the value estimate. Indeed the review process includes an *Appraisal Review Certificate,* signed by the reviewer, indicating that Uniform Standards of Professional Appraisal Review requirements have been followed.

POINTS TO REMEMBER

Uniform Standards of Professional Appraisal Practice (USPAP) standards developed and published by the Appraisal Foundation.

logic the study of a consistent, or compatible, set of beliefs.

deductive logic reasoning from a general principle to a specific case.

inductive logic a process of reasoning from repeated observations to the general case.

inconsistent conclusions conclusions, drawn from the given facts, which are not true.

ambiguous conclusions conclusions in which more than one conclusion follows from the evidence.

misleading conclusions conclusions that cannot be supported by the facts.

non sequitur errors conclusions that do not follow from the evidence.

nonrepresentative errors errors resulting from value evidence unrelated to the property appraised.

QUESTIONS FOR REVIEW

1. Give reasons in support of the appraisal review function.

2. Explain the three main functions of the appraisal review process.

3. Give three examples of technical detail that you would review in the valuation of a single-family dwelling.

4. What are the main elements of the checklist that reviews compliance with Uniform Standards of Appraisal Practice?

5. Explain and give an example of how an appraiser would value an income property using deductive logic; explain how the same appraisal would be completed by following inductive logic.

6. Explain common examples of appraisal errors in analyzing comparable sales.

7. Give an example of common appraisal errors in analyzing neighborhoods.

8. Explain and give examples of errors that illustrate appraisal errors in the categories below:

   inconsistent conclusions
   ambiguous conclusions
   misleading conclusions
   overextension of data
   non sequitur errors
   nonrepresentative errors

9. Explain the main elements of Standards Rule 3-1 covering review requirements.

10. Explain review requirements under Review Standards Rule 3-2.

11. What elements would you include in preparing your Appraisal Review Certificate?

PRACTICE PROBLEMS

1. You are presented with an appraisal report of a regional shopping center valued under the three approaches to value. Write your certificate of review covering points essential for a review of a regional shopping center appraisal.

2. Consider the appraisal review of an appraisal on a newly constructed $500,000 luxury dwelling of 5,000 square feet on 5 acres of land. For this appraisal problem, explain how the appraiser would avoid six common logic errors in completing this report. Give examples in illustration of your answer.

Appendix to Chapter 19   A Suggested Checklist that Complies with Standard 3*

Yes   No   *Review Item*

Standards Rule 3-1

_____ _____   Does the appraisal report adequately identify the real estate appraised?

_____

_____ _____   Does the appraisal identify the real property interest under valuation?

_____

_____ _____   Does the appraisal state the purpose and intended use of the appraisal report?

_____

_____ _____   Has the appraiser listed special limiting conditions?

_____

_____ _____   Is the effective date of the appraisal reported?

_____

_____ _____   Is the value reported defined in the appraisal report?

_____

_____ _____   Does the appraisal report indicate whether the market value estimate is the most probable price?

_____

* See Appendix IV, *Uniform Standards of Professional Appraisal Practice.* (Washington, D.C.: The Appraisal Foundation, 1990), pp. III-1 and III-2.

Yes	*No*	*Review Item*
―――	―――	Has the appraiser considered the cash equivalency value in estimating market value or in judging market data?
―――	―――	Are easements, restrictions, encumbrances, leases, reservations, covenants, contracts, declarations, special assessments, or ordinances considered in the appraisal report?
―――	―――	In the appraisal of a fractional interest, has the appraiser considered a partial holding that contributes *pro rata* to the value of the whole?
―――	―――	Is it indicated that a partial interest valuation cannot be used to estimate the value of the whole?
―――	―――	Does the appraisal report include personal property or trade fixtures in the value of the property appraised?
―――	―――	Has the appraiser correctly employed recognized techniques of appraisal?
―――	―――	Has the appraiser committed a substantial error that significantly affects the appraised value?

Yes	*No*	*Review Item*

_____ _____   Does the appraisal erroneously omit data that significantly affect
the appraised value?

_____

_____ _____   Does the appraisal include a series of errors which lead to
misleading appraisal conclusions?

_____

Appraisal Data Review

_____ _____   Have existing land-use regulations been considered?

_____

_____ _____   Have reasonably probable modifications of land-use regulations
been considered?

_____

_____ _____   Have possible changes in demand, physical adaptability of the real
estate, neighborhood trends, and the highest and best use estimate been considered?

_____

_____ _____   Has the land been considered as vacant and available for development at the highest and best use?

_____

_____ _____   Have land improvements been appraised according to their
actual contributions to the site?

_____

_____ _____   Is the site appraised by the appropriate appraisal method?

_____

Yes	No	Review Item
____	____	Have comparable cost data been analyzed to estimate cost new of the improvements?
____	____	Have comparable data been analyzed to estimate the difference between cost new and the present value of improvements?
____	____	Have comparable sales data been adequately identified and described?
____	____	Have comparable rental data been analyzed to estimate market rent?
____	____	Have comparable operating expense data been analyzed?
____	____	Have comparable data been analyzed to estimate rates of capitalization or rates of discount?
____	____	Are rent and expense projections based on reasonably clear and appropriate evidence?
____	____	Have lease terms been considered in valuing a leased fee estate or leasehold estate?

Yes	*No*	*Review Item*
_____	_____	Has the assemblage of various estates or component parts of a property been considered?
_____	_____	Has the appraiser avoided appraising the whole property only by adding values of the component parts?
_____	_____	Has the effect of anticipated public or private improvements located on or off the site been considered?
_____	_____	Has the appraiser considered physical, functional, and external market forces that affect value?
_____	_____	Have proposed improvements been valued only after examining plans, specifications, or other documentation?
_____	_____	Have proposed improvements been valued at the probable time of completion?
_____	_____	Have current agreements of sale, options, or listings for the property appraised been considered?
_____	_____	Has the suitability of appraisal data been judged and reconciled?

Yes	No	Review Item

_____ _____ Has the appraiser offered reasonably clear and appropriate evidence supporting development costs, earnings, occupancy rates, and market competition at the time of project completion?

_____

_____

_____ _____ For one- to four-family dwellings, have sales of the property appraised over the preceding year been considered?

_____

_____

_____ _____ With the exception of the property appraised of one- to four-family dwellings, have sales over the preceding three years been considered?

_____

_____

Standards Rule 3-2

_____ _____ Have I disclosed the extent of the review process?

_____

_____

_____ _____ Have I disclosed all information required under Standards Rule 3-1?

_____

_____

_____ _____ Have I given my opinions, reasons, and conclusions required by Standards Rule 3-1?

_____

_____

_____ _____ Have I signed the required review certificate?

_____

_____

C H A P T E R 2 0

Appraisal Ethics

After reading this chapter you will know:
- The concept of a profession.
- The meaning of ethics.
- The four ethical standards of professional appraisal practice.
- Limited exceptions allowed under Uniform Standards of Professional Appraisal Practice.

At the outset, the chapter reviews the meaning of ethics as a general appraisal policy. The main part of the chapter, however, focuses on four ethical standards. The chapter ends with a review of minor exceptions to ethical standards that guide appraisers.

Consider these scenarios: The market value estimate proves wrong but the appraiser is experienced. The market value estimate is grossly in error, but the appraiser is highly competent. The appraised value markedly departs from market value, but appraisal data–in every detail–is true and correct. These contradictions may be explained by the fact that the appraiser has not observed one or more ethical standards required by professional appraisal practice. Ethical appraisal standards are legally enforced to prevent these occurrences. Licensed and certified appraisers, organizations, institutions, and government agencies responsible for real estate appraisals must observe *Uniform Ethical Standards of Appraisal Practice.*

THE EMERGING APPRAISAL PROFESSION

Appraising as a recognized discipline began in the depression of the 1930s. The former Society of Real Estate Appraisers (now the Appraisal Institute) and the original American Institute of Real Estate Appraisers emerged from the 1930s depression to raise appraisal standards, because the unusual mortgage foreclosure rate created a need for accurate appraisals for residential mortgages. From this beginning, appraisers were hired as individual appraisers. With their developing skills, they were employed by federal agencies, local governments, and lenders to estimate market value. Appraisal organizations offered appraisal courses and published real estate appraisal textbooks. Appraisers were employed for their special training, their objective approach to value, and for their independence in working as individual appraisers who served many clients.

Today the working environment facing real estate appraisers has changed considerably. More appraisers work as members of an organization; the industry is highly organized. There are at least three explanations of why federal and state regulations strictly govern the appraisal industry.

First, the community relies more heavily on real estate appraisals. As real estate finance becomes more complex, business decisions increasingly depend on the estimated market value. Developers, commercial investors, and homeowners, by regulation, are granted real estate credit limited according to the appraised property value. Homeowners investing in residential property face substantial losses if the appraised value, which governs their mortgages and purchases, is in error.

Furthermore, real estate decisions, because of the large dollar amounts, are largely governed by estimated real estate values and their projection. Add to this the demand for accurate valuations by governments taking private property for public purposes that require competent appraisal estimates. Incorrect appraisals lead to expensive court litigation to determine just compensation paid to property owners whose property is taken for public purposes.

Second, professional appraisers today are likely to be employed by financial and other institutions that are highly impersonal and geared toward common business and profit goals. Ideas about what constitutes acceptable and professional appraisal practice may be influenced by business goals that conflict with the independent appraisals based on objective, impartial value estimates.

Third, appraisers and their parent organizations increasingly view themselves as a disciplined, professional group. Federal and state appraisal license and certification laws promote—and even require—professionalism in real estate valuation. Here the main question relates to how the appraisal industry generally meets the requirements of professional activity.

Requirements of a Profession

Appraising as a recognized discipline may be viewed as "professional work" if real estate appraising meets standards commonly associated with a profession. Professions generally meet commonly recognized criteria.

EXTENSIVE TRAINING

Recognized professions require extensive training as a prerequisite to professional practice. Among this group are architects, certified public accounts, lawyers, and the many disciplines followed in the health sciences. Usually these disciplines require an advanced college degree. It may be concluded that professional practice requires extensive training of a specialized type.

IMPORTANT SERVICES

Members of a profession provide important social services. This aspect of a profession segregates professionals from other disciplines that require specialized training, but training which society does not deem relatively important. Chess experts, while requiring many years of practice and training, are not deemed as important as medical doctors. In these terms, chess experts do not qualify as professionals.

INTELLECTUAL SKILLS

Followers of the professions practice disciplines that are largely intellectual. To be sure, skilled craftspeople such as woodcarvers, bricklayers, beauticians, and many others require years of training and experience. However, these disciplines focus mainly on physical talents. In addition, intellectual aspects of a professional usually mean that the "professional," like the real estate appraiser, advises others on issues that the layman does not understand.

Other Characteristics

Professional activities are usually licensed or certified—a trait shared by real estate appraisers undertaking an appraisal for a federally related transaction. Like other professions, practicing real estate appraisers must pass examinations that conform to federal law. While licensing or certification by the state is not always required—there is no licensing procedure required for college professors—generally, it is illegal to practice many of the recognized professions, such as pharmacist, medical doctor, and registered nurse, without a state license. Moreover, members of a profession form organizations that advance member goals; for example, the Appraisal Institute enforces an organizational code of ethics, sponsors educational programs, and supports research and publications for member advancement.

It has also been observed that professions operate with a high degree of freedom in exercising judgments and completing work assignments. They act independently and have considerable discretion in completing their commitments. While their activities must fall within acceptable boundaries of professional practice, they are specifically hired because clients want their individual and independent judgments.

Therefore, members of the appraisal industry share many characteristics common to the recognized professions. Central to performing professional services is the observance of a code of ethics. In this respect, the appraisal profession follows a recognized moral standard and ethics code.

ETHICS DEFINED

The concept of ethics is derived from the Greek word *ethos,* meaning character or custom. From this original definition, ethics has been extended to mean "moral right and wrong," "duty and obligation," and "moral responsibility." In real estate, appraising ethics has a more specific meaning.

Appraisal Ethics

To appraisers, ethics refers to acceptable or unacceptable appraisal reports, good or bad market value estimates and morally correct appraisal conduct. These ideas relate to individuals performing appraisal services independently and to organizations that require appraisals and related services for organizational purposes and clients. Appraisers, as individuals, observe appraisal ethics, while organizations that provide appraisal services for a profit must incorporate appraisal ethics as part of their business code of ethics.

The chapter, therefore, addresses conflicts between the individuals who pursue ethics common to the appraisal discipline and organizations that operate for a profit. For example, a business may lose a client if a $150,000 market value estimate is required to justify a $120,000 mortgage and the appraiser values the property at $100,000. The question of ethics applies equally to appraisal organizations and institutions.

Why Be Ethical?

The traditional view is that policies considered to be good ethics are considered to be good business. The lender who approves an $8 million loan on the basis of a $10 million appraisal, when the property only has a market value of $8 million, may eventually lose a profitable client. Overstated appraisals lead to financial losses; financial loss results in lost business. And while business decisions based on market value reduce risks, appraisals deliberately approved for more than the market value increase risks, damage reputations, and eventually cause losses to clients and others.

SOCIAL RESPONSIBILITIES

Failed real estate projects do not promote community interests. Mortgage foreclosures resulting from inadequate appraisals damage neighborhoods and surrounding property values. Therefore, ethical practices contribute to community welfare, and, on this point alone, seem justified. Truly, appraisers and their employing organizations share certain social responsibilities. These social responsibilities deserve the highest ethical conduct.

The argument rests on the notion of long-run self-interest. Appraisers, by being socially responsible, pursue long-term goals. An appraiser following this route creates a favorable image. The appraiser who assumes a social responsibility to report market value independently, impartially, and without bias, gains more clients and develops a favorable reputation among investors dependent on objective market value estimates.

More significantly, it can be argued that appraisal organizations, institutions, and agencies work with a valuable resource. Such organizations have moral obligations to base decisions on market value which may vary from the immediate self-interest of the organization or its clients. It is argued, further, that only in this way may appraisers and their associates attain their chosen goals to build favorable reputations and to be recognized for their authoritative opinions. In contrast, appraisers who commit fraud and follow deceptive practices undermine the confidence of their clients and the general public.

DECISIONS BASED ON CONSEQUENCES

The final implication is that not only is good ethics good business but, by pursuing ethical practices, individuals and their organizations enhance the general welfare of communities, neighborhoods, and their financial, governmental, and social institutions.

However, *it should not be concluded that ethical decisions made by appraisers are justified solely by their consequences.* The appraisal estimate is not to be judged according to whether it leads to good or bad outcomes as perceived by the organization or client. The sole question facing the appraiser remains:

Has the market value been estimated by following accepted appraisal practices and techniques? Of course, an appraisal of $30,000,000 may not satisfy a client who needs a $50,000,000 appraisal to meet minimum loan requirements. However, it is not the appraiser's duty to satisfy the need for a $50,000,000 appraisal; the duty is performed if the appraiser arrives at the estimate of market value according to acceptable standards of ethics and prescribed appraisal standards.

In short, the true value of appraisal services lies in conformity with appraisal principles and ethics rather than on the consequences of the appraisal. Again, it is not the responsibility of the appraiser to meet the $50,000,000 appraisal requirement of a client based on a distorted market value estimate. It is not the duty of the appraiser to base the market value estimate on the possible consequences of the estimated market value.

Like other moral guides, contractual obligations are to be satisfied and debts should be paid; it is the duty of persons to keep promises and to pay debts, not because of the good or bad consequences but because of the moral obligations inherent in contracts and loan agreements. To this extent, appraisal ethics do not consist merely of a set of rules that determine how appraisers should act; *appraisal ethics concern moral persons who pursue acceptable appraisal practices in all situations.*

Case Examples

The cases described here are taken from actual situations confronting real estate appraisers. Though the circumstances and values have been changed, each example indicates typical appraisal assignments that require the exercise of appraisal ethics.

CHASING SALES

Consider first the appraiser who was asked to value a new single-family dwelling recently sold for $250,000. The selling price was stated on the appraisal request. The buyer required a $200,000 loan based on a market-value estimate of $250,000. The new buyer had moved into the house, paying rent temporarily until the mortgage loan was approved and the sale was closed. In the course of the appraisal, the appraiser learned that the property appraised was in a subdivision of 50 houses constructed by the same builder over the last three years. There were numerous sales of the same house currently sold within the last six months showing a market value of $200,000 for virtually the same house, with the same floor plan in the same subdivision.

If the property was appraised for less than $250,000, the required loan for the buyer would be disapproved and the seller would be forced to move, renegotiate the sale price, or try to secure other financing. None of these alternatives would satisfy the buyer, the seller, or the lender. To report a market value of $250,000, the appraiser would be forced to secure sales in other (noncomparable) neighborhoods in which dissimilar houses sold for $250,000.

Therefore, the appraiser had the option of selecting comparable sales in the same neighborhood and reporting a value of $200,000—the true market value—or the appraiser, considering the consequences of the appraisal, had the option of listing dissimilar sales from another neighborhood to defend a reported value of $250,000—$50,000 more than the actual market value. Pursuing this option is known as "chasing sales."

Here the appraiser might reason that if the house was not appraised for $250,000, the lender would secure the services of another appraiser who would be willing to report a value estimate of $250,000. That is, the appraiser might conclude that, "If I don't report a value of $250,000, the lender will secure another appraiser who will report the required value of $250,000."

Therefore, it could be reasoned that, "It makes no difference whether I report a $200,000 market value (the true market value) or a $250,000 estimate since the lender will secure someone else to complete the required appraisal report."

Several arguments may guide the appraiser in these circumstances: *First,* appraising the property above the estimated market value would be a clear violation of Uniform Appraisal Standards. *Second,* suppose the appraiser concludes that it makes no difference if the property is appraised at the market value or $250,000, since the lender will secure services of a more cooperative appraiser. However, if *all appraisers* reason this way, the consequences could be quite serious: Competition between lenders would force above-market appraisals with the consequence of higher foreclosure rates, economic losses among buyers, and eventual property deterioration, higher neighborhood vacancies, and declining property values and neighborhoods.

Therefore, it could be concluded that an unethical act committed by one appraiser may be, in itself, insignificant. But *if the same practices are observed by all appraisers, the consequences would be quite serious.* Hence, it is invalid to reason that departure from Uniform Ethical Standards makes no difference. It is a false premise to follow this reasoning.

DIRECTED APPRAISALS

In the following case, reported values are changed, although the magnitude and relative figures are true. To settle a tax dispute, two appraisers were hired to value the property in question—one appraiser represented the property owner and the other appraiser represented a government agency. After six months of analysis, the appraiser for the government agency reported a market value of $400,000,000, while the appraiser for the taxpayer estimated market value at $95,000,000. The appraisal report prepared for the government agency complied with narrative appraisal report standards by an appraiser experienced in industrial property valuation. The appraiser for the property owner, who was equally experienced, was frequently employed by large corporations to appraise complex industrial properties. Before the controversy reached the court, the taxpayer settled out of court at the $400,000,000 appraised value estimate.

Why the wide variation between two appraisers that had the necessary experience to perform such appraisals? The answer probably lies in the fact that the owner's appraiser knew that juries, faced with complex valuation problems prepared by equally competent appraisers, would be likely to resolve the problem by averaging the two appraised values. Knowing this fact, the property owner's appraiser probably submitted the lowest possible appraisal in the expectation that differences of opinion would be averaged in a court of law. If true, this appraiser allowed the consequences of the appraisal to dictate the value opinion. On its face, this would appear to be a violation of appraisal ethics; in other words, the property owner, employed the appraiser to complete a "directed" appraisal.

The remedy lies in enforcing ethical standards among professional persons. By following a career that requires professional ethical standards, there is an implied *social responsibility* to observe the highest standards of professional ethics. The medical doctor does not reject a patient solely on grounds that the individual has no money to pay the doctor's fee. Members of the medical profession frequently perform services to indigent patients as a social responsibility. Similarly, appraisers, by assuming the responsibility to report market value, have social responsibilities to observe ethical standards like other professionals.

In short, there are strong philosophical grounds for appraisers to observe professional ethical practices. With new state and federal legislation, ethical appraisal standards are legal appraisal requirements. Figure 20-1 shows that the market value estimate follows from a combination of professional ethics and ethical guidelines that affect appraisals prepared for federally related transactions and various state enforced appraisal laws and regulations.

Figure 20-1   Real Estate Appraisal Ethics

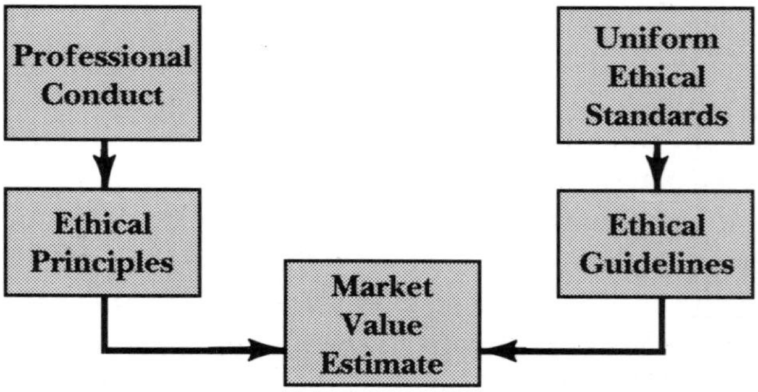

UNIFORM ETHICAL APPRAISAL STANDARDS

Ethical standards guide the preparation of appraisals, reviews, consulting services, and their administration. The standards are enforced against individual appraisers and their employing organizations. Ethical standards fall into four groups: appraisal conduct, appraisal management or administration, appraisal confidentiality, and appraisal records; these categories are treated as separate cases to show how appraisers comply with appraisal ethical requirements. See Figure 20-2 for summary of Ethical Appraisal Standards as developed by the Appraisal Foundation.

Figure 20-2   Ethic Provisions: A Summary

Uniform Standards of Professional Appraisal Practice

Conduct	:	Misleading
		Fraudulent
		Hypothetical conditions
Management	:	Compensation
		Predetermined value
		Directed appraisal value
		No undisclosed fees
		False advertising
Confidentiality	:	No disclosures except to:
		Parties authorized
		Third parties authorized by law
		Professional peer review committee
Record Keeping	:	Retain records five years after report completion
		Retain records two years after judicial proceedings

Other Provisions
  Competency
    Disclosure
      Describe lack of knowledge and steps taken to complete assignment
    Added personal study
    Association with others
  Departure Provisions
    Limited assignments
    Reports completed by reference
    Appraisal updates

Source: *Uniform Standards of Professional Appraisal Practice,* (Washington, D.C.: The Appraisal Foundation, 1990), pp. 1-2–1-3.

Case I: Appraisal Conduct

Like other economic pursuits, appraisers are governed by a general ethical standard that requires conduct that is not unlawful, unethical, or improper. These catch-all provisions enable administrators, clients, and administrative authorities to control appraisal acts that, generally, are dishonest or otherwise legally unacceptable.

Such catch-all provisions prohibit appraisers from undervaluing a property for possible sale to friends, relatives, or associates for later resale at a profit. Consider *fiduciary* responsibilities that prohibit acts hostile to clients. A fiduciary responsibility means that the appraiser holds a position of trust and confidence. The appraisal client acts with confidence, faith, and reliance on the appraiser's estimate of market value. The fiduciary relationship requires that appraisers act with good conscience in the interest of clients. In this application, the appraiser best serves the client with a supported estimate of market value.

The appraiser acts as a disinterested party in submitting an unbiased appraisal report, an appraisal review, or a consulting report. In each instance, ethical standards require appraisal standards to be executed with impartiality, objectivity, and independence. *Misleading conduct, fraudulent conduct,* or an appraisal based on assumed *hypothetical* conditions *violates* appraisal ethical standards.

MISLEADING CONDUCT

It is unethical to make a misleading oral or written statement. Statements that are not verified or that are based on mere conjecture would be considered misleading. For example, "Though I have conservatively capitalized the net income at ten percent, a capitalization rate of 12 percent would probably be justified"; such a statement added to the letter of transmittal would be grossly misleading—it is mere conjecture. Statements that are not verified by facts could be misleading and therefore unethical.

FRAUDULENT CONDUCT

Action may be brought against appraisers submitting fraudulent reports. A fraudulent report would be evidenced by a market value estimate in which certain operating expenses were deliberately understated or omitted. An overstatement of gross income, which clearly distorts the true facts, would be another instance of a fraudulent appraisal report. Appraisal clients expect appraisal reports to be impartially and objectively prepared and to be prepared independently and unaffected by personal interests of the appraiser.

HYPOTHETICAL ASSUMPTIONS

It would be unethical to base the estimated market value on hypothetical assumed events because if the hypothetical conditions are not met, the market-value estimate would probably be considerably lower. It would be misleading to hold that the current market value follows from an assumed hypothetical condition that may not exist.

Suppose the appraiser values a potential high-rise apartment site at $5,000,000 under the *assumption* that high-density residential zoning would permit a multiple-story elevator apartment building. Usually, zoning changes involving high-density land use are subject to public hearings and probable modification of the developer's original plan. However, to the client, the presumption would be that the market value is $5,000,000, although the assumptions of the appraiser would unlikely be realized.

Consider further the valuation of a 300-acre farm that is appraised as subdivision land with the assumption that:

1. Municipal and water sewage facilities would be supplied to the tract.
2. Residential streets, street lighting, and other municipal services would be available to the proposed subdivision.

Such an appraisal is largely dependent on the availability of off-site improvements (which do not exist). However, this conclusion rests on a mere *assumption* of their availability. With no supporting facts or strong indications that such facilities would be available, the appraisal report is based on mere conjecture, and since it is grossly misleading, it would be unethical.

It may be observed, moreover, that these examples of hypothetical assumptions are not based on the appraiser's highest and best use estimate. Under these examples, the market value estimate follows directly from the assumed hypothetical conditions. In these cases, the appraiser has not based the conclusion on the highest and best use estimate, but only on the unsupported, assumed hypothetical conditions. Clearly, there is a difference between the highest and best use estimate, which is adequately supported by the facts, and an assumed hypothetical condition.

Case II: Management Issues

Under this general topic, the appraiser commits an unethical act if:

1. Compensation is contingent on a predetermined appraised value.
2. Appraisal fees are contingent on a value that serves the cause of the client.

This ethical provision is directed to appraisers who accept certain appraisal fees granted only if the appraiser estimates value at some minimum or agreed upon amount. The appraiser may not accept an assignment in which the client states, "I will pay you an appraisal fee of $20,000 if you appraise this property at $15,000,000." Appraisal fees, based on a proportion of the appraised value or contingent on the value, are unethical. The appraisal fee should be based on a lump sum or on a basis other than a predetermined value.

Similarly, undisclosed fees, commissions, or other items of value paid for a "satisfactory" appraisal, review, or consulting assignment would be equally unethical. To avoid criticism of possible unethical conduct, such payments, if allowable under the Standards, should be disclosed in written reports or transmittal letters.

MULTIPLE APPRAISAL ROLES

This restriction, however, exempts appraisers who, in the normal course of their work, may not act in a disinterested manner. In this respect, appraisers could wear two hats. Real estate brokers, who are also appraisers, may form a limited partnership, acting as a general partner and perform brokerage services, cash-flow analyses, sales projections, and valuation reports. It is not expected that the appraiser assuming this general partnership role should act impartially. Contingent fees and compensation normal to a general partnership, if disclosed to limited and general partners, would not be unethical.

The same conclusion applies to others acting as asset managers. Asset and real property managers may assume consulting and other functions as part of their assigned duties. Management fees frequently are based on a percentage of gross income or other incentive fees. Appraisals and related reports prepared by consultants assuming a dual role, if fully disclosed, would be allowable under this ethical standard. The main point is that contingency fees should be fully disclosed to avoid criticisms of unethical conduct.

ADVERTISING

Ethics controlling appraisal management cover false, misleading, or exaggerated advertising, including solicitations of appraisal assignments. Groups or organizations undertaking appraisal assignments as part of their general real estate business may advertise and collect appraisal fees and other charges normal to the industry. For example, lender referral fees and loan origination fees are often based on percentages of the loan or market value. Individual appraisers working under these circumstances are responsible for observing ethical standards so that appraisal reports are completed with impartiality and reported independent of contingency or referral fees.

Case III: Confidentiality

The fiduciary relationship between appraisers and their clients requires that appraisal data must be treated as confidential. To this end, appraisers may disclose confidential appraisal data only to clients and their authorized representatives, third parties as required by law, and officially authorized professional peer review committees. In the latter case, members of a professional peer review committee may not disclose confidential appraisal data presented to the committee. Disclosure of such information represents an unethical practice.

The rule of confidentiality applies to the appraiser-client relationship. The appraiser does not have the ethical right to disclose appraisal information to others. Only the client can release the appraiser from this confidentiality rule.

The rule covers common appraisal-client situations. Appraisals to establish minimum bids acceptable at auctions encourage third parties to request confidential appraisal information. Confidential appraisals prepared for eminent domain are necessary for government agencies and utilities to negotiate just compensation for the taking of private property. By the same token, appraisals made in anticipation of a purchase or sale may serve as a basis for buyer and seller negotiations. Therefore, the confidentiality rule prohibits appraisers from disclosing information that could lead to irreparable economic loss.

Case IV: Record Keeping

The general rule is that appraisal records for valuation, review, or consulting assignments must be held for at least *five years* after completion or *two years* after final legal proceedings. The requirement applies to other storage devices—computer tapes, disks, dictation tapes, and the like.

Decisions based on appraisal reports may be subject to litigation, investigation, or review by government agencies, institutions, lenders, and others. Clients and other authorities are entitled to original records that may have influenced the market-value opinion. As a matter of professional policy, experienced appraisers keep working papers and other information used in preparing appraisal reports for at least five years.

The Appraisal Competency Rule

Appraisal-client relationships require that appraisers have the knowledge and experience to make competent real estate appraisals. If questions over the required experience or competency are in question, appraisers must:

1. Disclose the extent to which they lack knowledge or experience before accepting the assignment.
2. Explain the lack of knowledge and experience and the steps taken to compensate for these deficiencies.

Because the lack of background and/or experience can lead to inaccurate valuations, this rule deserves the strongest support. Faced with limitations in competency or experience, appraisers may retain others to assist in completing the assignment. For example, in estimating the market value of an oil refinery, the appraiser may employ a petroleum engineer to assist in the valuation.

The problem also arises in completing appraisal reports in foreign countries or in areas in which the appraiser has no recent experience. In these assignments, appraisers are advised to take additional time to review local markets and other factors that govern local real estate values. Affiliation with a qualified local appraiser represents another solution to appraising property in unfamiliar locations.

Limited Exceptions to Ethical Standards

Uniform Standards allow certain departures from specific guidelines provided:

1. The proposed assignment is not so limited in scope that the resulting service could mislead or confuse others.
2. The appraisal assignment requires less than the minimum requirements of Uniform Standards guidelines. Accordingly, the proposed report must clearly state the limited nature of the appraisal service.

Appraisers are frequently confronted by prospective clients unfamiliar with Uniform Standards and the nature of professional appraisal services.

Such client needs are often fairly limited. A brief discussion of typical cases illustrates *departure provisions* falling under guidelines of the Uniform Standards.

LETTERS OF OPINION

A client may approach an appraiser for a value estimate but states that because of the limited use of the appraisal, only a letter of opinion is needed. For instance, the client wants a professional opinion of value before offering property for sale. In the client's view only a letter of opinion would be required. Normally, a certified or licensed appraiser would reject the assignment since a letter of opinion would violate Standards Rules 1 and 2.

Note that a letter of opinion giving an estimate of market value accompanied with the comment, "Appraisal information that supports the market value estimate is on file" is generally insufficient to meet Uniform Standards, especially if such files do not directly relate to the specific appraisal assignment.

However, these standards may not apply if the assignment is fairly limited. For example, a lender may ask an appraiser to verify three comparable sales listed in an appraisal report prepared by another appraiser. Typically, the appraiser would locate each comparable sale and note any discrepancies between the property sold and the appraisal report description of each sale. County records would be reviewed to verify the date of sale, financing terms, and property rights conveyed. Here a letter of opinion summarizing results of the comparable sale review would be sufficiently limited so that the appraisal service furnished would not mislead or confuse others.

APPRAISAL UPDATES

Consider appraisal reports on complex developments where financing, land development, and environmental approval extends over several months. In these cases, clients may request appraisal updates to provide a current valuation opinion. Further, court cases may require valuation testimony several months after the date of valuation. Valuation updates of the original appraisal are permitted under Uniform Standards if the report identifies the property, states the current value, and supports the value conclusion *by reference* to a complete appraisal file and supporting current data on record and available for examination. By observing these latter requirements, the letter of opinion complies with departure allowances approved under Uniform Standards.

SUMMARY

Ethical appraisal standards are enforced, first, because the community is heavily dependent on real estate appraisals. Second, appraisers employed by institutions and government agencies may face conflicts between objectively prepared appraisals and organizational goals. Last, appraisal groups and legislation encourage appraisers to assume a professional stature.

Appraising has many of the requirements of a profession—primarily, *extensive training* as a prerequisite to professional practice. Besides, appraising is viewed as an important and essential social service. Add to these characteristics the intellectual skills which are common to both appraising and other professional activities and the fact that appraisers, today, are licensed or certified and that appraisers act with considerable independence.

Appraisal ethics refers to acceptable or unacceptable appraisal reports, good or bad market value estimates, and morally correct appraisal conduct. These ethical standards apply to individual appraisers and to their employing organizations, institutions, and agencies.

Appraisers adopt ethical standards because of large scale *social responsibilities*. Appraisers also base their market value estimates not solely on the consequences of their findings but on the question of whether the appraisal conforms with accepted appraisal principles and ethics. The practice of chasing sales or estimating values as directed or preferred by the client is clearly unethical.

In short, Uniform Ethical Appraisal Standards govern appraisal conduct that is not unlawful, unethical, or improper. Such conduct must conform to the *fiduciary responsibilities* that prohibit acts hostile to clients. Misleading conduct, fraudulent conduct, or appraisals based upon hypothetical conditions violate appraisal ethics.

Uniform standards relate to certain appraisal management issues: Compensation should not be contingent on a predetermined appraised value, and appraisal fees must not be contingent on values that serve the special interest of clients. In this regard, uniform standards require appraisers to observe the ethical standard of *confidentiality*. Only the client may release the appraiser from this ethical rule. Ethical standards require further that the appraiser maintain appraisal records for at least *five years* after the appraisal completion or *two years* after final legal proceedings.

Other ethical appraisal standards cover appraisal competency. If there are questions over the required experience necessary for the assignment, appraisers must disclose the extent to which they lack knowledge or experience before accepting an assignment; they must explain the lack of knowledge or experience and the steps taken to compensate for these deficiencies; or they may employ qualified appraisers to assist in assignments where additional experience is recommended.

Limited exceptions to ethical standards allow certain departures from ethical guidelines, provided the proposed assignment is so limited that the resulting service would not mislead others, or the appraisal assignment, by its nature, requires less than strict observation of Uniform Standard guidelines.

Generally, *letters of opinion* are not accepted unless the appraiser can certify that the value conclusion is supported by reference to appraisal files and associated data on record and is available for examination. Appraisal updates are treated in the same manner.

POINTS TO REMEMBER

profession a profession is associated with extensive training, important social services, intellectual skills, a high degree of regulation, and considerable freedom in exercising professional judgments.

ethics a term that refers to moral right and wrong, duty and obligation, and moral responsibility.

appraisal ethics a term that refers to acceptable reports, "good" or "bad" market value estimates, and morally correct appraisal conduct.

chasing sales the practice of basing market value on the sale price of the property appraised.

directed appraisals the unethical practice of basing the market value estimate on values or conditions predetermined by the client.

appraisal conduct conduct which must not be unlawful, unethical, or improper according to Uniform Ethical Appraisal Standards.

misleading conduct conduct which is likely to mislead clients or the public, as prohibited by Uniform Appraisal Standards.

confidentiality because of their fiduciary relationship, appraisers must hold appraisal data in confidence. Only clients may release appraisers from this rule. The rule excepts third parties as required by law and authorized professional peer review committees.

appraisal competency rule the ethical rule that the appraiser must have the required knowledge and experience to make a competent real estate appraisal.

QUESTIONS FOR REVIEW

1. Explain why federal and state laws regulate the appraisal industry.

2. What are the main elements of a profession? In your view, are these elements typical of the appraisal industry? Why or why not? Give reasons for your answer.

3. Explain reasons why appraisers should observe ethical standards.

4. Give an example of appraisal conduct that would be unethical under the Uniform Appraisal Standards.

5. Describe appraisal assignments that violate management issues regulated by Uniform Ethical Appraisal Standards.

6. What steps are appraisers advised to take to comply with management ethical issues?

7. Why do the Uniform Appraisal Standards require that appraisals be held confidential? What are the exceptions to this rule?

8. Explain what is meant by the Appraisal Competency Rule. Give examples in illustration of your answer.

9. Give two examples of allowable exceptions to ethical appraisal standards.

CASE PROBLEMS

1. A national corporation purchased 5,360 acres of wetlands for $2 million. Because environmental protection laws prohibited planned development, the company donated the land to a government agency as a watershed. The company then hired a real estate appraiser to value the property as "a milled peat harvesting operation." The appraiser subsequently valued the land at $24 million for a corporate income tax deduction.

   Critically evaluate the ethics of this appraisal assignment. In your answer, consider whether the appraiser valued the property at the highest and best use and whether, from the facts as stated, the appraiser followed Uniform Standards of ethical appraisal practice. Give reasons for your answer.

2. Give an example of unethical appraisal practices for the four main violations of appraisal ethics under Uniform Appraisal Standards. Explain how you would revise appraisal practices to conform to the intent of the four main guidelines to Uniform Ethical Appraisal Standards. Explain thoroughly.

A P P E N D I X

Uniform Residential Appraisal Report
(Freddie Mac Form 70; Fannie Mae Form 1004)

The uniform residential appraisal report form is required by the Federal National Mortgage Association and the Federal Home Loan Mortgage Corporation. This form has also been adopted by the Veterans Administration, the Federal Housing Administration, and the Farmers Home Administration.

Properly completed, the form conforms to current appraisal standards. The form is sufficiently flexible to be universally used for single-family dwellings. Other forms are available for multiple-family dwellings and condominiums. Additional forms for photographs, floor plans, and added explanations are available. The two-page form (front and back), devotes the first page to descriptive data on the neighborhood, site, and building. The second page provides space for a building sketch, an estimate of the depreciated reproduction cost new, and the comparable sales analysis. On this page, the reconciliation and certificate of value require signatures of the appraiser and appraisal reviewer, if any.

For this appraisal example, explanations accompany each valuation section of the Uniform Residential Appraisal Report.

SUBJECT

This section of the report identifies the property appraised. The address of the property, the census tract, the legal description, name of owner or occupant, and map reference allow lenders and others to locate and review cited references. The source of information, real estate taxes, property rights, and certain lender information are provided.

SUBJECT				
Property Address 2468 Main Street		Census Tract 9911	LENDER DISCRETIONARY USE	
City Macon	County Bibb	State GA Zip Code 30501	Sale Price	$ 134,500
Legal Description Lot 99, Blk. 2, Hidden Harbor Subdivision			Date	4/91
Owner/Occupant Seller/Seller		Map Reference Q-6	Mortgage Amount	$ 108,000
Sale Price $ 134,500 Date of Sale 4/91		PROPERTY RIGHTS APPRAISED	Mortgage Type	conventional
Loan charges/concessions to be paid by seller $		[X] Fee Simple	Discount Points and Other Concessions	
R.E. Taxes $ 1,400 Tax Year 1990 HOA $/Mo. N/A		[ ] Leasehold	Paid by Seller	$ None
Lender/Client First Federal Mortgage Company		[ ] Condominium (HUD/VA)		
Information obtained from closing attorney		[ ] De Minimis PUD	Source First Federal	

Property Address

The subject area identifies the property. The property address must be sufficient to enable others to locate the property. Rural box numbers and post office box numbers are unacceptable. The location of the property should be identified if rural route numbers are necessary. The address, legal description, and map reference numbers, i.e., census tracts, zip codes, and map references, should be consistent with local tax records, the sales contract, and other documents. Current real estate taxes are obtained from local public tax records. For condominiums or planned unit developments, the home owners assessment (HOA) is stated as a monthly charge obtained from project offices. Note that the form states the property rights appraised, usually the fee simple estate.

Financing

The section on financing information is discretionary with the lender. The appraiser does not complete this portion of the report.

NEIGHBORHOOD

This portion of the report assumes critical importance to lenders. Accurately completed, lenders may be forewarned of potential mortgage risks by data of this section. The critical analysis of neighborhood factors, and their interpretation as indicated by comments added by the appraiser, leads to accurate mortgage risk assessment.

LOCATION		Urban		X	Suburban		Rural	NEIGHBORHOOD ANALYSIS	Good	Avg.	Fair	Poor
BUILT UP	X	Over 75%			25-75%		Under 25%	Employment Stability		X		
GROWTH RATE		Rapid		X	Stable		Slow	Convenience to Employment		X		
PROPERTY VALUES		Increasing		X	Stable		Declining	Convenience to Shopping		X		
DEMAND/SUPPLY		Shortage		X	In Balance		Over Supply	Convenience to Schools				X
MARKETING TIME		Under 3 Mos.		X	3-6 Mos.		Over 6 Mos.	Adequacy of Public Transportation		X		

PRESENT LAND USE	%	LAND USE CHANGE		PREDOMINANT OCCUPANCY		SINGLE FAMILY HOUSING PRICE $ (000)	AGE (yrs)	Recreation Facilities			X	
Single Family	98	Not Likely						Adequacy of Utilities	X			
2-4 Family		Likely		Owner	X			Property Compatibility	X			
Multi-family		In process	X	Tenant		$90 Low	New	Protection from Detrimental Cond.	X			
Commercial		To: Residential		Vacant (0-5%)	X	$300 High	10	Police & Fire Protection	X			
Industrial		from Rural		Vacant (over 5%)		Predominant		General Appearance of Properties	X			
Vacant	2					$175 —	7	Appeal to Market	X			

Note: Race or the racial composition of the neighborhood are not considered reliable appraisal factors.

COMMENTS: The subject property is not within walking distance of grade and high schools 5 miles north of the property. This does not affect value since school buses serve the area. Recreational facilities are few but typical of a suburban area and do not detract from market value.

Neighborhood Location

Location data conforms to the usual appraisal practice: *Urban* refers to a city location; a *suburban* location covers neighborhoods adjacent to a city, while the *rural* location includes areas outside suburban areas. While appraisers are not confined to statistical or census definitions, they must follow customary concepts in classifying residential property according to these categories.

Neighborhood Trends

The next five entries help lenders identify valuation trends, and therefore, mortgage risk. The appraiser indicates the degree or percent of neighborhood build-up. A neighborhood showing an over 25 percent rate of build-up may indicate a mature neighborhood with stable or even declining values. Similarly, a neighborhood listed as under 25 percent built-up, with a slow growth rate, probably indicates an unsuccessful, new subdivision. In contrast, a neighborhood built-up over 75 percent, with declining property values, warns lenders of possible high mortgage risks. Such a neighborhood may have reached the end of the neighborhood life cycle.

Conversely, a built-up rate under 25 percent with a rapid growth rate and increasing property values would be indicative of a favorable mortgage risk–especially if the appraiser indicates a supply shortage and a marketing time of less than three months.

In the present instance, the subdivision is 75 percent built-up with stable growth rates and property values, and with demand/supply in balance. The marketing time falls between three to six months. A review of this example suggests that the property appraised is in a subdivision nearing the peak of its life cycle. Expected values are stable where growth rates show no rapid rising nor declining values.

In short, this section requires that the appraiser provide data to judge the risk of a future decline in value and the probability that values will be rising or stable in the foreseeable future. The appraiser's judgment over location variables, in combination, helps third parties validate the market value estimate.

Neighborhood Analysis

This portion of the neighborhood section requires a personal value rating. *Fair or poor ratings require explanation in the neighborhood comment section.* The example indicates that poor convenience to schools is typical of a suburban area but is offset by the availability of school busing. The appraiser concludes that this lack of convenience to schools does not affect value. Similarly, the limited recreational facilities are explained as fairly typical of a suburban area and do not detract from market value.

It should be added that conventional practice follows the ratings as defined below:

Good: A good rating indicates that neighborhood characteristics are outstanding and superior to characteristics of competing neighborhoods.

Average: An average rating indicates that the neighborhood is equal to typical neighborhoods for the market area. An average neighborhood conforms to competing residential neighborhoods.

Fair: A fair rating indicates a neighborhood inferior to competing neighborhoods.

Poor: This rating shows a neighborhood substantially inferior to neighborhoods found in the local market. Such a rating indicates that the value of single-family dwellings are adversely affected by a poor neighborhood rating.

Present Land Use

The present land use, shown in percentages, indicates the property mix and possible encroachments. The appraiser indicates a vacancy rate so that the percentages add to 100. For example, a single-family dwelling neighborhood has a land use of 98 percent single-family dwellings and a vacancy rate of 2 percent, totaling 100 percent.

Other Neighborhood Factors

Here the appraiser judges the probability of land use change. In the example above, the appraiser indicates that the suburban location is in an area undergoing a transition from rural to residential suburban land. The predominant owner occupancy and low vacancy rate are indicative of suburban neighborhoods with low mortgage risks.

The price brackets show value ranges from the lowest value to the highest value. The typical values and housing age for each group give further insight into market value. An appraiser who estimates value above or below the stated ranges in value must explain the effect of nonconformity in the house appraised with neighborhood values. This section of the report indicates whether the house under value is an "over" or "under" improved dwelling.

Finally, the comments in the neighborhood section must provide further understanding of those facts that significantly bear, positively or negatively, on the appraised value. The appraiser indicates that the estimated market value is relatively free of detrimental factors and that favorable valuation trends support the estimated market value. These judgments are entered in the comment section.

SITE

The site section lists data that supports the highest and best-use estimate. Further, data entries indicate the degree to which the site is adapted to residential use. The example below illustrates these points.

Dimensions 204' x 233.3' x 180' x 190.6'						Topography	Above street grade
Site Area 0.93 acres; 40,511 square feet			Corner Lot No			Size	Typical of area
Zoning Classification Residential, single family			Zoning Compliance Subject complies			Shape	Rectangular
HIGHEST & BEST USE: Present Use Single family use			Other Use None			Drainage	Good from side to back
UTILITIES	Public	Other	SITE IMPROVEMENTS	Type	Public	Private	View Average
Electricity	X	Underground	Street	Asphalt	X		Landscaping Good
Gas	X	Natural	Curb/Gutter	Concrete	X		Driveway Concrete
Water	X	Municipal	Sidewalk	None			Apparent Easements None
Sanitary Sewer		Septic Tank	Street Lights	Mercury Vapor	X		FEMA Flood Hazard Yes* ___ No X
Storm Sewer	X	to Oconee River	Alley	None			FEMA* Map/Zone N/A
COMMENTS (Apparent adverse easements, encroachments, special assessments, slide areas, etc.): Wooded lot; well landscaped. No adverse easements or encroachments or other detrimental conditions noted.							

Site Data

The dimensions for an irregularly shaped lot lists lot dimensions starting with the street frontage. The example shows a total square-foot area of .93 acres, or 40,511 square feet. The highest and best use estimate shows that the dwelling conforms to the single-family dwelling zoning classification.

Site characteristics include available utilities and other site improvements. Note that the appraiser lists the topography, size, shape, and drainage characteristics. The view, landscaping, driveway, and easements observed are listed in this portion of the report. In the present case no apparent adverse easements, encroachments, or other detrimental conditions were noted.

Deficiencies in the site would be explained in the comment portion of this section. If the property is in a flood hazard area, the map and zone number would be entered. The flood hazard reference refers to the map area as designated by the Federal Emergency Management Agency (FEMA). Flood insurance is required if the property is in a flood hazard area designated by zones: A, AO, AH, A1-30, A-99, V or V1-30. These zones and map areas are shown in Flood Insurance Rate Maps (FIRM) obtained from the Flood Map Distribution Center, Baltimore, Maryland, or their local agents.

IMPROVEMENTS

The improvements are described according to a general description and to descriptions of the exterior, foundation, basement, and insulation. The appraisal form provides information for brief entries.

GENERAL DESCRIPTION		EXTERIOR DESCRIPTION		FOUNDATION		BASEMENT		INSULATION		
Units	1	Foundation	Poured Concrete	Slab	No	Area Sq. Ft.	1,344	Roof	Good	X
Stories	1	Exterior Walls	Masonite	Crawl Space	No	% Finished	576 s.f.	Ceiling	Good	X
Type (Det./Att.)	Detached	Roof Surface	Asph/Shingle	Basement	100%	Ceiling	7'	Walls	Good	X
Design (Style)	Ranch	Gutters & Dwnspts.	Aluminum	Sump Pump	No	Walls	Plasterboard	Floor	Good	X
Existing	X	Window Type	Casement	Dampness	None	Floor	Vinyl Tile	None		
Proposed	–	Storm Sash	Thermopane	Settlement	None	Outside Entry	Rear	Adequacy	Good	X
Under Construction	–	Screens	Inside	Infestation	None	entrance; basement		Energy Efficient Items:		
Age (Yrs.)	10	Manufactured House	No			room used as study		Recommended "R"		
Effective Age (Yrs.)	8							Values		

General Description

The general description portion shows the character of the dwelling unit. Since the form covers one-to-four family units, the general description identifies the number of residential units appraised. The number of stories and whether the property is detached or attached (row house) indicates the type of dwelling appraised. The design or style falls in broad categories—typically, ranch, contemporary, bungalow, Spanish stucco, and other locally recognized dwelling architecture.

Detail for other building components shows whether additional explanation is required. *Deficiencies in these areas require special comment.* For example, dampness in the foundation or basement or foundation settlement would require detailed explanation. Similarly, finished basement rooms of less than the standard square-foot area (100 square feet) or ceilings of less than seven feet require explanation.

The part on insulation would include R values if known. R values rate the thermal efficiency of insulation or building materials. These values are available from building suppliers and contractors. Minimum recommended R values depend on climatic zones designated by geographic regions.

Entries for the actual and effective age indicate building condition. If the appraiser indicates an effective age that closely approximates actual age, the building would be well-maintained. A building with an effective age of 15 years and an actual age of 10 years indicates poor maintenance. *The lender requires appraisal comments and explanations of the discrepancy between actual and effective age.* An effective age considerably less than the actual age would result from remodeling or rehabilitation which corrects for obsolete design and worn out building components.

ROOM LIST

The room list identifies rooms by floor level and basement areas. The form requires the number of square feet of heated, enclosed space (outside dimensions).

ROOMS	Foyer	Living	Dining	Kitchen	Den	Family Rm.	Rec. Rm.	Bedrooms	# Baths	Laundry	Other	Area Sq. Ft.
Basement							study				Gar.	1,344
Level 1	1	1	Combo	1				3	2	1		1,344
Level 2												
Finished area **above** grade contains:	7		Rooms;	3		Bedroom(s);	2		Bath(s);	1,344	Square Feet of Gross Living Area	

The room list identifies rooms common to single-family dwellings. The last category, "other," provides for enclosed space such as studies or other special purpose rooms not listed in Form 70. Space is provided for additional floors above the second floor.

It should be noted that rooms entered in this section of the report must conform to typical, minimum room requirements—mainly, a minimum area of 100 square feet including closet space and minimum clear ceilings of seven feet. Space that does not conform to these standards would be listed as storage space for valuation purposes.

INTERIOR AND AUTOS

The section identifies interior surfaces, auto storage, and building equipment. Since the arrangement for automobiles varies widely, special entries are required for automobile storage. Finally, this section of the report includes an improvement analysis with a rating system similar to the rating given neighborhoods. These examples follow.

SURFACES	Materials/Condition	HEATING		KITCHEN EQUIP.		ATTIC		IMPROVEMENT ANALYSIS	Good	Avg.	Fair	Poor
INTERIOR Floors	Carpet/Wood Good	Type	Hot water	Refrigerator	X	None	X	Quality of Construction		X		
Walls	Drywall/Good	Fuel	Oil	Range/Oven	X	Stairs		Condition of Improvements		X		
Trim/Finish	Wood Trim/Average	Condition	Good	Disposal	X	Drop Stair		Room Sizes/Layout	X			
Bath Floor	Vinyl Floor/Ave.	Adequacy	Yes	Dishwasher		Scuttle		Closets and Storage	X			
Bath Wainscot	Shower only/Ave.	COOLING	Yes	Fan/Hood	X	Floor		Energy Efficiency	X			
Doors	Hollow Core/Ave.	Central	Yes	Compactor		Heated		Plumbing-Adequacy & Condition	X			
Bathroom Linen Closet/Ave. quality		Other		Washer/Dryer	X	Finished		Electrical-Adequacy & Condition	X			
		Condition		Microwave	X			Kitchen Cabinets-Adequacy & Cond.	X			
Fireplace(s)	#	Adequacy		Intercom				Compatibility to Neighborhood	X			
AUTOS CAR STORAGE:	Garage X	Attached		Adequate	X	House Entry		Appeal & Marketability	X			
No. Cars 1	Carport	Detached		Inadequate		Outside Entry		Estimated Remaining Economic Life	60			Yrs.
Condition Ave.	None	Built-In	X	Electric Door	X	Basement Entry	X	Estimated Remaining Physical Life	60			Yrs.

The section on interior surfaces applies to the walls and floors including bathrooms. The trim and its finish and the type of doors and fireplaces cover important value determining features. The type of heating and air conditioning systems and their adequacy is listed under the heating section.

The area for *kitchen equipment* requires special comment. The appraiser indicates the availability of refrigerators, sink disposals, dishwashers, washer/dryers, and microwave ovens. These items may be personal property included in the appraisal or fixtures specially adapted to the dwelling. Ordinarily, kitchen equipment does not have a contributory value if appliances are more than three to five years old. Older equipment in this category, while listed in the appraisal report, may have nominal value. Good-quality kitchen equipment of less than three years, in excellent condition, may warrant an added value as explained by the appraiser under comments to this section.

Because of the wide variation among attics, the form provides space for appraisers to indicate finished attic rooms and their access. The type of automobile storage is identified according to the number of cars. A garage or carport of unusually narrow dimensions or inappropriate for the house appraised deserves explanation.

These judgments are summarized in the *improvement analysis rating*. The quality of construction allows the appraiser to rate the property according to the quality of materials. Space is allowed for an evaluation of present building condition. Other elements affecting building utility are listed in the rating improvement analysis—for example, the room sizes and layout, and the adequacy of closets and storage. Other building systems are similarly judged—energy efficiency, the electrical system, and kitchen cabinets.

Finally, the appraiser must indicate how the dwelling conforms to the neighborhood. Note also that if the dwelling lacks current marketability because of depressed market conditions, this fact would be *explained under the comment section*. The data on the remaining economic and physical life relates to property in poor repair or property which has been extensively remodeled.

COMMENTS

The comment section allows the appraiser to list additional features not accounted for by the appraisal form.

COMMENTS	Additional features: _Exterior and interior materials and condition conform to neighborhood. An unroofed deck, 15' X 30'_ _sets above_
	Depreciation (Physical, functional and external inadequacies, repairs needed, modernization, etc.):
	General market conditions and prevalence and impact in subject/market area regarding loan discounts, interest buydowns and concessions:

Since most appraisal reports cover existing properties, lenders and others expect a statement from the appraiser on observed depreciation and how it was estimated. Space is provided for describing current market conditions, including the effect of loan discounts, interest buydowns, and other marketing concessions. This part of the report allows the appraiser to distinguish between sale prices and favorable credit terms.

COST APPROACH

This portion of the appraisal report, starting on the second page, provides for a building sketch showing the gross living area above grade and the estimated reproduction cost of improvements. This section requires an estimate of the indicated value under the cost approach, and other data important to property standards and construction of warranties.

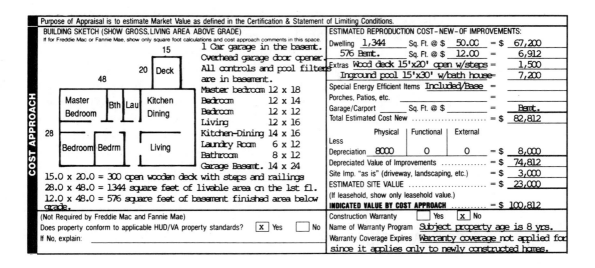

Purpose of Appraisal is to estimate Market Value as defined in the Certification & Statement of Limiting Conditions.

COST APPROACH	
BUILDING SKETCH (SHOW GROSS, LIVING AREA ABOVE GRADE)	**ESTIMATED REPRODUCTION COST-NEW-OF IMPROVEMENTS:**

BUILDING SKETCH (SHOW GROSS, LIVING AREA ABOVE GRADE)

If for Freddie Mac or Fannie Mae, show only square foot calculations and cost approach comments in this space.

1 Car garage in the basement. Overhead garage door opener. All controls and pool filters are in basement.

Master bedroom 12 x 18
Bedroom 12 x 14
Bedroom 12 x 12
Living 12 x 16
Kitchen-Dining 14 x 16
Laundry Room 6 x 12
Bathroom 8 x 12
Garage Basemt. 14 x 24

15.0 x 20.0 = 300 open wooden deck with steps and railings
28.0 x 48.0 = 1344 square feet of livable area on the 1st fl.
12.0 x 48.0 = 576 square feet of basement finished area below grade.

(Not Required by Freddie Mac and Fannie Mae)

Does property conform to applicable HUD/VA property standards? [x] Yes [ ] No

If No, explain: _____

ESTIMATED REPRODUCTION COST-NEW-OF IMPROVEMENTS:

Dwelling	1,344	Sq. Ft. @ $ 50.00	= $	67,200
	576 Bsmt.	Sq. Ft. @ $ 12.00	=	6,912
Extras	Wood deck 15'x20' open w/steps		=	1,500
	Inground pool 15'x30' w/bath house		=	7,200
Special Energy Efficient Items	Included/Base		=	
Porches, Patios, etc.			=	
Garage/Carport	Sq. Ft. @ $		=	Bsmt.
Total Estimated Cost New	....		= $	82,812

	Physical	Functional	External	
Less				
Depreciation	8000	0	0	= $ 8,000

Depreciated Value of Improvements	....	= $ 74,812
Site Imp. "as is" (driveway, landscaping, etc.)		= $ 3,000
ESTIMATED SITE VALUE	....	= $ 23,000
(If leasehold, show only leasehold value.)		
INDICATED VALUE BY COST APPROACH	....	= $ 100,812

Construction Warranty	[ ] Yes	[x] No
Name of Warranty Program	Subject property age is 8 yrs.	
Warranty Coverage Expires	Warranty coverage not applied for since it applies only to newly constructed homes.	

The Building Sketch

An appraisal prepared for the Federal National Mortgage Corporation or The Federal National Association shows only the square-foot gross living area calculation. Building sketches must be attached to supplemental sheets. For others, the building sketch shows the floor plan and calculation of the total gross living area.

Estimated Reproduction Cost of Improvements

Certain special requirements cover the reproduction cost new estimate. For appraisals of new buildings, the Department of Housing and Urban Development does not require this section to be completed; only the estimated value of the site is shown. In this case, for new construction and buildings of less than one year old, appraisers complete and attach the Marshal and Swift Appraisal Form 1007 to Form 70. For appraisals submitted to the Federal National Mortgage Association, a typical site value for the neighborhood must include an explanation of how the noncomparable site value affects marketability.

Estimated Reproduction Costs

The cost-new estimate per square foot should agree with the local market. Likewise, the land value should agree with comparable land sales and should show a land-building value ratio typical of the locality.

The appraisal form shows the estimated replacement or reproduction cost new as of the date of the appraisal. For extra items, the appraiser must add for energy-efficient construction, porches, patios, and in this case, a swimming pool. Since the present house is only eight years old, the appraiser deducted a lump sum allowance for physical depreciation. The depreciated improvement cost is added to the site value to give the reproduction cost new, less depreciation for the property appraised.

SALES COMPARISON ANALYSIS

Probably the most critical section of the appraisal report, the sales comparison analysis, includes sufficient detail on three comparable sales which are compared directly to the property appraised. Additional comments allow appraisers to expand on the indicated value under the comparable sales approach.

Sales Comparisons

While the appraisal report requires a minimum of three comparable sales, additional sales may be listed on continuation sheets for added market value support. Preferably, the sales should be completed within the last three months. Reasons for relying on sales of more than six months deserve explanation.

There is a further problem of the proximity of comparable sales to the property appraised. Generally speaking, if the comparable sale is more than one mile from the subject property, the appraiser must explain why such comparable sales were used. Regulations generally provide, therefore, that comparable property should be located near the subject property, recently sold, and that the sales selected have been completed and closed. Real estate listings or offers to sell are generally not allowable.

The undersigned has recited three recent sales of properties most similar and proximate to subject and has considered these in the market analysis. The description includes a dollar adjustment, reflecting market reaction to those items of significant variation between the subject and comparable properties. If a significant item in the comparable property is superior to, or more favorable than, the subject property, a minus (−) adjustment is made, thus reducing the indicated value of subject; if a significant item in the comparable is inferior to, or less favorable than, the subject property, a plus (+) adjustment is made, thus increasing the indicated value of the subject.

ITEM	SUBJECT	COMPARABLE NO. 1	+ (−) $ Adjustment	COMPARABLE NO. 2	+ (−) $ Adjustment	COMPARABLE NO. 3	+ (−) $ Adjustment
Address	2468 Main St. Macon, GA	33 High St., Macon, GA Slr. R. Simpson to J.Murphy		100 East St., Macon, GA Slr. R.Clark to J.Carbine		74 Elm St., Macon, GA Slr. K.Woods to M.Hall	
Proximity to Subject		.7 miles to subject prop.		1 mile to subject property		.5 miles to subject prop.	
Sales Price	$ 100,000	$ 106,000		$ 101,500		$ 101,000	
Price/Gross Liv. Area	$ 74.00	$ 106.00		$ 67.67		$ 75.15	
Data Source	Sales Agreement	Personal Inspection		Personal Inspection		Personal Inspection	
VALUE ADJUSTMENTS	DESCRIPTION	DESCRIPTION	+ (−) $ Adjustment	DESCRIPTION	+ (−) $ Adjustment	DESCRIPTION	+ (−) $ Adjustment
Sales or Financing Concessions		Conventional None Known		Conventional None Known		Conventional None Known	
Date of Sale/Time	April 30, 1991	March, 1991		March, 1991		March, 1991	
Location	Average to Good	Equal		Equal		Equal	
Site/View	103 x 150 Avg.	2 Acres Excellt	−8000	100 x 150 Avg.		120 x 130 Equal	
Design and Appeal	Ranch Average	Ranch Average		Ranch Average		Ranch Average	
Quality of Construction	Avg.Wood Frame	Avg.Wood Frame		Avg. Wood Frame		Avg.Wood Frame	
Age	10 years	10 years		9 years		11 years	
Condition	Average to Good	Average	+2000	Average to Good		Average	+2000
Above Grade Room Count	Total 7 / Bdrms 3 / Baths 1	Total 6 / Bdrms 3 / Baths 1		Total 7 / Bdrms 3 / Baths 1		Total 6 / Bdrms 3 / Baths 1	
Gross Living Area	1344 Sq. Ft.	1000 Sq. Ft.	+3000	1500 Sq. Ft.	−2000	1344 Sq. Ft.	
Basement & Finished Rooms Below Grade	Rec.Rm.or Office 576 Square Feet	Equal 1000 Square Feet	−1000	Inferior	+4000	Equal 1000 Square Ft.	−1000
Functional Utility	Average	Equal		Equal		Equal	
Heating/Cooling	Oil Forced H/W	Equal		Equal		Hot Air Heating	+1500
Garage/Carport	1 Car In Basemt.	2 Car Detached	−4000	1 Car Attached	−3000	2 Car Detached	−4000
Porches, Patio, Pools, etc.	Deck 15x20 Open 15x30 Inground	Equal Inferior	+3000	Equal 15x30 Inground		Equal Inferior	+3000
Special Energy Efficient Items	Thermopane wind. Full Insulation	Equal Equal		Equal Equal		Equal Equal	
Fireplace(s)	None	Equal		Equal		Equal	
Other (e.g. kitchen equip., remodeling)	400'Drilled Well Domestic Hot/Wtr	Equal Equal		Equal Equal		Equal Equal	
Net Adj. (total)		− $ 5,000		− $ 1,000		+ $ 1,500	
Indicated Value of Subject		$ 101,000		$ 100,500		$ 102,500	

SALES COMPARISON ANALYSIS

Comments on Sales Comparison: The comparables used in the above report were considered to be the most compatible ones at this time and best indications of value of the subject property. Please note the proximity of the comparables to the subject is within 1 mile. It should also be noted that the appraiser made an inspection of the three comparables.

Financing Concessions

Financing concessions include below-market interest-rate mortgages, interest-rate buydowns, loan discount points, loan origination fees, and other concessions granted by the seller. The critical question relates to how typical concessions are negotiated in the current market. Some concessions are normal-to-market negotiations. Other exceptionally large sales concessions may lead to sales price distortions.

In this regard, the appraiser adjusts sales to show differences between what the comparable sales actually sold for *with sales concessions* and what they would have sold for *without sales concessions.* In short, no adjustments to sale prices are necessary for those costs which are normally paid sellers in the local market. The appraiser considers comparable sales that sold for all cash or with cash-equivalent financing—if they are the best indicators of value.

Sales Adjustments

In making adjustments, appraisers follow certain standard rules:

1. The property sold is adjusted to the sale on a percentage basis rounded to the closest $100, $500, or $1,000. Adjustments are based on market data as documented by the market evidence.
2. Adjustments to each comparable sale that are *superior* to the property appraised are adjusted with a *negative* dollar adjustment; all comparable sale items *inferior* to the property appraised are adjusted upward with a *positive* dollar adjustment.
3. Appraisers avoid excessive adjustments. Generally, large adjustments indicate noncomparable sales. As a rule, total gross adjustments should not exceed 25 percent of the comparable sales price. Individual adjustments generally must not be greater than 10 percent of the sales price.

Form 70 provides space for 17 sales adjustments. To expedite the adjustment process, the subject property with its 17 characteristics is listed for each comparable sale. In this example, the property appraised sold for $100,000 which is equal to $74.00 per square foot of living area. The date of sale, the data source, and location serve as a basis for making sales comparisons.

Following the rule that the comparable sales should be selected for the least number of sales adjustments, it will be noted that the first required adjustment is made for the two acres of Sale One. Because this is a *superior* feature, the appraiser has *deducted* $8,000 for the difference in land area which is within the 10 percent maximum adjustment allowance.

The appraiser considers the property appraised as average to good condition, which for the average condition of comparable Sale One calls for an *upward* adjustment of $2,000. The same relationship applies for the 1,000 square feet of the property sold (comparable Sale One) which, compared to the property appraised, requires another adjustment of $3,000. Differences in the 1,000 square feet of basement finished rooms relatively to the 576 feet of the subject justifies a *downward* adjustment of $1,000. Again, the superior feature of a two-car detached garage compared to a one-car basement garage justifies a *negative* downward adjustment of $4,000 for comparable Sale One. To account for the added value of the deck and pool, the appraiser has adjusted Sale One upwards by $3,000. In this instance, therefore, after adjustment, the $106,000 sale of comparable Sale One indicates a value of $101,000 for the property appraised.

Comparable Sale Two, calling for a net adjustment of $1,000 to a sale of $101,500, indicates a value of $100,500. Note that for comparable Sale Two, the one-car attached garage has a lower sales adjustment relative to the two-car detached garage of comparable Sale One. Such an adjustment seems reasonable in view of these facts. Note also that Sale Two is equivalent with respect to the swimming pool which further justifies the pool allowance of comparable Sale One.

Comparable Sale Three, within one-half mile of the subject property, has a less favorable condition and has hot-air heating rather than the oil-forced hot-water heating of the property appraised; and no swimming pool or deck requires a positive adjustment of $6,500. After making negative adjustments for the added square foot area in the basement and the two-car detached garage, net adjustments for comparable Sale Three are $1,500, giving an indicated value of $102,500.

Normally, the appraiser would select real estate sales that show lower and higher values than the estimated value of the property appraised. In this instance, however, the sales prices closely approximate the property valued; they are sold within the last 60 days, and they are within one mile of the property appraised. Further, the comparable sales approximate the age of the property valued. Therefore, though the sales prices are not "bracketed" around the property appraised, they require only reasonable net adjustments and strongly support the estimated market value.

These facts are noted in the comment section of the sales comparison. Comments on the sales comparison approach should support comparable sales adjustment. In the case at hand, the appraiser has noted that each of the three comparables is within one mile of the property appraised. The appraiser indicates that information on comparable sales was secured from a personal, interior and exterior inspection. The indicated value by the sales comparison approach listed at the end of this section gives the appraiser's final opinion of value under the sales comparison approach.

The example further shows that the estimated market approach, using the monthly gross income multiplier of 125 and a rent of $800 a month equals an indicated value of $100,000.

RECONCILIATION

In the final section, under the reconciliation section, the appraiser "reconciles" each approach to value in making the *final estimate of market value*. The comments provide a concise summation of appraisal conclusions.

INDICATED VALUE BY SALES COMPARISON APPROACH	$ 100,500
INDICATED VALUE BY INCOME APPROACH (If Applicable) Estimated Market Rent $ __800__ /Mo. x Gross Rent Multiplier __125.00__ = $ 100,000	

This appraisal is made [X] "as is" [ ] subject to the repairs, alterations, inspections or conditions listed below [ ] completion per plans and specifications.

Comments and Conditions of Appraisal: The subject is a one story home with 7 rooms, 3 bedrooms and 1 bath. It is typical of many in the area. Maintenance & repairs = $20 mo. Heat and utilities = $125 mo. Real Estate Taxes = $125 mo.

Final Reconciliation: The most weight was given to comparable #2, the $100,500 estimate, due to the lowest percentage of adjustments. This estimate is well supported by the cost and income approach estimates. The largest adjustment was on comparable #1, $8000, for two acres of land. The dwelling on comparable #1 was in center of lot, no subdivision.

This appraisal is based upon the above requirements, the certification, contingent and limiting conditions, and Market Value definition that are stated in

[X] FmHA, HUD &/or VA instructions.

[ ] Freddie Mac Form 439 (Rev. 7/86)/Fannie Mae Form 1004B (Rev. 7/86) filed with client __April 30,__ 19 __91__ [X] attached.

I (WE) ESTIMATE THE MARKET VALUE, AS DEFINED, OF THE SUBJECT PROPERTY AS OF __April 30,__ 19 __91__ to be $ 100,500

I (We) certify: that to the best of my (our) knowledge and belief the facts and data used herein are true and correct; that I (we) personally inspected the subject property, both inside and out, and have made an exterior inspection of all comparable sales cited in this report; and that I (we) have no undisclosed interest, present or prospective therein.

Appraiser(s) SIGNATURE *John Doe*   Review Appraiser SIGNATURE _____ [ ] Did [ ] Did Not
NAME John Doe, SRA   (if applicable) NAME   Inspect Property

In the final reconciliation statement, the appraiser in the illustration above explains that the second comparable sale is given the greatest weight since this sale requires the least net percentage adjustments. The appraiser further explains that the final value of estimate is strongly supported by the cost and income approach estimates. Note further that the $8,000 adjustment under comparable Sale One is explained as the result of the larger two-acre land site. In the final statement of market value, the appraiser provides the date of valuation and the final value estimate which is verified by the appraiser's written and typed signature. Space is provided for signature and name of the review appraiser.

In short, Form 70 gives a concise and current description of the neighborhood, the site, buildings, the final market value estimate, and the marketability of the property appraised. The end result provides the market value estimate: not more than the market value and not less than the market value.

G L O S S A R Y

A

adjusted cost basis the original cost, less accumulated depreciation taken over the investment holding period.

age-life depreciation depreciation based on a proportion of the estimated cost. The proportion is based on the present age relative to the expected age. Both the present and expected age are variously defined for specific purposes.

air rights the right to use air space above the land surface.

allocation technique a method of valuing sites by applying the prevailing land/building ratio to properties of known value.

ambiguous conclusions conclusions in which more than one conclusion follows from the evidence.

amenities the intangible benefits of home ownership.

amortized mortgages mortgages that provide for monthly payments that cover partial payment of principal and interest payments on the remaining mortgage balance.

annual debt service monthly mortgage payment times 12. Annual debt service includes the total annual mortgage interest and principal payments.

annual gross income annual gross income that would be earned if the property were fully occupied.

anticipation a principle that refers to prices as an expression of the present worth of the future benefits of ownership.

appraisal competency rule the ethical rule that the appraiser must have the required knowledge and experience to make a competent real estate appraisal.

appraisal conduct conduct which must not be unlawful, unethical, or improper according to Uniform Ethical Appraisal Standards.

appraisal ethics a term that refers to acceptable reports, "good" or "bad" market value estimates, and morally correct appraisal conduct.

Appraisal Foundation a nonprofit corporation originally chartered by eight national appraisal organizations to promote "uniform standards of professional appraisal procedure."

appraisal process a procedure that appraisers follow in providing appraisal reports that conform to a standard, logical format.

Appraisal Qualifications Board a board appointed by the Appraisal Foundation to study and recommend education, experience, examinations, licensing, and certification of appraisers.

appraisal report an unbiased written estimate of value.

Appraisal Standards Board a board appointed by the Appraisal Foundation to establish and improve standards of professional appraisal practice.

Appraisal Subcommittee the Committee includes the Board of Governors of the Federal Reserve System, the Federal Deposit Insurance Corporation, the National Credit Union Administration, the Office of the Comptroller of Currency, the Office of Thrift Supervision, and the Resolution Trust Corporation.

arithmetic mean the sum of each value divided by its number.

asbestos natural minerals that separate into strong and very fine fibers that are heat-resistant and extremely durable.

assessed value the value determined by the tax assessor for property tax purposes.

assessment discrimination the over- or underassessment of taxable property for property tax purposes.

avigation easements the right to use air space above the glide path extending from airport runways.

B

back-land theory the concept in which frontage taken for a right-of-way is assumed to have the value of the rear portion of the property.

balloon mortgages mortgages that require a lump sum payment at the date of maturity.

band-of-investment a method of estimating capitalization rates by calculating the weighted average of mortgage yields and the yield on the equity interest.

base year the calendar year in which the lease is executed.

break-even point the sum of the annual debt service and annual operating expenses divided by the annual gross income.

building codes local regulations that enforce minimum building materials and construction standards in the interest of public safety.

building life building life may be actual age—the number of years from the date of construction to the present; or the economic life—the period over which improvements contribute to market value.

building residual capitalization a method of allocating income to land and capitalizing the remaining income to the building. The sum of the building value and land value equals the estimated market value.

bundle of rights a concept that treats real estate ownership as a collection of numerous property rights, much like a bundle of sticks.

C

cash equivalent value a sales price that has been adjusted for below-market financing.

chasing sales the practice of basing market value on the sales price of the property appraised.

colinearity the tendency of two property characteristics to occur together.

community property a right granted by selected states that treats property acquired by either spouse during marriage as community property belonging to both persons as co-owners. Community property does not include the right of survivorship.

comparable sales recent sales of land and buildings that are reasonably similar to the property under valuation.

composite tax rate a local property tax rate consisting of the sum of tax rates separately levied by local agencies.

comprehensive zoning codes zoning codes that regulate building bulk, minimum building standards, and land- use districts.

comprehensive (general) plans general plans coordinate public and private agencies in developing land for recreation, public, commercial, and industrial use.

concurrent ownership joint ownership by two or more persons.

condominium bylaws regulations that establish management rules and condominium authority.

condominium interest a fee interest in a condominium unit and an undivided interest in common elements. Common elements include land and other improvements with use-rights shared with other condominium owners.

condominium ownership ownership in a unit with an individual interest in the common elements.

confidentiality because of their fiduciary relationship, appraisers must hold appraisal data in confidence. Only clients may release appraisers from this rule. The rule excepts third parties as required by law and authorized professional peer review committees.

consequential damage payments for the decrease in value of real estate, no part of which was taken for public purposes.

contract rent rent determined by a lease.

cooperative ownership a nonprofit corporation that issues ownership shares equal in value to a given unit. Cooperative owners acquire possession under a proprietary lease granting exclusive use and occupancy of a selected unit.

corner influence an increment in value assigned to a corner lot.

cost approach a market value estimate derived from the sum of the estimated land value and the depreciated building cost.

cost indexing a method of estimating the current cost of construction by multiplying original cost by a cost index showing the change in construction costs from the original date of construction to the present.

curtesy a life estate granted to husbands on real estate owned by the wife during marriage.

D

debt-coverage ratio the annual net operating income divided by the annual debt service.

declaration the instrument that creates a condominium entity.

deductive logic reasoning from a general principle to a specific case.

deductive reasoning the process of reasoning from the general case to the specific case.

deed restrictions restrictions placed on land use by the seller as a condition of sale.

deficiency judgment a personal judgment granted if proceeds of a foreclosure sale do not satisfy the mortgage debt.

demand a schedule of increasing quantities that buyers would take at the same time at a series of decreasing prices.

demographic data population characteristics showing expansion or decline and pressures that determine trends.

depreciated book value the book value less the accrued depreciation allowable for accounting purposes.

depreciation a loss in value from any cause; the loss in value is equal to the difference in value between the property under appraisal and the value of a new, substitute building.

descriptive statistics measures of central tendency and their dispersion.

development rights rights to convert vacant land to urban use according to allowable building densities.

directed appraisals the unethical practice of basing the market value estimate on values or conditions predetermined by the client.

dollar adjustments dollar adjustments in the sale price to account for differences between the property sold and the property appraised.

dominant estate an interest of the person benefited by an easement.

dower rights the interest of the surviving wife in land acquired by the husband during marriage.

due on sale clauses the right of the lender to payment of a debt on sale or transfer of real estate.

dwelling services the division of single-family dwellings into three functional areas—the sleeping area, the living area, and the service area.

E

easement a nonpossessory interest to use property for a specific purpose.

easement by condemnation a right held by state-regulated utilities and government agencies to acquire easements for right-of-way or other public use.

easement by necessity an easement created to allow access to a public road.

easement by prescription an easement acquired without written permission, provided requirements of state law are met.

easement by reservation an easement

created by a conveyance instrument that reserves the right to an easement.

economic base the sum of all human activity engaged in earning a living.

economic building life the time in which a building has no economic value.

effective age the age indicated by the present building condition.

effective buying income personal income, less personal taxes and nontax payments (disposable or after-tax income).

effective gross income annual gross income less annual vacancies and bad debts.

effective gross income multiplier (EGIM) the ratio of effective gross income, less vacancies and bad debts, to sales price.

electric transmission line easement the right to erect, construct, operate, and maintain electric transmission lines over private property.

eminent domain the right of government agencies and regulated public utilities to take private property in the public interest.

encroachments a building, fence, wall, or other improvement that extends over the property of another.

equity dividend rate the yield on the equity interest. It is also called the cash-on-cash return.

equity of redemption the right of the borrower to redeem the mortgage before foreclosure by paying the full amount of the debt, including interest and expenses of the lender.

escalation clauses clauses that adjust rents for increases in selected expenses or for the total annual operating expenses.

escheat the power of the state to take property of a deceased person without a will or legal heirs.

escrow funds funds collected monthly by the lender to pay yearly taxes, hazard insurance premiums, and monthly mortgage insurance premiums.

estate for years a leasehold estate that continues for a definite period of time.

ethics a term that refers to moral right and wrong, duty and obligation, and moral responsibility.

excess rent rent that exceeds market rent.

external obsolescence the loss in value caused by forces unrelated to the property appraised—an external cause.

extraction method a method of valuing sites by subtracting the building "contributory value" from the property value.

F

federally related transaction a real estate transaction in which a federal institution or agency or the Resolution Trust Corporation engages in contracts for the sale, lease, purchase, financing, investment, or exchange of real property.

fee simple absolute the maximum ownership in real estate that conveys title over the life of the owner. It may be inherited without restriction.

fee simple determinable an estate that terminates on the occurrence of a known event.

FHA-insured mortgages mortgages insured by the Federal Housing Administration.

fixed expenses expenses that do not vary with the occupancy rate.

fixture an article, which was formerly personal property, permanently installed or attached to land or buildings.

flowage easements the right to flood private property for flood control or water reservoirs.

forecast an estimate of future events derived from past data modified according to current conditions.

foregone opportunities opportunity costs in which costs are equal to foregone alternative opportunities.

freehold estates an interest in land for an indefinite period.

functional obsolescence the loss in value resulting from changes in style or design.

functional obsolescence, curable the loss in value equal to the cost of remedying functional obsolescence.

functional obsolescence, incurable the loss in value which is not feasible to correct. It is estimated by capitalizing the rental loss caused by functional obsolescence, incurable.

future value factor (FVF) the amount one dollar increases at a given interest rate over a given period, earning compound interest.

future value of an annuity factor (FVAF) the sum an ordinary annuity accumulates, assuming that periodic payments are invested at a given interest rate.

G

general data a part of the preliminary analysis which includes appraisal data of a region, city, or neighborhood.

government rectangular survey system a method of identifying land by reference to principal meridians and base lines.

graduated leases leases in which rents vary at stated intervals over the lease.

gross capitalization rate the reciprocal of the gross income multiplier.

gross income multiplier (GIM) the relation between annual gross income and selling price expressed as a ratio. Property sold for $10,000,000 with a current annual gross income of $1,200,000 illustrates a GIM of 8.3 ($10,000,000/$1,200,000).

gross leases leases in which the landlord assumes all net operating expenses.

gross living area square-foot floor area indicated by the outside dimensions of heated areas.

gross possible income annual gross income assuming full occupancy. This term is also known as the *gross potential income.*

ground lease a lease covering land only leased to tenants who construct buildings on leased land.

ground rent net annual rent for vacant land which may be capitalized to estimate site value.

H

highest and best use the use which is reasonably probable and legally permissible and must prove physically possible and economically feasible. The highest and best use results in the highest land value.

homestead right limited protection granted by selected states to protect the family home from creditors.

housing codes local regulations that keep minimum occupancy standards and a minimum quality of housing.

I

implied easement an easement created by the nature of a right-of-way which is implied by observation and use.

improved land land improved with building structures or other land developments, including leveling, drainage, curbs, paving, and the like.

inclusionary zoning zoning in which zoning approval requires developers to build a certain proportion of housing for low- or middle-income groups.

income approach the estimated market value equal to the present value of an annual net income.

inconsistent conclusions conclusions, drawn from the given facts, which are not true.

index leases leases that adjust rent according to changes in the selected price index.

inductive logic a process of reasoning from repeated observations to the general case.

installment of one factor (MC) a factor that gives the payment necessary to repay a debt of one dollar at a given interest rate and a given number of repayments.

insurable value the reproduction cost new, less the cost of the foundation and less the cost of building plans.

interim use a temporary use prevailing until a more intensive use is economically justified.

intermediate lien theory states states which establish mortgages as liens on the borrower's title. On default, the title passes to the lender.

internal rate of return (IRR) the yield rate which equates discounted after-tax cash flow with the equity interest.

interval ownership an undivided fee simple interest to each purchaser of a condominium as a tenant-in-common.

J

joint tenancy ownership by two or more persons who have a unity of interest and title and who have acquired property at the same time. Joint tenancy includes the right of survivorship.

just compensation payment for the taking of private property by government agencies or regulated public utilities for public purposes.

L

land residual capitalization capitalization by allocating income to the building and capitalizing the remaining income to the land. The sum of the building value and land value equals the estimated market value.

leased fee estate the interest held by the lessor.

leasehold interest the interest held by the tenant-lessee.

lessee the tenant who holds the leasehold estate.

lessor an owner who leases real estate.

license a temporary use of private property.

lien theory states states that treat mortgages as a lien on the title.

life estate interest an ownership that terminates upon the death of the person whose life measures the estate.

limited partnership title held as a limited partnership provides for general and limited partners. General partners assume management, while limited partners provide capital. The liability of limited partners is limited to their interest.

limiting conditions a statement of limiting conditions that the appraiser makes in estimating market value. The market value estimate is valid only to the extent that limiting conditions prevail.

loan assumption a real estate purchase in which the buyer assumes an existing mortgage and agrees to repay the debt personally.

loan forbearance special forbearance privileges prevailing under FHA-insured mortgages for temporary mortgage delinquencies.

loan-to-value ratio the mortgage loan expressed as a percent of the estimated market value.

loan value a value based on a percent of the market value.

location map a map showing the site location in relation to other community facilities.

logic the study of a consistent, or compatible, set of beliefs.

M

management agreement an agreement defining duties of the manager to condominium owners.

market analysis the collection and analysis of data to estimate current and projected real estate markets.

market equilibrium a market where all buyers who wish to buy at the market price are satisfied, and all sellers who wish to sell at the market price find buyers.

market indicators economic data that show current market changes in supply or demand.

market value the most probable sales price for which the property will sell in a competitive market, with the buyer and seller acting knowledgeably and with neither party acting under duress.

maximally productive the use in which land earns the highest income; the proposed highest and best use represents the optimum use that produces

the highest income, and therefore the highest land value.

measures of dispersion measures that show the scatter, or variation, of items from a measure of central tendency.

mechanics' liens liens filed by persons who have performed work or furnished materials in the erection or repair of a building.

median the middle item of a series ranked according to their magnitude.

member designations appraisal membership designations awarded to qualified members who have obtained the minimum required appraisal experience, passed the required examinations, and submitted other evidence of their qualifications for a member designation.

metes and bounds a method of describing land area by describing boundary directions and their turning points.

minimum property standards minimum property requirements for FHA-insured mortgages.

misleading conclusions conclusions that cannot be supported by the facts.

misleading conduct conduct which is likely to mislead clients or the public, as prohibited by Uniform Appraisal Standards.

mode the most frequently occurring value.

monthly gross income multiplier (MGIM) the relationship between monthly gross income and sales price.

mortgage assignment the right of the lender to transfer the mortgage to others without the borrower's consent.

mortgage buydowns payments to the lender by the seller, builder, or buyer to reduce mortgage interest rates and, therefore, monthly payments.

mortgage discount a discount required by the lender to increase the effective mortgage interest rate. A one-point mortgage discount equals a one-percent reduction in the mortgage principal.

mortgage release the right of the borrower to have the public record cleared of the lender's interest in mortgaged property.

mortgage a pledge of a real estate interest as security for a debt.

multiple coefficient of determination (R^2) a statistical measure that indicates the variation in the dependent variable explained by a set of independent variables.

multiple regression analysis the statistical technique of predicting market value from a group of independent variables or property characteristics.

N

neighborhood a local community in which land uses are homogeneous.

net ground lease a lease covering land leased only to tenants who construct buildings on leased land.

net income ratio the complement of the annual net operating expense ratio.

net leases leases that shift part or all net operating expenses to tenants.

net operating expense ratio total annual operating expenses expressed as a percent of reported gross annual net income.

net present value discounted after-tax cash flow less the equity interest.

non sequitur errors conclusions that do not follow from the evidence.

non sequitur literally meaning "it does not follow," a non sequitur refers to a market value estimate that does not follow from the sale price.

nonrepresentative errors errors resulting from value evidence unrelated to the property appraised.

nonrepresentative sales property sales which are not drawn from openly negotiated sales between buyers and sellers who have a reasonable knowledge of the market.

O

off-site improvements sidewalks, streets, street width, storm sewers, street lighting, and other neighborhood facilities that serve the site that is under valuation.

opportunity costs the sacrifice of opportunities or the cost of options foregone in maximizing choices.

over improvement the allocation of excess capital to land, with the result that the return to land is below market value.

overage rents rents that exceed the minimum rent.

overall capitalization rate the annual net income expressed as a percent of the selling price.

overextension of data false conclusions resulting from the "extension" of data to other unknown factual relationships.

P

percentage rents rents based on a specified percentage of tenant gross sales; also known as overage rents.

percentage sales adjustments percentage adjustments in the sales price to account for differences between the property that is sold and the property appraised.

performance zoning local zoning ordinances that base land use on performance and not land-use districts.

periodic tenancies leases that continue until one of the parties of the lease gives notice of termination.

physical depreciation the loss in value caused by physical conditions arising from wear and tear, action of elements, and catastrophic events.

physical depreciation, curable the depreciation measured by the cost of remedying the observed physical defect.

physical depreciation, incurable depreciation which is not economic to cure; incurable depreciation may apply to *short-lived* building components or *long-lived* building components.

pipeline easements an easement for the construction, operation, patrol, maintenance, and replacement of pipelines across private property.

plottage value the added value resulting from the assembly of small sites into a larger parcel. Plottage value arises from the change in use from that assigned to smaller parcels.

police power the right of government to regulate property in the public interest.

potential gross income multiplier (PGIM) the ratio of annual gross income at full occupancy to sales price.

prepayment privileges the right to prepay the mortgage before the due date.

present value factor (PVF) the present value of a future sum or reversionary value.

present value of an annuity factor (PVAF) the present value of the right to a future income.

preservation easements an easement right in which the property owner gives up the right to modify structures, to use a historically significant structure, or to use land in a way that is harmful to the preservation of the site.

price value expressed in money.

principle of change real estate markets are subject to continually changing economic, legal, social, and environmental forces.

principle of competition competitive forces tend to reduce unusually high profits.

principle of conformity real estate that conforms to surrounding property assumes maximum value.

principle of contribution component parts of real estate assume value according to how much they contribute to market value.

principle of diminishing returns the increase in total utility resulting from an additional unit. It is implied that utility decreases as units are added.

principle of proportionality a principle that states there is an optimum combination of land and capital that maximizes income.

principle of substitution real estate may be substituted for other real estate providing for similar utility or income.

process layout an industrial building constructed for manufacturing multiple products.

product layout a floor plan for industrial buildings adapted to assembly-line production in which machinery is laid out according to a sequence of operations.

profession a profession is associated with extensive training, important social services, intellectual skills, a high degree of regulation, and considerable freedom in exercising professional judgments.

profit maximization the tendency of the market to allocate land to uses that earn the highest income.

profitability index discounted after-tax cash flow divided by the equity.

promissory note a personal promise to repay a debt.

property residual capitalization capitalizing annual net income to the property and adding the present value of land at the end of the building economic life.

purely competitive markets a market in which the quantity demanded equals the quantity supplied.

Q

quantity survey a cost estimate based on a detailed list of materials and their cost, labor costs, and overhead and profit.

quartile range the difference between the low-end and high-end values after eliminating the lowest 25 percent values and the highest 25 percent values.

quit claim deeds deeds that convey only an interest in real estate. The seller makes no warranties of title.

R

radon radioactive gas formed by the decay of uranium atoms in rocks and soils.

range the range is the largest value, less the smallest value.

ranges lines running north and south at six-mile intervals measured east and west from the principal meridian.

real estate land and its attachments.

real estate cost the cost of land, land improvements, and building costs including certain "soft costs."

real estate investment trust ownership in real estate acquired by share interests that exempt owners from federal corporate net income taxes, provided the trust observes IRS requirements.

real property legal rights associated with land ownership.

reappraisal leases leases that base rent on periodic reappraisals to establish the fair market rent.

reconciliation evaluation of the evidence of the three approaches to value offered in support of the final estimate of value.

recorded subdivision a method of identifying lots and blocks in subdivisions recorded in public records. Each lot is described by a metes and bounds description.

recovery fund a (Florida) fund consisting of monies raised by appraisal fees and assessments. The purpose of the fund is to satisfy claims against appraisers for negligence, fraud, and other damages suffered by appraisal clients.

remaining economic life the economic life remaining at the date of appraisal.

rentable square-foot area the square-foot area, including a pro rata share of common areas such as washrooms, corridors, and service areas for full-floor tenants.

replacement cost the cost of creating an equally desirable building with the same utility as the property appraised.

replacement cost of equipment the annual cost of replacing equipment according to its replacement cost and economic life.

reproduction cost new the value based on the cost of reproducing or constructing an exact building replica.

required yield rate the yield required by a typical real estate investor.

reserve for replacement the average annual cost of replacing personal property.

residual value the amount of variance unexplained by multiple regression analysis.

return on equity the annual net operating income divided by the value of the equity.

reversionary value the present value of property reverting to the lessor at lease termination.

right of acceleration a clause that gives the lender the right to demand full payment of the remaining mortgage balance.

right of eminent domain the right of government and regulated public utilities to take property in the public interest.

right-to-use timesharing the right to a timeshare interest governed by a lease, license, or club membership.

S

sales comparison approach the estimate of value derived from recent sales of similar property.

second-lien financing financing that includes a mortgage loan subordinate to the first mortgage.

sections sections are approximately square-mile areas in a 36-square-mile township, numbered from the upper right hand corner down in a serpent-like manner to section 36.

servient estate the interest of a person who grants an easement.

severance damages damages from the loss in value to the property remaining after a partial public taking of private property.

short-lived building components building components that have an economic life less than that of the building.

simple regression analysis the statistical association between market value and a property characteristic; the relationship between an independent variable (property characteristic) and a dependent variable (sales price).

simple regression a method of prediction based on a relationship between two variables that is expressed by an arithmetic function.

sinking fund factor (SFF) the amount that must be deposited in an interest-bearing fund to recover a given sum.

specific data data that includes a description of the property appraised and appraisal data that applies directly to the market value estimate.

standard deviation a measure of dispersion derived from the square root of the variance.

standard error of estimate a statistical measure that indicates that the predicted value would fall within 68 percent of the cases.

state plane coordinate descriptions a method of identifying land by longitude and latitude that accounts for curvature of the earth.

statutory right of redemption the right of the borrower to redeem the property by paying the foreclosure sales price plus interest and expenses after the foreclosure sale.

subdivision layout the general plan of a subdivision—i.e., square lots and blocks or a curvilinear layout plan.

subdivision regulations local regulations that ensure that subdivisions comply with traffic patterns, minimum physical requirements, and public utilities.

subdivision restrictions also called subdivision covenants, subdivision restrictions preserve the character of the neighborhood, reduce property depreciation and increase community amenities. Usually, restrictions affect the *aesthetic* qualities of the subdivision.

subject to refers to borrowers who buy real estate subject to an existing mortgage but who do not personally assume responsibility for the unpaid debt.

subleases a lease in which the lessee leases to a third party. The lessee remains responsible to the original lessor.

summation appraisal method another term for the cost approach in which market value equals the sum of the depreciated building value and land value.

supply a schedule or quantity that sellers offer at a given time under a series of increasing prices.

T

10-90 percentile range the difference between the lowest value after eliminating the lowest ten percent of observations and the highest value after eliminating ten percent of the highest values.

tax levy the tax rate or levy imposed against real estate for property taxes.

taxable capital gains the sales price, less the adjusted cost basis.

taxation government has the inherent right to tax private property.

tenancy at sufferance a tenancy created when a tenant, who enters the premises lawfully, holds over without permission of the owner at lease termination.

tenancy at will an estate created lawfully with the consent of owner and tenant that may be terminated by either party upon proper notice.

tenancy by the entireties ownership by husband and wife treated as ownership by one person. The tenancy includes the right of survivorship.

tenancy in common ownership consisting of two or more owners with an undivided interest that may be owned in unequal shares, acquired at different times with the right of partition.

term mortgages mortgages that do not amortize the principal. Payments cover interest only.

time series analysis data charted over successive periods to predict seasonal patterns, cyclical variations, and trends which are expressed by an arithmetic function.

timesharing interest an ownership of a condominium or a hotel unit for a given time.

title theory states states in which mortgages transfer title from the borrower to the lender.

townships property reference lines, under the rectangular survey system, that run east and west at six-mile intervals, north and south of the baseline.

trade market area an area consisting of the geographic area served by a shopping center.

trust deeds written instruments in which a borrower transfers title to a trustee who holds title in trust for a lender as security for a loan.

U

under improvement the term refers to insufficient capital to develop land, with the result that land earns a below-market yield.

Uniform Standards of Professional Appraisal Practice (USPAP) standards developed and published by the Appraisal Foundation.

unit comparisons cost estimates based on the building cost per square foot or cubic foot.

unit-in-place cost cost of materials and labor of each building component.

usable square feet the area for tenant use, not including public and service areas.

use value the value to a particular user.

utility the power to increase satisfaction or decrease dissatisfaction.

V

vacancy and bad debts an allowance deducted from annual gross income, which gives the effective gross income.

value the power of a good to command other goods in exchange.

variable expenses expenses that vary according to the occupancy rate.

variable interest rate mortgages mortgages that vary interest rates according to changes in an interest index. Mortgage payments vary according to the frequency of the interest rate changes and the magnitude of the allowable rate change.

variable payment amortization mortgages that cover a fixed payment to principal. Under this plan, mortgage payments are relatively large during the earlier years of the mortgage.

variance the sum of squared deviations from the mean, divided by their number.

Veterans Administration guaranteed loan loans that are guaranteed by the Veterans Administration for eligible veterans.

W

written appraisal a written statement that is independently and impartially prepared by a licensed or certified appraiser giving an opinion of defined value of an adequately described property, as of a specific date, and supported by analysis.

INDEX